QUADERNS D'ARQUITECTURA I URBANISME
n. 271 — Autumn 2018

Biannual magazine by COL·LEGI D'ARQUITECTES DE CATALUNYA (COAC)
Issue directed by XAVIER MONTEYS

This issue is devoted to the relationships between food, architecture and the city. The name is taken from the album that appeared in 1978—exactly 40 years ago—, *More Songs About Buildings and Food*, from the american rock band Talking Heads, formed by musicians who had met at Rhode Island School of Design. As soon as we think so, our cities are basically formed by these two things, buildings and food, to express it crudely. This issue of *Quaderns* seeks to help formulate an opinion, if not architectural, at least 'spatial' of food and eating. Architects have an innate sense of the scene that comes from our habit of placing things into space, and we have the obligation (and the necessity) to open our field of interests by expanding it into all that which, one way or another, is tied to space, and food cannot escape from this *mise-en-scène*.

These pages bring together several articles. A talk by Nuria Ortigosa and David Steegmann with Carolyn Steel, the architect from United Kingdom who has most emphatically shown the connection between food and the city. This link is expanded on by two articles, that of Eulàlia Gómez and Pere Fuertes on the role of food in the organization of the city—where the markets of Barcelona are their expression—; and that of Magda Mària, which shows through images of paintings, drawings and photographs found in museums and collections of the city, a long tradition of the presence of food and eating in Barcelona. Also discussed are some of the current transformations that affect the organization of collective spaces, such as markets, especially that seen in relation to La Boqueria by David Steegmann; as well as the changes that affect the home due to the growing influence of home-delivered food, in the article by Nuria Ortigosa. Finally, through two reflections by Roger Sauquet and Núria Salvadó, we see the impact of food to the territory.

We can add to these contributions two articles that discuss the conception and organization of the house through two essential elements, the dining room and the table. These can aid in thinking about the need for a center in the contemporary home and to seriously review the limitations that modern architecture has in this respect, as it too often seems that the presence of food in the home comes almost exclusively from the kitchen. The case of Lisbon is presented by Carlos Dias Coelho, who links changes in the dining room with the urban fabric, and a small collection of European tables gathered together by Stephen Bates. And finally, an article by Gianluca Burgio about the literature on eating and food as a motive for reflection, which broadens the cultural dimension of food as related to space.

Xavier Monteys

Xavier Monteys

The Architecture of Food

9

Food is the place from which to observe the city and the home. It is the reason behind many of our actions and it is impossible not to see its political dimensions, with repercussions on the environment, health, and the economy. But food also suggests an order, it is the reason for and gives meaning to many of our actions, and it involves a spatiality that the city embraces and architecture *dresses*. The following are some of the reasons why architecture should address and incorporate it.

Food marks the timetable of our activities, of our life, especially of our life in common, both in the city and at home. The city is different at breakfast, lunch or dinnertime, and the expression of those same hours varies depending on whether it is a weekday or weekend. During those times, the city changes itself, as if it were a stage, and its *scenery* varies. What we do in the streets at those times is also different, and the background music and the smell of the streets change. Thus it seems that the rhythm of the city is determined by food, more so than by work or school hours, which after all are subordinated to food. As accustomed as we are to observing public space and thinking about it in an operative and functional way—in which more than walking around or being in it, it seems that we only pass through it—, food provides an element that forces us to consider it as simply part of our life. This fact, that food is presented on a schedule, gives public space a living dimension, clearly linked to an action. It allows us to see public space, in short, as a stage that, although of indisputable importance, is nothing without the performance that takes place on it every day. It is not a matter of resorting to physical elements, such as what we usually call *urban furniture*, not even to the recognizable patterns of public space design and its countless improvements and renovations, but of appealing to the movements, gestures, and clothing of people who are called to these spaces for food at different times of the day. The outward appearance that various places in the city acquire thanks to food—seen through movements of provisioning, supply and pickup, and those who eat standing up at temporary counters, sitting on benches, stairs, in parks or in sidewalk cafes, and the sounds that accompany these actions—leads us to invoke them as an inseparable part of the city, without which it would be reduced to a mere grotesque model.

In our cities, food is an obvious element, and not only because the ways to provide it have grown through multiple means that infiltrate public space in a positive way, but because we ourselves are now clearly sensitized to this phenomenon and, consequently, it is now noticed, it is not observed distractedly as a set of isolated events, but as part of a clearly urban phenomenon of which we are aware. Food arrives in the city, is distributed, and that distribution affects the city on all levels, from small local shops to supermarkets, which come in all possible styles, and the smaller they are, the more they seem to be almost prolongations of the sidewalks. We see food in the texts of public spaces, the announcements, the offers, the menus written on signboards placed in the street, and in countless words that dot the street-side commercial strip that we scan with our eyes: Burgers, Chips, Sandwiches, Steak, Pizza, Creole Empanadas, Kebab, Paella, Baked Potatoes, Squid, Rotisserie Chicken, Bread, etc. It is impossible not to associate them with the urban settings of our cities.

Linked to these two factors, the opening hours and the elements, eating on the street at sidewalk cafes and pedestal tables has become a practice of which we still partake despite growing regulation. At certain hours, the sidewalks become dining rooms that bring a domestic atmosphere into the street and, in that contrast, we cannot fail to think about something similar to a house relocated into the street. Passers-by become curious when they see the street theater alive with almost domestic performances, and the diners add spectacle and a certain exceptionality to the everyday act of eating. That is perhaps the moment in which they own the city, appropriating it by leaving their homes. We eat out an average of 3.5 times a week.[1]

The city adds to its traditional role as food supplier a new role that has grown exponentially in recent years: food that is pre-cooked and ready to take home. Today it is no longer just pizzas, until now the urban food par excellence; today any restaurant will cook anything to take home depending on the conditions set by the different apps and companies (Glovo, Deliveroo, Just Eat...) that connect homes with nearby restaurants. Proximity is determined by the condition that the food arrives hot, thus forming a "hot food neighborhood" around the home, and opening a new dimension to the provisioning aspect of the city, that of the kitchen-city. Home delivery provides an exotic, different, and informal meal at the doorstep that impacts the manner and style of eating. An urban phenomenon, added to decidedly by the fact that it is transported by bicycle.

This last aspect of food brings into question the idea that we have had until now of our kitchens, which have never been the subject of adequate reflection. Almost always, the reflections have been limited, limited to the field of rational design, which has now been joined by analysis from a gender perspective, but which have almost never focused on food. The category of food, whether it is fresh or processed, cooking times, the predominance of one type or another of preparation, portions and serving sizes, the eating habits of those who live alone, as a couple, or as a family, and the weight of logic of the supermarket in the organization of the kitchen and its storage, have not been taken into account adequately, and today make the well-known "Frankfurt Kitchen" an antiquated fossil. In our kitchens today, we cook for a direct-to-table lifestyle, or pre-cooked take-home food

1
As reported in the "Study of the Restaurant Industry in Catalonia. Behavioral Habits and Tendencies," carried out by the company Hamilton, for the Departament d'Empresa i Coneixement of the Generalitat de Catalunya. In it, it is striking that the percentages of eating breakfast, lunch, and dinner away from home decrease in that order during the week and are reversed radically on the weekends.

is arranged or heated, or there is a mixture of both approaches. Very different products coexist in kitchens and are cooked using both recipes and the instructions on the packaging of the processed or manufactured products that we buy in supermarkets. Kitchens cannot be, are not really, like those of thirty or forty years ago. Nevertheless, we continue to design them in

practically the same way; only the materials change, which are a function of updated options. Our kitchens must be open to new possibilities, and escape from the stigma of style and coordinated and modular space; they should look more like a DIY workshop than a laboratory, and are more a DIY product than an architectural project.

Supermarkets have evolved into a multiple reality that makes us question whether the word supermarket is capable of containing so many varieties of formulas and stores. Today in their maturity, in our country, they have begun a new reformulation that brings them closer to the traditional small local shops, presenting fresh, processed or cooked products in their stores. These new supermarkets also incorporate horizontal surfaces in the center for fresh products that are no longer exhibited only on typical store shelves. This small revolution seems to be aimed at disproving what Michel Pollan sagely pointed out in *The Detective in the Supermarket* (2008) about the display of products on these sales surfaces, inviting consumers not to trust what was displayed on the central shelves, but only products available against the perimeter walls, since this was the traditional place for fresh, refrigerated (plugged in) products. Today the appearance of tables—many of them sprayed with water—with products in the center of these businesses opens the door to considering them as a place where a fusion between two different ways of selling food is being attempted, mixing the spatial organization by "street"—as in a city—of produce markets with a model based on aisles of shelves, like those of any library. These stores represent miscellany par excellence, and we could say that they anticipate contemporary recipes, using fresh products and combining them with pre-cooked ones. This mixture of elements and food

products prefigures an eclectic and practical kitchen that the design of our home kitchens still does not seem to have discovered, remaining anchored in functional, modular and ergonomic rationalism in which the word food hardly ever appears. All these stores contribute to a validation of the presence of street food, which is made especially evident by the policies of many of these businesses, of long opening hours, without doors, and literally overflowing onto the sidewalks.

Food, and mealtimes, as a common space par excellence, has been appropriated by various artists and performers to turn it into a field of activity with a notable spatial connotation taking advantage of one of its perhaps most important qualities: to create a vocabulary. This quality makes it absolutely compatible with public space, in the street; it can color any urban place turning it into something that hardly needs translation. Artists Antoni Miralda and Daniel Spoerri have worked with food. The latter has contributed to the idea of the food on our tables appearing as one of our most obvious cultural fingerprints. As Valentín Roma says in *Communication + Exchange + Perception = Miralda* (2011): "In this sense, food is, perhaps, the first and most essential element of community cohesion, as it reflects collective social, economic and ideological conditions; however, at the same time, it gives them a new meaning, placing them in a scenario devoid of political inflations or media hyperbole." The line that separates this form of *performance* from the meals typical of popular celebrations—in which protest gatherings can be included—is very thin, and

they have in common the use of food to give identity to the chosen street or urban location, making it into a space for the relationship. FADFEST 2016 organized an open-air meal for 900 diners, named *Assaig General*, and brought together various elements: recycling—both discarded food and dishes, cutlery and utensils—, merging the banquet with awareness; it is an example halfway between a performance and a popular meal—from which, in fact, it took its format. Among the events that have used food to raise awareness is *Enemy Kitchen*, which dealt with the cuisine of countries with which the United States was at war, sponsored by the Museum of Contemporary Art in Chicago in 2017. In it, a converted food truck that was part of the exhibit served Iraqi food on printed paper plates that were replicas of the china from Saddam Hussein's palace.

To this consciousness-raising dimension of food, we must add the presence of urban gardens that are grown by neighborhood organizations and protest movements. These vegetable gardens have become one of the favorite proposals of these movements for colonizing the so-called urban voids that appeared a few years ago, considered as a block, for which the Barcelona City Council used bid processes to grant their management. These gardens, especially these, show a genuine side of food in an urban context and demonstrate the certain knowledge of the origin of the produce. They are the raw manifestation of so-called proximity (local) foods. The food is displayed in this way online and allows the public to literally see

how it grows, which fits perfectly with the ideology of many urban activism collectives. These same gardens have also been installed on the roofs of buildings, one of them on the roof of the Vall d'Hebron Market renovation project, where it is easy to imagine the boxes of fruits and vegetables from the interior stands as replicas of the rectilinear order of the furrows planted on its roof. Food is thus used to educate.

Food itself also advances, and it is invigorating to observe it in its architectural dimension, represented, for example, in the shapes and varieties of cooking vessels, which function as authentic kits or extensions of the different appliances: silicone cases—such as from the firm *Lékué*—to cook in the oven, *tajine* ceramics, couscous-makers, and traditional steamers, and others that have appeared hand-in-hand with new types of food, which embody users' curiosity and desire to have fun with food and that has reached the point of us wanting to make our bread ourselves. We now pay attention to the forms we create or assemble: sheets of pasta that we fill, fold, and seal to make empanadas, gyozas, or tacos, balls that we manipulate to make meatballs or croquettes, or rice and fish cylinders wrapped in seaweed. In this way, we expand the set of forms with which we make individual food items or snacks. They are the new types that we have added to those of homemade pastry and which end up providing the table with a collection of elaborated foods that transform it into something similar to fantasy cities. The Rome of the engraving of Pirro Ligorio, interpreted by Le Corbusier in one of his well-known drawings appearing in *La leçon de Rome* of *Vers une architecture* (1923), is shown in a naive way, and we remember the architectures presented by Marie-Antoine Carême—who had

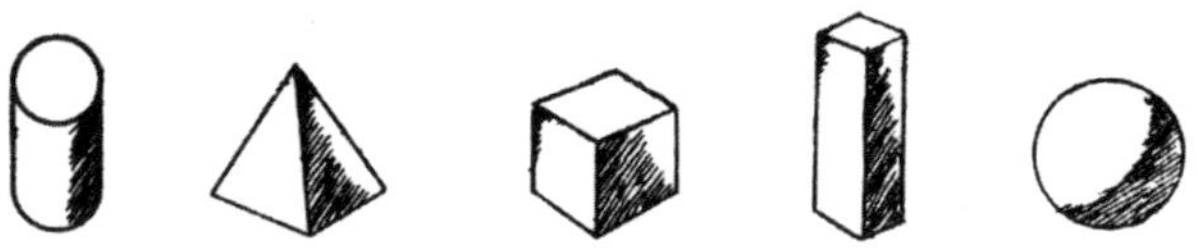

studied architecture—as models to inspire pastry students in his treatise *Le pâtissier pittoresque* (1815). At the same time, the famous page of the magazine *AC* No. 4, 1931, GATEPAC, showed an image that superimposed a two-story cake onto the residential building on the corner of Aribau Street and Avenida Diagonal in Barcelona—known as Cake Model 1931. The image now seems to us a scolding that we cannot resist disobeying in all senses—both by wanting to eat the cake, and by considering architecture as an example of something that also gives character to our cities. We are more interested in the imagination that brings pastry to architecture than Rationalist puritanism.

Food is an excuse to meet almost anywhere, and is able to transform and give meaning to those spaces. But for this, the table—which we alluded to before—must act as a catalyst between prepared foods and the space. Even when it does not exist, the tablecloth seems to represent a *tabula rasa* on which the plates and food are arranged and around which diners sit, as we can see in public parks on Sundays. With the table—or only with its representation—, a space, a place is given meaning. There is much ritual in this, and in our culture it transports us to the altar and the Eucharist. Tables, even when out of place, have an undeniable magnetism as creators of space that kitchens have never had, transferring interest in food in a biased way towards its production in a, we could say, Calvinist way, leaving aside aspects such as the gathering, the celebration, and pleasure, one debt more that the uncritical devotees of the Modern Movement have with everyone. For example, the celebration of a Christmas meal that has been revived year after year since 1982 in the church of Sant Just i Pastor in Barcelona, in which the community of Sant Egidi offers a meal to people who cannot celebrate the ritual on that day or who simply would not otherwise be able to eat. It is surprising how easily the tables available in the nave fit into this new and unusual situation, and it is also surprising how the nave so naturally encompasses this banquet, and how the architecture, altar and lamps give it an absolute plausibility, and

we are left to think that almost any space can be transformed into something so intrinsically human. The cultural weight, in the broad sense of the word, engendered by a table set for eating and those who meet around it makes it almost universal—at least in the part of the world that uses chairs to sit. It is similar to writing a word about these spaces that does not need translation. The films *Darkest Hour* or *The Terminal*—to choose two with scenes set in an airport—and many others, use cinema to show the ability to create a true domestic scene in any place and under adverse circumstances. The ritual theatricality of a meal is called upon in these examples, a scene that we reproduce when we meet at home, unconsciously unaware of the value it possesses and its invaluable contribution to our being able to say something as simple as: "We are here and this is a home."

18

Nuria Ortigosa

Home Food Delivery

19

TAKE AWAY
SUPERMARKET
NEW ORDER ONLINE
amazonfresh
FRUITS & GO
MENU
TAKEAWAY
HOT
DOG

94 % of orders for prepared food in Spain are for home use.[1] In turn, 25 % of users who request home food delivery do it once a week and 11 % of users from 2 to 4 times. This implies that, if we ask for home food delivery, we are not using our kitchens and that the ones that we are using, however, are spread across the city and not necessarily in the same place. The food we eat today is not only moving from the kitchen to the living room or dining room, but also traveling through the city and arriving directly at our tables.

The growing boom that home food delivery is experiencing within and outside of Spain has urban and domestic effects that we cannot ignore. If previously the city landscape in this context was mainly made up of women who carried shopping home in bags and carts with fresh produce peeking out, today the situation is different, and we see bags with packaged products—packaged lettuce, tomatoes inside of transparent plastic boxes, pre-cut fruit, etc.—and a high number of food transport options, from the recognizable supermarket distribution van to the recently-arrived bike or moped riders with backpacks that transport ready-to-eat food.

Frequent meals away from home—in Catalonia 3.5 times a week—[2] mean that our daily diet is more and more habituated to certain types of menus. The "home-cooked" is gradually becoming the special event of the week, thus inverting the assumed order of traditional family events in which the special day was the meal eaten out, usually during the weekend, or the day when home food delivery was ordered to gather in front of the television.

The "home delivery" effect is increasingly recognizable in large cities, such as London,[3] and is made evident in the city by queues of riders waiting for orders at restaurant doors at certain hours. In this sense, the time of home food delivery has become one of the elements that typify everyday urban life, in the same way that we have incorporated certain visual factors into the collective imagination when it comes to the time to go to work or school that determine and make what is happening recognizable.

The street

Home food delivery is somewhat domestic, but also tremendously urban. The packaged food moves through the streets in light transport, motorcycles, and bicycles, icons of the current urban scene. The moment of this boom in prepared food delivered to homes coincides with the arrival of the bicycle as a means of transportation in the modern city. This urban phenomenon is defined by the distance within which the home food delivery options are found, that is, where and how far away our new kitchens are. In

1 Data extracted from the annual study of home-cooked food 2016 conducted by Just Eat.

2 Data extracted from the "Estudi de la restauració a Catalunya. Hàbits de comportament i tendències", report prepared by the Hamilton Consultancy for the Direcció General de Comerç of the Generalitat de Catalunya, with the collaboration of FIHR, l'Associació d'Empresaris d'Hostaleria i Turisme del Moianes i d'Osona, and of the Gremi de Restauració of Barcelona in 2018.

3 In large capitals such as London it is no longer enough for a restaurant to cook to take away, but satellite kitchens of these restaurants have recently appeared, the so-called dark kitchens, installed inside shipping containers in residual areas of south London dedicated exclusively to preparing take-away food.

this sense, the size of the neighborhood is not determined by the limit established by municipal zoning, but by the maximum distance at which such kitchens are found. The parameters that measure these "neighborhoods" determined by food are others, and issues such as "it must arrive hot" or "it can't go soft" have more weight than the dividing line between districts.

Perhaps the most critical factor in the delivery of home-cooked food is that the order arrives still warm. In fact, William Ritchey Newton, in *Derrière la façade: vivre au château de Versailles au XVIIIe siècle* (Behind the facade: life in the Versailles palace in the 18th century), 2008, speaks of the great number of kitchens, not considered in the original plans, that arose distributed throughout the different wings and apartments of the palace of Versailles, which, based on its size, could be compared to any of the neighborhoods that make up our cities. Some of these kitchens, all installed in spaces initially not designed for them or in huts built against the walls of the inner courtyards, were improvised, while others were clandestine or *de tolérance*, and all were generally intended to prepare light menus or reheat food before being served. The operation of a palace like Versailles was undoubtedly closer to the operation of a city, in relation to its number of inhabitants, "public" spaces, and distances, than to a large house. So much so that probably the distance to travel between the original kitchen and the different areas of the palace were longer than from our houses to the restaurant kitchens located in our neighborhood. In addition, while in Versailles these trips were made on foot, in the present city they are generally made by bicycle, thus shortening the delivery times.

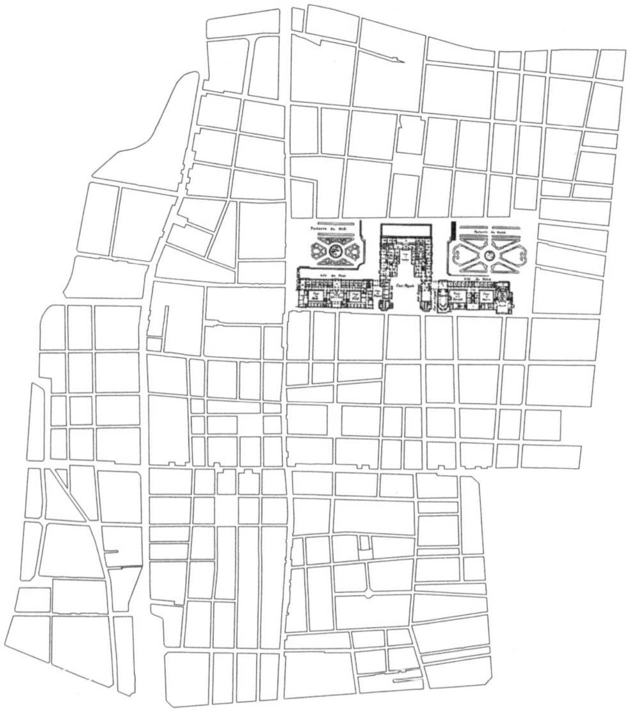

On Parliament Street in Barcelona there are 34 restaurants, and 34 kitchens, and some of them also cook to take away. This leads us to think that, probably at some time of day, there are more kitchens operating at street level than on any of the upper floors of residential buildings on a street like Parliament or Enric Granados. And that, in addition, the amount of food we eat prepared in these "downstairs kitchens" and in our own private kitchens is very close. In this sense, we could think of a house as a series of interconnected parts regardless of their location, not just in the same building, but in the city as well. The "ground floor kitchen" would constitute in this case one more room, such as the parking lot or the storage room,[4] with the advantage that it is also shared.

Two kitchens compared shows the plan of a hypothetical domestic kitchen organized according to current lifestyles, and the kitchen of a London restaurant that only prepares take-away food. If we would compare them without knowing which was which, we could confuse them and curiously

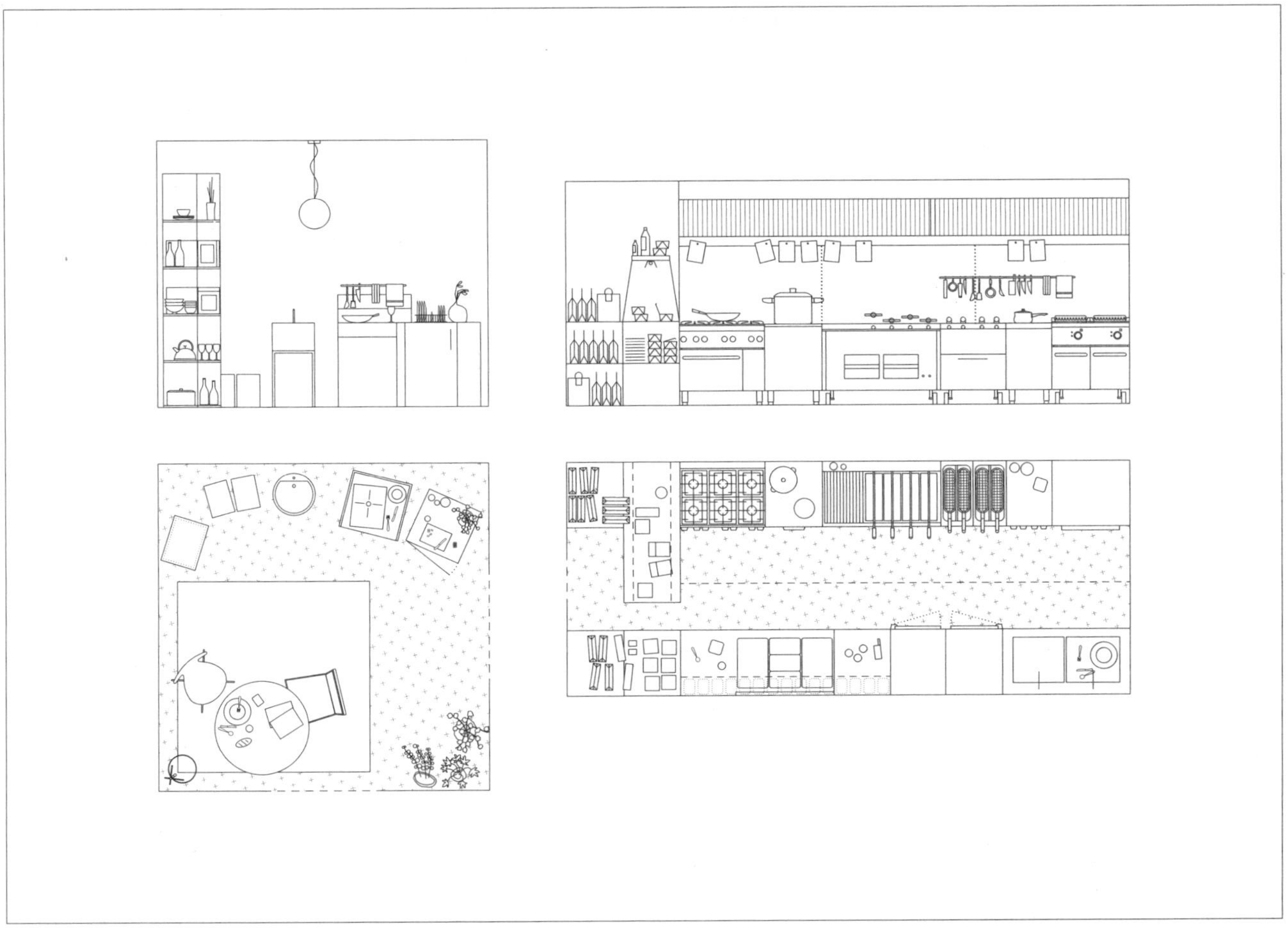

we would probably assume the take-away kitchen is the traditional one instead of the kitchen we actually need in our homes. In the first, the only fixed element necessary—for technical reasons—would be the sink; the rest could appear and be located according to the changing needs of its users. The cooktop could be portable and hang like one more of the utensils that are used to cook, just like the saucepan or pot. The appliances are confused with stackable furniture or objects on shelves, and the refrigerator works as a refrigerator on par with an auxiliary table. It is a kitchen made by and for people who use it, which could be located somewhere in a traffic-flow area and have several doors. In contrast, the second is a kitchen designed in an explicit place with a single entrance, where everything has a site defined independently of the real need. In this sense, this comparison between the adapted kitchen and the planned one only emphasizes that our home kitchens are closer to impersonal assem-

4
Xavier Monteys and Pere Fuertes, in *Casa Collage*, 2001, propose a rethinking of the housing block: "House, study or office, apartment for the eldest children or parents, storage room, DIY workshop, and even parking for the car or *Roulotte*, or a private terrace on the roof, can be made available by the building without having to be part of a compact house".

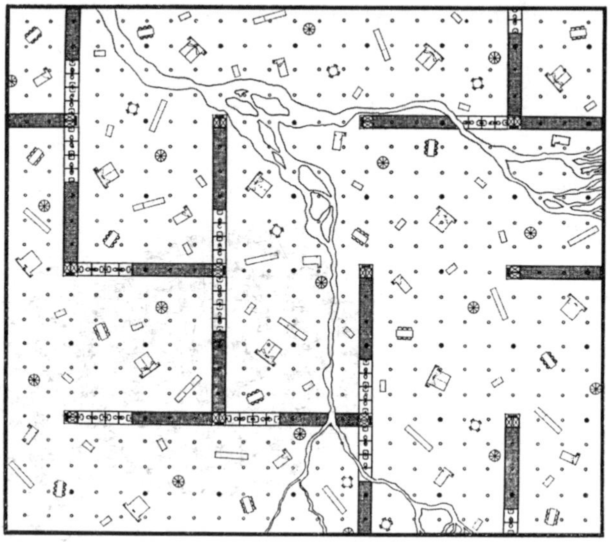

bly lines than to the uninhibited and practical domestic life in our homes. Also, the role that the smartphone has acquired in our current relationship with the city and with our homes is decisive. The whole city is virtually part of our homes and vice versa, a kind of *Non-stop City* from the Italian avant-garde group Archizoom, in which technology eliminated the need for a centralized modern city, and where the city could be extended infinitely through the sum of homogeneous elements adapted to a variety of uses. We work from home, rent rooms that we do not use, we eat cooked food outside of what is conventionally assumed to be our home, and our purchases are delivered even when we are not at home. The limits of the domestic sphere have changed.

Revisiting Lubetkin

Revisiting Lubetkin has redrawn and updated the domestic protocols of the last eighty years, in which the traditional model of delivery, preparation, cooking and service have become much more direct, contributing in turn to the disappearance of certain rituals and furniture associated with housing. In the original drawing for Highpoint II, Berthold Lubetkin—who in the same way that Le Corbusier, among others, was helped by drawing to explain how their buildings work—explained the operation of these houses that were uncommon for the time. In his drawing, the protocols established for the home, and even the spaces themselves, are very segmented. The space reserved for delivery is exclusively outside the home, adjacent to the preparation and washing area, mainly because the products that arrived at the house were generally fresh and needed some elaboration prior to being consumed; this is unlike what is happening at present, when food arrives practically on a plate or, at least, in a container that can go directly to the table. Next, we find a space for cooking equipped with a central kitchen and a smoke extractor in the ceiling. These two areas were used solely and exclusively by the domestic service personnel; in fact, the door is the service entrance, a figure less common in today's homes. The smaller space that current homes have tend to be due to the value of the land and new occupancy models[5]; together with the informality in our current habits and the number of ready-made products we consume, this means that areas such as the scullery[6] have disappeared or become another thing. If previously the ritual was divided into a series of processes and spaces—similar to the characteristic serial processes of the Modern Movement—up to the point when the food reached the table around which the whole family met, nowadays the situation is very different. The dining table is usually in a place where more activities are carried out; and while in Lubetkin's drawing a room is dedicated entirely for eating, today, that same space would probably have been converted into an office or an improvised bedroom, because the house is a shared environment and we need to take the best advantage of the space. Furniture, objects, books are mixed in the same room where, in addition, you can heat up and prepare something. It no longer makes sense to install over-equipped kitchens with fixed elements. The figure of the woman or the service dedicated exclusively to daily cooking for the whole family is out of date and as a consequence, so is the entire mechanism that this requires.

The model of the family gathered in front of a television does not exist anymore. Now each person connects to a technological device to fill their free time. Our rooms are becoming more generic and we could carry out any activity in any of them. A room is a kitchen if you put a stove/oven in it, and a table is a dining room table if we eat on it, as shown in the pro-

5
30.6% of Spanish households are occupied by two people and 24.8% by a single one. The average occupation is 2.51 people. Data extracted from the National Institute of Statistics (2014).

6
According to the Real Diccionario de la Lengua Española—*scullery*: "Space that is attached to the kitchen and in which the table service is prepared". Currently there is an incorrect meaning of this space, encouraged by decoration magazines, which define it as a space within the kitchen to take small meals, such as breakfast or snack (eat-in kitchen).

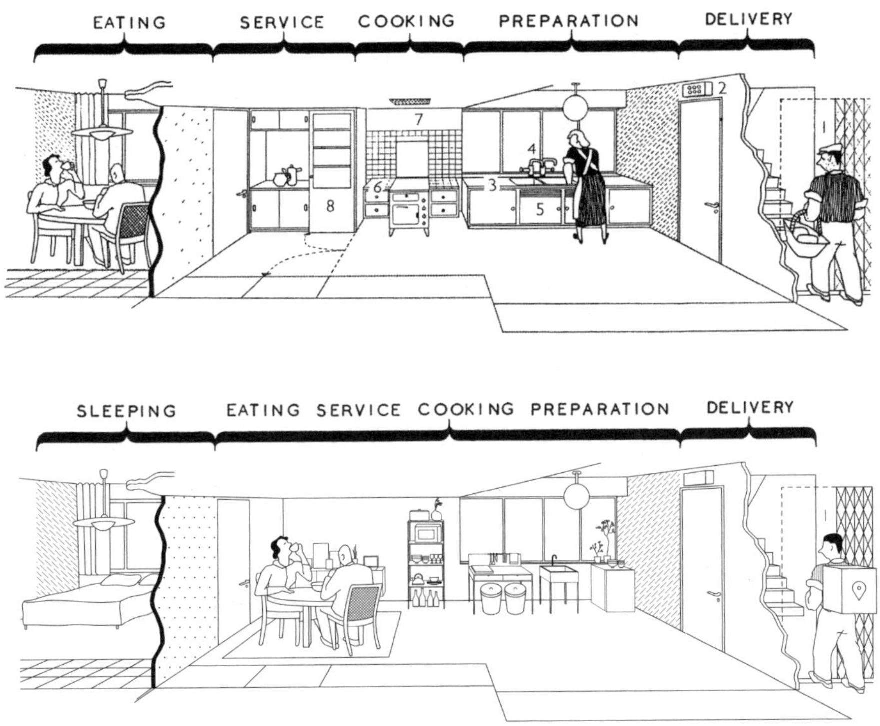

motional video of the Ikea 2017 catalog, Dining Room Timelapse. This video is a reflection of what happens in our homes, and shows the daily activities of a family and how a single table in the same room can accommodate all of them, from lunch or dinner, to study, work, or leisure. New forms of home occupancy and current lifestyles may not only require a smaller number of rooms and more generic ones, but it may be more flexible to take advantage of the square meters dedicated to the kitchen for other things, using furniture that can house some portable appliances instead—like that of Andy Warhol or the Kitchen Set, designed by Sam Chermayeff for his own home, that has mobile partitions that separate rooms but that maintains a kitchen of fixed elements that are oversized with respect to their real use. S. Chermayeff defines this kitchen as a series of parts and appliances or expandable furniture, like a series of objects that make it so that essential components do not define the design itself, and allow for a malleable program in areas corrupted by use.

This incipient dissolution of the kitchen has caused subtle changes in our homes, mainly the appearance and disappearance of certain objects associated with that usage. The scullery or the pass-through—one of the icons of the domestic modernity of the 1930s—as designed by Berthold Lubetkin for the Green Spa (1938) building in London, or by Alfred Roth, Emil Roth and Marcel Breuer for the Dodertal apartment houses (1935) in Zurich—are elements that are becoming less common in our homes and, in a way, could be compared to the refrigerator-backpacks used to carry prepared food home and thanks to which we practically do not need to use our dishes. The home landscape no longer needs space for dry-salting of products, but there are other objects, such as microwaves or trash cans for different types of recycling that now occupy this place. Instead of storage cabinets, it would make more sense to have a wall equipped with refrigeration and heating together with the access system of our homes, a kind of reception port for all home-delivered products, such as the one already planned

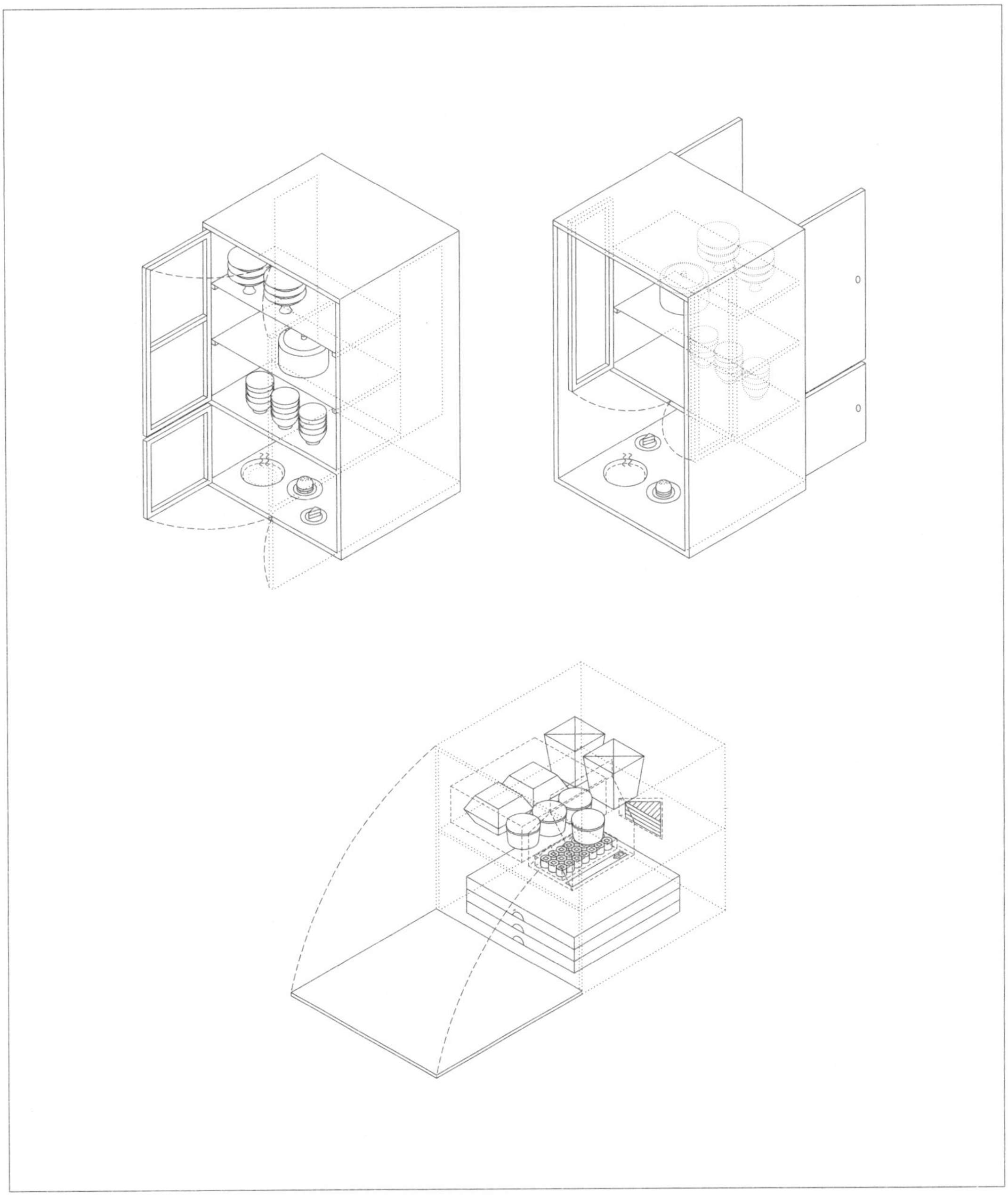

by Le Corbusier in the Unité d'Habitation, which housed a small door that directly connected the *rue intérieure* with a fridge installed inside the apartments, which allowed the dairyman to leave the fresh milk every day.

Take-away

The consumption of prepared food has historically been associated with the classic fast food model, in which burgers, chips, or pizza have been the most recognizable take-away icons. The burger box, the pizza box, marketed as we know them today from the sixties, or that of donuts and take-away coffee popularized by American cinema, are part of the traditional collective image of take-away food. We all know what is in those boxes, even without opening them. The new archetypes in the field of food, gourmet food and the awareness of healthy food habits, together with the globalization to which our cities are subjected, have led to home-delivered food having

evolved from fast and ordinary food to other types of healthier, elaborate, and exotic dishes. Not only do we recognize and receive at home a certain type of packaging associated with a single meal, but other more generic containers have appeared that can accommodate almost any type of food. The design of both the packaging and the food itself have evolved exponentially if we compare them with that of the kitchen. We eat more and more

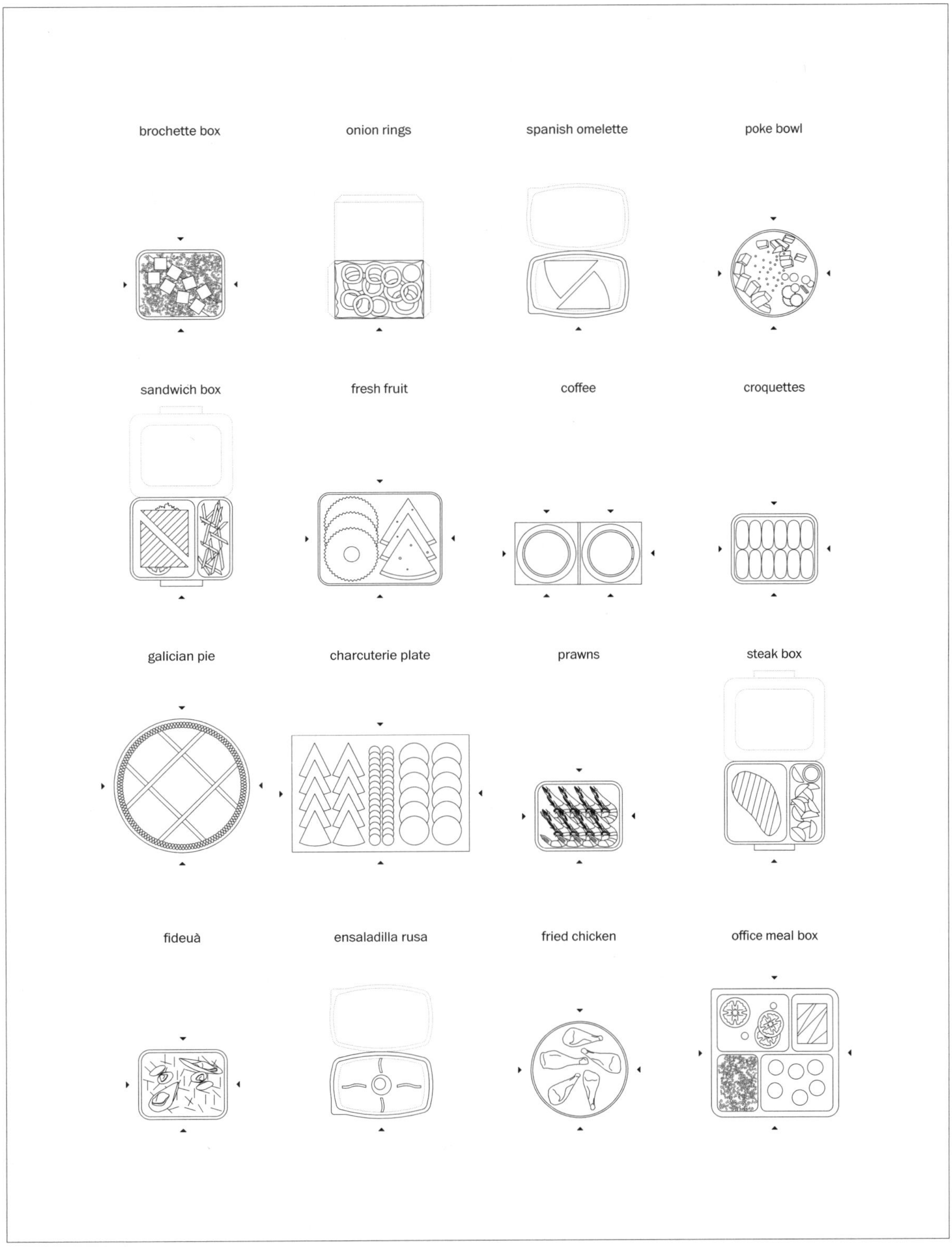

designed and individual "objects", adapted to current lifestyles. From the aforementioned classic burger, single-serving sushi, or an individual miso soup, to the office meal box with different types of food packaged in the same container each day.

What we know about take-away food is not just about what we eat, what we ingest, but involves the assumption of a certain implicit informality in this type of food and that which comes to us from the street. Food nowadays involves a more nutritious cultural phenomenon, as Massimo Montanari explains in *Food as Culture*, 2006: "In this way, food is defined as an exquisitely cultural reality, not only with respect to the nutritive substance, but also to the way of assimilating it and everything that surrounds it. Substance and circumstance assume a significant value, usually connected to each other because the language of food cannot—unlike verbal languages—dispense with the concrete object, the intrinsic semantic value, predetermined in some way, of the instrument of communication". The arrival of prepared food in our homes, starting with the classic American TV dinner in the 1950s—which just needed to be heated and generally eaten in front of the television set—changed our habits and our language—even our body language—within the home.

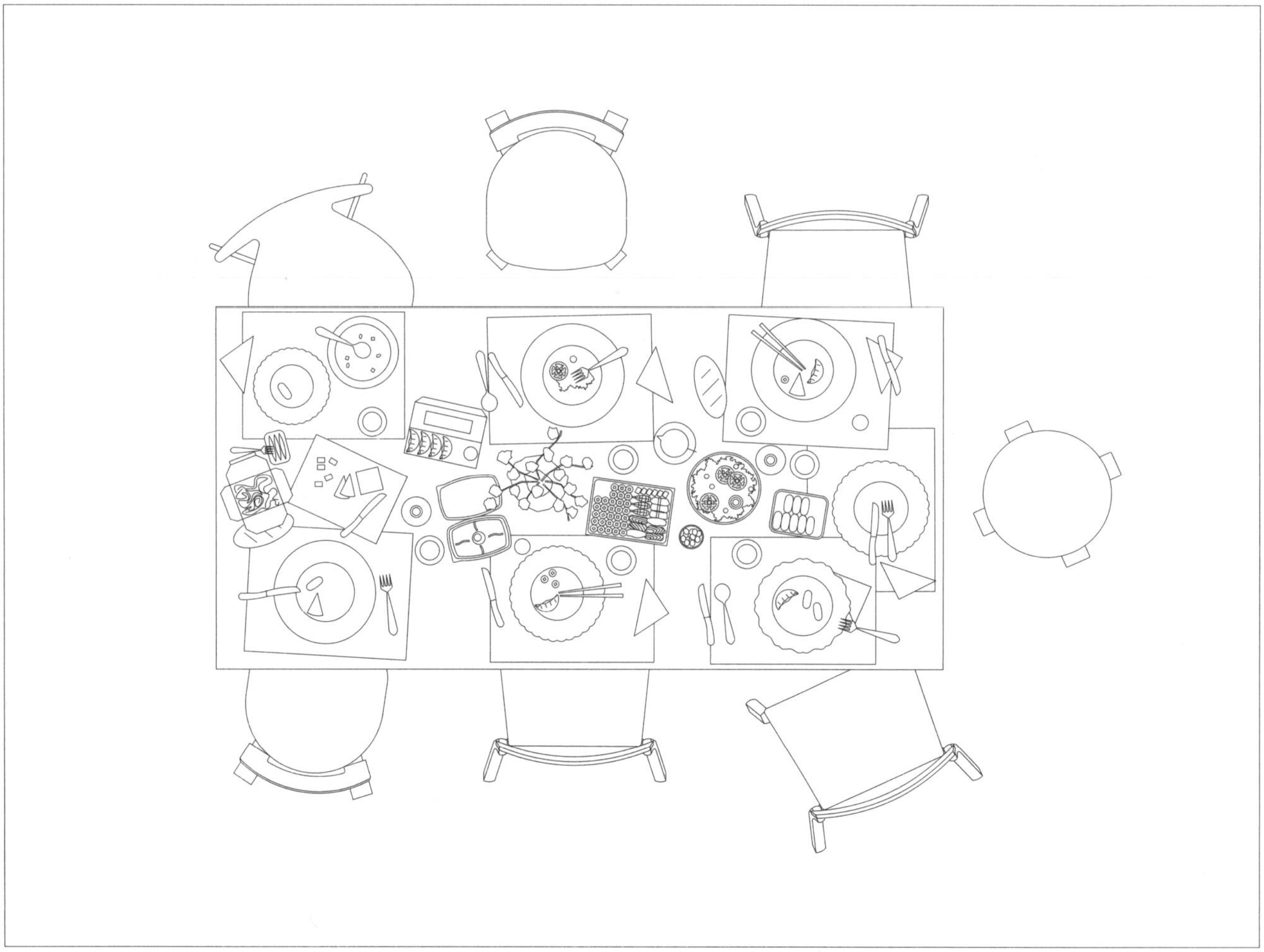

What happens at our tables is a reflection of what happens in our homes and, by extension, in our cities. Nobody finds it strange to attend a dinner in which there is not a single casserole, but instead a series of them semi-finished at home and many others to share brought from the street, either delivered or purchased on the way home from work. These dishes are mixed with things to be served, and, in turn, with other extremely domestic things, such as the cheese—cutting board or a piece of bread broken by hand. Different chairs and utensils, forks and chopsticks, and disposable napkins are some of the elements that portray our current home habits. And food is perhaps the most significant element of the intrinsic relationship that exists between the home and the street, on which, in a certain way, the opposite also happens: the meaning, and above all the table habits learned at home, also are spread out into the streets via what we eat.

The Bainton family in the dining area of their living room in Collingbourne Ducis, Wiltshire, with a week's worth of food. Peter Menzel, *Hungry Planet: What The World Eats*.

Nuria Ortigosa
David Steegmann

Interview with Carolyn Steel

Q. C.S.

You have stated that meat and urbanism are rising hand in hand. Can you explain this idea?

Yes, it's very odd isn't it? Well, this is rather a long story. The first thing to say is that we humans evolved through the sharing of food. Our ancestors were nomadic hunter-gatherers, and when they learnt to control fire everything changed, because for the first time they were able to cook food, which allowed them to specialize. While the men were out all day hunting, the women would gather tubers from the ground and cook them, which meant that, whether or not the hunters were successful, there was always some kind of meal waiting for them in the evening. So out of this deal "I cook, you hunt", as it were, came society, language, economics... That's the first part of the puzzle: we are evolutionarily hardwired to want to eat meat.

When we humans began to farm, one of the first things we did was to domesticate animals. If you look at the animals we domesticated historically they have different benefits: pigs, chickens and goats have the great advantage that they are omnivores, so they can eat the same food that we eat. We can feed them our food scraps, and when they are grown, we eat them. Sheep and cattle have a different benefit: they eat grass. So that's fantastic, because they can eat something that we can't. And that, really, was the deal through most of history: we grew grain, and we might have offered some of it to pigs and chickens, but mostly we ate the grain ourselves, while sheep and cows ate grass. So this was the basis of a sort of mixed farming approach, and that's basically how everybody farmed. Farming also made cities possible. Because people had to guard and protect their fields, they started to camp next to them, and these encampments evolved into farming villages which, over time, gradually grew bigger and more complex until they were effectively cities.

So the first silos were the first cities. You talk about Ur.

Yes. When Sir Leonard Woolley first excavated Ur in the 1920s, he said that the temple looked more like a kitchen than a temple! This was because the temple was responsible for bringing in the harvest, storing the grain and baking it into bread. So what we learn from this is not only that farming and cities evolved together, but that *grain* is the food of cities; this is actually significant in answering your question, and also to understanding the evolution of cities as a whole. If we fast-forward a couple of thousand years, it explains why most cities didn't grow very big: it was because they struggled to get enough food into town.

Yes, there was a theory of Johann von Thünen, which talks about the maximum radius of a city, and its productive hinterland.

Exactly. Most cities were very small in the pre-industrial era, the best-known exception being Rome. Von Thünen was the first to explain why. In his 1826 work *The Isolated State*, he analysed the productive hinterland of the city, which was usually organized in a series of concentric rings. The innermost one consisted of market gardens, orchards and dairies, which were luxury foods whose profits were high enough to pay the rent close to the city. Beyond that was a band of about thirty kilometres of grain production: the most important food, but heavy and bulky in relation to its value, so it had to be grown close enough to the city to make its transport economically feasible. In the outer band there would be livestock production, and after that, wilderness. So these productive rings effectively limited the size to which cities could grow.

If we compare these two pictures of the Thames in London and the Seine in Paris from the pre-industrial era, we notice that London is full of oceangoing ships, while Paris only has canal barges. This is because the Seine is not navigable by oceangoing vessels, which meant that Paris could

William Daniell, *View of the River Thames*, 1804, Port of London Authority.

The Grève or Port aux Blés in Paris, looking toward the Pont Marie, 17th century engraving.

only feed itself from the surrounding countryside. The city had to impose its will on its hinterland, which it did through a 'grain police' headed up by the King himself, who was held responsible for feeding the people—we all know how that ended! London, on the contrary, was always able to import food easily from overseas, so no English monarch took responsibility for feeding London. In this way, we can see how geography led directly to politics. Food physically shaped the city, it shaped politics and the landscape, and at the heart of everything was the relationship between the city and the country. Then the railways come along and everything changed. Because food could be easily transported quickly over long distances, cities were no longer constrained by geography, so they could grow much bigger and agricultural landscapes could also expand.

This picture of Chicago Union Stock Yards reflects what happened when the American Midwest was converted into grain production. What do you do with grain if you've got too much of it to feed people? You feed it to cows. This was the beginning of cheap meat. In the pre-industrial era, you couldn't keep your herd of cows going over the winter because there was nothing to feed them, so most cattle were slaughtered in the weeks

John Vachon, *Chicago Union Stock Yards*, 1942.

leading up to Christmas. Everyone had a big feast, and then there was very little meat for several months. When the railways came, however, there was plenty of grain to feed to cows, and despite the fact that cattle are not designed to eat grain, they will eat it, because to them it is like fast food. For the first time, huge amounts of meat were available all year around, which was exported to the east coast of America and Britain, and ultimately all around the world, forging the link between cheap industrial meat and city dwellers that exists today.

Don't you think that, somehow, this evolution has led us to the loss of cooking skills, to the loss of knowledge about food, and, consequently, to the loss or transformation our kitchens?

Yes. Industrialization essentially moves people from the countryside to the city, changing them from primary food producers to consumers—that's essentially what it does. Since food comes from the countryside, the change often leads to a loss of skill and knowledge. The modern urban condition is therefore one of ignorance about food.

The industry is feeding you and is cooking for you.

Q. C.S.

Yes, and that's very interesting. In my new book, actually, I'll talk about the evolution of home as a place where you can feed yourself. When most people were farmers, they were mostly self-sufficient, but when you live in the city you are dependent on others to feed you, which actually makes you rather vulnerable. In the modern city, you also lose sight of food. This is actually the second big shift that occurs with the railways. If you think of living in London in the 19th century, food was all around you; but when the railways came, food began to travel along special, hidden routes—what we now call 'food logistics'—and so it became invisible to most people. The last thing that changed was that historically politicians were in control of food, but when the railways came, they were happy to let the new food industries take over and, very quickly, the companies were controlling food: they had the power, creating a gap between political control and the food supply.

Can self-production be a possible future solution for cities' food supply? If the necessity of bringing food into a city, as you have written, has slowly moulded its shape, can this new phenomenon, as an internal urban mechanism, be significant in future city development?

Yes, but only up to a point. And it's very important to understand why—and also to realise why some degree of self-sufficiency also matters.

The first thing to say is that people have always produced food in cities. I mentioned pigs and chickens earlier: people used to keep them in their houses, because they were the ideal food recyclers! If there was open space in the city, people would have grown fruit and vegetables too, they would have grown their own food. Many city-dwellers also had orchards, vineyards or fields just outside. Aristotle wrote about this: his concept of "oikonomia" (which means household management, the root of our work 'economics') talks about an ideal scenario in which every citizen would have had a house in a town, but also a farm in the country, and would have managed the relationship between the two. So "oikonomia", the ideal of the city-state of the Greek polis, aimed at self-sufficiency and independence from foreign trade, because being dependent meant weakness.

In the pre-industrial city, many citizens had a small patch of land outside the city that they farmed. So there was always a strong personal connection between growing food and living in cities which, of course, disappeared with industrialization: cities got bigger, so people couldn't reach a piece of land so easily.

Our cities no longer have physical barriers, but the barrier is even longer. The distance is the barrier.

Exactly. This is why my favourite image of the feeding of the city is *The allegory of the effects of good government* by Ambrogio Lorenzetti, because if you're really looking after the city, you have to look after the countryside: it's all about that relationship. It's so clear what the image means: that one can't exist without the other. Everything is about balance.

One really strong thing that these pictures show is that nowadays all those crops would be for feeding animals, not for feeding people.

Ambrogio Lorenzetti, *The Effects of Good Government on City and Country* (1338). Detail from *The Allegory of Good Government*, Palazzo Pubblico, Siena.

Yes. Around 95 percent of the meat we eat now is grain-fed, yet it takes 10 times as much grain to feed us if it goes through an animal first. So we could feed 10 times as many people if we just ate bread.

So, must we be vegetarians in the future?

Yeah, pretty much. Meat needs to be a luxury.

What's interesting about growing your own food is that many people do it for fun, not for necessity.

As you rightly say, there's more interest in growing your own food now than there was, let's say, twenty years ago. It is partly a realization that you have no control over what you eat if you go and just buy it in the supermarket.

Growing food was always part of the city anyway, but it was never how cities were really fed. They've always needed the countryside. Actually, we're as dependent on the countryside now as we were when most of us lived there. Cities have never fed themselves. They've always had this rural hinterland; and the idea of the *polis* was that city and country were understood as one symbiotic entity. Industrialization has brought a totally different model in which cities can grow as big as they want, and the food supply is no longer considered a problem thanks to new methods of transport. This is what I call the 'free trade' attitude, and it's also the industrial attitude: the food system is designed by market demand, rather than by political or social constraints. What's happening now, however, is that by following this model we are trashing the planet. Feeding people was always a politician's hardest job. But when the food industry came along and the market took over, politicians absolved themselves of this task.

Q. C.S.

Many people agree that we can't go on feeding cities like this. But there is divided opinion about what we should do about it. Some people believe that vertical farming is the answer: bringing all food production back into cities, so we can release nature back to being wild again. I don't think this is going to work, not least because you can't actually feed a city from within itself. I do think that growing food in cities is important, but for me this is mostly because it makes food visible again: it can educate us, get kids involved, allow people to engage with food again. We will only be able to feed a proportion of the city from within the city, but this still matters because of the way it can help build food-aware communities.

Food consumption in public and collective spaces seems to be a rising phenomenon. In this context, some markets—such as La Boqueria, in Barcelona, or San Antón, in Madrid—are introducing more and more prepared food in their offer and installing tasting spaces. Compared to other times, how do you think the role of food has changed in urban daily life?

The first thing to say is that they always did that. When ancient cities such as Ur and Pompeii where excavated, they found shops selling what we now call "fast food". This was because most people lived in tiny houses without kitchens, so from the very beginning, they had to buy prepared food. As

Fast food in Pompeii, unknown source.

you can see in this picture of a shop in Pompeii, there is a counter onto the street with different holes in it where there would have been containers of hot food that people could choose from to take away, just as we do today.

So we could say fast food is the first food of the city. We always relate it to the modern city but, in fact, it's pretty old.

Yes, you could say that. There is plenty of evidence that eating together in public was a totally common thing in the past. If we look at this 1611 map of Pye Corner in Smithfield, it tells you everything you need to know. These are taverns, and these big red objects are public ovens: they belonged to the tavern but they produced huge amounts of pies and roasted joints and so on that you could either eat there or take away.

Historically, the urban food supply was mostly controlled by the city authorities and centred around the market. The reason for this was that they wanted to control the quality of food being sold. Once food is cooked, it could be anything; so the market had this sort of official status as the place where you could go to buy raw ingredients, and it was overseen by the city authorities.

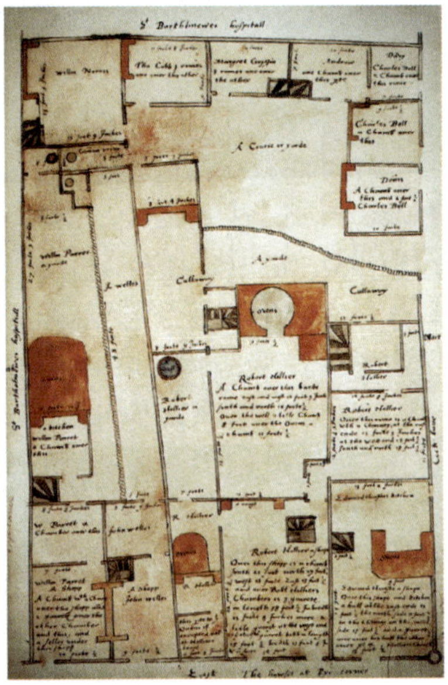

Ralph Treswell, *Survey of Giltspur Street and Cock Lane ('Pye Corner')*, 1611, Christ's Hospital and Guildhall Library, London.

So the market had this vital function of feeding the city, but it was also where you went to experience public life. What's missing today is that, even though people still go out to eat, it's a totally different phenomenon, because the civic aspect is missing, the seasonal aspect is missing and the sense of it being something that brings everybody together. I often say, "food is what used to animate the public space of the city". You went out not just to buy food but to meet people: food animated lots of things. Now it's all Starbucks or similar, so it's a chain, it's not personal, it's not seasonal, and you could argue it's not social either because we're all just sitting there staring at our smartphones. It's not a part of building civic society.

Part of the problem is that nowadays just a few companies control the food supply. This is called 'vertical integration' in the food chain. Very interestingly, in pre-revolutionary Paris, it was forbidden for bakers and millers to do one another's job, for the simple reason that being both a miller and a baker would give you too much control of the bread supply. So this was forbidden. But, of course, they found lots of ways of getting around it. Now we have complete vertical integration in the food system,

Q.   C.S.

Smithfield Market (c.1830), Aquatint by R. G. Reeve after James Pollard, The British Museum, London.

so mega-companies control everything from the field to the table. And, globally, these companies have incredible power. We have forgotten that control of food is power.

The supermarket has changed significantly through its history, from a pretty sober and cheap post-war supply solution, gradually, to a more sophisticated and warmer place. It seems like these spaces are now mirroring old markets, trying to make shopping a more pleasant experience. On the other hand, the so-called 'dark stores' seem to be rising fast as a practical shopping solution. Do you imagine a future where streets have only 'funny' and 'interesting' food shops and all the boring shopping is done online?

That's where it's going. The whole question of what a city is for, I think it's being challenged by the Internet. Historically what made cities wonderful was that the social encounters that we had gave rise to institutions, they gave rise to markets, libraries, concert halls. And now, it seems that we can replace that kind of activity with just pressing a button online. The Internet is having a devastating effect on the high street, and, interestingly, it's also threatening supermarkets. There have been many stages in the evolution of supermarkets. It began when the railways came and markets, these amazing places of sociability and celebration, got challenged by local high streets, when cities like London grew too big to be served by just a handful of central markets and there was a proliferation of unregulated local food shops.

Next came supermarkets, which were explicitly invented as a dehumanizing mechanism. In traditional grocery stores, customers were served by assistants from behind the counter and you couldn't touch the products. Then Clarence Sunders, an American grocer, invented the Piggly Wiggly, the first self-service supermarket, where instead of being served by assistants, customers helped themselves to the food and paid at the checkout—saving Saunders a lot of money. The next phase was out-of-town supermarkets, where instead of walking to the city centre to shop, you drove to the outskirts—which, when you think about it, is a complete reversal of the original logic of the relationship between food and cities: you could even go as far as to call supermarkets anti-urban.

Today, online shopping is replacing the supermarket and out-of-town supermarkets are really struggling, because why would you drive out there when you can get your food online? The high street is an even bigger problem. The UK government has constant research projects about how to save the high street: we have to rethink what our city centres are for. A lot of restaurant chains in the UK are closing as well, partly because of services like Deliveroo, which bring you restaurant-quality food on the back of a bike. But a lot of that food is not actually cooked in restaurants at all, but in so-called "dark kitchens": portacabins underneath motorway flyovers are really destroying restaurants, so it's a big issue.

In fact, I have recently read some news about these "dark kitchens", which are placed in south London. Londoners spend on take away food more than 200 pounds/month, which is more than the double of the national average. We would like to know what you think about this.

Well, Londoners tend to be more employed than people elsewhere in the UK and have more disposable income, but the bigger issue for me is the way in which we value food in the UK. I think it's a real sin that we don't value food here, that we don't understand it, we don't value the people that produce or prepare it for us.

For me the Deliveroo thing is another sinister development because it's a bit like milk cartons with 'happy cows' on the front, grinning at you from a grassy field. It's propaganda. It's the same with Deliveroo: you know and trust the restaurant brand, and think that the chef is cooking for you in between serving his or her other customers... but no, they're underpaid chefs often working in windowless, overheated shipping containers under motorway intersections. It's really shocking.

We need to remind ourselves that food consists of living things that we kill in order to live, so it isn't just an amazing metaphor for life; it is actually *life itself*. So for us to believe that food should be 'cheap' tells you everything. Something is seriously screwed at the heart of our value system, and we need to question how we got here, and why we allowed this to happen. It's a really revealing series of processes, of which politicians stepping away from responsibility for food is a major one. We have structured society so that we can't see the true cost of our own lives, and food is the most powerful way of understanding that. So if you see a chicken on sale for 2 pounds you know something is wrong, if you pay 20 pounds for dinner in central London restaurant, you also know something is wrong. We have to wake up to the fact that we're living on the back of ecological destruction and quasi-slavery. It can't go on. Food shapes everything, so if we don't value food, everything gets damaged.

If we look at history, it seems that currently we eat very differently than in past times, particularly if we think of some manners and traditions that have given way, at least in most of our collective meals—like when we have a dinner with friends at home—, to more informal events. Do you think this can be an influence on how food consumption has developed in collective spaces, like fast food restaurants, during the 20th century?

Yes. I mean, we totally eat very differently now. But how does the way we eat shape wider society? My favourite statistic, which I learned from an interview with Michael Pollan, is that 20 % of meals in America are now eaten in cars. We evolved as social beings through the sharing of food, yet now we share through money, which is about as unlike food as it is possible to be: ephemeral and invisible. Our transition from eating together to eating individually is very understandable, because we now have a socio-economic model that basically excludes the human and tells us that we have no time for anything, because we have to be productive, and so on.

Under globalization, food contents are slowly homogenizing worldwide. Is this true in your opinion?

Yes.

Do you think, for example, that Europe's southern countries are still significantly different than northern ones?

Yes they are, but they are under threat. The key figure is the cook. Without the cook's skill we can't eat. Without the cook's knowledge we can't get good ingredients. Without the cook's engagement there can't be a vibrant market. In other words: you can't grow good food if nobody values it, and the cook is the one who values and confers value on food.

The question that we have to ask is "what relationship with food do we want, and what role does food play in our idea of a good life?". We have to ask what a good life might look like in the 21st century, not just individually, but collectively. For me, the shorthand is that we have to value food.

If you value food, if you don't externalize the true cost of living well, but you internalize it, then food would become expensive again—which in turn would mean that we would need a more equal society, so that everyone could afford to eat. I think that if everybody eats well, you have a good society, because to eat well means a lot of things.

To me, the question is how do we get there, given our very different social conditions now. One of the things we have to ask ourselves is whether all the technological innovations that are happening now are really good. Of course technology is wonderful, but we have to find a balance between what technology can do for us, and what it actually gives us amazing pleasure to do for ourselves. For example, I grow special Danish pickling cucumbers on my roof; I don't have to do it, but it gives me enormous pleasure. In fact, probably more pleasure, in terms of that sense of being alive, of being part of an earthly cycle, than anything else I've ever done. That's really beautiful, and I think we've lost sight of simple pleasures like that. Food, for me, is the most obvious way that we can reconnect with those kinds of pleasures: growing it, cooking it, sharing it and taking time for it.

To welcome back the table as a communal space. Have you seen—it's not new anymore—this commercial of Ikea? Ikea is talking about the table again and they don't talk about the kitchen anymore. They talk about the table, like a communal space where you can do a lot of things. You can work there, you can eat there... Not a specific space, but a generic space, that we have to recover.

Yeah, that's really interesting. You're absolutely right. I should tell you about Sitopia, maybe, this invented word of mine, which is in the last chapter of *Hungry City*. The reason I invented it was because I was researching "Utopia", and Utopians talk endlessly about food. They talk about farming, about sustaining the community, about waste or communal dining, but they never saw food as an overall connecting principle. And it just struck me, when I realized that Utopia was a joke word that could either mean a "good place" or "no place", that it can never exist and it made me sad, but it occurred to me that we could have an alternative, by recognizing how deeply our lives are shaped by food, and use that as a multidisciplinary way of thinking about how we should live instead. That's why I invented the word, which comes from Greek *"sitos"*, food and *"topos"*, place. The whole point about it is that we already live in Sitopia; just a bad one, because we have not made it consciously. Tiny changes can immediately make it a better Sitopia, and that's the great thing. Food is a practical tool for making real change, and we can all use it right now—which is why it's so powerful.

Stephen Bates

On the Table

The domestic rituals that we all share in our everyday lives lie at the heart of housing design and any consideration of home as a cultural notion. It is through an understanding of how these activities play out and a willingness to allow them to find their form in space that design can be meaningful. This requires empathy, treading in the footsteps of others and seeing the world through their eyes, in order to offer possibilities that might go beyond our own imagination as designers. To do this, it is important not only to recognize the origins of these rituals, their evolution and relevance, but also to acknowledge that specific forms and objects have over time become inextricably connected with many of these activities. [Fig.1]

A central thread to the idea of domesticity is the condition of companionship, the sharing of time and place with others. The word 'companion' evolved through Middle English and Old French from the Latin *companio*, formed by the word *con*, meaning together, with, and *panis*, bread, or more generally, food. The idea of 'breaking bread with someone' lies at the root of our idea of companionship: coming together at the table, sharing food, com-

Fig. 1: Farmhouse near Parma, from Aldo Rossi, *A Scientific Autobiography*, MIT Press, Cambridge, Massachusetts and London, England, 1981.

ing within touch of others. Similarly, the term 'convivial', indicates a sociable, friendly, enjoyable atmosphere, and is based on the Latin *convivium*, for a feast or banquet and, more broadly, for living together, from *con* + *vivo*.

The table is central to our notion of domesticity, and has evolved over time from a practical device providing a working surface and support for domestic implements to a space-making object that reinforces social and emotional bonds. It is perhaps the most significant communal object in a home, a signifier of intimacy, which, while in origin indicated by the sharing of food, has evolved in parallel with contemporary lifestyles to accommodate other rituals. Amidst the increasingly private spaces of the contemporary home, the table endures as a communal docking point, for feasting or romantic dinners for two, for homework or as a place to 'spread things out'. It reinforces the bonds of companionship, providing a venue for togetherness and a catalyst for family gatherings and household activities.

In the domestic setting of the fifteenth century and for over a hundred years afterwards, the table was demountable, a flat surface supported on

Fig. 2: The Hall, Penshurst Place, Kent.

trestle legs, to be stacked against the walls of the room along with benches, and brought out when necessary. Fig. 2 For the medieval home was a public, rather than a private place, and in most houses the large ground floor room or hall was in constant use for cooking, eating, entertaining, for business and even for sleeping. Domestic space needed to be used in numerous ways over the day and night, for various activities which often occurred in close succession and required rooms to be quickly re-organised. No attempt was made to form permanent arrangements of furniture, as constant improvisation was required; the table itself was used for preparing food, eating, counting money and even for sleeping on.

The French and Italian words for furniture *meubles* and *mobili*, both derive from the Latin *mobilis*, movable. Demountability also suited the semi-nomadic lifestyle of the nobility, who moved from residence to residence with their household, furniture and furnishings in tow. Unlike the 'master bed' or the 'armchair', the table was treated more as a piece of equipment than as a prized possession.

Fig. 3: Mary Ellen Best, *An Interior*, 1837–1840, New York, Cooper-Hewitt, National Design Museum, Smithsonian Institution.

The evolution of the table from a temporarily useful tool in the Middle Ages to a more permanent fixture, as we know it in the twenty-first century, occurred in parallel to a number of overlapping phenomenological developments within a relatively short period of time in the mid-eighteenth century: the development and refinement of the chair for comfortable sitting, the assigning of certain rooms to specific uses reinforced by furniture dedicated to specific functions, and the development of 'society' gatherings which focused on conversation, card playing, embroidery, tea drinking and debate. As the 'home' became more a place of leisure and rooms became connected one to another within a ritualized continuum, the objects placed in them came to signify their use, as the objects themselves (the table, for instance) became traces of specific functions. Such change in signification required the formal appearance of the table to change from a lightweight demountable element to one endowed with weight and physical presence. The development of the drawing room in the last quarter of the eighteenth century is an example of this: in this room, which became mainly

Fig. 4: Carl André, *Aluminium Square Nine*, 2006.

the domain of the women in the house, tables and chairs were permanently located at the centre of the room, rather than against the wall. [Fig.3] The room was consciously arranged to denote a certain decorum and the status of the hostess, and so the table became more elaborate, often heavier as an object, and was no longer used as a merely functional object, but also to define the actual space around it.

The known use and signification of a room were reinforced by furniture and provided inhabitants with a common code that gave spatial structure to the domestic setting. It also gave them intellectual control over architectural space, for example to withdraw into a more private space, or to engage in a more intimate dialogue with others. Parallel to this personalization of space was the evolution of the concept of 'self', which first emerged during the Enlightenment and by the mid-eighteenth century was being redefined from a scientific concept to an anthropological and social state. Interior spaces came to relate to the idea of 'interiority', addressing not only the challenges of comfortable spatial arrangements

Fig. 5: Luigi Caccia Dominioni, annotated plan.

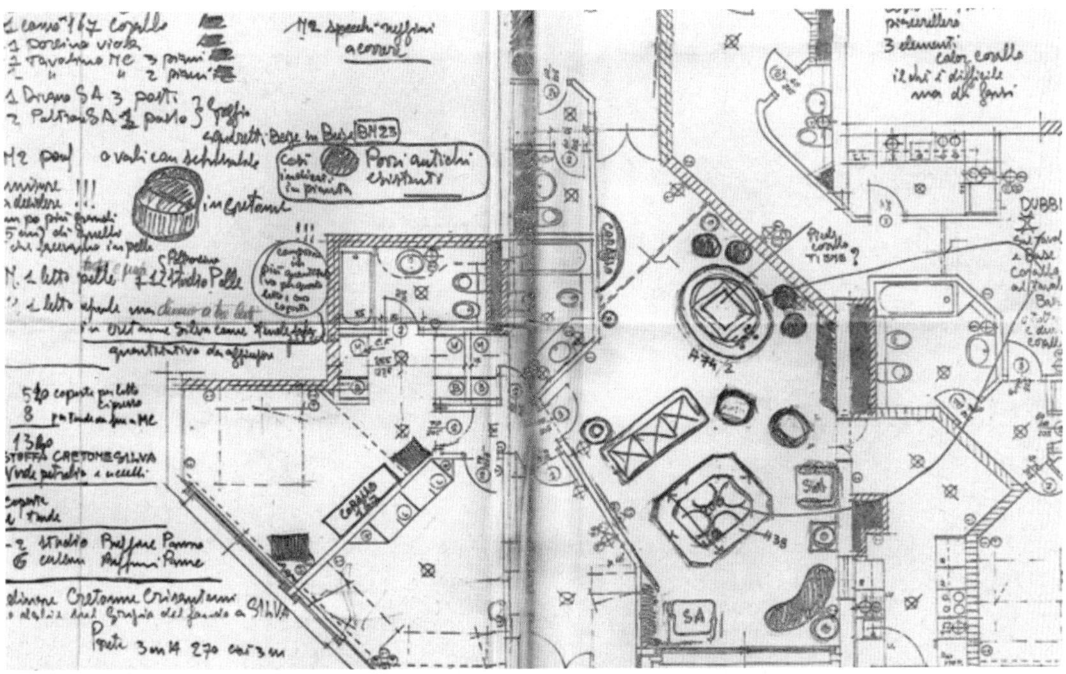

but also the question of staking out a personal territory, giving it meaning and representing it. The way we live became a sign of the way we think, feel and imagine the world. While representing our view of the world, furniture also provided the prop for such speculation within a protected interior, an ergonomic support for thinking or writing. These reflections on the evolution of the meaning of furniture, and of the table in particular, create a context for working as a designer. They explore the complex and multi-layered condition we call domesticity and offer insights into our embodied relationship with furniture and space.

The floor installations by Carl André are used to occupy space: his sculptures in iron, steel, copper, aluminium, sawn timber and clay 'seize and hold' the surrounding space. Fig. 4 In accommodating and reflecting the dimensions and form of the room in which the work is placed, André makes the place itself an essential component of his sculpture. His works are set out in such a way that the observer is encouraged (sometimes forced) to walk over or around them. These works highlight the setting they occupy,

Fig. 6: From Georges Perec, *Species of Spaces and other pieces*, Penguin Books, 1997.

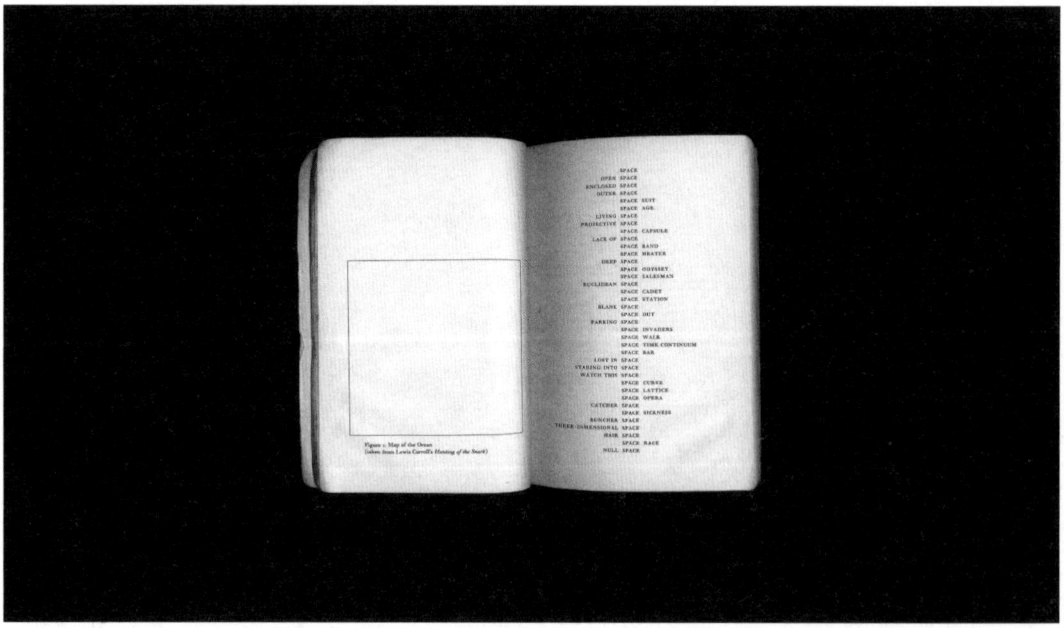

or rather they give those who experience them a heightened awareness of the surrounding environment. At the forefront of Minimalism in the 1960s, André explored the idea of an 'active' observer whose perception of the work, the surrounding space and of oneself is sharpened through the experience. Inspired by Maurice Merleau-Ponty's *Phenomenology of Perception* André recognized that perception is not just a visual phenomenon but involves the entire body. His sculptures are not just about the physical objects themselves, but about the space around them and about the observer's physical engagement and encounter with them. In this sense the object educates the participant.

Similarly, the Milanese architect Luigi Caccia Dominioni explored the relationship between space and furniture in the pursuit of domestic comfort in his interior architecture between the 1950s and 70s. In 1947, at the start of his career Caccia Dominioni concentrated on furniture design and, together with Ignazio Gardella, Corrado Corradi Dell' Acqua, Maria Teresa and Franca Tosi, established Azucena, a company manufacturing bespoke

Fig. 7: *Mansion block*, Fitzjohn's Avenue, Hampstead, London, Sergison Bates architects.

furniture for residential clients. Combining his educational background in functionalism and his bourgeois upbringing with its focus on ritual and leisure, Caccia Dominioni was able to see the inter-relationship between the objects in a room and the room itself. In the context of a weak post-war economy and widespread housing scarcity, with apartments and rooms diminishing in size, Caccia Dominioni prioritized the optimization of space and sought to create a perception of generosity and comfort in his work.

As a self-styled *pianista* (a pun which conflates the idea of the piano-player and the planmaker) he approached the domestic plan as a spatial continuum to be experienced by the individual in an uninterrupted flow, as if in constant movement. He declared, "I am an architect to the core and I find urbanism everywhere... In reality, the apartment is a micro city, with its paths, its constraints, its public and private spaces. I have always had a passion for small spaces and have always done all I can to make them feel larger, for example by extending the routes, contrary to a certain trend to reduce them. I don't like a direct entry into the living room, because then

Fig. 8: Kettle's Yard, Cambridge.

there are no surprises, while the role of the architect, I believe, is also to evoke a sequence of emotions. (...) my entrances, my staircases, even the furniture are urban solutions" (quoted in M. A. Crippa, *Luigi Caccia Dominioni. Flussi, spazi e architettura*, Torino: Testo e imagine, 1996, p. 9).

In designing apartments, Caccia Dominioni imagined invisible pathways that connect spaces with moments of encounter and surprise, such as curved stretches of walls or small niches, to evoke emotions and to amuse the owner. These pathways reveal themselves only gradually, creating scenographic impressions and disclosing unexpected details. Fig. 5 Furniture pieces provide settings that establish distinct territories and prompt a variety of possible uses. In contrast to straight sightlines, which immediately show what is to come, his plans work with diagonal views and segmented routes between spaces, enriching the character of an apartment without limiting its sense of spatial generosity. On entering, one catches a glimpse of a series of spaces but it is never clear where they actually end, so that the apartment feels bigger than it actually is. Through the shap-

Fig. 9: St. John Restaurant, Smithfield, London.

ing of the rooms, the placing of furniture and the control of sightlines, the dimension of the interior is not fully revealed, but unfolds as one moves through the plan and new vistas open up.

In *Species of spaces and other pieces* (Penguin Books, 1997), Georges Perec presents the interior as a serialization of objects, movements and operations, which become ultimately and intimately linked to the inner life of the mind. Referring to his own writing table, he emphasizes that this is not simply an object on which he writes, but a carrier of specific types of imagination. Perec was aware that the domestic interior, like the table, has always been a metaphor for consciousness in all its dimensions. Fig. 6 Interiority is a space where all the trajectories of consciousness as intentional experience unfold, from awareness to remembrance and imagination.

The work of such artists, designers and writers feels relevant and informs our work in the making of domestic arrangements. The object—the table, in this case—and the space are entwined, as the object gives both purpose and meaning to the space around it. Today, in the context of compact

Fig. 10: Maggie's Centre, Fulham, London.

house planning, the evolution of complex households and our increasing dependence on digital communication (both infrastructural and social), the table remains a central element of the home. Despite the strangely conservative and slow-moving development of spatial alternatives to established domestic arrangements, its role as a setting for bringing people together on the one hand, and for making space on the other, has endured. While it continues to multi-task, the table is still the main catalyst for convivial gatherings in a domestic setting. Coming together at the table still marks moments of intimacy in our increasingly secluded domestic world.

Thinking about different ways of organising a house, perhaps in resistance to the often impotent tendency to follow linear patterns established by Modernist principles based on identifying 'functions', the placing of a table contributes to a densification of thought.

With the table at the centre, the plan can radiate outwards transforming a compact plan into an interconnected domestic landscape of views and cross views, of 'almost rooms' and transitional spaces. Fig. 7

Fig. 11: Table and banco, Wooden House by Norbert Fritz, Innsbruck, Austria.

Tailored in size and shape to fit the space around it like a glove, the table creates a setting in which it is the 'room' itself—a micro environment within a structure of surrounding spaces. Fig. 8 A table can be made to ensure the greatest proximity with your companion(s), so narrow that it dissolves habitual expectations of physical distance, and dining becomes an intimate exchange, with dining plates, glasses and cutlery forming overlapping patterns. Fig. 9 Or it can be dimensioned so that there is no 'head' but only a shared end—a rectangle that wants to be a square—encouraging inclusivity and a comfortable distance between those sitting across the table. Fig. 10 A table can be so small that it is really the domain of an individual, placed to interlock with a banco against the wall to provide a protective vantage point, with natural light from the side. Fig. 11

The table may be transformed, moved, folded in parts or rotated, reacting to and interacting with the user in unexpected ways. In so doing, it forms a kind of landscape of events in itself—it can change every day—transforming the space in which it is set. Fig. 12 The form of a table is some-

Fig. 12: Enric Miralles, *Mesa Inestable*.

times adjusted to respond to the constraints of a particular space. In turn, such modifications influence the dynamics of the relationships that are created between those who sit around it. This is particularly evident when the table is placed in a different space, and the original constraint removed. Fig. 13

The long table can be many things at any one time, a placing for a meal for two, a stacking place for books, a perch for a dozing cat, a place to drop the post and keys—a docking point that confirms you are now home. And at another time, a surface cleared for a banquet. Fig. 14 The social potential of the table becomes relevant beyond the single-family house or apartment, for new models of collective living that quietly invite greater interaction between people. Fig. 15

Domesticity is a specifically human language, where spatial and symbolic arrangements transform mere space into a home. To be a home, a house needs stability and sense of time—a strong embodied relation between an interior space and the sense of interiority that memories and desires bring. The table is a crucial focal point in the home: it carries the

Fig. 13: Table in use at TU München.

memory of conviviality, the promise of intimacy as well as the potential for concentrated activity—in the most fundamental way, the table embodies the many ways we inhabit space.

Fig. 14: Marie-José Van Hee, House on Pig Street, Gent.

Fig. 15: Co-op housing at River Spreefeld, Berlin, by Carpaneto Architekten, Fatkoehl Architekten, BAR Architektend.

Carlos Dias Coelho

Organizing the City Around the Dining Room

Why the dining room?

The study of the home has already covered all its spaces, functions and evolution over time and cultures. The interpretation of its uses has already been questioned, evaluating the intended use and versatility of its different spaces. The spatial and functional essence of the home has been sought many times and the kitchen has been chosen as the essential and fundamental space of the "home" in its practical sense, without dissociating it, however, from a religious meaning.

Less importance has been given to the dining room[1] in the organization of urban housing in the bourgeois and industrial city, at a time when the city grew the most in the West. Fig.1 Nowadays, in a time that we could call *post-living*, the topic of subdivided spaces, apt for specific functions, is once again on the agenda.

We must not forget that households that had a dining room as an essential space, produced for close to 100 years in the second half of the 19th century and the first half of the 20th, are still not only an important reference for the production of domestic space, but are still lived in and reused, in overwhelming numbers among inhabited homes in the contemporary European city.

The dining room in the home

The projects and research that historically address this room identify their appearance in our society around the 18th century. After passing through indistinct spaces of the house and having left the "chambers" where people slept, received, and ate, the function of eating moved on to the antechambers and gained a space with a more specific purpose. In this way, we can place its consolidation in Paris, at the end of the Old Regime, as a specialized part of that typological invention that is the *hôtel particulier*, from which it was passed on to the apartment building.

However, the practice of "setting the table" in the different rooms of an *enfilade* did not disappear and the orientation of a unique and exclusive space towards this function took place very slowly.

European elites progressively promoted the appearance of this space of coexistence, with eating as the great excuse. In less than a century, its victory was redundant, extended to an urban bourgeoisie, numerous and influential, and even in some cities such as Lisbon it became part of an essential space in the organization of the home during a specific era.

The popularization of this room, which became essential, came about in response to the social practices of an emerging class and went through

1
The compartment that in Spanish receives the name of 'dining room', a generic name for its function, is related in French, German, and Danish with the space/function association (*salle à manger, esszimmer, spisestue*) and in English, Italian and Portuguese , with space and 'one' of the specific parts (dining room, *pranzo* room, or *jantar* room).

the different economic levels through which the bourgeoisie was distributed. With different dimensions, accessories, and adornments, the dining room constituted an unrivaled domestic space, where a family showed itself off to others, interacted with them, and practiced their "urbanity". It was not in the more open "salon", which before the arrival of the telephone could be accessed without invitation or appointment, although at defined times, but in the dining room where the family chose those who it wanted to honor, providing the best it could offer: good food in a prepared setting and with choreographed rituals, where the social and economic position of the person receiving guests, and the one being received, could be decoded. [Fig. 2]

Fig. 1: "le Dîner"—Claude Monet, 1869. Bührle Foundation, Zürich, Switzerland.

At a time when Western society grew as never before and accommodated this emerging and numerous social class, such an outstanding novelty had to be supported by expeditious methods that could respond to this new demand. Thus, the serialized, we could even say industrialized, nature of the response was remarkable. Spatially, the housing of expansion districts was produced from standardized types, as we will see later on for the specific case of Lisbon.

Fig. 2: Victorian dining room, Berkley House. cerca 1900. Great Britain.

This space had to be defined—and for that, decorated, furnished, dressed, and equipped—so all the "civilized" nations developed a relevant manufactured production. If we exclude a small elite that could afford to commission a comprehensive project for a dining room, the overwhelming majority resorted to what the market provided. [Fig. 3]

In short, this room was furnished with a "stylish" setting, that is, resorting to a simplified "revival" vocabulary, and was expressed more commonly in the "Henry II", "Dutch style" ensembles, [Figs. 4 and 5] among many other national variations. Beyond the essential pieces consisting of table and the chairs, there were three support pieces, a side table, carving board, and china cabinet, which housed the porcelain, glassware, and cutlery services, adapted to the possibilities of each family. A set of decorative pieces, such as embroidered linens, complemented the necessary furniture

Fig. 3: Masson dining room 1903–1906. Art nouveau project of Eugène Vallin and Victor Prouvé. L'École Museum in Nancy.

for the grand staging of guest reception and the celebration of the most important family rites. Fig. 6

Fig. 4: A Jacobean style English dining room.

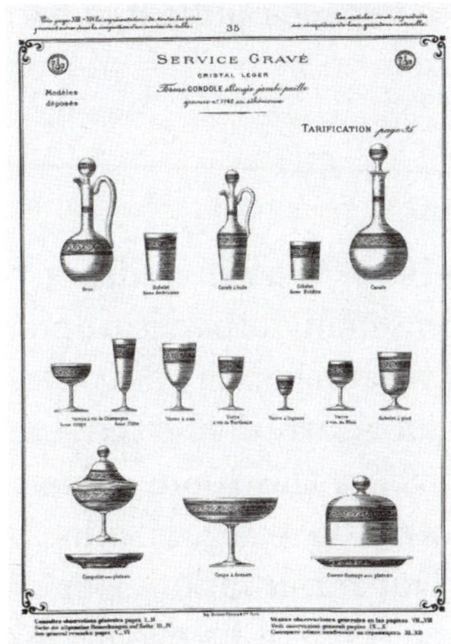

Fig. 5: "Service gravé"—Baccarat Catalogue 1907.

Strange late arrival

The force with which the dining room was popularized and contributed to the organization of urban housing from the second half of the 19th century is not strange, considering the roots of our civilization. The strange thing is, on the contrary, the fact that this phenomenon happened so late. If we think about the cultural foundations that many consider to be the two great pillars of Western civilization—classical antiquity and Christianity—we easily reinforce the feeling of incomprehension towards the recent arrival of this domestic space.

Since the late Middle Ages, monastic groups were organized based on fixed rules for each order, whether urban or rural, hermit or gregarious. The organization of the buildings of each religious community is clearly recognized, which, despite the distinctions, included—beyond the temple—the cloister, the chapter house, the cells or dormitories, and the refectory as its own space, predetermined and specifically organized for the purposes for which they were intended.

From the other pillar we can consider the organization of the *domus*. Although the Roman house was organized around a patio, it was oriented on an axis that crossed the house from the entrance to the *triclinium*, the latter being the most important and ceremonial room in the house, specifically dedicated to meals. If we wanted to further complicate the importance of this room/function and the contamination between these two cultural pillars of our civilization, we could discuss the constitution of the church itself as a space in the Roman Empire.

Fig. 6: "Dinner at Haddo House"—Alfred Edward Emslie, 1884. National Portrait Gallery. London.

The origin of the great Christian basilica, conceived after the official recognition of Christianity, is usually recognized as being the pagan basilica that served as a spatial reference. However, the local church had an earlier origin, when the cult was still clandestine and was carried out in private homes. The case of Santa Maria Antiqua, in Rome, is illustrative of the metamorphosis of a *domus* into a church, verifying the evolution of the *impluvium* to constitute the nave, the galleries as lateral aisles, and more surprising, the *triclinium* as the main chapel. Much could be speculated about the metamorphosis of a space intended for *real* food into a space conceived for mystical sustenance. In this way, it is surprising that neither in the Middle Ages, a period marked by the influence of the religious orders that organized much of the European space, nor later in the Renaissance, with the reintegration of many components lost or relegated in the classical culture of the West, was there a contamination of the domestic space and the creation of a room exclusively for food, instead relegating this function to shared spaces, almost indistinct in the whole series of rooms of a house.

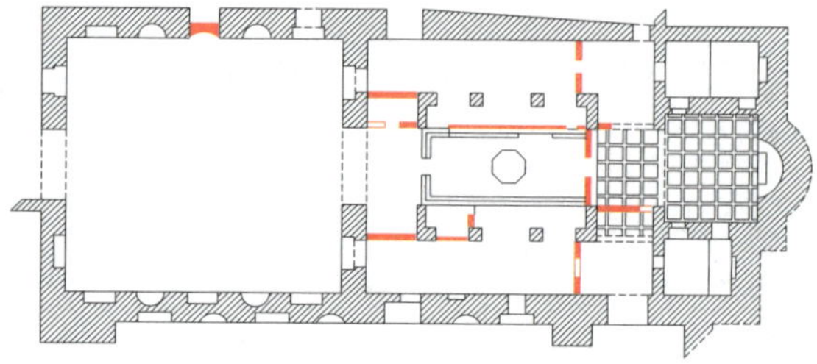

Santa María, Ancient Rome. Superposition of paleo-christian strata in the Roman house.

Acts of an appearance

The issue we will address has a specific scenario, Lisbon, as one case among many other European cities. Like all of them, it presents traces that we can identify as common, but also specificities of its own. In Lisbon, we can clearly define the stages that mark the evolution of collective housing, where this room gained such importance that it came to determine the structural organization of the entire home.

Our observation does not attempt to explain the appearance of the dining room or its evolution as a function or room, but to verify how, at a certain moment, this space contributed to, if not led, the organization of the current household. Finally, an interpretation will be made based on some examples that, in some way, crystallized into a continuous movement and that, in spite of appearing simultaneously, can be distanced some decades in time.

Thus, we will start the topic of the dining room with a prologue, that is, when the function existed independently of its exclusive location in a specific space, and we will conclude with an epilogue, when ideologically we want to eliminate the dining room as an autonomous space in the house.

Pombaline Lisbon

The city of Lisbon presents the peculiarity of having resorted in a systematic way to the production of serial housing before the Industrial Revolution. This was not due to an advance in ideas about urban production or as a consequence of an explosive growth resulting from a new economic cycle, but to the fact that the city suffered the impact of a great earthquake that destroyed it in 1755. After a short wait, the decades that followed saw feverish construction that, to ensure its effectiveness, involved the conception of an urban, architectural, and construction solution that allowed for a reconstruction of the city based on principles of standardization and prefabrication. The complex operation was led by the Marquis of Pombal, whose name today adorns the neighborhood, the design, and the process (Baixa Pombalina, Pombaline building, pombaline reconstruction).

The reconstruction involved the realization of a plan, fully executed in the La Baixa area of Lisbon, and that, in broad strokes, required the conception of an urban layout, including a rigid definition of streets and blocks; of a facade design, which characterized each of its streets by its importance; and of a construction technology, imposing the execution of a wooden "cage" inside the masonry as a form of seismic prevention, thus making possible the resistance of the buildings in the event of a new catastrophe.

These rules were applied to an entire building system that included a commercial floor and four housing floors above, including an attic. As the plan did not foresee or design plans for the typical home, but only for cases of great exceptionality, and the size of each building, uniform in its depth, varied enormously as a result of a redistribution that re-drew the property lines from what existed before the catastrophe, the result was a home of very elastic size, given proportion by the windows of the façade and conditioned by the size of those wooden structures that ended up being called "pombaline cages". The result was a home made up of rooms of similar size, three deep and an undefined number along the façade, creating three hierarchical levels: the front rooms, which faced the facade of the building, the rear rooms, which overlooked the patio, and the interior rooms.

This solution, consisting of a juxtaposition of similar spaces of varying importance, is notable for the versatility of uses and dimensions in which all the rooms can be assigned any function, and the size of the spaces can be doubled or tripled by the simple opening of the doors that join them, both in the longitudinal direction of the façade and transverse to it, in depth. On this chessboard, in which there are different combinations, there was only one previously assigned space: the kitchen.

It is not clear if there was a space intended for dining, although we know that the function was gradually consolidating into a specific room in large aristocratic residences and that, although without any original intention, ended up being fixed, a fact that can be seen from the decoration added in later times.

One hundred years after the earthquake, in the mid-nineteenth century, Lisbon followed the trend of European cities to open new expansion districts, in this specific case developing new areas not along the river, but for the first time to the north and inland. The houses of this bourgeois city of tree-lined avenues that came to be called Avenidas Novas ('New Avenues') no longer followed strict rules similar to those of a reconstruction process, but rather rules of a typological series that consistently repeats the application of a readable and understandable archetype that gradually adapts to the fluctuations of a society's desires and possibilities.

The main features of the nineteenth-century expansion districts are present in the case of Lisbon: broad, tree-lined avenues, defined by long blocks and with large inner courtyards, suitable for receiving buildings that, without being equal, were limited and regulated in the alignment of their façades and in their height, and which respected an established type.

In the organization of housing, the relatively small size of internal spaces survives, but their organization is already substantially different, with the appearance of two different spaces that determine the organization of the home: the hall and the dining room.

In a century that came between the two moments that we present, the organization of the home was gradually altered, highlighted by a certain specialization of its rooms, verifiable more by the decoration of the tiles, frescoes, and stuccoes that enriched them than by configuration, size, or relative position in the house.

Probably the size of the blocks in the Avenidas Novas—of similar size to those of a block of the Eixample of Barcelona—allowed and originated buildings with depth, with the existence of two ventilated and illuminated facades, although hierarchically very different, and the resource of the lateral or interior patios, which was aimed at improving the health conditions of the interior rooms.

The organization of the home was built around a new space—the corridor, which ran the entire depth of the building—and included opposing rooms on the main facade, where the reception room was generally located, and the two main rooms of the rear façade, which faced the interior of the block, where the kitchen was located along with a room specifically intended for dining.

The importance of this space, the dining room—the only room with a specific destination other than the kitchen—was reinforced not only by the size, being always the largest of all the rooms of the home, but also by the decoration applied to it, particularly painstakingly done and always allusive to the act of eating.

We must highlight some notes in the interpretation of the organization of this type of home. The first is the endurance of this type, which survived for nearly half a century and crossed various architectural periods, expressing itself in different styles such as end-of-century eclecticism, Art Nouveau or Decó, and even in the first examples of residential buildings that adhered to a modernist aesthetic. In the same way, it is seen in buildings of different quality, more current or erudite, with the differences concentrated in the details of the spaces, the design of the main facade, or finishes and interior decoration, rather than in the organizational logic of the home. Finally, it is worth noting the irrelevance of the segregation of housing areas by the nature of their use, intimate/private or public/collective, in favor of the hierarchical relations established by proximity to the facades, concentrating the reception areas at both ends of the building, and relating the dining room with the service, that is, the kitchen.

The Lisbon of "Soft-Portuguese" style[2]

The second act of this story begins with the condemnation of the courtyard as a supposedly unhealthy space. Indeed, the victory of the social hygiene movement's ideas that imposed a supply of ventilation and natural light to all the rooms of a house had its origin in the social and regulatory rejection of the possibility of organizing a home based on internal or lateral courtyards.

The systematic construction of multi-family housing buildings of a type that became established in the early 1940s and lasted two decades, which modern architects contemptuously call *Rabo de bacalhau*,[3] was the result of the consolidation of a conservative political and bourgeoisie regime that congratulated itself over a pacified society.

These residential buildings recover a language of academic inspiration and react to the first modernist essays, which in Lisbon have above all a "plastic" flavor of exploration of a new material—concrete—and its aesthetic possibilities. All this architectural production, mistakenly considered anti-modern for its apparent containment and recovery of traditional values, was called *Soft-Portuguese.*

The reason for the exploration and arrival of this type of housing, called *rabo de bacalhau*, is none other than the opening of the side yard to the inner courtyard of the block. This approach has a scholarly parallel in the proposals of the *a redant* buildings of the early twentieth century. However, if the origin of the French *redant* was a scholarly speculation on how to enhance the lighting and ventilation of a building by trimming its street-side facade, and which consumed itself in specific cases, the appearance

2
"Soft Portuguese" is an expression used vulgarly to define this 1940's era Portuguese architecture of commitment that never had the radicalism of the Italian or the monumentalism of the German. It was used because it was the name of a very popular cigarette brand that was called *Português Suave*.

3
The *rabo de bacalhau* gets its name from the shape of the floor of these houses, which narrows to the side of the block's patio, and which bears a certain resemblance to a salted whole cod. Portugal is a large consumer of cod.

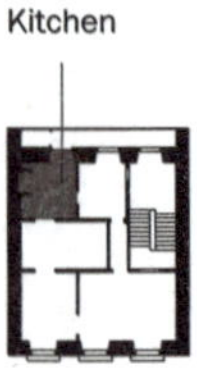

R. Augusta 109–113

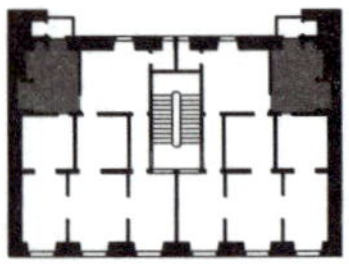
R. da Prata 210–220

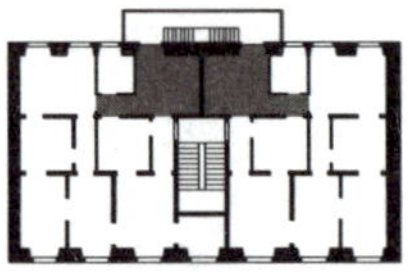
R. Augusta 170–182

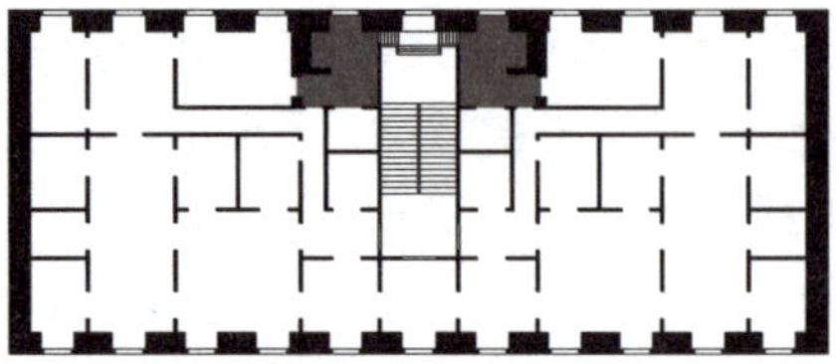
R. dos Franqueiros, projecto, 1805

Pombaline Lisbon

Lisbon of the Avenidas Novas

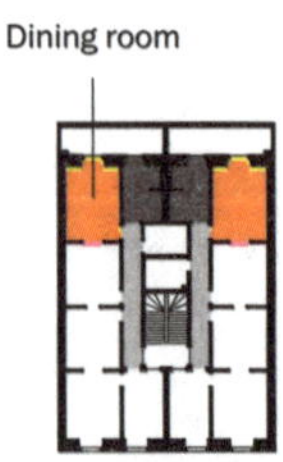

R. Bernardim Ribeiro 22

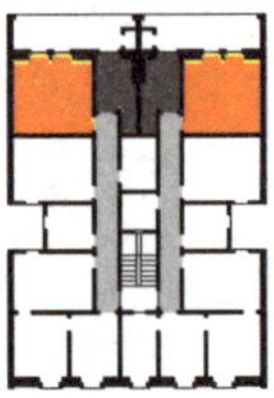
R. Bernardim Ribeiro 22

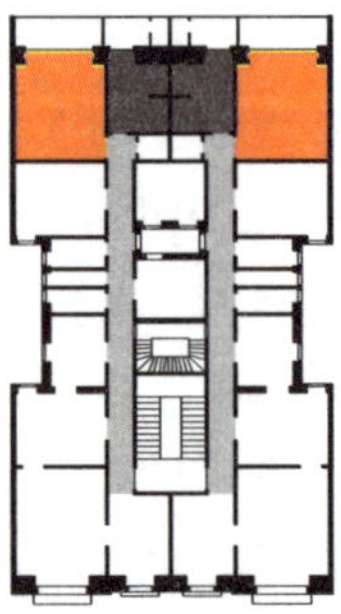
Av. da Liberdade 23–23A

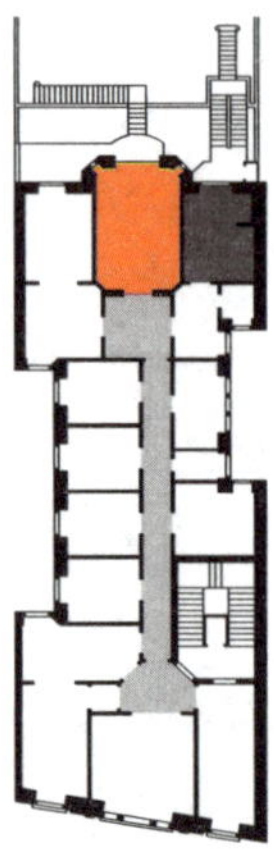
Av. Duque d'Ávila 26–30

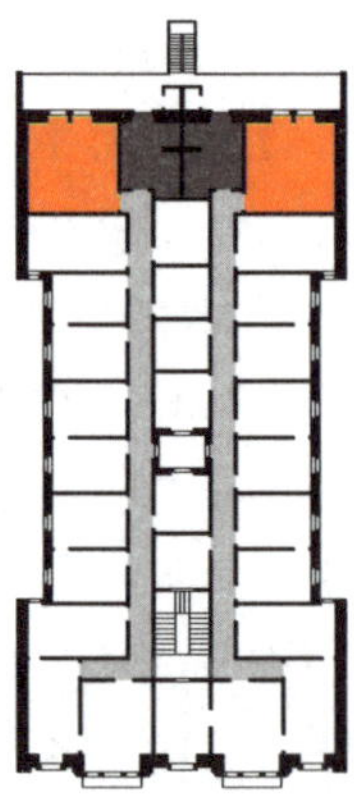
R. Braamcamp 10

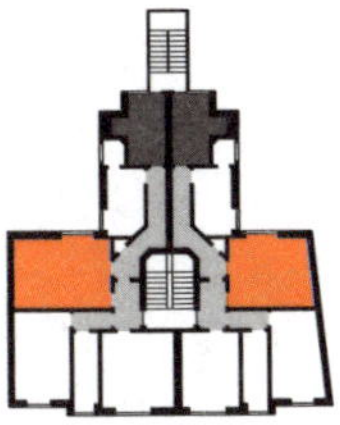

R. de São Ciro 58

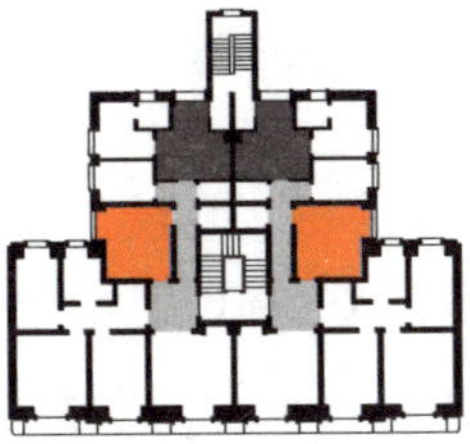

Av. Guerra Junqueiro 15

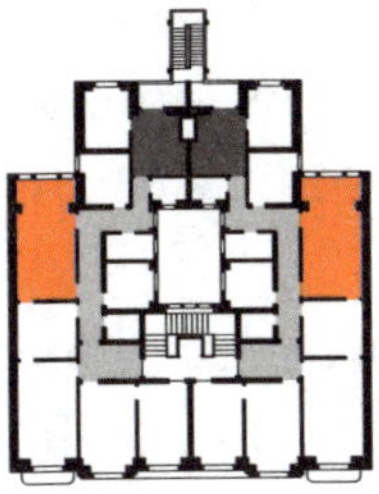

R. Rodrigo da Fonseca 75

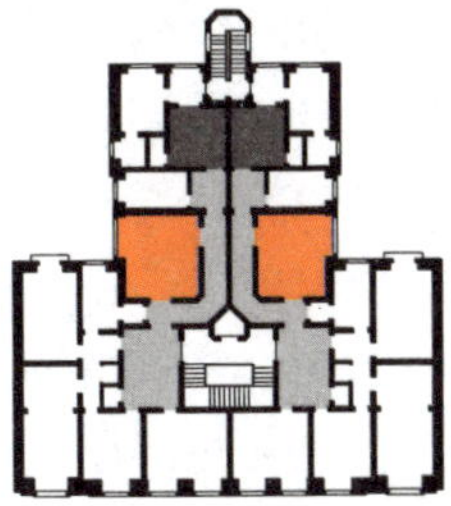

Al. Dom Afonso Henriques 78

Lisbon of "Soft-Portuguese"

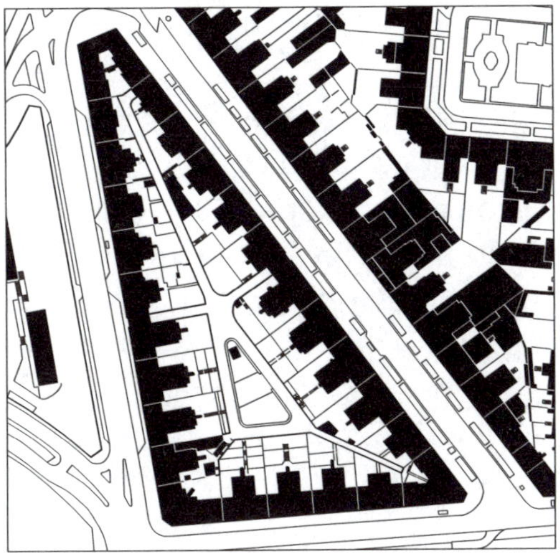

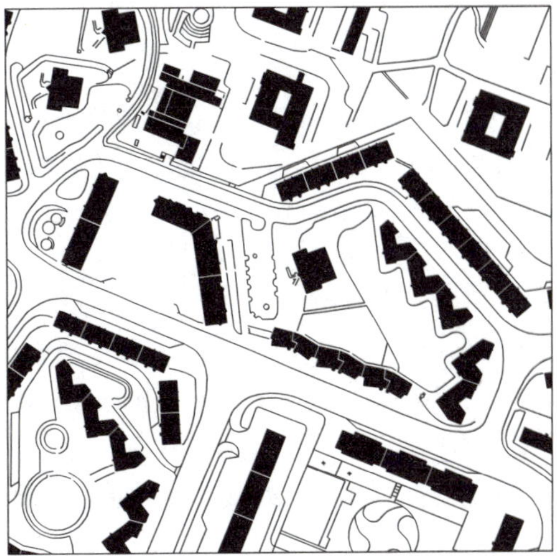

Modernist Lisbon

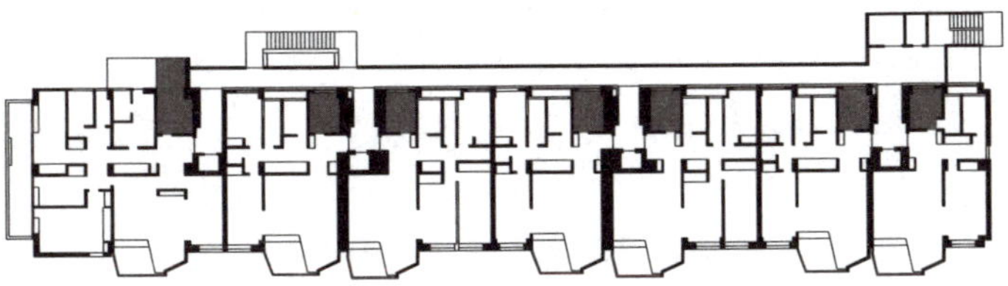

Bloco das Águas Livres, Pç. das Águas Livres 8–81

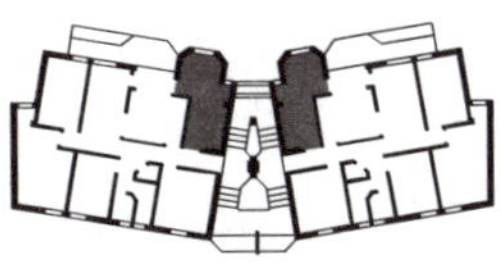

R. Cidade de Moçâmedes 242

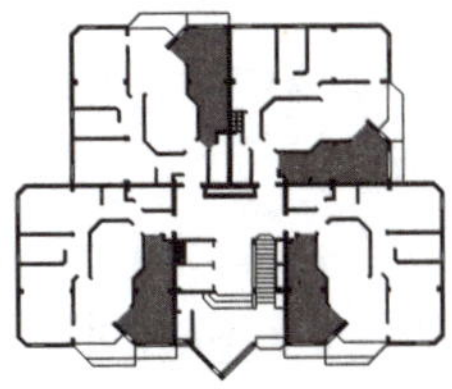

R. Cidade de Carmona 240

of the *rabo de bacalhau* in Lisbon, which is nothing more than a *redant* that faces the interior of the block, did not have previous theoretical support, although it became widespread, coming to characterize the new neighborhoods of the city.

The solution explored by *rabo de bacalhau* allowed for the illumination and ventilation of all the rooms of the home, including the bathrooms, without the building losing its character and its traditional relationship with the street, starting from an aligned and continuous façade. It was organized in two perpendicular volumes, depending on the depth of the block: one along the length of the facade and the other, a "tail" extending into the backyard. The two bodies were oriented towards different functions, with the street-side facade keeping the functions of rooms and bedrooms, almost comparable to the organization of the pombaline building, and, in the tail, the functions linked to the entirety of building services, where the kitchen and annexes, the service staircase, and the maid's quarters were located.

The unique feature of the typology lies in the articulation between the two bodies and the way to make it a reality. In fact, this articulation is done by means of the room intended for dining, which is directly related to the entrance of the house as well as connected to the kitchen area and annexes via a system of broken corridors that guarantee the independence of the service areas from the front of the house.

When looking at the plans for some buildings of this type, we understand the key role of the dining room in the organization of the home and the distinct and effective way of relating the two bodies of the building. We can even note that the room retains the importance of being the largest room in the home, although, due to its position, its configuration has been altered slightly, approaching a square shape more so than the elongated rectangle of the buildings of the Avenidas Novas.

The opposing nature of the building sections is evident and does justice to the name attributed to this period of "Soft-Portuguese". The street-side facade is organized based on regularity and the repetition of openings, through a classic and discreet language, often without being able to determine which rooms are located behind each window of the main facade.

In contrast, the inner body of the block is clearly treated with a facade that is not public and that identifies, through the size of the windows, all the rooms and volumes that comprise it, be these service stairs, the kitchen and its gallery, or bedrooms, and particularly identified by the largest opening: the dining room. This type of solution lasted approximately two decades and disappeared with the arrival of the second modernism, at the end of the 1950s.

The death of *rabo de bacalhau* occured, above all, for ideological reasons. The fight for the modern and the architects who wanted to implement a new form of housing were opposed to the bourgeois and traditional life that supported that type of housing. It was condemned as an architecture of concessions from which the aesthetic and ideological vanguard was excluded.

Inspired by the great international debates and the architecture that rebuilt Europe after the destruction of World War II, the architects of this new period applied a new idea of home organization to housing production, whose only possibility for acceptance was with many adaptations, in a country that in reality remained in another era.

The history of modernism and modern housing has been the object of all kinds of interpretations and here we will only highlight the aspects that contributed to the condemnation and death of the dining room as an autonomous room. Indeed, the modern home is organized around a distinction between the private and group spaces of the home, and in the latter the living or common room prevailed, that is to say, a generic space that contained all the collective activities of the house characterized by the functions of "being" and "eating".

The impact of a typology that intended to educate instead of responding to the wishes of society explains why the first large trials were carried out in buildings intended for an economically and culturally privileged social class. On the other hand, the fact that these buildings continued to have large areas dedicated to home service functions, mainly large areas for the kitchen and servants' room, explains the need for concessions, but also the markedly ideological nature of the combat against the dining room as an autonomous room.

When looking at the plans of the homes in the Aguas Libres building, designed in 1956, which includes a remarkable typological variety, we see that only the biggest home, with four rooms, includes the living room as a space that could be interpreted as more autonomous.

The large urban operation in the neighborhood of Os Olivais—markedly modern in appearance, although influenced by naturalistic ideas of Scandinavian urbanism—brought this new model of home to buildings of a more social nature, which questioned the rules of the traditional city, but in which the home, by not having a dining room, organized the common room in a compound way in order to allow one of its corners to be destined for this purpose.

In the plans of the buildings in this neighborhood, built for a population that was less culturally integrated into European intellectual currents, this multi-spatial composition of the common room is curiously more evident, even though, in many cases, the home no longer realistically contemplates any service room beyond the kitchen.

The revenge of the real

If lifestyle habits and social practices sometimes change very quickly, the built city resists beyond the functions and objectives that were granted at a given time.

The homes that were organized without a space dedicated to dining received or adapted one when the moment demanded it. On the other hand, households that were conceived or organized taking into account the existence of this room, continue to be part of the majority of the built fabric of this and other cities.

What we have explained with a succession of phases is, in fact, a superposition of layers that coexist and are part of our daily life. The question is to know how this ritual of meals in common is present today and in the near future in the different ways of life found in an urban population, and how those spaces specifically planned for a function can be adapted, transfigured, and used for other purposes, or returned to the initial use.

David Steeggmann

The New Meaning of a Collective Space: La Boqueria Market

The last five decades have put the survival of the local market in check. It has been a period in which these old facilities, the nerve center of the city since antiquity, have gradually been losing importance in the urban food supply chain, in many cases disappearing. In this context, in Barcelona and in cities around the world, a good number of markets are still standing at the expense of changing their traditional fare, offering an increasing presence of prepared food. Halfway between the supermarket, the mall, and the restaurant, many of them stand today as a new urban space for the sale and consumption of food considerably removed from its original function.

Characterized by the sale of unprocessed fresh produce, market fare has been linked to activity in the kitchen, while many of the supermarket products, often created in response to the emergence of certain lifestyles, have facilitated an increasingly lighter use of that space. The prosperity of the supermarket—as opposed to the decline of the traditional market—derives from important changes in the food dynamics of contemporary society. We can say that one of the most notable of these, due to its influence on the landscape that makes up the collective space of the city, is the increase in meals away from home, an phenomenon inseparable from the progressive loss of culinary skills in the domestic sphere, as Michael Pollan reminds us.

The inertia of the market, in these cases, seems to continue to reside in the socializing factor of the space, still in the idea of the square, but associated with the development of new patterns, dynamics, and forms of consumption of the urban population.

Market, supermarket and restaurant

The consolidation of the gastronomic era, inaugurated by the enlightened thought of Brillant-Savarin nearly two centuries ago, has put food at the center of the scene. Contemporary urban society has developed what François Ascher calls the eclectic individual, characterized, in his own words, by not possessing an exclusive taste and instead projecting on the city various systems of values and references. Possibilities of choice have permeated the urban space, converting it into a reflection of the preferences of its inhabitants. In the context of a consumer society, the figure of the restaurant, paradigm of the individualization of food, seems to have come to stay. The growing number of spaces dedicated to the restaurant industry is turning this service into the most important in many cities. In Barcelona, for example, many streets seem to be leaning towards specialization in this sector, as is the case of Blai, Verdi, Parlament or Enric Granados.[1]

1
Enric Granados Street in Barcelona, for example, currently has 42 stores dedicated in one way or another to the restaurant sector, many of them opened between 2008 and 2012, when fifteen years ago there were only a handful. Since then, the number of bar and restaurant openings in the city has not stopped growing, today totaling more than 7,400 establishments. Currently, the regulations of the Eixample district, at the top of the ranking of openings, establish control protocols in the face of the proliferation of this type of monoculture, and you cannot open a business of this type if there are four others in a radius of 50 meters.

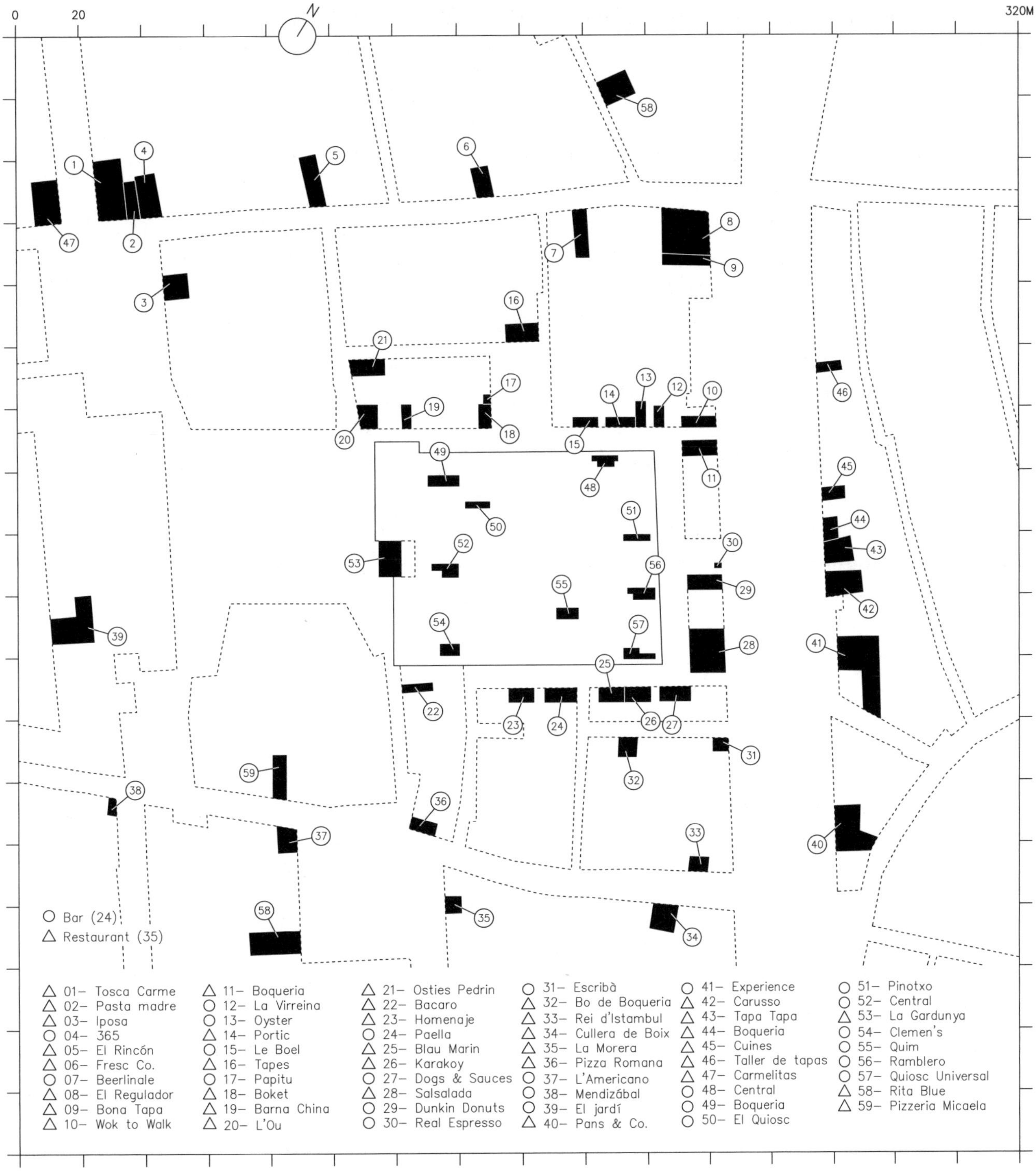

BARS AND RESTAURANTS WITHIN THE BUSINESS PERIMETER OF LA BOQUERIA 2018

Globally, the supermarket has been stalked for years by the boom in the restaurant sector,—if we eat out, we do not do so at home—that's why prepared food has more and more presence in its display cases. Some markets seem to be following the same path in their struggle for survival against the same adversary. In cities around the world, these markets are consolidating into a new urban figure, as Carolyn Steel has described it, not so much a place dedicated to the food trade as to the celebration of food. The appearance of more and more food stalls prepared in different formats is one of the most evident features of this change, which seems to follow a common pattern regardless of where we are and which, in many cases, is directly related to the transformation of the neighborhood itself in which these markets are located.

In contrast with the inaction of many cities, Barcelona has opted for trade in small format and proximity, promoting legislation that is friendly to the market. As a result, this city currently has 39 neighborhood supply markets spread across all its districts. Even so, many of Barcelona's markets have been changing their fare, focusing on the new model, especially those located in areas with a high influx of tourists, such as the district of Ciutat Vella.

A market in transformation

The market of Sant Josep, better known as La Boqueria, is an example that is worth examining closely. The increasingly evident effects of its progressive transformation, especially over the last decade, have attracted the attention of the media, the City Council and citizens themselves. The opening of more and more prepared food stalls, generally for take-away, and the sale of snacks as a complement to the business of traditional stalls, are giving this space an environment that is increasingly different from that of a traditional food market. During this time, many surrounding spaces have been converted into improvised outdoor dining rooms, such as the recently inaugurated La Gardunya Square, which shows the impact of market changes on the city.

The current increase in the supply of prepared food in many markets around the world is related to several factors that operate simultaneously. The most obvious, in the case of La Boqueria, is undoubtedly tourism and its growing influence in that part of the city. The limitation of guided visits to small groups on certain days of the week allows us to intuit the magnitude of the accessibility problems in a place like the market caused by the widespread growth associated with this phenomenon. But tourists not only occupy space, their presence generates business expectations that

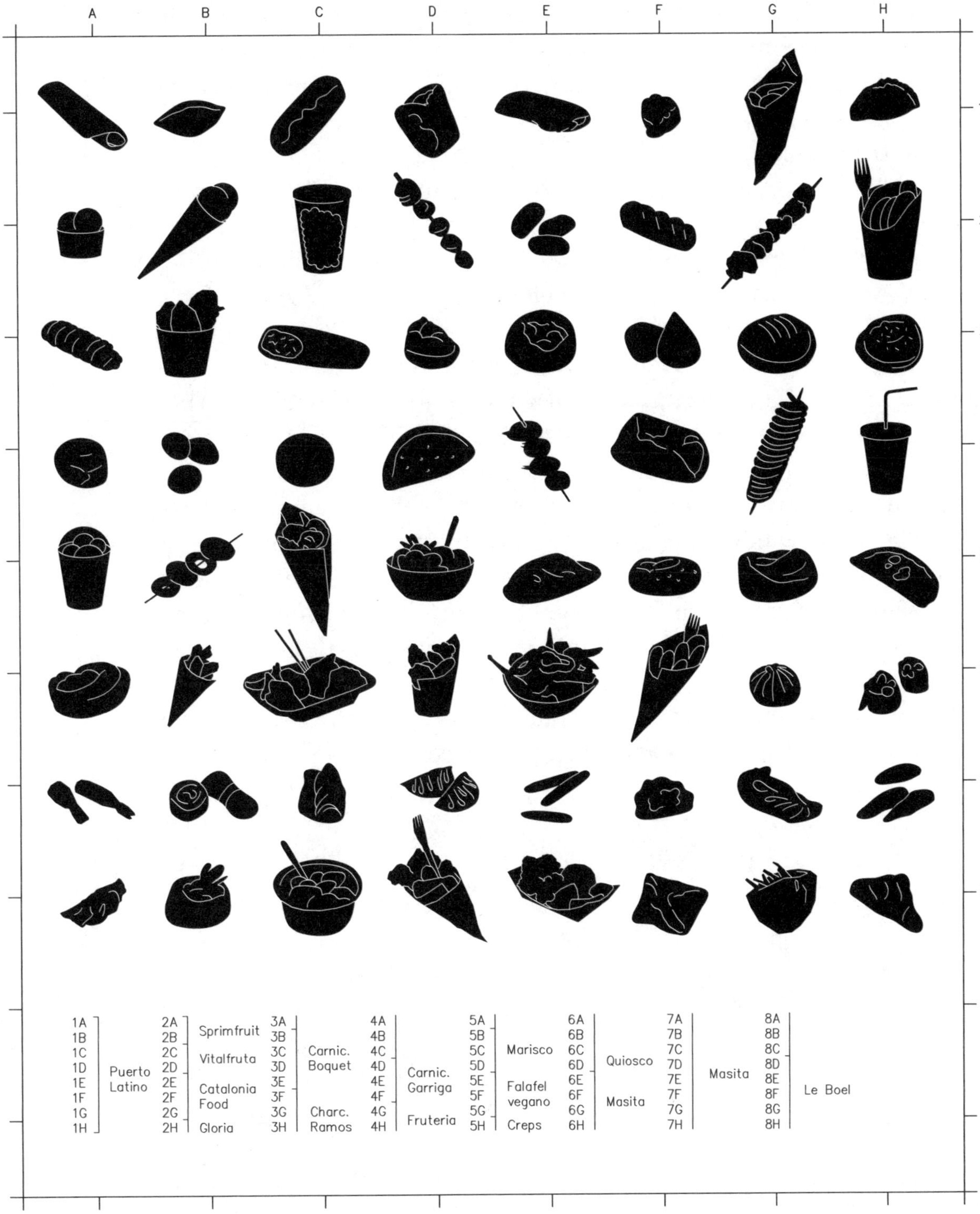

COLLECTION OF FOOD OBJECTS FROM LA BOQUERIA 2018

encourage the incorporation of new content. In the case of La Boqueria, this began to become evident with the proliferation of stands selling fruit cut into containers to carry, a product blatantly focused on the provisioning of the visiting masses that years ago began to invade many of the traditional fruit shops.

In addition to the growth of tourism, the decrease of daily purchases is a factor. In the case of La Boqueria, the shortage of regular customers, widespread in all markets, is explained, in part, by its current oversizing. In the mid-nineteenth century, the Barcelona City Council defended the existence of only three major supply markets: La Boqueria, Santa Caterina, and Sant Antoni, and allowed them to grow beyond the needs of their environment, thinking of them as markets on a scale for the whole city. At the end of the century, however, these three were joined by those of each new population annexed into the city, so that, since then, with a much more diluted clientele, they have continued to operate with a size greater than necessary. The latest renovations of Santa Caterina and Sant Antoni reduced the number of stands, restoring, as far as possible, the balance between supply and demand. In La Boqueria, however, in the absence of a major reform project, the number of stands is still far higher than necessary.[2]

Another factor in the decline of the market business, linked to the inclusion of new food content as an adaptation strategy, is the incorporation by the city of an increasingly complete system of food businesses. La

FOOD BUSINESSES IN THE AREA OF LA BOQUERIA 2018

Boqueria has ended up surrounded by a swarm of businesses dedicated in one way or another to food, a context where the limits of the market are blurred. The Barcelona Special Food Equipment Plan (PECAB) recognizes what it calls "functional commercial polarity perimeters", which in the case of La Boqueria corresponds to the area of almost 4 hectares that extends between Hospital and Carme streets, La Rambla and the old Hospital of Santa Creu. This is an area that, at present, functions as a thematic space almost entirely dedicated to restaurants and the sale of food products.

Social groups, lifestyles and new forms of consumption

Phenomena such as increased life expectancy and falling birth rates also have a direct influence on the functioning of the market. In the neighborhood of La Boqueria, El Raval, the marked aging of the population is combined with the arrival of young people who increasingly take longer to have children. On the one hand, the increase in longevity is causing more and more elderly people to live alone, especially in cities, creating a population sector whose food consumption is usually based on a small daily purchase that often, for convenience, is done at the nearest convenience store. This is a type of business that has proliferated in different parts of the city during recent years, especially in the district of Ciutat Vella. On the other hand, the increase of couples without children among the neighbors and potential customers of the market decreases their business expectations, being family units with low levels of domestic cooking habits.

The transformation of this and many other markets has to do, therefore, with the appearance of new lifestyles associated with new forms of consumption. Fewer and fewer people eat at home three times a day, as evidenced by the extraordinary proliferation of restaurants in the city. In the urban environment, we have delegated many of our meals, which has gradually changed the meaning of collective spaces, including that of some markets. In addition, many of our meals away from home occur during leisure time, via weekend trips, where experiences linked to food have become a form of entertainment, which has led to the growth of this service in the city.

Metropolitan regulations attempt to guarantee a balance between consumer needs and the professional profitability of the food trade. In the case of La Boqueria, this policy puts the increase in prepared food under the magnifying glass, as it is an offering that is not only growing thanks to new licenses, but is being incorporated into many of the traditional stands, such as those of salted fish or delicatessens, where products for tasting

2
To address this problem without resorting to a major renovation, the City Council has been buying licenses from this market for years. The surface area of the acquired stands is intended for public space use, which would allow for a widening of the current interior passageways of the market, often saturated by the current number of visitors.

SUPERMARKETS AND CONVENIENCE STORES IN THE AREA OF LA BOQUERIA

2018

have been sold for some time together with the usual fare. In addition, in many of these cases the products have not been cooked in the stand, but are produced in off-site kitchens distributed throughout the neighborhood, which frees the sales points from having to comply with certain regulatory standards. This way of organizing productivity allows us to think of the market as a dispersed entity, which is evident every morning through the noise and smell that comes from the hustle and bustle of cooked product carts moving towards the stands.

The new meal formats can substantially alter the characteristic fare of some shops, as in the case of many of the fruit shops in the area of the market closest to La Rambla, where between juices and containers of cut fruit you can no longer buy a simple apple. But the constant flow of tourists, the proliferation of stands dedicated entirely to prepared food and the shortage of consumption of traditional market products push merchants to try their luck with this other type of offering. For this reason, the City Council is trying to control the phenomenon with relative tolerance, determining the amount of prepared food that can be exhibited and sold at each stand based on its characteristic fare, which is possibly the only solution if you want to allow traders to be able to continue doing business with tourism and adapting, as seems inevitable, to the new consumer dynamics of the local population. Even so, beyond prohibition, any form of control of such a complex phenomenon can easily entail a level of monitoring that is difficult to imagine.

On the other hand, another factor for change in La Boqueria, as in many other markets, is the gentrification process,[3] which involves the incorporation of new urban elements according to the tastes and needs of new population groups. Sharon Zuckin, who has spent years studying this problem in some neighborhoods of New York, calls this phenomenon *domestication by cappucino*, emphasizing the close relationship that exists between the development of this phenomenon and the variation of food supply in specific places. The arrival of new inhabitants with a certain purchasing power to working class neighborhoods, as is happening throughout the district of Ciutat Vella, is also reflected in the market, shifting the nature of its fare towards new sensibilities, such as the nutrition movement. In La Boqueria, some current stands represent this linkage of the market with new lifestyles, putting, for example, fast food and health food in the same plane.

In the Raval, on the other hand, immigration has increased significantly in recent decades as compared to other city neighborhoods, from 10 % of the population in 1995 to 49 % today—compared to the growth of 13 % that Barcelona has registered in that same space of time. The neighborhood has been filled with all kinds of shops selling products from different

3
From gentry, a word related to the minor British nobility.

parts of the world. This map of food businesses reflects the multi-ethnicity of the population, and introduces contents that are quickly absorbed by the city, whose variety of supply never stops expanding. The opening of the neighborhood to other food cultures has also influenced La Boqueria, with varying degrees of adaptation. While the butcher shops serve cuts characteristic of other countries, such as the strip or entrails, immigrants from different parts of the world have been opening stands with their own products, and most of the new prepared food stands are also foreign cuisine, so that traditional market cuisine has long been living alongside an increasingly diversified offering.

Nevertheless, the explosion of multicultural cuisine is not only related to immigration, but also to the growing development of the gastronomic leisure sector and the need to offer an increasingly wide range of experiences. The market, in this sense, is only adapting to the general trend of the city, where the variety of global cuisine continues to expand.

Towards a new model

A good percentage of the booths in La Boqueria are dedicated today, in one way or another, to the sale of prepared food—in total, more than 25 establishments of the nearly 200 that the market has today. That does not count the number of stands that have included different prepared food products along with their original fare, which would substantially increase the total surface area of displays dedicated to this type of fare. To this we must add that many of the stands in the perimeter colonnade, a space directly related to the market since its last major renovation in 2001, have gradually been occupied by bars and restaurants. These data considerably alter the contents of the traditional market, heralding a new meaning for this collective space.

The transformation of La Boqueria, like that of many other markets, has been linked to the loss of values associated with traditional commerce, which has been happening as a result of the progressive closure of emblematic shops in the city, raising concerns of their owners and others. But the loss of identity seems inevitable if authenticity is necessarily linked to everyday patterns that tend to disappear. In any case, it seems necessary to rethink the usefulness of certain preservation protocols. The current Boqueria is just a reflection of the city that now surrounds it, far beyond the growth of tourism, the influence of which, divided among multiple variables, seems to be far from what we can or should even try to control.

On the other hand, many markets in the city continue to operate similarly to how they have always done, even though they have considerably

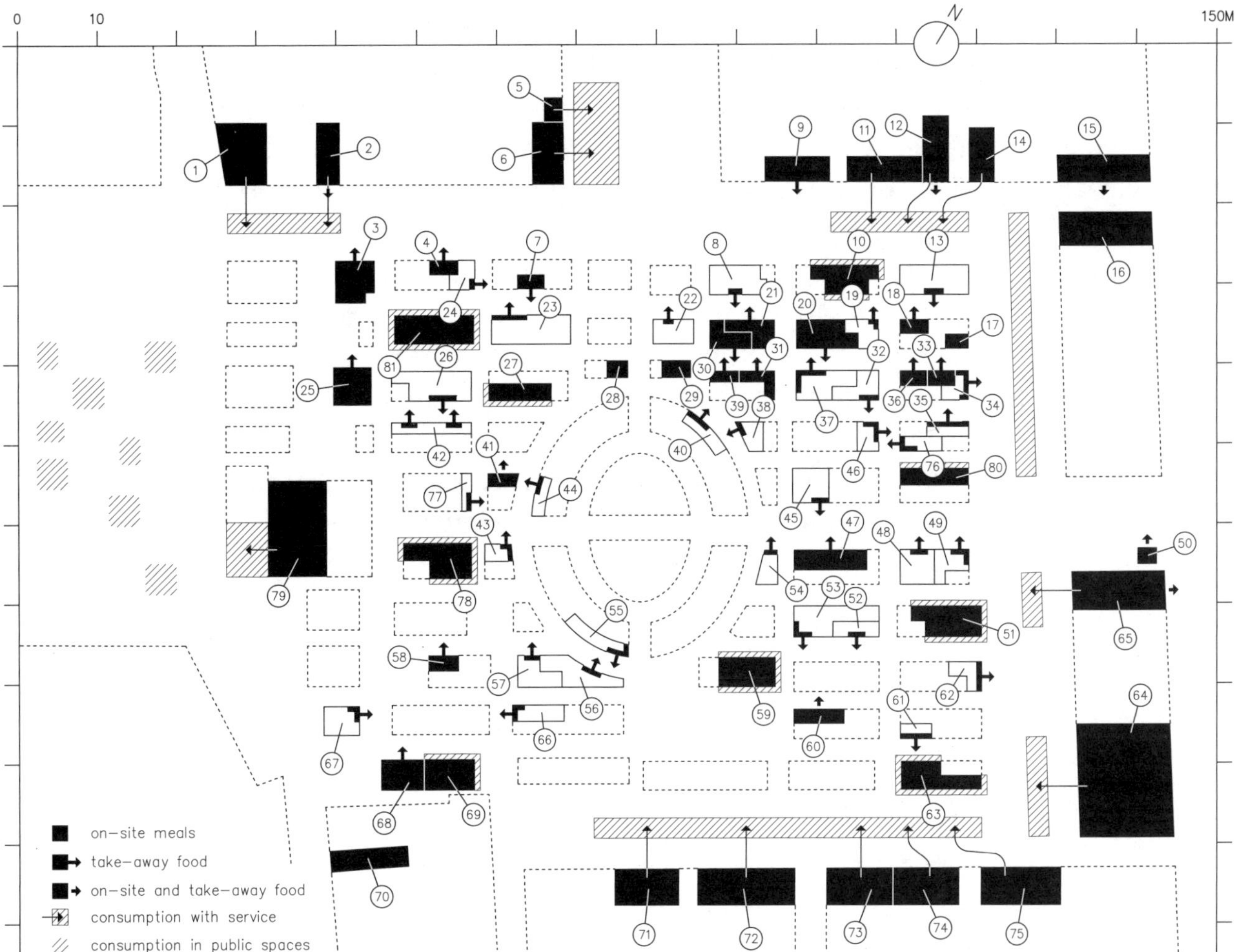

01– L'Ou restaurante
02– Barna China restaurante
03– Organic
04– Falafel vegano
05– Bar Papitu
06– Boquet restaurante
07– Catalonian food
08– Charcutería Josep
09– Le Boel boulangerie
10– Bar central

11– Portic Boqueria restaurante
12– Oyster bar
13– Charcutería Can Vila
14– La Virreina café bar
15– Wok to Walk
16– Boqueria bar restaurante
17– Frutería El racó de la Tere
18– Creps Boqueria
19– Frutería Esencia Frutal
20– Frutería Vitalfruta

21– Frutería Fruits de la terra
22– Charcutería Ramos
23– Carnicería Boquet
24– Carnicería Garriga
25– Masita Take Away
26– Charcutería Mas gourmets
27– Bar Quiosc modern
28– Pollería Gloria
29– Verdulería Jaime i Montse
30– Puerto Latino

31– Verdulería Alfonso i Conchi
32– Frutería Micó
33– Frutería Pedro i Carmen
34– Frutería Natura Fruits
35– Frutería Xavi
36– Frutería
37– Verdulería Jaime i Montse
38– Frutería Germans Pasqual
39– Puerto Latino
40– Marisco Juani

41– Slice Pizza
42– Carnicería Barrachina
43– Frutería Alfonso
44– Pesca salada Martínez
45– Frutería Morilla
46– Frutería Diego i Nuri
47– Sprim Fruit
48– Soley Boqueria
49– Frutería Vidal Pons
50– Bar Boqueria 887

51– Bar Ramblero
52– Charcutería Mas gourmets
53– Verdulería Mercedes
54– Verdulería Peña
55– Marisco Luci i Noemi
56– Panadería La Torna
57– Verdulería Maria Pujol
58– Asador Ramón
59– Bar El Quim
60– Zumos Simó

61– Zumos Juicy Juice
62– Frutería Alfonso
63– Quiosco Universal
64– Salsalada restaurante
65– Dunkin coffee
66– frutería El Ahreche
67– Carnicería Soler Capella
68– Paella Molt bo
69– Bar Clemen's
70– Bacaro restaurante

71– Homenaje restaurante
72– Paella Bar
73– Blau Marin restaurante
74– karakoy restaurant
75– Dogs & Sauces
76– Verdulería J. Carro
77– Frutería Alfonso
78– Bar Central
79– La Gardunya restaurante
80– Bar Pinotxo
81– Bar Boqueria

BARS, RESTAURANTS, TAKE-AWAY FOOD, AND OUTDOOR CONSUMPTION AREAS IN LA BOQUERIA 2018 reduced their turnover. Meanwhile, markets such as La Boqueria and Santa Caterina, among others, seem to have ceased to be something essential from the point of view of fresh product supply, focusing on a new business model. The important growth of meals away from home has placed on the city the responsibility of meeting this new demand, calling for new and different business models based around food, a business niche that has been quickly occupied by everything that has found in it an opportunity.

The act of eating, projected in a thousand ways on the map of the city, has become one of the most important expressions of humanity as a collective. Therefore, instead of judging this transformation from a nostalgic point of view, it is possible that it should be understood as the birth of a new urban space, which may be worth observing with at least as much attention as we have devoted to the model it leaves behind.

Pere Fuertes
Eulàlia Gómez-Escoda

How Fresh Food Shapes Barcelona

In the markets we can see the pulse of Barcelona. The relationships they establish with the city, the street, and the home can be described by means of nine terms that define the urban profile that fresh food helps shape: organize, cover, extract, attract, overflow, equip, fit in, cooking, and food. The market has an ability to attract due to the sensations awoken by food on display, to establish a bridge to the home kitchens where food is prepared, to overflow activity towards the streets and squares that lead to it, and to help the city fit into its surroundings. The renovations that started two decades ago have significantly transformed the role of the markets with the aim of guaranteeing their survival and keeping them alive under roofs that in the past determined the relationship between the city and food, due to the removal from the streets of the inconveniences traditionally linked to the food trade. While other European cities that built a network of public markets have given up due to changes in the commercial distribution of food, Barcelona has come to terms with this phenomenon and, at the beginning of the 21st century, maintains and renovates its 38 municipal markets, a living heritage that provides a strategy for access to fresh foods and which, through food, conditions the city around them.

Organize Walking through a market is to wander between displays that are no more than one meter and a half tall and that display the fare of butchers, delicatessen shops, poultry stalls, and preserves, fruits and vegetables on tables, and fish and seafood on beds of ice. The care in the display of food at each stand—fish lined up in parallel, pieces of fruit in pyramids, in a matrix, or stacked according to size, meat dissected in parts, the sausages displayed by shape and length of the meat—requires time every day to arrange, stack, or hang the food before market gates are opened for buyers.

During the first third of the nineteenth century, Barcelona began to systematize the organization in market spaces and did not do so through the use of these strategies of geometric design and layout of food—which existed since the beginning of commerce—but by removing them from the street to enclose them in regulated and specialized spaces: the market squares. Sant Josep and Santa Caterina are an example: they follow the footprint of the cloisters of underused convents and convert them into porches, which establish an enclosure with the rhythm of the columns along the perimeter and draw a set of defined geometries contrasting with the complicated geometries of the surrounding streets. The market squares offered in their interior a mix of food, conversations, people and, above all, shelter for commercial exchanges.

Initiatives to organize market squares were due to a need for urban order, but also for reasons of hygiene and control of sales, transportation, and tax payments. The first municipal ordinances already defined what foods could be sold at the market and under what conditions—fresh, preserved, cooked or prepared—, what minimum and maximum weights should be and how they should be displayed in the stalls. The city imposed an order in this way on the promiscuous relationship between food and the street and started down the path towards the appearance of market buildings, by which it intended to deprive the street of one of its reasons for being: sales.

Cover In just a few years, the new market squares began to be covered with permanent structures. The awnings of the stalls, which had to be mounted and disassembled on a daily basis, gave way to a shelter that protected the entire space and which, over time, would lead to the iron and glass buildings that began to be built during the Restoration, influenced by the modernity of French models: the Born market (1876), Sant Antoni (1882), Barceloneta (1884), Hostafrancs, Concepció i Llibertat (1888), Clot i la Unió (1889), and the Abaceria Central de Gracia (1892), followed by other examples at the beginning of the twentieth century, such as the first market of Sant Gervasi (1913).

In this context, the Boqueria market followed a unique path, probably due to the close relationship that had been woven with the Plaza de San José, which gave it limits without defining it as a building; an ambiguity that allows us even today to understand it as a covered square. The first roof in 1874, the metallic structure of Antoni de Falguera in 1914, as well as the cleaning and renovation of Lluís Clotet and Ignacio Paricio—finished in 2001—, and the expansion in 2015 towards the Plaza de la Gardunya, by Carme Pinós, have managed to maintain this hybrid character, free of closures, which assures a good interaction with the city.

Overall, the covers of these markets can be understood as thermodynamic devices that allow for heat dissipation and air renewal, creating a fresh atmosphere according to the nature of the products that are bought there. Their height and openings offer to the market a quality of light that preserves the feeling of open space. They are covers that protect buyers from the weather and food from the adverse effects of the sun. Scenes of poultry or fish hanging outside, which still survive in other nearby cultures, are no longer socially acceptable.

Under these protective covers, the market is organized in an open space, occupied by busy food tables—which no longer need awnings—and a whole host of buyers and sellers that surround them. Despite the progressive transformation of the stalls into devices equipped with roofs and enclosures, which contribute to the fragmentation of space, and the massive incorporation of electric lighting over the food, it is still possible to recognize and evaluate a large part of the qualities that these covers provide. It could be said that they cover the very act of selling and, in that sense, they are a city.

At the same time, covering the market—protecting it—can also be synonymous with meeting demand. This has historically been the expression of a commitment that the city has assumed—and reinforced during several periods of expansion or crisis—in order to guarantee all its residents access to fresh food. Although it is a process that must be considered and evaluated in all its complexity, the renovations of markets over the last three decades has moved away from this goal, fomenting a heterogeneous model under one roof.

Extract Covered markets with facades are buildings that are isolated from the outside, aimed at removing from the streets exchanges that until then had invaded them. The original intention was to eliminate the dirt and noise of the market from the public space, but this process of extraction also weakened the relationship between the street and food established naturally up to then via smells, colors, and the constant presence of food on any corner and clinging to any facade. The markets were public buildings and, to strengthen them during the first years, the City Council regulated competition around them based on the distances within which fresh foods could not be sold on the street. In this way not only was activity moved away from the squares, but in the streets that led to them mobile carts were prohibited and stands with food were no longer allowed.[1] They were measures aimed at leaving the surrounding streets empty of commerce in favor of the new network established between the stalls inside the market, although the expansive nature of commerce would resist these goals.

Concentrating sales in a closed space is the best way to centralize them: to guarantee competitive prices and fair weights, and, above all, to isolate everything that inconveniences the street and bring it together in a single place: the unloading of food and the collection of waste. In Barcelona, the markets built in the second half of the 20th century and the successive renovations that have taken place to the earlier markets, channel most of these operations of delivering food and extracting waste via underground routes, so that distribution flows are concentrated around the ramp from the street to the underground level, or the freight elevator to the sales area. The public space inside the markets has inherited the desire for order and aseptic conditions by removing the street food trade, closing it in buildings, and modernizing the city by cleaning it.

Thus the market left the street and the food gained protection from the sun, rain, and temperature, but, at the same time, lost the more immediate benefits granted by the outdoors; artificial light, covered space, and regulated temperature stabilized the environment in the interior and took from the market the connection with the passage of the day and the change of seasons.

Equip Before the advent of market squares, the location of the market had been at the gates of the city, such as the Mercadal—the current Plaça de l'Àngel—at the gate of the Roman site or the Boqueria plain, in front of the Jaume I wall. They were such vital points of confluence and exchange between the city and the countryside that they persisted, even when urban growth had swallowed them. The markets extended linearly along the access roads, and the progressive formalization of squares modeled on this allowed a greater and more effective concentration of grid-organized stops. In this density and intensity of activity there was the seed of the current market: many regularly grouped stands are more competitive and controllable than an endless line. In fact, most of the eighteen markets built in Barcelona through the middle of the 20th century are the result of previous outdoor activity, the traces of which can be felt in the configuration of the building itself and, above all, in the nature of its surroundings.

However, the 20 markets erected after 1957 no longer have any relationship with previous activity or with a fabric that had evolved in parallel. They were planned as new autonomous buildings far from the ambiguity of the covered squares. They offered a service aimed at guaranteeing the supply of fresh food to the population of an expanding city before the arrival of supermarkets and self-service locations, introduced slowly from the end of the 1950s.

At a time when the number of markets in Europe was waning due to the rapid modernization of commercial distribution, as recalled by Manel Guàrdia and José Luis Oyón, [2] Barcelona consolidated its role as a network of facilities aimed at strengthening neighborhood centers, occupying spaces that responded to the opportunity and availability of land in dense urban areas. To a certain extent, a mental model has been exported, originated and developed under very diverse conditions, but now without the necessary complicity of the city to welcome it, and with uneven results.

The most recent turning point occurred in 1991 with the creation of the Municipal Institute of Markets, which proposed updating the inherited model according to changes in consumer habits. Following in this line, the reform of the Concepció Market in 1998 established a pattern that, with variations, has been maintained for twenty years until the reopening of the Sant Antoni market in 2018: a reduction of the number of stands and expanding their area, management of unloading and residues via the basement, and incorporation of a supermarket, a public car park and,

1
On April 28, 1827, following the opening of the new Sant Josep market, the edict of the Marqués de Campo Sagrado was published, which prevented the sale of food products elsewhere on the Rambla (Barcelona City Council, AMCB).

2
Manuel Guàrdia and José Luis Oyón with Nàdia Fava, "The system of markets in Barcelona". *To make a city via the markets*. Europe, 19th and 20th centuries. Barcelona: MUHBA, 2010.

The city without markets. Beyond the part of the city supplied with fresh food—represented by the streets that are less than 5 minutes on foot from a market—there are urban areas where the distance to the nearest market is more than 10 minutes. They are central areas such as Entença Street, the two ends of the Diagonal, and neighborhoods such as Poble Sec, Vila Olímpica, Vallcarca, La Mercè, and Vallbona. In this scenario, there is also a constellation of supermarkets• and food shops° that extend throughout the city.

occasionally, other non-food stores or restaurants. They want to respond to the urban sprawl of which they are part through an agglomeration of services typical of a mall. Despite the renewed capacity for attraction within the neighborhood itself, markets face a decreasing share of sales[3] and show the contradictions inherent in a model that has undergone so many processes of adaptation.

Fit in The markets are the public space where one goes to buy fresh food. They are a part of the area of the city where they are located and established according to the zoning rules that apply in each case. There are markets that, despite the passage of time, continue to be covered squares—such as Liberty, Abaceria, San Andres, El Clot, La Barceloneta, the Union, and La Boqueria—and there are those that respect the map of streets, and substitute in shape, dimensions, and height what could have been a square block of houses—such as Sants, Hostafrancs, Sant Gervasi, Galvany, Sant Antoni or Horta. The most recently constructed are located in parts of the city where the size of the open space imposes itself on the network of streets and the markets are just another building—such as Bon Pastor, Canyelles, Trinitat, Vall d'Hebron, Provençals, Navy, Meridian City, Besòs, Felipe II, Guineueta, or Montserrat. Other examples occupy fragments of street blocks, corner-intersection properties, or are attached to buildings with other uses—such as Santa Caterina, Concepción, Ninot, Tres Torres, Estrella, Les Corts, Lesseps, Carmel, Sant Martí, la Mercè or Sarrià. The latest versions even include the market as one of the parts of a puzzle that includes various facilities: combined with a primary care center, an elderly residence, a civic center, a library, or a nursery school—Guinardó (2015), Sagrada Familia (2007), Fort Pienc (2003). They are examples of how domestication of ordinary market activities has reached the point of allowing it to share a roof with other activities and how its architecture has moved away from the monumental to look instead towards a mix of users and density of activities.

The most intimate link between the market and the city are the access doors. They have gone from occupying the entire street—when the animal-drawn trolleys crossed the market and unloaded their merchandise in front of the stand—to open up to only pedestrians—the renovations with ramps and elevators have made accessible the markets that had a sales floor different from the street level. The buildings of the late nineteenth century with iron structures freed up the perimeter from being loading areas and the facades could be as transparent as needed, with unlimited openings in terms of number and dimensions. While, in the first markets, people and food entered at the same place, today the logistics have become more complex and the access points have been segregated, so that the rear façade has disappeared and the entire perimeter has been gained as an urban facade. The position of the doors depends on the market´s interaction with the surrounding city, which is made more intense by the passage of people attracted by the market. The activity overflows and the food emerges, as it has done from the beginning, into the streets.

Attract The market is, in the words of Carolyn Steel, a "city of food";[4] A world of temptations for the senses. The structure of streets and stalls is translated into an organization of food displayed before the eyes and nose of the visitor analogously to a well-stocked buffet; an enveloping still life that suggests the image of abundance itself. Cheeses of different origins arranged in shades of yellow by degree of curing or type of milk, families of fruits and vegetables carefully arranged in ranges of bright colors, the vastness of the sea visible at one glance, meats and sausages overflowing the physical area of the stand. The diversity of the fare has increased markedly, but the quantity continues to be a characteristic long associated with the markets. According to the economic historian Francesc Valls, in 1849, and with a population of 186,000 people in Barcelona, there were annually "about three and a half million kilograms of lamb, beef, and veal [...] almost fifteen thousand pigs and a difficult number to specify of birds [...] that would include, among others, two hundred thousand chickens".[5] In these conditions of abundance and diversity, fresh food can easily become an engine capable of activating the city around it, thanks to its potential for attraction.

The transition from renovated markets to a model with a higher presence of quality and gourmet food—which would push out other more basic or secondary foods—calls for the presence of a trusted vendor, who knows the product well, and a commercial system capable of incorporating traceability, concern for diet, and ecologic production. The demand for local foods, however, is limited in practice of the amount of land cultivated in relation to the population that is fed,[6] an inverse situation to what was common when the first market buildings were erected, with farmers who sold their production and livestock that entered the city on their own.

In this change to the current model, we can sense the influence of a generational shift of buyers and stand-holders coupled with new lifestyle habits that should be carefully evaluated. It is true that younger consumers value, above all, the quality of the offering, but it is at least, or more, significant that almost one in four Barcelona residents never goes to the market.[7]

Under these conditions, the market loses influence in daily supplies and a gradual drift towards exceptional or sporadic purchases could be expected—those that compete with specialty stores and not with super-

3
According to the report *Consumer Habits and Commercial Polarity in the city of Barcelona* (2017), municipal markets sell 44.4 % of fish and seafood, 35 % of meat and pork and 23.2 % of the fruits and vegetables that are consumed in the city. Five years ago, the same study indicated that the sale of fruits and vegetables was 27.9 %.

4
Describes the London Borough Market as "a seething, hissing, sizzling city of food". Carolyn Steel, *Hungry City: How Food Shapes Our Lives*. London: Vintage Books, 2009.

5
Data extracted from the *Statistics of Barcelona* (1849), by Laureà Figuerola. Francesc Valls, *"Geography of food supply around 1850". To Supply Barcelona: The municipality and the city's food, 1329–1930*. Barcelona: MUHBA, 2013

6
According to *Mercabarna's Statistical Yearbook*, 2017, only 14.2 % of fruits and vegetables and 12.5 % of distributed fresh fish and shellfish originate in Catalonia. They are the relative minimum values of the last ten years.

7
Report *Consumer habits and commercial polarity of the city of Barcelona*, from 2017.

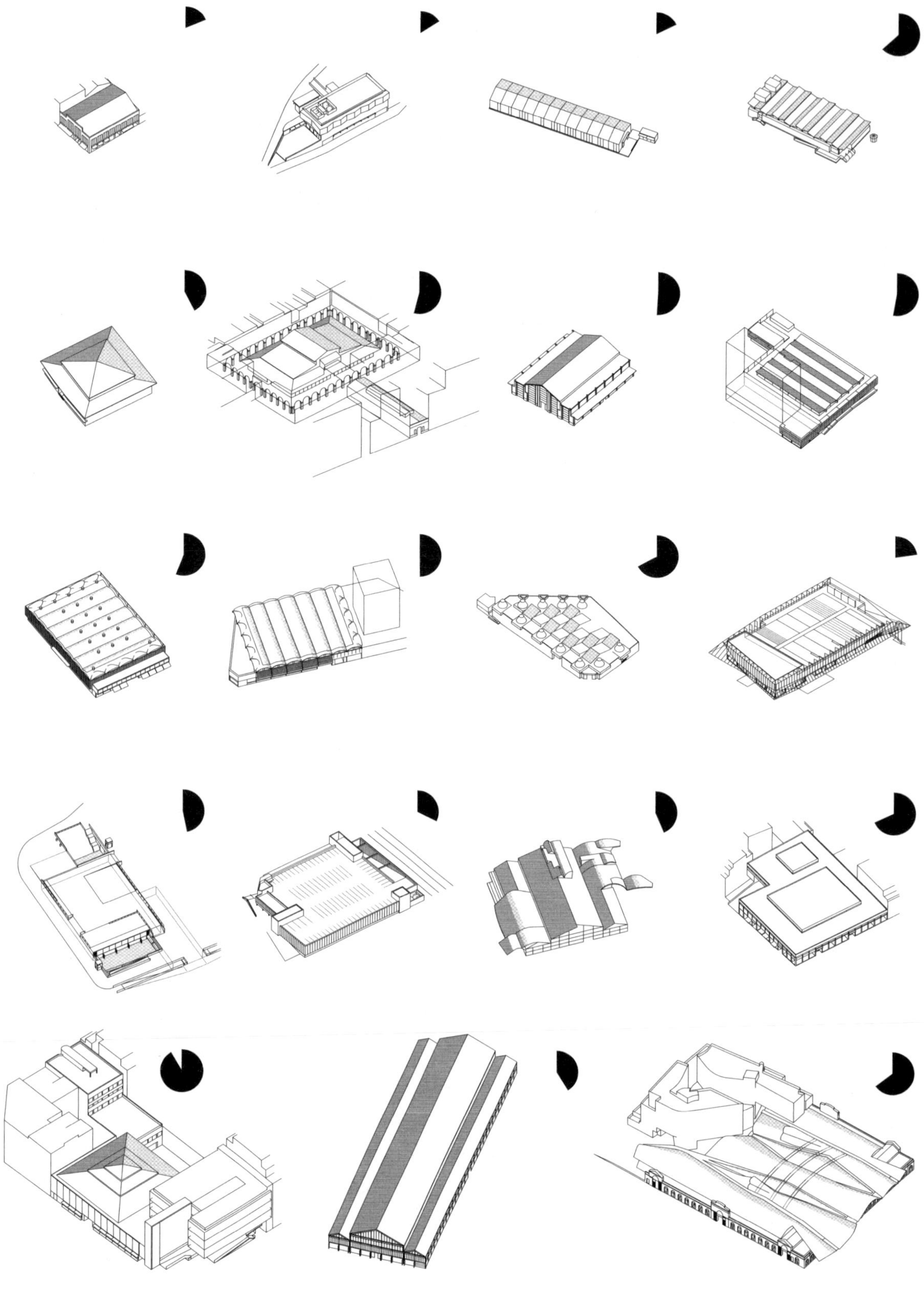

38 markets for 380,000 Barcelona residents. The image of the 38 markets on the same scale (from left to right and from top to bottom: Tres Torres, Ciutat Meridiana, Bon Pastor, Sant Gervasi, Lesseps, Clot, L'Estrella, Sarrià, Horta, Sant Andreu, La Unió, Sant Martí, Guinardó, Fort Pienc, Canyelles, Trinitat, Les Corts, La Mercè, Felip II, Vall d'Hebron, Galvany, Llibertat, Besòs, Montserrat, Marina, Provençals, Barceloneta, Carmel, Hostafrancs, Guineueta, Sants, Abaceria, Sagrada Familia, La Concepción, Santa Caterina, El Ninot, La Boqueria, and San Antonio) shows the relative independence between the size of the infrastructure for the sale of fresh food and the density of the population to be served (represented by areas of circumference that relate households served in the area close to each market with the maximum number of households served by the market that supplies the most homes, Sant Antoni). Sant Antoni is the market with the most homes within a maximum distance of five minutes on foot (20,686) and Ciutat Meridiana

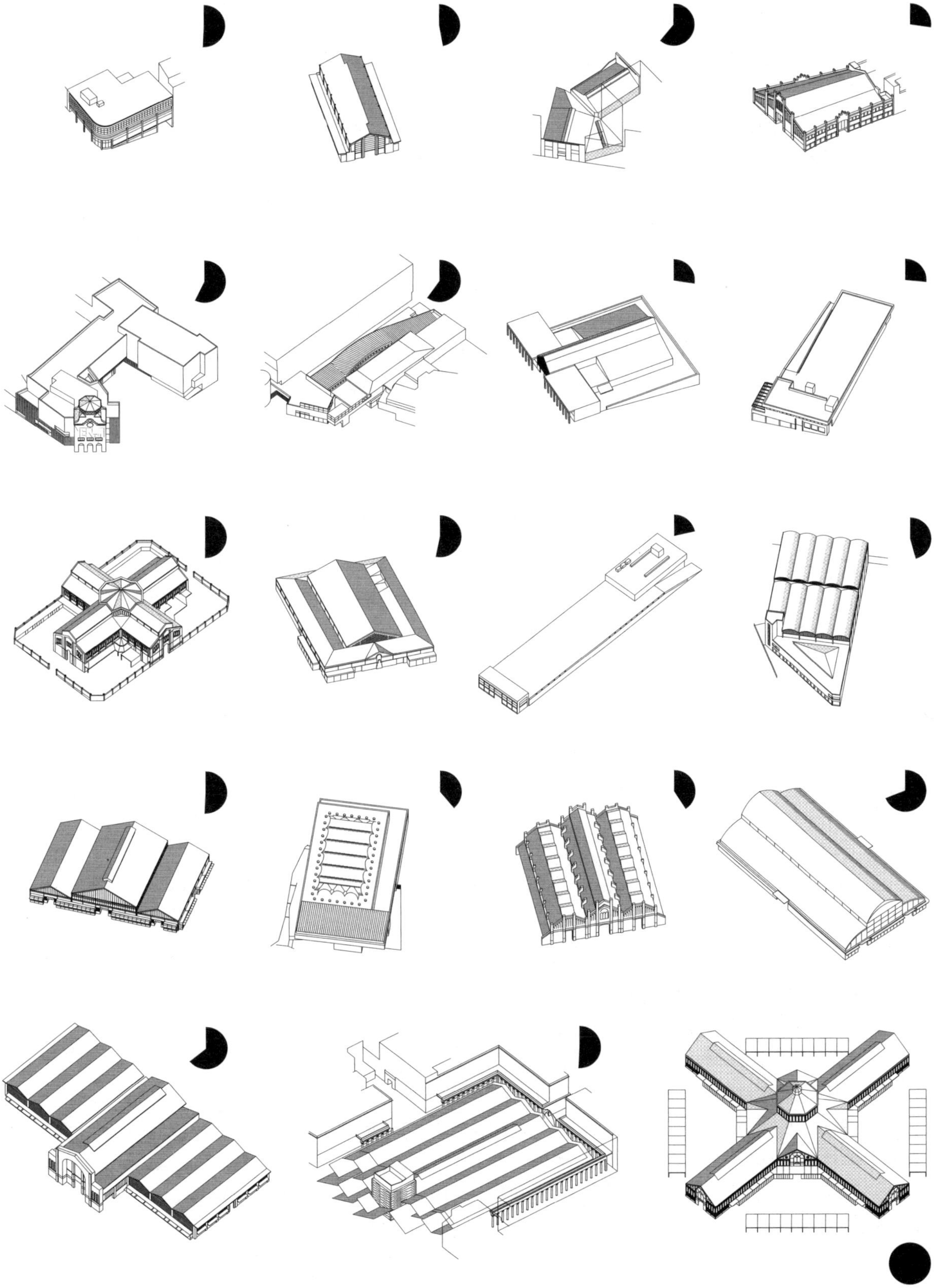

(3,280, one sixth) the least. In between, Bon Pastor has 3,677 homes within the same distance, Tres Torres 3,872, Besòs 4,435, Vall d´Hebron 4,696, Trinitat 5,479, Sarrià 5,628, Canyelles 5,674, Provençals 6,616, Guineueta 8,025, Sants 8,424, La Concepción 8,472, Horta 8,754, La Barceloneta 9,017, Montserrat 9,427, Marina 9,659, Clot 9,742, La Mercè 10,306, Galvany 10,366, Hostafrancs 10,489, Lesseps 10,517, La Boqueria 10,524, La Unió 10,905, Sant Martí 11,016, Llibertat 11,199, Sant Andreu 11,538, Les Corts 11,876, Guinardó 12,395, Fort Pienc 12,442, L'Estrella 12,636, Sant Gervasi 13,039, El Ninot 13,333, Santa Caterina 13,411, Felip II 13,853, El Carmel 14,134, Abaceria 14,306, and Sagrada Familia 18,937. Also, the type of markets explains the different ways in which, at different times, architecture has responded to the same need: to supply the city with fresh food. Calculation of the number of households based on the "Urban data of the square blocks of the city of Barcelona", updated on May 3, 2018.

markets. In fact, more than half of the weekly purchases are concentrated between Friday and Saturday,[8] when interference with working hours is minimal, and time and means can be devoted to weekend social dining. However, the growing presence of single-serving and semi-prepared foods in the market, ready to be cooked or heated without any additional preparation, is aimed at guaranteeing the presence of regular buyers, attracted by fare that takes into account the scarce time available during the week and the demand for a diet based on fresh products.

Overflow In the city, food is not produced, it accumulates and is distributed. Barcelona began to be a large food supply storage site in 1329 with the *Vi vel gratia*, granted by Alfonso IV, which allowed it to prepare for times of scarcity by accumulating inventory, to prohibit the departure of grain from the area, and to subsidize its imports.[9] The consequence of this centennial municipal commitment to guarantee access to fresh products has remained in collective memory over the years, so that the scattered food stores side by side with the markets—fruit shops, butchers, fish shops, delicatessen shops—responds today to a tradition of buying food in specialty shops, despite the appearance of supermarkets and self-service locations and the convenience of packaged and precooked food.

Access to food is guaranteed by a constellation of establishments spread throughout the city[10] which, in some cases, are concentrated near the markets, touching the walls, or on lower floors, and which take advantage of both the flow of people to the market as well as the prestige of the food that they provide. The fruit and vegetable stands on the outside are the most elementary part of this overflow: Sant Galdric Square, at the back of the Virreina and next to La Boqueria, or the long facade of the Abaceria on Puigmartí Street conserve this urban face made of ordered groups of fresh produce on tables supported on the cardboard and plastic boxes that served to transport them. The market building is also transformed by this overflow effect: the exterior facade becomes thick in some cases and is packed with florists, herbalists, clothes stands, and household utensils. They are complementary uses that do not have a space among the food stands and that are set up in daily folding kiosks, which look out onto the perimeter streets. The latest renovations of municipal markets, however, have not trusted that this magnet effect would take place and, given the doubt that the user figures would not meet expectations and the markets would make a desert of the areas around them, they introduced supermarkets inside to attract consumers. With this strategy, they invaded structures that already had activity overflow—the markets—with structures that are alien or even contradictory in the products they offer, the way to present them, and the system used to sell them.

Overflow implies that the market does not satisfy the entirety of the demand or all of its expressions. This is the case of specialties that cannot find a suitable format in the stand system, such as bakeries—which cannot be operated—, wine shops, or delicatessen boutiques—which do not want to depend on market opening times—or franchises—which do not qualify due to surface area or by regulation. In these cases, the immediate environment embraces the dispersion, and some of these establishments are located close to the doors and along the access roads. The PECAB[11] establishes perimeters around 31 markets of the city—with a specific shape in each case decided by the existing shops and accessibility in the area—in which it regulates the opening of new food stores to form an area of polarity complementary to the municipal market fare. The inheritance of this urban policy of keeping the markets strong is very clear in some cases, such as Boqueria, Hostafrancs, Abacería, Concepción, Libertad, Ninot, and Tres Torres, where sales overflow the market and colonize the ground floors nearby.

Cooking In Barcelona there are 822,719 households with their respective kitchens, of which almost half have a market less than 400 meters away[12]—that is, five minutes on foot. We can expand the radius and the proportion would change, but we must take into account that the vast majority of Barcelona residents buy fresh food in the immediate vicinity of their home[13]. The idea of supplying housing systematically with a network of local markets was already present in the plans for the Eixample, d'Ildefons Cerdà, although the estimated distance on that occasion—a grid of 10 by 10 square blocks[14]—is appreciably higher, in line with other mobility standards. In this scenario, it is possible to establish a potential relationship, on an urban scale, between each of the kitchens that are within the radius considered and the covered space of the market, in the manner of an umbilical cord that links them directly. In this sense, the market itself can be understood as an extension of the home; a vast collective refrigerator that provides food and which can be used regularly, whether directly from home or on the way home from work. The area of influence of each market allows one to see clearly the scope of this link and detect, as a result, the urban fragments that are not covered by the expansive wave. In these cases, alternatives could be accepted—as PECAB does with certain commercial centers—or the opening of new markets could be considered, as has happened with Fort Pienc (2003), built sixteen years after the last market.

In a scenario of mutual dependence between market and domestic kitchen, however, there are several distorting factors caused by the ongoing changes in social structure, consumption habits, and working hours.

8
Ibídem.

9
Mercè Renom explains (2016) *To Supply Barcelona: The municipality and the city's food, 1329–1930*, Barcelona: Ayuntamiento de Barcelona and MUHBA, where the food supply of the city is defined as "a more urban that rural need [...] the local governments of towns and cities had—and still have—among their essential functions the one to guarantee the subsistence of their inhabitants".

10
A non-universal access according to *the Survey of living conditions and population habits* made by IDESCAT in 2011. In the city of Barcelona, 70,130 households acknowledged renouncing a meal of meat, chicken or fish at least every two days for economic reasons.

11
Special Plan for Food Commodity Facilities of Barcelona, drafted by the City Council, in force since 1986 and with a latest review in 2011.

12
Based on the *"Urban data of the city blocks of Barcelona"*—updated on May 3, 2018, and available at http://opendata-ajuntament.barcelona.cat/data/ca/dataset/taula-map-illa—the number of households has been calculated within an effective radius around each market, stating that 47% of the city's homes are included in this proximity perimeter.

13
Report *Consumption habits and commercial polarity of the city of Barcelona*, 2017.

14
Francesc Magrinyà i Salvador Tarragó, Cerdà. *City and territory. A vision of the future*. Barcelona: Electa, 1994.

As a result, an average of 3.5 meals a week are eaten outside the home[15]—one in six, considering breakfasts, lunches and dinners—a figure that must be added to the growing practice of replacing or combining daily cooking with take away or delivered dishes and, of course, purchases made outside the market. The umbilical cord is thinner than a decade ago, but not necessarily less intense, if we consider that buying at the market implies cooking at home, and the availability to do so includes meals with family or friends on the weekend. The very aisles of the market, especially when they have been expanded according to the current reform policy, seem to be saturated on these days of maximum activity, when neighbors arrive at the same time, with an identical intention that underlines the collective nature of their activity.

Food The expression "market cuisine" refers to a set of dishes made with products available at a given moment. Traditionally, these have been seasonal foods, fresh and abundant but limited in time. The technical and scale changes in food distribution and preservation put this relationship into crisis in the vast majority of cases, except for some fruits and other foods that persist in seasonality. However, Massimo Montanari explains the dependence on time when he says that "in the food calendar, cultural aspects have prevailed over natural ones", so we have tended to modify foods to preserve them beyond the limits of natural availability; in the past, only the elites were allowed the consumption of fresh fruit and vegetables out of season, bringing them from far away.[16] According to this logic, today everyone would behave like those elites, but at an unsustainable environmental cost.

We link market cuisine—with the mentioned nuances—to domestic food and, above all, on some restaurant menus. In the case of the Barcelona markets, renovations such as those of Santa Caterina (2005), Barceloneta (2007), and Ninot (2015) have incorporated restaurants under the same roof as part of a renewed offering. They are restaurants that open to the outside—which guarantees a range of timetables—but with an implicit link to the environment in which they are found, which allows them to show off "an element of quality, the offer of cuisine tied to the territory and the fresh food of the market; a substantially innovative option nevertheless based on traditional elements."[17]

In this logic of bringing sale and consumption together, an alternative long called for by La Boqueria as a response to tourist pressure—and that has also been tested in the case of the Ninot—is the tasting of specialties at the stand itself, which is already defined and foreseen, under certain conditions, in the market ordinances. There have always been restaurants and taverns in the immediate vicinity of the market, some of them with tables near its façade. What is really significant is that now the same fresh product can be bought to cook at home or to eat directly at the stand, immersed in the atmosphere and activity of this city of food. Josep Pla referred to the agricultural landscape as a domestic symphony and to the market as its logical urban expression, while enjoying a *de forquilla* breakfast at Fonda Europa, before the formidable scenario of the weekly outdoor market in Granollers.[18] In this sense, the validity of the markets could be understood as a result of this association with the territory, culturally rooted in its continuity over time, despite the current origin of many products that no longer fit in this equation. Eating at the market transgresses the direct relationship of fresh products with home cooking and, despite being a recent addition—perhaps the newest of all—, it is part of a demand for quality that makes it understandable.

15
Hamilton, *Study of the restaurant sector in Catalonia. Behavioral habits and trends*. Department of Enterprise and Knowledge, Generalitat de Catalunya, 2018.

16
Massimo Montanari, *Il cibo come cultura*. Rome-Bari: Laterza, 2006.

17
Ibídem.

18
Josep Pla. *Three guides*. Complete Works, volume XXX. Barcelona: Destino, 1976.

Magda Màrià

Barcelona Eats

Art and food have always had a close relationship. Due to its presence in everyday habits, food has, over time, been an unlimited source of inspiration for art in many of its manifestations: from the murals of Roman villas to the thematic genres that emerged in the 16th century, when food moved from being objects to subjects in still life paintings. Food became the center of the artistic story in paintings of bucolic scenes, banquets, kitchens, the sale of food in public spaces, or in terraces and cafes.

In Barcelona, the relationships between food and the city have been immortalized throughout the twentieth century by artists and photographers who, using classic thematic genres or by considering new ones, have reflected their personal points of view onto the manners, time, and activities related to food and urban life. All of them have demonstrated their ability to transcend the mere scenic description, transmitting a wide range of situations in the production, sale, or consumption of food. Painters have described with sobriety and realism, but also with humor and mischief, scenes in which food is part of everyday habits and social customs of well-off and working classes. Photographers have captured with exceptional sensitivity domestic scenes, but also situations in public establishments and urban environments, where food plays a leading role in our lives. Some artists have represented meals as objects of extraordinary beauty that, at the same time, awaken our senses. In all these works the food is poor and rich; slow and fast; routine and festive; individual and social; nutrition and waste; survival and abundance; work and rest; the food is sweet and salty; field and sea; vegetable and animal; fresh and packaged; business and offering; loading and unloading; exhibition and consumption; market and store; home and street; food is, ultimately, life.

In this article, we bring together diachronically paintings, drawings, and photographs from different milieus of Barcelona, made throughout the twentieth century by established artists in the city, that show the ability of food to activate and transform the space in which it is found. In five sections, the repercussion of food as merchandise in establishments and surrounding streets is presented; the preparation and consumption of food in bars and restaurants but also in public spaces; the context where food is celebrated as a collective ritual; household space in relation to food; and the qualities of the food itself through still-life representations. In all of them, the interest generated by food in artistic output is confirmed, but also the profusion and intensity of its presence in different environments of the city, whether popular or bourgeois. And we can observe how food has always used space as a support, testing it, energizing it, and optimizing its contributions, thereby modifying its perception and use.

Food has come into the city from diverse backgrounds and via means of transport that have varied substantially over time. Depending on their nature—meat or vegetable—, during the first decades of the 20th century, products came through the port or were transported in cars or motor vehicles, from orchards and farms in the vicinity or from other parts of the country. Numerous images document the unloading of food at the docks, the fish auctions at fishery ports, or the harvesting of vegetables on the outskirts of the city. Progressively, food was gathered in large wholesale centers, such as El Born at the beginning of the century or, starting in 1967, Mercabarna, from where it was distributed to different points of sale. Of all of them, the markets are the most ancestral. Their surroundings have always been places "contaminated" by food. The accumulation of cars, the transfer of boxes or large baskets, parallel activities during market hours on adjacent streets, and the combination of farmers, shopkeepers, street vendors, and consumers, have attracted the attention of photographers and artists who have reflected the changes that all of this generates in an environment that acquires another meaning with the vitality that is activated.

For centuries, the food trade was carried out in the city squares, and it did not move into the markets until the middle of the 19th century. Even so, the sale of outdoor food coexisted in Barcelona. The narrow streets of the Raval, for example, hosted all sorts of stands that were built according to the linearity of the road, forming a "soft" domain that mediated between the vertical hardness of the facades and the central pedestrian passage. Often these stalls were equipped with lightweight structures that supported awnings that protected products from the sun and, at the same time, created a shady area that included both vendors and customers. The character of the street changed substantially, approaching the domestic. Especially interesting are the images of wide lanes where the sellers of melons and watermelons were gathered. The spherical volume of these fruits, the unique structures in the form of cumulus clouds resulting from their piled arrangement, and the appearance of the public space invaded by circular units similar to cannonballs, offered photographers undeniably inspiring scenes, comparable to performance activities.

Even so, most of food sales were concentrated in markets prior to the appearance of the first supermarkets in the 1950s. These "covered cities", with "main streets" and secondary ones, were organized by food sectors, as if they were neighborhoods. Artists throughout the 20th century showed, through the energetic tracings of the drawings or the impressionistic brushwork of oils and watercolors, the activity and atmosphere that these open spaces welcomed. Some images focus on the close links between the sellers and their stalls or on the exquisite placement of the foods in the small space available to them. Starting in the 1960s, photographers accentuated the lighting and atmospheric conditions of the indoor areas, or focused on the voluptuousness of the fare: fish and seafood set in a fan on ice trays, sausages or game hanging on hooks, or fruits and vegetables piled in layers in a fragile balance. Nowadays, many of the markets combine the sale of fresh products with tasting, which can also be seen in numerous photographs.

At designated times, food product fairs were organized on certain avenues in the city that attracted the attention of artists and photographers. The images that came from the exhibition of live animals were especially attractive due to the coexistence between two contrasting realities: the urban, with dressed-up families shopping, accompanied by curious children, and the rural, with peasants and living beasts jumbled together between hay bales. These still exist today, with fairs such as those of Sant Ponç or the Tres Tombs displaying candied fruit stalls or bread rings, changing the ambience and character of the streets.

FRUTAS

Barcelona has been, for centuries, a city of bars and restaurants.[1] In these establishments, the space where the manipulation and transformation of raw materials into delicious dishes is done is the kitchen, where the chef is the master of ceremonies. His activities, centered on the elaboration of the meals, extend to utensils, casseroles, stoves or countertops, but also to the entire space that houses them, and which together achieve an inseparable entity. This atmosphere has been shaped by numerous images in which the modulation of color or the drama of black and white captures the essence of the atmosphere and places all the protagonists and the space that surrounds them at the same level of significance. Lately, the transformation of kitchens reflects the paradigm shift that is affecting the sector. Although, as of the 1950s, there were numerous radio shows and programs featuring renowned chefs, the photographs show us workshops, hidden from the eyes of guests and ruled by anonymous gifted professionals. Nowadays laboratory kitchens are frequent, visually connected to the dining room, with famous chefs who act directly in front of the clientele.

Historically, the city's restaurants and dining venues combined perfectly their culinary service with the economic level, food needs, and space requirements of diners. The dining room was usually a medium-sized family-style room. And home-style food, cooked by chefs, was served by professional waiters. In the 1960s, locations appeared that combined the restaurant service with other consumer and leisure options. At the Drugstore Passeig de Gràcia you could eat at any time, but also buy other products. At the moment, the mystification of uses and activities, including the restaurant business, has been spreading to all types of facilities. At the same time, other meal sampling formulas have emerged within premises that have been transformed, incorporating counters where dishes prepared for direct consumption are displayed, without the intervention of waiters. In these cases, unlike the past, photographers and artists do not focus as much on the general environment of the establishments as on the details of the food and its composition.

There are also terraces in Barcelona, which extend the restaurant activities into the street. In past decades, the extension of awnings marked out a shady transitional space that restrained the accelerated urban pace, and under which food and drink became the excuse for both conversation and looking and being seen. Nowadays, parasols have replaced the awnings, moving the activity away from the facades, and changing the attributes of both the terraces and the street itself.

In strategic places where the fabric of the city is diluted, bars and restaurants were installed that turned their terraces or gardens into emblematic spaces. The limits of the port, Montjuïc, or Tibidabo, but also urban parks or properties in the upper area of the city, were colonized with extensive platforms from which views and the outdoors could be enjoyed. Also, the working classes moved to popular places on the outskirts of Barcelona where outdoor dining was available. The scenes of tents and snacks, as well as picnics in Les Planes or Trencaones, with informal crowds of people, folding chairs, baskets, and food, have been collected in numerous images.

In spite of everything, for decades, eating in the public space outside establishments was not well looked-upon. If you ate in the street or in the open, it was because of need or lack of money. Even so, there were strategic temporary sale points that provided food and drink, expanding food's range of influence to people's walking routes. Drawings and paintings of coffee cups with milk, photographs of beverage kiosks in Las Ramblas, or current images of *churros* stands testify to this.

1
But also of taverns, cafes, hotels, cabarets, amusement parks, or gardens that offered the combination of leisure and free time.

A.H.C.R.I.S.

Food, as well as being a constant in our basic anthropological structure, is a social and cultural factor. As a general rule, important events, whether they are public or private, base their ability to create social connections on a grand meal. Naming events, welcoming events, farewells, or inaugurations are accompanied by food and drink. And the same happens in family celebrations, from the most private to the most multitudinous, such as weddings, baptisms, communions and, in other times and societies, burials.

From the anthropological perspective that analyzes customs, including food, as socially relevant historical and cultural indications, the frequency of public meetings organized around food was especially prominent in Barcelona.[2] Throughout the 20th century, great banquets were common that brought together dozens or hundreds of citizens around long tables arranged in the huge halls of the best hotels in the city, or in environments that were usually used for other functions. Theaters, courtyards, large halls, shipyards, or box seat areas welcomed diners who made the banquet the motivation for their periodic gathering. Food thus became part of the place where the great meal was celebrated, modifying its organization from both functional and perceptual perspectives. Some of these banquets were sheltered under spectacular tents specifically built for the occasion, such as the one that was set up in Parc Güell in 1916. At another level, these community lunches or dinners contributed to forging links between the members of a group, and were celebrated, pragmatically, inside the workplace, often between tools and machinery, demonstrating again the capacity of food to test the versatility of a space.

Changing customs have led to replacing the long tables of the first decades of the twentieth century with generally circular ones that seat a maximum of ten or twelve people. The spaces gain in inner mobility but lose their strong sense of being a unit. On other occasions, these meals are celebrated standing up, and this gives flexibility to both the food routes and diners' mobility, which allows them to spread out throughout the reception area.

Local neighborhood festivals are also examples that show how Barcelona has used food linked to urban space as a means to cohesion among neighbors. Periodically, group meals were held on the street, and these are still held today. The fact of eating together was, by its very nature, a sign of closeness. One of the most common were the children's snacks, in which candy and sweets were distributed among the kids, or long tables were set up where hot chocolate and pastries were served. The streets were transformed into large communal dining rooms, whose walls were the facades of the houses.

In different work or institutional environments, the daily meals involved a whole group gathering around a table. The image of impeccably dressed cooks eating before beginning their workday is a good example. In the case of schools, photographs of their lunch rooms from different periods reflect how different pedagogical systems influenced both eating habits and the size and organization of the spaces where the meals took place. Especially delicate are the images of domestic dining rooms in the active teaching schools of the 1930s, with children sitting around tables arranged in environments similar to those of a house, while their teachers watched them discreetly, eating in the same space; or those of open-air snacks, where glasses of milk extend their domestic dimension to the environment.

2
The Latin word *convivium*, which means 'to share life', is more explicit than the term banquet when describing these great meals, since it implies that eating together is a sign of union and friendship. See Merton, Thomas, The Living Bread. New York, 1956. Spanish version: *El pan vivo*. Madrid: Ediciones Rialp, 1963.

The structural differences between social classes, which in public were more widespread, could be seen in Barcelona essentially inside the homes. It is no coincidence that there are few graphic testimonials of the different domestic areas of working class homes. And, if there are any, it is of the dining rooms, which, during the 20th century, spatially revealed a family's social level. In pictures of humble or official protection housing, the kitchen, dining room, and living room occupied the same room where, in addition, clothes were washed and ironed and other domestic or work activities were carried out, as shown in some of the few existing photographs. On the other hand, in middle-class homes or bourgeois residences, the space used for daily meals occupied a more or less luxurious space, depending on economic status, which was furnished and decorated with chests of drawers, side tables, paintings, and objects related to food and its adornment. The appearance of food was common, not only in kitchens and dining rooms, but in other areas of the home. Various paintings and photographs showcase the coexistence of furniture, lamps, books, various objects, and some piece of food, in the most unexpected corners of houses. It is precisely the food that, in these cases, with its colorful and luminous presence, gives the scene life.

Mealtime was the time when the family met around a table. This family habit required that the table be set, using the necessary trappings for each occasion, which were stored in the scullery, in the dining room side tables, or in the kitchen. It was a ritual that, as simple as it was, always involved an order of processes and elements that, from the perspective of painters and photographers, could be transformed into something sublime. The cleanliness of the tablecloths, the layout of dishes, cutlery, and food or the transparency and reflections of glasses and bottles had the ability, in the light of these artists, to evoke the best moments of daily domestic life around a table that, with the excuse of eating, became the center of family life.

On special days, or when the family received guests, setting the table meant displaying the best tablecloths, tableware, cutlery, and glassware that were only used on special occasions. The table was also decorated with candleholders and floral arrangements. In contrast to daily meals, which were faster and more functional, during these evenings built around food, time extended and diners were fed not only with the meals on their plates, but also with conversations and ramblings around the table. The atmosphere in the dining rooms during these festivities has been the subject of different kinds of drawings, paintings, and photographs that explain, among other things, the joy of the occasion, the protocol of the event, the quality of the table settings, or the properties of the food and beverages. But they also showed how everything interacted to activate and change the space that surrounded it. Other images depict with acute psychology the personality of the various characters who, in traditional families of the time, were used to playing a decisive role.

Currently, due to the lack of time, family dispersion, and the advent of more practical and quicker lifestyles, the daily routine of setting the table or domestic meals that were held on specific dates where the best trappings were exhibited, have, with honorable exceptions, disappeared from the homes of Barcelona.

The images of objects, flowers, and food without people are known as still lifes—because they are composed of lifeless bodies—, or *bodegons* in Spanish, which, for centuries, showed simple utensils and food found in wineries (*bodegas*).[3] Especially evocative are paintings and photographs from the first half of the 20th century in Barcelona, which inherit the traditional monastic composition of the 17th century Spanish *bodegons*,[4] meticulously describing food and humble objects against a blurred or darkened background. These compositions, which with modulation of the colors or dramatic use of light manage to prolong the solitude and silence of the inert bodies, become almost supernatural scenes.

Far from disappearing, this artistic genre, which was initially undervalued, is in constant evolution. The artistic avant-gardes of the 20th century rescued it and turned it into one of its main thematic subjects. The simple morphology of fruit, bottles, glasses, or other objects allowed them to be subjected to geometrical abstractions or deformations, eliminating their boundaries, distorting the perspective and incorporating time in their simultaneous understanding. In parallel, the pioneers of photography experimented with compositions that underlined the volumetric texture, lights, shadows, and reflections of their components. Currently, both artists and advertisers continue to use the great expressive potential that food has in transmitting wellbeing, pleasure, harmony, voluptuousness, or sensuality. Particularly interesting are the images that, by means of photography or hyper-realistic painting, portray the contemporary pantry with a classic composition, combining fresh products with other packaged fare, in a postmodern exercise that fuses tradition with an expiration date.

In the *bodegons* and still lifes that were created throughout the 20th century in Barcelona, some foods appear more frequently than others as they were, probably, identifiable from the city's markets and tables. Fish has starred in a good number of images. Salt herring, mullet, or lobsters, due to their morphological, structural or chromatic characteristics, or to represent the paradigm of humble, popular, or luxurious food, have been represented in oils, watercolors, and photographs. The hunting of fur and feather, with the stunning presence of the sacrificed animal deposited on a table with other objects or hanging on a hook, has also been very present in the genre. More current photographs, such as ham bones suspended against a dark background, show an artistic interest in continuing to shape the paradoxical contrast between the violent destruction of animal life and human dietary needs. Also eggs, with their oval shape, have been drawn, painted, and photographed on several occasions in the company of dishes and pots, embedded in the traditional Easter pastries, or without the shell, about to be beaten. As to fruit, representations of grapes, apples, oranges, pomegranates, and pumpkins stand out due to their spherical nature and chromatic variety, or watermelons, due to the contrast between the smooth, bright, green exterior, and the red interior, fleshy and sprinkled with seeds. In contrast, some artists have preferred other less attractive vegetables such as mushrooms, berries, or autumn fruits, such as quince in the process of decomposition, to indicate the temporary nature of food and, therefore, the ephemeral nature of life.

3
Among the recent bibliography that refers to this artistic genre, we can highlight, among others, Berger, John; Calvo Serraller, Francisco; Castilla del Pino, Carlos *et al.*, *El bodegón*. Madrid/Barcelona: Fundación Amigos del Museo del Prado/Galaxia Gutemberg, 2000. Bryson, Norman i Coll, Miguel A., *Look again: four essays on the painting of still lifes*. Madrid: Alianza Forma, 2005. Schneider, Norbert, Still life. Köln: Taschen, 2009.

4
Calvo Serraller, Francisco, *"El bodegón español"*. *In El bodegón Español. De Zurbarán a Picasso*. Exhibition catalog. Bilbao: Museum of Fine Arts, 1999.

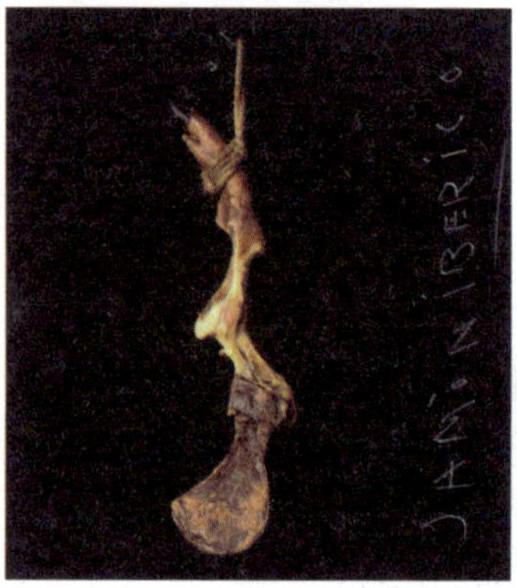
JAMÓN IBÉRICO

Núria Salvadó
Roger Sauquet

Two Considerations on the Impact of Food

surrounding agricultural area located, in particular, on the fertile plain of the Llobregat, an environment too often strangled by the growing needs of the city that it feeds.

Summer Dinner. Green salad (lettuce, tomato, onion, and olives), potato omelette, black cold cuts, sheep cheese, anchovies from L'Escala, bread with tomato, and yogurt with strawberries. Accompaniment: cruet (oil, salt, vinegar) and white wine.

8
Sources used to create the graphic:

Besse, Jean. *La alimentación del ganado [The feeding of livestock]*. Mundi-Prensa, Madrid, 1986.

García Menacho-Osset, Vicente. *El Gallinero ecológico. La fertilidad de la tierra [The ecological henhouse. The Fertility of the Earth]*, Estella, 2013.

Maynegre Santaulària, Jordi; Nogué Ribas, Moisès. *Dades i resultats de la gestió econòmica a les explotacions de vaques de llet a Catalunya 2016 [Data and results of the economic management of dairy cattle farming in Catalonia 2016]*, Generalitat de Catalunya, Department of Agriculture, Livestock, Fisheries and Food, Barcelona, 2017.

VV. AA. *Informe anual del sector porcí 2016 [Annual report on the pig farming sector 2016]*, Generalitat de Catalunya, Department of Agriculture, Livestock, Fisheries and Food, Barcelona, 2017.

VV. AA. *Producció d'ous de gallina per a consum humà a Catalunya 2017 [Production of chicken eggs for human consumption in Catalonia 2017]*, Generalitat de Catalunya, Department of Agriculture, Livestock, Fisheries and Food, Barcelona, 2018.

VV. AA. *Superfícies, rendiments i produccions dels conreus agrícoles a Catalunya 2017 [Surface area, yields, and production of agricultural crops in Catalonia 2017]*, Generalitat de Catalunya, Department of Agriculture, Livestock, Fisheries and Food, Barcelona, 2018.

Basic course in ecological agricultural production. Agro-ecological production cycle, IES Castellar del Vallès (thanks to professor Anna Cáceres).

The Ukita family in their dining room in Kodaira City, Japan, with a week's worth of food. Peter Menzel, *Hungry Planet: What The World Eats.*

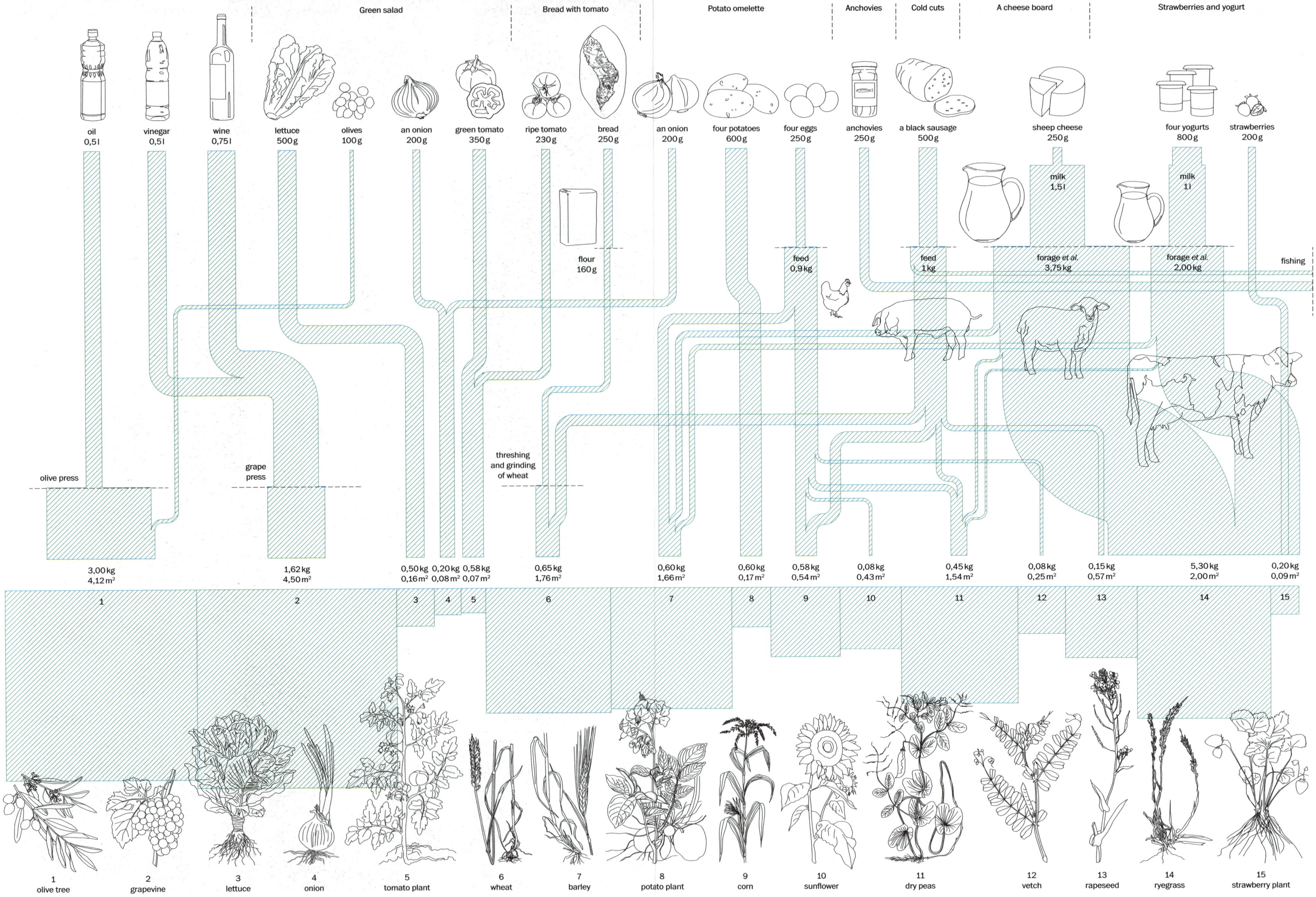

Green salad
Bread with tomato
Potato omelette
Anchovies
Cold cuts
A cheese board
Strawberries and yogurt
oil 0,5 l
vinegar 0,5 l
wine 0,75 l
lettuce 500 g
olives 100 g
an onion 200 g
green tomato 350 g
ripe tomato 230 g
bread 250 g
an onion 200 g
four potatoes 600 g
four eggs 250 g
anchovies 250 g
a black sausage 500 g
sheep cheese 250 g
four yogurts 800 g
strawberries 200 g
milk 1,5 l
milk 1 l
flour 160 g
feed 0,9 kg
feed 1 kg
forage et al. 3,75 kg
forage et al. 2,00 kg
fishing
olive press
grape press
threshing and grinding of wheat
3,00 kg 4,12 m²
1,62 kg 4,50 m²
0,50 kg 0,16 m²
0,20 kg 0,08 m²
0,58 kg 0,07 m²
0,65 kg 1,76 m²
0,60 kg 1,66 m²
0,60 kg 0,17 m²
0,58 kg 0,54 m²
0,08 kg 0,43 m²
0,45 kg 1,54 m²
0,08 kg 0,25 m²
0,15 kg 0,57 m²
5,30 kg 2,00 m²
0,20 kg 0,09 m²
1
2
3
4
5
6
7
8
9
10
11
12
13
14
15
1 olive tree
2 grapevine
3 lettuce
4 onion
5 tomato plant
6 wheat
7 barley
8 potato plant
9 corn
10 sunflower
11 dry peas
12 vetch
13 rapeseed
14 ryegrass
15 strawberry plant

It is difficult to get an idea of how much land is occupied by what we eat. By means of two different approaches, the agricultural expanse necessary to feed us is shown here. The first relates the city of Barcelona with the nearest agricultural area that has historically supplied it: the *Agrarian Park* of the Llobregat Delta. The second, on a smaller scale, is a research exercise on the area necessary to obtain the ingredients for a *Summer Dinner*.

In 1932 GATCPAC proposed the development of a city for rest and holidays for the city of Barcelona in the Llobregat Delta area, between Castelldefels and El Prat, with an area of 1,200 hectares and the capacity to accommodate 300,000 visitors. One particular feature of this city was that it would allocate 1/3 of its area for rental gardens located behind the residential area. This measure was not insignificant, as the *city* was surrounded by an agricultural area that occupied practically the entire Llobregat plain. Therefore the gardens became a transitional zone between the recreational space and the productive space. The project was never carried out, and the Delta was progressively occupied by large infrastructure projects, to the extent that in 2004 it was decided to protect it under the umbrella of the Agrarian Park of the Llobregat Delta. With an expanse of 3,348 hectares, with 2/3 currently being cultivated, and where the most significant crops are artichokes, tomatoes, and potatoes,[1] the Park distributes 70 % of what is produced through Mercabarna, (the largest market within reach of Barcelona and the entire metropolitan area). But despite the fact that the area of the Park is extensive, it is clearly insufficient to supply the city, and the fact is that in Mercabarna 85.7 %[2] of vegetables and fruits come from outside Catalonia, and that the only product produced in El Prat that is exported is the artichoke.[3] Mercabarna, strategically located at the gates of the city of Barcelona, between the Agrarian Park and the port,[4] acts as the intermediary between production in the fields and retail sales in the neighborhood markets of Barcelona.

According to a study conducted in 2011[5] by the Universities of Groningen, Graz, and the Institute of Social Ecology of Vienna, the cultivated area needed to feed a citizen of southern Europe for a year is approximately 3,500 m². [6] Taking the Agricultural Park area, and assuming that it does not specialize in vegetables, this could only feed the equivalent of the population that lives in 15 square blocks of the Eixample annually. If the Agricultural Park only cultivated the vegetables and fruit trees that we need to eat for a year, (200 m² according to the same study), this population would expand to 167,400 people, which would be equivalent to the average population that lives in 236 square blocks of the Eixample.[Fig.1] And if, returning to the GATCPAC idea, the Agrarian Park were to be reconfigured as family garden parcels for the population of Barcelona, 2/3 of the city's families[7] could have a garden of about 60 m² for seasonal produce.[Fig.2]

1
VV. AA. Surfaces, yields and productions of agricultural crops in Catalonia 2017, Generalitat de Catalunya, Department of Agriculture, Livestock, Fisheries and Food, Barcelona, 2018.

2
Statistical yearbook of the Mercado Central de Frutas y Hortalizas de Mercabarna. Statistical book 2017.

3
Instituto Cerdà; 'The economic dimension of the food system in the metropolitan area of Barcelona: scope, challenges and opportunities', Metropolitan Area of Barcelona (AMB), March 2017.

4
According to the traffic statistics of the Port of Barcelona of the year 2017, 19.1 % of the products that enter the Port of Barcelona are of the agro-livestock and alimentary sector. They only exceeded by energy products (21.2 %) and vehicles and transport elements with 20.5 %.

5
Global changes in diets and the consequences for land requirements for food'. Kastner, Th. Ibarrola, Mª J., Koch, W. & Nonhebel, PNAS; volume 109, No. 18, p. 6868–6872 S. Edited by B. L. Turner, Arizona State Univeristy, May 2012.

6
The data includes both food and drink.

7
According to IDESCAT data, Catalan families are made up of an average of 2.6 people. In agricultural areas, 20 m² have been affected by roads, highways, and other areas. (There are 418,500 vegetable fields in the Agrarian Park of the Delta del Llobregat).

The second consideration is on a smaller scale. Starting from a random meal, a *Summer Dinner*, the field area necessary to produce it can be calculated. The meal consists of simple dishes such as a green salad, bread with tomato accompanied by potato omelette, black sausage, sheep cheese, anchovies from L'Escala, and yogurt with strawberries for dessert. To find out how much field you need to produce these products, the recipes have been reviewed, as well as preparation stages, the composition of feed and animal fodder, and crop performance data.[8] To facilitate the calculation, excessively elaborate products (pastries, or preserved sauces) and products that cannot come from the peninsular area have not been used.

This exercise is reflected in the graph that accompanies this text. The conclusion reached is that the field area required to produce this *Summer Dinner* is about 18 m². The data are absurd, because we would never cultivate only what is necessary for a specific meal. It is obvious that in order to obtain the oil inside a half liter bottle, it is necessary to have an olive tree that will produce much more oil than that in this container. Likewise, to obtain the tomatoes, we would need a tomato plant that will give us 14 times more tomatoes than those used in this dinner. And it is obvious that no one cultivates a square meter of wheat to make a single loaf of bread. However, the data help us to understand the scope of what we eat and compare it with spaces we are familiar with. 18 m² would be the size of, for example, a living room or a kitchen-dining room. We could, therefore, affirm that the space necessary to produce the *Summer Dinner* coincides with the size of the room where we normally eat.

The graph also shows quantitative phenomena typical of the transformation of food. Salad, for example, consists of ingredients that come directly from the field. The weight of these products as harvested in the fields is the same as when they arrive at the table. They are irrigated products that need a lot of water but little cultivated area. On the other hand, the ingredients of the second dish have a less obvious origin. Generally, they are foods generated by the transformation of products from extensive dry land crops. Bread, for example, is obtained from flour that is milled and pressed wheat. And the omelette, sausage, and cheese come from the eggs, meat, and milk of animals that eat a specific proportion of ingredients. Pig feed consists of more than 5 crops, whereas feed for ewes or cows is basically forage. Now, to get 500 g of black sausage just 1 kg of feed is needed, while to get 250 g of cheese 3.5 kg of ryegrass is needed.

Both analyses put the area of production, the fields, the scope of consumption, and the city in the same picture. Knowing the area that what we eat occupies in the territory helps us to understand the impact that any home or city has on agricultural land, exemplified here by Barcelona and the

1 km
Sagrada Família
El Ninot
La Concepció
Sant Antoni
Gran Via
Mercabarna
Gardens
1.500 m
Resting Cure Area
Baths Area
Weekend Area
Residential Area
5.700 m
2.200 m

Fig. 1

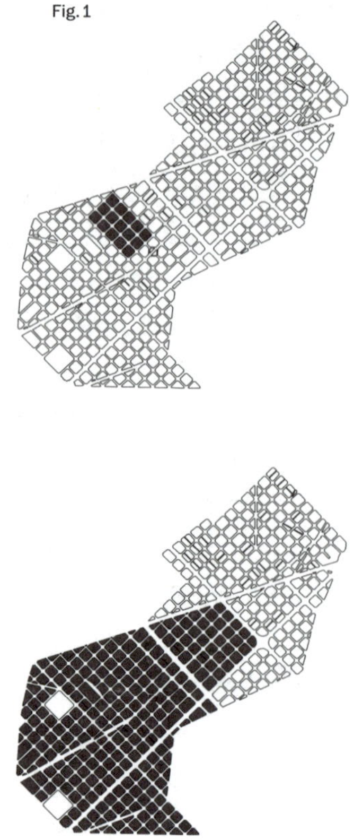

Fig. 2

Gianluca Burgio

Food, Books and the Crust of the World

133

If we had to build a bibliography using the usual scientific criteria about "food and space", we would have to compile a very long list that could be boring and, in a way, unhelpful. Books are tools that, in our opinion, serve to subvert reality and understand the world, or parts of it, and are, ultimately, living instruments, not just cold verbal concatenations that satisfy thought through scholarly accumulation. "The vertigo of lists", to paraphrase Umberto Eco, only makes sense if it whets our appetite for knowledge. It could be said that an annotated bibliographical selection is, in itself, a good critical exercise. We would like to avoid a scientific adhesion to the subject that would force us to exclude some seemingly distant texts, which, nevertheless, would help to delineate a genealogy—a kind of multiple narration, from different origins—of concepts that support the idea of a relationship between the inhabited space and food.

In a classic bibliography on subjects of this type, Carlo Ginzburg and James Joyce probably would not find a suitable place, and perhaps would cause a grimace of disgust on the faces of the most orthodox. The literature on food is vast: during recent decades, especially at the beginning of this century, food has literally invaded our imagination. It has invaded our mind, changed our material practices and influenced the way we inhabit space. The relationship between inhabited space and food can be traced in the aforementioned extensive literature, but when it is not clear, we must help it emerge with operations analogous to those in the kitchen, selecting products (texts and books) and manipulating them until the desired result is achieved. Roland Barthes, in his book *Lo obvio y lo obtuso* (1986), helps us explain this idea when he compares writing to cooking, identifying both with the origin of painting since, after all, cooking manipulates the ingredients through various actions. Barthes refers to those "practices that tend to transform matter according to the full range of its consistencies, thanks to multiple operations, such as softening, thickening, liquifying, granulation, and lubrication, to produce what in gastronomy is called the anointed, the bound, the thickened, the creamy, the crispy, etc."

We propose here a manipulation, a cultural operation done via an intentional selection of some texts, from the most recognizable because—directly and undoubtedly—they relate food and space, to those that—like truffles—we must look for with a little knowledge, intuition, luck, and a delicate sense of smell. Our proposal, therefore, moves on another level; metaphorically, we think of books, texts, and fragments as foods that nourish us. All that remains is

to find the right gastronomic ideas to elaborate them and propose appropriate recipes that make sense and are palatable, satisfying the taste and demands of those readers who want to dig deeply into the relationship between space, the city, architecture, and the food that nourishes us daily.

Perhaps one of the most brilliant books in this line is that of an artist of French cuisine, Marie-Antoine Carême—the famous chef at the service of the powerful in nineteenth-century France—, who in 1815 wrote an extraordinary pastry book which presented an unusual relationship between sweets and architecture.[1] It is a unique and absolutely rare book that talks about pastry through architecture: *Le pâtissier pittoresque* (1815) begins with a surprising statement by Carême himself who says that the most useful thing he can do for his apprentices is to explain the classical orders through a *Traité d'Architecture*. In his opinion, the rules of composition, proportion, and distribution were more useful than any other manual for young people who wanted to approach the art of confectionery—by the way, very well detailed in other volumes by Carême himself. Despite his name, which translates as "Lent", the French chef's arts do not deny or forbid anything; In fact, the elaborate sweets built by Carême employ a complex configuration made using tools, techniques, and craft skills that are a triumph of abundance.

In contrast, much more austere is the gastronomic art presented by Roland Barthes when he describes, in *L'empire des signes* (1970), the spatial composition of Japanese food. An almost natural meal, sometimes raw, cut with mastery and always very elaborated; a kind of painting on the plate whose order of ingestion is delegated to the one who eats it, who can proceed in the order that pleases him most."The dish is no longer an objectified product whose preparation is, for us, discreetly remote in time and space (pre-prepared meals behind the wall of a kitchen, a secret room where everything is allowed, as long as the product comes out composed, embellished, embalmed, prepared). Hence the living (which does not mean natural) character of this meal". Two completely opposite visions of the world and space, the Japanese and the western one of *Monsieur* Carême; two visions that recreate a cosmos and a spatial order on the plate and in pastry that go beyond the biological needs to which food responds, and that also introduce the metaphorical value of food.

That the world can be seen as a prepared dish might be surprising. However, cultures from almost all latitudes have always been accustomed to using the metaphor of food to define the space in which they live. And so the cosmos represented as a cheese, in which the inhabitants are wonderful worms born within it, is not especially strange or completely original. This is the image that Carlo Ginzburg presents in *Il formaggio e i vermi* (1976). Menocchio, a sixteenth century miller, saw the world as this special food and imagined the inhabitants of this cosmos as beings who fed on it. The poor miller could have chosen a thousand other metaphors (which might not have brought him before the Inquisition), but he adopted precisely that of cheese, the metaphor of a food. Ginzburg argues that this type of gnoseological analogy was present in other cultures: "In proposing this analogy, Menocchio, without knowing it, echoed ancient and remote myths. In an Indian myth, mentioned in the Vedas, the origin of the cosmos is explained by the coagulation—similar to that of milk—of the waters of a primordial sea, whipped by gods of creation. According to the Calmuchis, in the beginning of time, the waters of the sea were covered with a thick layer, like the one that forms on milk, from which sprouted plants, animals, men, and gods. 'At first, this world was nothing, and... it was beaten from the sea water like a foam, and it coagulated like a cheese, from which then a great number of worms were born, and these worms became men, of which the most powerful and wise was God'. These had been, more or less, [...] the words spoken by Menocchio".

All this is not a coincidence: rather it is a profound demonstration that food is linked anthropologically to our lives and also to the space in which we live and to the places that have produced it. The crucial facts of the Book of Genesis, which mark the life of man after Creation, are linked to food: the original dwelling has its privileged place in Eden; however, the arrogance of Adam and Eve, the greedy attraction to a fruit, determines a new way of inhabiting the Earth. The expulsion from Paradise leads to humankind's new home, the place in which he himself must procure his food for survival; through his own efforts, he must cultivate the land to obtain bread, which in the Christian tradition becomes Eucharist.

Bread is an elaborated food, and behind this food there are millennia of cultural and agricultural evolution, experiments, and territorial conquests. This is so ingrained

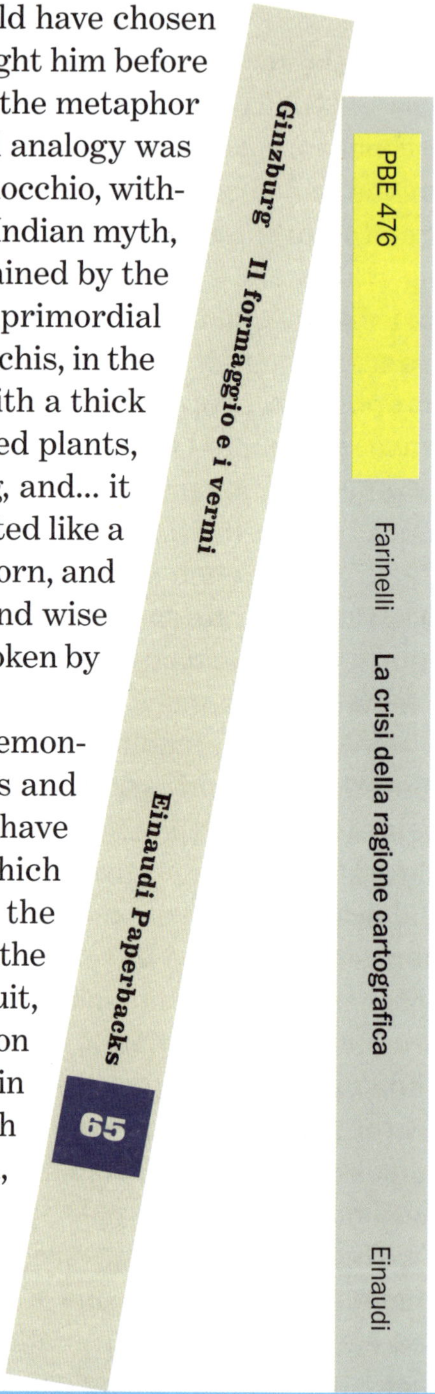

in Western cultures that, over time, it has become synonymous with life and home. In fact, bread becomes a descriptive model, as Franco Farinelli demonstrates in *La crisi della ragione cartografica* (2009). Then, the bread becomes a kind of map, a primordial cartography that defines the world: it is born from the geography of a place, its waters, its seeds, and its land, and ends up being, through its synthetic form, a cartography that is also possible to read in section. Says Farinelli: "He taught an ancient interpretation: Scripture is bread, and it has crust and crumb; the crust is equivalent to the literal meaning, the crumb to the intellect (*intellectus*) hidden in it".

There is a passage, very well represented precisely by bread, which, according to anthropologists, marks the moment of transition between eating as a biological necessity and cooking as a sociocultural fact. In both cases, however, the organization—or, at least, the control—of space is present. Specifically, Carolyn Steel, in *Hungry City* (2009), argues sharply about how food gives more form to a city than urban planning. It is interesting to find the trace of food, hunger, and the need for foodstuffs in urban planning.

The city and food are certainly related. Table habits are defined as urbane,[2] the table is a representation of social coexistence between citizens who have the right to occupy that space. But beyond metaphors, it is clear that the city is fed and takes shape through food, as Carolyn Steel explains: the image that opens her book is that of the "Allegory of Good Government", by Ambrogio Lorenzetti, in which the cities and the countryside feed each other with food that becomes an element of inclusion and construction of the urban space. However, food has not always been considered inclusive and, in many cases, it has become a divisive element: the cheese described by Piero Camporesi in *Le officine dei sensi* (1985) is a food that separates people. Cheese was often considered a food for semi-wild populations, more similar to animals than to men; thus, cheese marked a separation between urban spaces (sophisticated and cultured) and the undefined and unprotected spaces of that human consortium (wild and uneducated) that were considered outside civilization. Urban culture should be kept away from possible contamination caused by food, such as cheese, from peripheral and non-urbanized populations. The issue of limits, of the border, is not only an abstract issue, but becomes concrete and objectified in foods such as cheese and bread itself, which was the reason for the separation between classes identified via white bread, for the well-off classes, and the black bread fed to the less wealthy.[3]

Between Carolyn Steel and Piero Camporesi, in a kind of dialogue of three (or maybe it would be better to say four) that brings together the city, food, and the concept of inclusion/exclusion, Marcel Detienne and Jean-Pierre Vernant could also participate. In *La cucina del sacrificio in terra greca* (2014), they show us how the founding of the *polis*—the city-state—is linked to cooking to the point of stating that cooking is political. The founding acts of the cities, the definition of the limits between sacred and profane spaces, the division into social classes, had as a principle, among the ancient Greeks, a ritual meal in most cases preceded by an animal sacrifice, so that: "to found a colony [...] it is sufficient to bring from the mother country a spit and a pot with fire"; two kitchen utensils and fire, which enable the transformation of food and the definition of the urban space.

Food is undoubtedly the cause of many of the social and spatial divisions that take place in the urban environment. But there is also another very important issue that induces inclusion/exclusion mechanisms: contamination. In fact, the separation between what is clean—edible, without doubt—and what is dirty and should be avoided or eliminated, is well known. This distinction is usually anthropological and has strong repercussions on the spatial organization of places where food is prepared and consumed. The cultural variations that define and distinguish what is pure from what is not, and the edible from what cannot—or should not—be eaten, often have religious origins. Mary Douglas, in *Purezza e pericolo* (1988), explains the sacred reasons for this distinction that distances certain foods from the table and defines the space within which some of these foods can remain. Starting from religious origins, the cultural concepts of cleanliness/dirtiness have been gradually secularized and, in many occasions have become medicalized, becoming hygienic problems. The organization of cooking spaces and of the *salle à manger* (when it exists) also depends on the routes by which products can enter the house. The sphere of restaurant cooking also has, as a result of regulations, a spatial arrangement similar to that of a hospital, in which the clean and the dirty must never cross paths.

In light of this idea of border and separation suggested by the English anthropologist, it is interesting to read some reflections by Gianfranco Marrone, who, in *Gastromania* (2014), observes how street food is usually placed in areas outside the city or in places that mark the urban accesses. It is not new that food finds its favorite places at the entrances to the city: Massimo Montanari, in *La fame e l'abbondanza* (1997), relates the words of the Minister of the Ostrogothic monarch Cassiodorus, who lived in the sixth century AD, who recommended to the prefects charged with supplying the cities of the kingdom of Teodorico that the transit of food be located just in the obligatory passages of the city: "in its own throat", that is, near the access doors. Ultimately, it is a form of control to protect the urban community, according to a secular system in which the urban boundary is a dike of defense and verification. The danger of contamination is the line, material and cultural, that defines spatial organization. Contamination is kept away if what is potentially dangerous is kept out of the city: this is the reason why markets and some peculiar food preparations often have, as a final border, the doors of the city. However, contamination is also one of the reasons for the complex organization of food, which, according to Mary Douglas in *Antropologia e simbolismo* (1985), defines what is admissible—and what is not—in a Jewish meal. In a very brief passage, although very incisive and plastic in its descriptive capacity, Mary Douglas speaks of the Hebrew dietary rules, comparing them with a classic poem by a Chinese author, Lu Ji, who defines poetry as the link between the infinite world and the human gender; in the same way, the Israelite table itself contains infinite space because it is, in itself, a representation of the world. All the rules applied to food tend to defend the sacred integrity of physical forms, so that all who are pure can have access to the Temple and its altar; and here we return to the topic of inclusion/exclusion to which we referred earlier.

To the *gastro-nomy* of which Mary Douglas speaks in her anthropological research, a reply can be found in Claude Fischler's *gastro-anomy* ("Gastro-nomie et gastro-anomie").[4] If the western urbanity of the enlightened city in the eighteenth and nineteenth centuries corresponds to a series of rather rigid and defined *gastro-nomic* rules, an evident *gastro-anomy* applies to the contemporary dispersed city and its spatial deregulation: cities have become a kind of nutritional juke-box, widely spread out, in which the logic of access to food à la McDonald triumphs. Somehow, the progressive atomization of eating habits, increasingly individualistic, has reconfigured the location of food places in cities, causing a kind of food sprawl.

But where and in what spaces do people who decide to use the city as an alternative to their home eat? Excluding from this reflection restaurants, cafes, and bistros, and all those closed spaces in which you can eat almost like at home, it is evident that nowadays you can eat almost anywhere in the city, except where it is explicitly prohibited or in those places—such as sacred or institutional spaces—where the sense of convenience intuitively excludes the inappropriate presence of food. Thus, food trucks, kiosks, and beach bars are widespread, especially in large cities, and have redesigned the public space, if not directly in its configuration, then in the geometries imposed by their use. Food has become spatialized (in the sense that it has occupied new spaces or that these have been modified) and, among its many attributes, it has also become street food, according to Gianfranco Marrone in *Gastromania*. Among the many reflections of the Italian semiologist, there is one related to the way we eat this food: “Travelers and indigenous, pilgrims and residents, meet and mingle from time to time in front of the beach bar that offers alternatives to homemade food [...], they all congregate there to take bites, rigorously standing, of greasy garbage...”. Like Marrone, also Claude Fischler, in *Les alimentations particulières* (2013), emphasizes the increasingly widespread habit of eating standing up, a fast way of feeding that is part of a less regulated and more *gastro-anomic* system: “Eating while standing, in many cultures, is strongly disapproved of, perhaps precisely because the standing posture contrasts with the sitting posture, the only one permitted in the circle of the table”.

The fragmentation of meals has led to a loss of structure of schedules and modes of eating; Claude Fischler, to describe this phenomenon and contrast it with regular dining habits, has used in *Gastro-nomie et gastro-anomie* a concept from ethology, called vagabond feeding: “Baboons in freedom tend [...] rather towards vagabond feeding: they feed in solitary, at irregular intervals but more frequently, in small amounts, and at random while wandering”.

Fischler’s idea is that regular dining habits actually arose after vagabond feeding, as primates would show. *L’origine des manières de table* (1968) by Claude Lévi-Strauss, together with the other writings that make up the *Mythologiques*, demonstrates a progressive structuring of feeding behaviors that, nevertheless, have been changing over the last few decades; consequently, Fischler states that “the urban-industrial civilization provokes a return to the archaic, a kind of ‘phylogenetic regression’”.

The gradual disappearance of food structures increases 31
the entropy of the world of food and has strong consequences for the established order of urban environments and domes-

tic spaces. Public and private places are mutually modified in terms of food: the way in which the space (domestic or public) is entered, the way people move, the means of processing and consumption, profoundly transform the places where people live. Again Fischler, in another text,[5] observes that today "eating is no longer so identified with domesticity." This is a statement that accurately portrays the current situation in which, as we said before, it is possible to eat anywhere: the consequence is that typically domestic space has exploded and spread out and extended into thousands of other places.

In the 1990s, more than half of French homes—a phenomenon that extended equally to the rest of Europe—were equipped with microwave ovens and freezers. From the presence of these devices we can deduce that both the food supply and food processing spaces have changed profoundly. Spatial *deregulation*, caused by differences in food consumption, has transformed the typical binomial of the bourgeois house *cuisine/salle à manger*. This has been broken apart and reconfigured in other ways: kitchen/sofa; kitchen/bedroom; fridge/sofa; microwave/dining room, etc. In addition, new spaces have appeared that could be defined as kinds of outsourced kitchens of which, for example, new binomials appear, such as the supermarket/dining room or restaurant/sofa, thanks to the intervention of food delivery companies.

There could be many more combinations, as we can imagine, and in addition, all point towards the atomization of regular eating patterns. Once again, Fischler speaks in *Les alimentations particulières* of a progressive individualization of food that profoundly alters the meaning of eating together (regular dining habits): the Roman *mensa*—the word from which table derives—was the place shared by diners where they had space, food, and experiences in common. Today, the dining space is often reduced to a lunch-box that contains vegan food for some, oriental or macrobiotic food for others. The contemporary experience of eating can dispense with the table and its shared space, a bit like headphones connected to a music player that dispense with the shared experience of an auditorium.

In general, the global organization of contemporary domestic space is changing to a greater or lesser degree. The hearth is no longer the center of the home and, in fact, the house can almost do without the kitchen, as it had been understood and conceived up to now. The space of the Kabyle house described by Pierre Bourdieu in “La maison ou le monde rénversé”,[6] is based around the so-called *foyer*, the fireplace, governed and controlled by women. The house is (or was) built around the fire, which acts on the raw ingredients and turns them into dishes. Home, food, and domesticity met in a well-defined part of the domestic space, and the *foyer*, or hearth, represented the center. The expression *manger hors foyer*, for the French, means ‘eating away from the hearth’ and today, increasingly, means staying away from the hearth as a source of heat and a tool for food processing. Rem Koolhaas, in *Fireplace* (2014),[7] shows in a very clear diagram how *fire* and *place* have been separated progressively, forming other elements that influence the space and its use in a completely different way.

The individualization, even spatial, of meals had already been identified by Georg Simmel who, in “Sociology of food”,[8] stated that the plate “points out that this portion of food has been isolated exclusively for that person. [...] The line of the circle is the most closed drawing, its content is the most concentrated into itself, while the source of food available to all is rectangular or oval, that is, it is less jealously closed on itself”. The kitchen objects that mediate between the public space of the table and the private space of our body provide us with other opportunities for reflection. Roland Barthes, in *L’empire des signes*, describes Japanese chopsticks in this way: “[...] in all the gestures involved, the chopstick stands in contrast to our knife (and its predatory substitute, the fork): it is the utensil that refuses to grasp, cut, or mutilate to separate [...]; for the chopstick, food is no longer a prey on which violence is exercised [...], but a substance transferred harmoniously...”.

However, there are places that summarize the complexity of contemporary food by bringing together the behavior, often schizophrenic, of the so-called *hypermoderne mangeur*, so well described by François Ascher in the book that has this same phrase as its title. The *bistrot* mentioned by Marc Augé in the *Un etnologo al bistrot* (2015), is a place where individualism can coexist with communal dining, and private space is confused with public space. The owner of the bistrot constructs a spatial device that allows these opposites to come together and find a kind of citizenship right without “any clear inter-

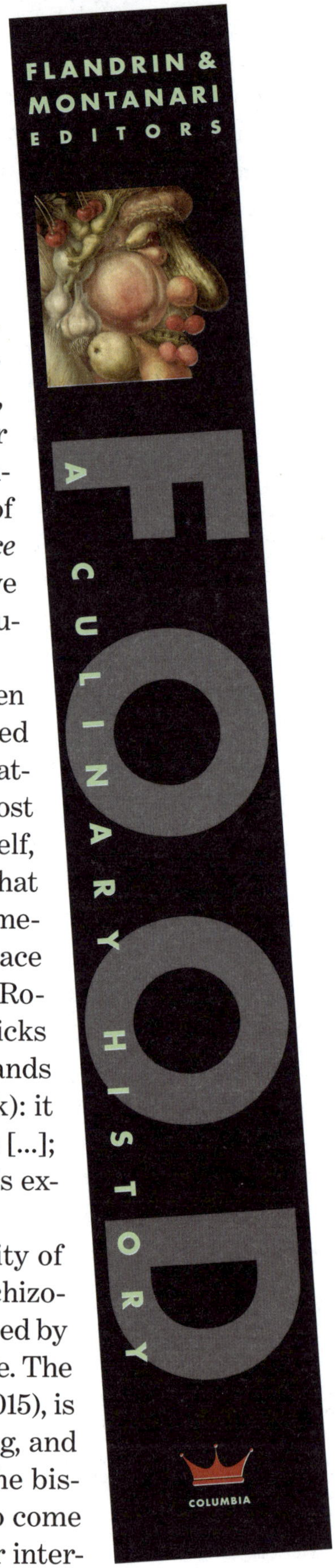

ruption, but only thresholds and passages; a space that does not own or exclude anyone".

But perhaps the most interesting spatial device—for the symbolic, cultural and metaphorical force that millennia of use have given it—is the table, on which the disposition of the elements and the diners defines the urbanity of the meals. A suggestive image of the table is offered by David Leatherbarrow in *Table Talk*:[9] "Throughout the meal, some things or objects, such as the centerpiece, maintain their fixed position; others, such as the bread basket, the wine bottle, salt and pepper, migrate. Place setting elements may not be anchored in a specific place, but the relationships between them are relatively stable [...]. However, the permanence of the place is not permanence in time, because some things appear at different times and then are distributed everywhere; others are removed; while others, like the tablecloth, are always present, either covering a small table in the kitchen or laid on the ground during a picnic. These comings and goings are governed by the relationships between the various elements of the situation. Some elements belong to sets of things, others are isolated elements; in addition, some are shared, others are not, because the dining room table also configures public and private spaces".

Equally significant are Luce Giard's observations in the second volume of *L'invention du quotidien* (1994), written together with Michel de Certeau and Pierre Mayol. For Giard, the table—sometimes compared by Levi-Strauss with the bed—is a social machine that encourages cooking, makes people talk, and pushes them to reveal secrets: "the table is a place of pleasure, it is an old discovery, but it keeps its truth and its secret because eating is always more than simply eating". In fact, the table is the reflection of human and urban relationships; the table in its very different forms—from the sacrificial altars to the Roman table, passing through the individual tables of fast food restaurants, to contemporary lunch-boxes—is the city.

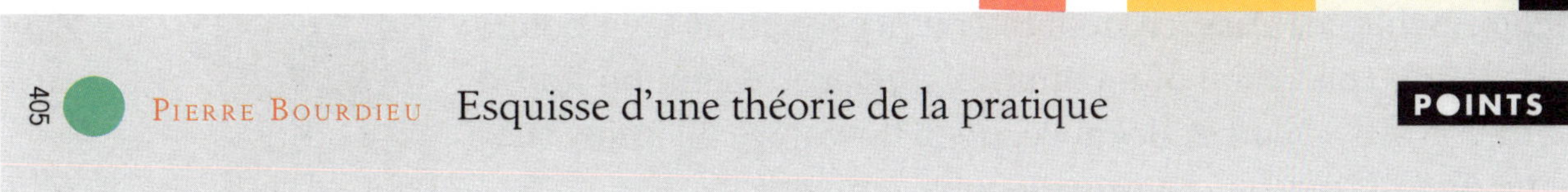

With its objects, it represents the dynamics of use, organizes spaces, separates and includes, defines a private space within the public space, such as a restaurant, or converts a park bench, when used as a table, into a domestic space. Montanari says, in *Il cibo come cultura* (2011), that food is grammar. Its anthropological value makes it capillary, it penetrates into the depths of urban dynamics and contributes, as Carolyn Steel argues, to shaping the space in which we live.

This text hides a kind of invisible and very precarious architecture, very similar to the structure of a conversation between diners around a table, in which we have participated countless times. The beginning of the talk is often linked to observations about the dishes, to the Proustian cupcake effect that can be caused, for example, by a cheese: on the table—starting from an almost random element—, the infinite space of other places, stories and experiences that come to life every day through the daily act of eating. The dialogues at the table overlap, sometimes chasing each other, repeating themselves, leading to arguments that seem unrelated and that, nevertheless, contribute to broadening the view and opening up new topics. Therefore, conversation is rarely linear; in fact, it proceeds by jumps and fragments, tedious digressions and formidable intuitions, a bit like the breakfast of Leopold Bloom, described by Joyce in *Ulysses* (2016), who goes from the point of cooking the kidney, to the bedroom and the bed where his wife is sleeping. A way to err, like that of Ulysses, whose main concern—each time he stepped ashore in a new land—was to find bread and a human community organized around it. Pierre Vidal-Naquet, in *Il cacciatore nero* (2006), talks about this heroic figure who wanders through a mythical geographical space, populated by non-human peoples who feed differently: they eat men, flowers of oblivion or ambrosia, the nectar of the gods; nevertheless, the Greek hero hopes to find fields of wheat and populations that eat bread; but the non-humans he meets are relegated to a space devoid of this cultural product.

Josep Pla seems more fortunate when he relates, in *Illes mediterrànies* (1986), his experience, similar to that of Ulysses, and yet with more positive results. During his travels he observed that, somehow, the Mediterranean people share a recognizable identity, thanks to the presence of fava beans that define the space of a common culture. When he found them, Pla felt at home. Because, deep down, we all know that living and eating, on many occasions, coincide.

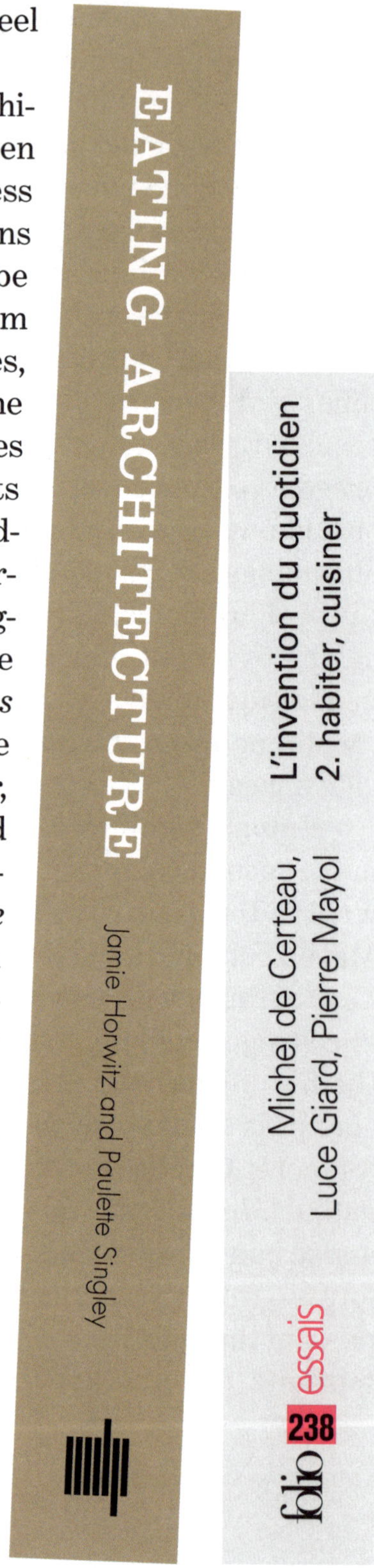

Note:
The editions of the books and articles consulted are those cited in this essay. The translations of the cited texts are those of the author.

1
After all, our intention in this text is, in a way, similar to that of *Monsieur* Carême and, for others, symmetrical and opposite: we will talk about food through space and space through food. This might be a little disorienting to our readers, but we will probably offer a different point of view—*à la Carême*—on the themes of eating and living.

2
Among the many testimonies that prove it, we remember that of Erasmus of Rotterdam, who wrote an educational text for children entitled *A Handbook on Good Manners for Children* (De civilitate morum puerilium, 1528).

3
Piero Camporesi documents this in the chapter entitled "*Il pane fuggente* ('the bread that flees')", from the book *Il pane selvaggio*, 1980.

4
The article "Gastro-nomie et gastro-anomie" can be found in *Communications* magazine, No. 31, 1979, edited by Fischler himself.

5
Claude Fischler, "The McDonaldization of the Culture", in Massimo Montanari and Jean-Louis Flandrin, *Food. A Culinary History from Antiquity to the Present*, Columbia University Press, New York, 1999, e-book.

6
"La maison ou le monde rénversé" is found in Pierre Bourdieu, *Esquisse d'une théorie de la pratique,* 2000.

7
It is one of the volumes of the series *Elements*, published by Rem Koolhaas and Amo for the Venice Biennale 2014: "From the caveman to the toaster, the fireplace is the catalyst of cultural evolution. Throughout history, its various functions branch off into discrete devices, so that the fireplace, which we thought had disappeared, proves remarkably persistent and versatile in its multiple offshoots, even those that reach back into a more primitive history...".

8
The essay "Sociology of food" is found in Georg Simmel, *El individuo y la libertad*, 1998.

9
This text is found in Jamie Horwitz, Paulette Singley (eds.), *Eating Architecture*, The MIT Press, Cambridge-London, 2004.

Publisher
Col·legi d'Arquitectes de Catalunya

Quaderns #271

Managing Editor
Francisco Rei

Director of this issue
Xavier Monteys

Essays by
Stephen Bates, Gianluca Burgio, Carlos Dias Coelho, Pere Fuertes i Eulàlia Gómez-Escoda, Magda Mària, Xavier Monteys, Nuria Ortigosa, Núria Salvadó i Roger Sauquet, David Steegmann, Carolyn Steel

Design
Bendita Gloria

Translations
David C. Ambler

Proofreading
Stephanie Jennings

Printing and binding
Arlequín, Barcelona

Other Photo Credits:
Pages 9–18: Images taken from chicagoreader.com, wired.com, *Le pâtissier pittoresque*, *AC* No. 4, Le Corbusier *Vers une architecture*, Bauhaus Archiv Berlin, Eroski mediakit, Comunitat de Sant Egidi.

Pages 19–31: Images courtesy of the author plus images taken from june-14.com, arqueologiadelfuturo.blogs.com, upcommons.upc.edu, *MacGuffin* No. 4, Lecrere maison de ventes.

Page 54: Camiel Van Noten; 55–58: Stephen Bates; 59: Simon Burko; 60: Sergison Bates architects; 61: Ute Zscharnt.

Pages 102–123: Images courtesy of Arxiu Fotogràfic de Barcelona (AFB), Arxiu Històric COAC, Arxiu Nacional de Catalunya (ANC), Institut d'Estudis Fotogràfics de Catalunya (IEFC), Museu Nacional d'Art de Catalunya (MNAC), Marc Llibre Roig, Germans Santilari i Galeria Artur Ramon.

Pages 3, 150: Adobe Stock.

ISBN: 978-84-343-1377-4
Dep. Legal: B-47269-2018

Subscriptions

Artbooks
mag@artbooks.es

Bruil & Van de Staaij
info@bruil.info

Publicaciones de Arquitectura y Arte
publiarq@publiarq.com

Acknowledgments

This issue of *Quaderns* wouldn't have been possible without the coincidence of several things. First, the grant awarded by RECERCAIXA to Habitar research group from UPC, won by public competition in 2016, in order to develop the project *El menjar i l'espai públic urbà a Barcelona* (LCF/PR/RC16/10100009). This grant has been the main inspiration of some of the articles of this issue.

Second, the decision of the jury of the COAC, who selected this atypical editorial initiative. Also, the institutions, archives and museums that gave us permission to reproduce images free of rights. The Barcelona-based graphic design studio Bendita Gloria who has fitted this puzzle and, obviously, the authors who agreed to collaborate in this issue. To all of them, thanks.

Xavier Monteys

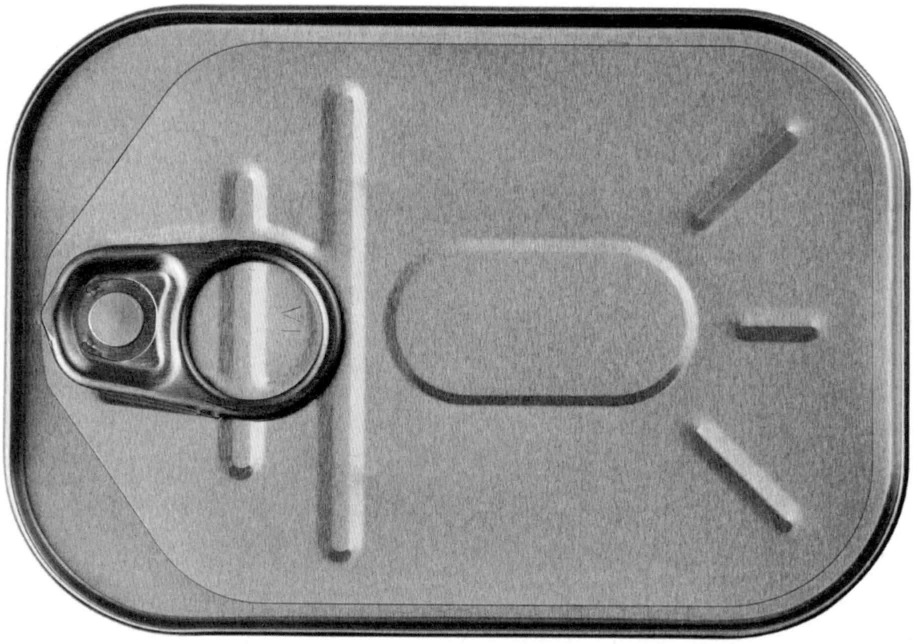

Sabadell
Professional

Una cosa és dir que treballem en PRO dels professionals. Una altra és fer-ho:

Compte
Expansió Plus PRO

Bonifiquem la teva quota de col·legiat

1 / 6

Aquest nombre és indicatiu del risc del producte. Així, 1/6 és indicatiu de menys risc i 6/6 és indicatiu de més risc.

Banco de Sabadell, S.A. es troba adherit al Fons Espanyol de Garantia de Dipòsits d'Entitats de Crèdit. La quantitat màxima garantida actualment pel fons esmentat és de 100.000 euros per dipositant.

10% de la teva quota de col·legiat màxim 50 euros* el primer any.

+ 0 comissions d'administració i manteniment.

+ Remuneració fins a 3%TAE Primer any fins a 2,74% TAE. Saldo màxim a remunerar 10.000 euros.[1]

+ 1% de devolució en els principals rebuts domiciliats i sobre les compres amb targeta de crèdit en comerços d'alimentació[2], màxim 50€ bruts al mes.

Truca'ns al 900 500 170, identifica't com a membre del teu col·lectiu, organitzem una reunió i comencem a treballar.

*Bonificació del 10% de la quota de col·legiat amb un màxim de 50 euros per compte amb la quota domiciliada, per a nous clients de captació. La bonificació es realitzarà un únic any per a les quotes domiciliades durant els 12 primers mesos, comptant com a primer mes, el de l'obertura del compte. El pagament es realitzarà en compte el mes següent dels 12 primers mesos.
1. Per tenir accés a aquesta retribució, els titulars han d'haver fet amb les seves targetes cinc compres en el mes anterior al mes a remunerar i tenir un saldo mitjà mensual al banc superior a 30.000 euros en recursos, calculat com la suma de saldos del mes anterior de comptes a la vista, dipòsits, renda fixa a venciment, assegurances de vida-estalvi, fons d'inversió, valors cotitzables i no cotitzables, plans de pensions, plans de previsió d'EPSV i BS Fons Gran Selecció. No es tindrà en compte per al còmput del saldo mitjà el saldo existent en aquest Compte Expansió Plus ni en cap altre de les mateixes característiques en el qual els titulars siguin intervinents. Sí que es tindrà en consideració el nombre de cotitulars, de manera que el saldo mínim existent a l'entitat com a requisit serà el pres proporcionalment per a cada cotitular. No es remuneraran els saldos durant el primer mes de vida del Compte Expansió Plus.
En cas que no s'arribi per part dels titulars al saldo mínim que dona dret a la retribució del Compte Expansió Plus, la liquidació es farà al 0% per aquest concepte.
Rendibilitat primer any: per al tram de saldo diari que excedeixi els 10.000 euros: 0% TIN. Per al tram de saldo diari des de 0 fins a un màxim de 10.000 euros: 2,919% TIN, 1,8191% TAE (calculada tenint en compte els dos tipus d'interès per al supòsit de permanència del saldo mitjà diari durant un any complet des de l'alta del compte). Exemple de liquidació: saldo al compte de 15.000 euros diaris, saldo diari sobre el qual es remunera: 10.000 euros; freqüència mensual; interessos liquidats a l'any: 270,82 euros; data contractació: 30/06/18; data primer pagament d'interessos: 31/08/2018; data final primer any: 30/06/2019.
Rendibilitat resta d'anys: per al tram de saldo diari que excedeixi els 10.000 euros: 0% TIN. Per al tram de saldo diari des de 0 fins a un màxim de 10.000 euros: 2,919% TIN, 1,9910% TAE (calculada tenint en compte els dos tipus d'interès per al supòsit de permanència del saldo mitjà diari durant un any complet a comptar des del segon any del compte). Exemple de liquidació: saldo al compte de 15.000 euros diaris, saldo diari sobre el qual es remunera: 10.000 euros; freqüència mensual; interessos liquidats a l'any: 296,77 euros; data inici segon any: 30/06/19; data primer pagament d'interessos: 31/07/2019; data final segon any: 30/06/2020.
2. T'abonarem fins a 50 euros bruts al mes, sempre que l'import de la devolució sigui igual o superior a 5 euros i hagis fet cinc compres durant el mes amb les teves targetes.
- Rebuts domiciliats de llum, gas, telèfon fix, mòbil i Internet.
- Rebuts domiciliats que corresponguin, com a emissor, a organitzacions no governamentals (ONG) registrades en l'Agència Espanyola de Cooperació i els rebuts de col·legis, escoles bressol i universitats carregats durant el mes. S'ha de tractar de centres docents espanyols (públics, privats i concertats) i en queden excloses les despeses d'acadèmies particulars, col·legis professionals o despeses diferents a les d'escolarització. Tampoc s'hi inclouen les despeses en concepte de postgraus, màsters i doctorats.
- Operacions de compra fetes amb targeta de crèdit incloses en la liquidació del mes, amb les targetes modalitat Classic, Or, Premium, Platinum i Shopping Or el contracte de les quals estigui associat a aquest compte, en determinats establiments comercials d'alimentació inclosos i que es poden consultar a la pàgina www.bancosabadell.com/cuentaexpansionplus.

Oferta vàlida per a nous comptes oberts des del 24/04/2018 fins al 31/12/2018 amb la domiciliació en el Compte Expansió Plus PRO d'una nova nòmina, pensió o ingrés regular mensual per un import mínim de 3.000 euros (se n'exclouen els ingressos procedents de comptes oberts en el grup Banc Sabadell a nom del mateix titular). També cal haver domiciliat dos rebuts domèstics en els dos últims mesos.
Els titulars d'un Compte Expansió Plus PRO en podran disposar d'un altre d'addicional sense requisits de domiciliació de nòmina, pensió o ingressos mensuals recurrents. I, a més a més, tots els Comptes Professional que vulgui, sense comissió d'administració i de manteniment (rendibilitat Compte Professional: 0% TAE).
Pot fer extensiva aquesta oferta als seus empleats i familiars de primer grau.

sabadellprofessional.com

Banco de Sabadell, S.A., av. Óscar Esplá, 37, 03007 Alacant. Inscrit en el Registre Mercantil d'Alacant, tom 4070, foli 1, full A-156980. NIF A-08000143 Condicions revisables en funció de l'evolució del mercat. S'aplicaran les que estiguin en vigor al banc en el moment de la formalització. Document publicitari. Fecha de emisión: Octubre 2018

Lisbon ArchiTecTure Triennale

The PoeTics of Reason

3 OCT – 2 DEC 2019

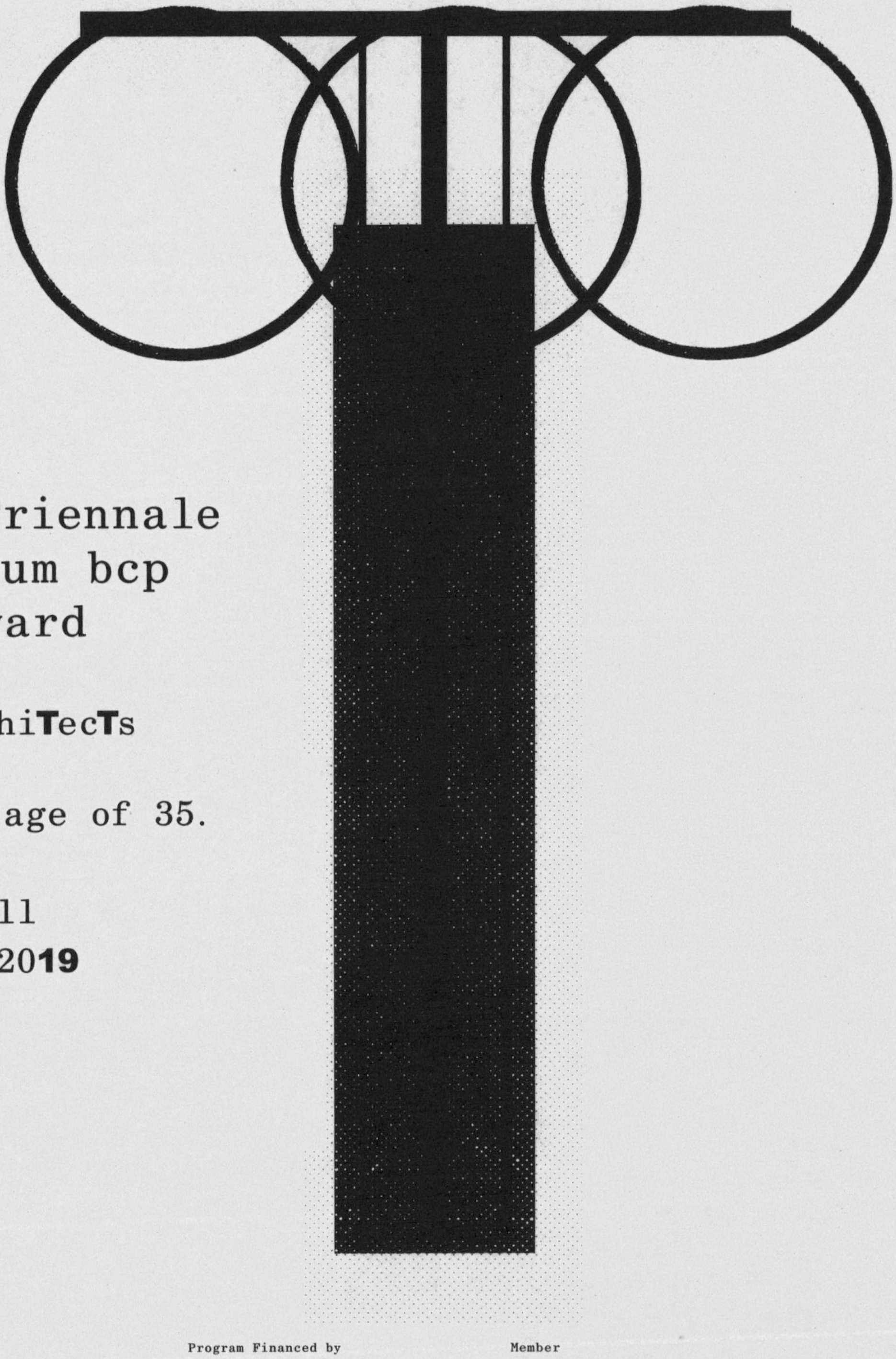

Lisbon Triennale Millennium bcp Début Award

Is for archiTecTs
& sTudios
up To The age of 35.

→ Apply Till
March 26, 2019

Artwork: Marco Balesteros (LETRA).

shower technology
ONE-TOUCH SHOWER CONTROL
TRES
TRES has revolutionised the way you can interact with your tap. Technology and design come together for a new way to thoroughly enjoy your shower. This is SHOWER TECHNOLOGY. Electronic thermostatic control for enjoying a shower with complete peace of mind.
www.tresgriferia.com

OBLIQUE EXPERIMENTS

OBLIQUE EXPERIMENTS

CLAUDE PARENT'S ARCHITECTURAL INSTALLATIONS (1969–1975)

IGOR SIDDIQUI

CONTENTS

PROLOGUE

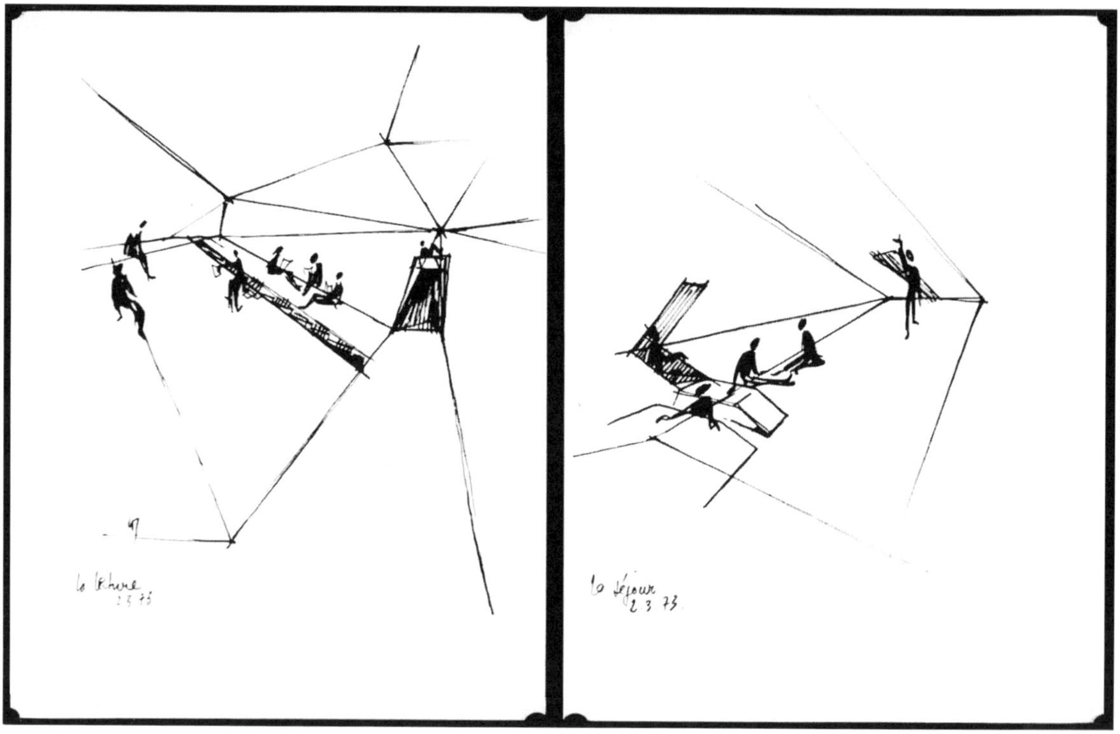

Sketches from the CPA 473 folder *Dessins utopiques de Claude Parent (1966–1982), Fonction oblique: Vivre à l'oblique (1973–1975)*, part of the Claude Parent Archives housed by the Kandinsky Library at the Centre Pompidou in Paris.

> Sigurður Guðmundsson, *Study for Horizon*, 1975.

CPA 473: The call number for one of nearly five hundred folders that comprise Claude Parent's digitized archive housed by the Kandinsky Library at the Centre Pompidou in Paris. Part of a larger section dedicated to the French architect's graphic works in the archive—identified as *dessins utopiques*, or utopian drawings—the folder contains photographically reproduced sketches of imagined spaces shaped by angled floors, walls, and ceilings. Titled according to daily activities like work, play, and eating, and populated by scale figures suggesting such uses, the hand-drawn perspectives depict interior environments in which architecture acts as furniture and vice versa. These archived documents, dated between 1973 and 1975, are a record of Parent's exploration of oblique living, that is, his total vision of life on sloped surfaces that contributed to his reputation as a radical architect.

CPA 473 contains evidence of Parent's thinking about interiority, an aspect of his experimental architecture that was at times overshadowed by the monumental forms that emerged in many of his speculative drawings. Since this is one of the things that particularly interests me about his work, encountering these sketches was a step in the right direction for my research. Browsing through the folder for the first of many times, I eventually reached the last of the thirty-six images. In lieu of one more drawing, I was surprised to find another kind of image: a black-and-white negative of a photograph showing a man standing on a beach, his figure

juxtaposed against the flatness of the sea level in the background. Rather than standing upright his body slants forward, astonishingly parallel to the oblique angle of a wood post in front of him. A single line of text below the picture, "Study for horizon," turned out to be its title, a self-portrait by the Icelandic artist Sigurður Guðmundsson from 1975.[1]

At first, I had no idea how the image ended up in Parent's archives, much less in this specific folder. However, the fact that it did immediately made sense to me, almost as if it were a matter of fate. Someone, I guessed, must have been amused by the resonance between Guðmundsson's tilted stance and Parent's explorations of oblique architecture. Perhaps the artist and the architect's apparently shared interest in defying the normative orientation of horizontals and verticals inspired someone to place the photograph among the collection of drawings, highlighting this observation. I later discovered a miniature reproduction of the same picture in Parent's 1981 monograph *Entrelacs de l'oblique*, where, instead of being identified by title or author, its brief caption only notes that the artist in question participated in the Venice Biennale—conceivably the place where the architect first saw it.[2] In any case, my unexpected encounter with this particular image, in this very folder, at this very archive, helped me grasp the sense of serendipitous displacement—or the fortuitous outcome of being out of place—that ripples through the various layers of my research that became this manuscript.

For one, unexpectedly finding within Parent's vast oeuvre a small opening (Guðmundsson's photograph) that leads to a view of oblique living beyond architecture, encapsulated in a single moment the kind of relationship between specificity and expansiveness that had already existed in my own engagement with the architect's work. The truth is that while my initial interest in oblique architecture stemmed from the challenge that it posed for building interiors, its underlying theoretical principles simultaneously prompted me to contemplate the potential of obliqueness not only as it applies to inclined ground—which is how it appears in most standard accounts of Parent's work—but also, interpreted more broadly, as any vector whose direction deviates from an already established expectation, reference, datum, or norm. I was working through my ideas about obliqueness in relation to my own design practice, publicly lecturing and publishing on the subject as early as 2017.[3] Such a path, I later realized, is not unlike the experience of looking through Parent's sketches but somehow ending up following the lead of a misplaced picture.

I came to the Pompidou archive to see if I would find in Parent's body of work the very thing that his buildings, drawings, and writing inspired me to look for elsewhere. Moreover, I sought to identify any overlaps between such expanded expressions of obliqueness and his oblique interiors, as if trying to posit a fraction of his practice into a vast landscape formed by broader interpretations of his theoretical principles. These objectives led me to Parent's architectural tour of France from the early 1970s, throughout which he designed a series of temporary interior installations as public explorations of oblique living. As the book's primary subject, this episode of his career captured what I consider to be an oblique approach to practice—the tour was, in a sense, very much a detour—while also yielding a series of interior experiments.

As an architect, I typically spend most of my time in the design studio rather than in the archive—the space of research where

I eventually arrived through my design practice, as if following the oblique path of a wormhole. The memory of coming across Guðmundsson's image stayed with me in part because its placement reminded me of my own position in the archive, both out of place and with a purpose. The artist's posture in the photograph likewise embodies a mixture of adaptation and defiance, a type of productive displacement that defines oblique practice. And if my own departure from the comfort zone of my usual habitat in order to pursue this research was in this sense oblique, so were Parent's traveling experiments during which he left his Parisian atelier behind in order to figure out an alternative form of architectural practice in a different kind of environment. Along the way, he challenged himself to redefine not only the role of architecture but also that of the architect. If the transformed silhouette of such a figure were visible, it would likely appear no less oblique than his architecture.

INTRODUC-
TION

COLLECTED OBJECTS AS MODELS OF A PRACTICE

Parent testing a mocked-up slope with his collaborators while designing the oblique installation for the 1970 Venice Biennale.

> Parent sitting on the sloped floor among the audience in Amiens, c.1973.

Suppose that most of life took place on sloped surfaces instead of flat ground. Imagine buildings without any level floors. How would it feel to live in an environment that inspires movement even in moments ordinarily associated with rest? What if everything straight were oblique?

Such speculations invite an engagement with the work of French architect Claude Parent (1923–2016) who in the 1960s started exploring the use of angled planes in reshaping both architecture as a habitable terrain and its effects on those who inhabit it. As part of his ongoing investigations of such an architecture—which he pursued through various modes of practice, including writing, drawing, and building—Parent designed a series of temporary installations with which he intended to introduce his avant-garde ideas to popular audiences. Produced between 1969 and 1975, these pop-up architectural interventions—referred to, in French, as *praticables*—were designed for various sites throughout France (as well as featured at the 1970 Venice Biennale), usually accompanied by related public programs. In addition to helping promote Parent's theories and bringing them closer to reality, these itinerant endeavors served as a form of observational research through which the architect sought to gain insight into how people responded to his work. The installations were thus instruments for imagining, questioning, feeling, testing, and verifying the potential of life at oblique angles. *Oblique Experiments: Claude Parent's Architectural Installations (1969–1975)* is the outcome of collecting these objects and examining them as a cohesive series.

In French, the word *praticable* stands for a floor or platform on which an activity occurs, such as a theatrical performance or gymnastic routine. As a matter of décor or scenography, a *praticable* is also an element that exists three-dimensionally rather than being painted on or depicted through a flat image. The adjective form of the word references something

Studies for a practicable installation, 1973.

passable—like a path—or, in another sense, something that is possible to put into practice, as in "feasible" or "achievable."[1] The equivalent English term used to describe theatrical props and scenery is "practicable," although the adjective's abbreviated version, "practical," is more common today.[2] In the book *Practicable: From Participation to Interaction in Contemporary Art,* the adjective "practicable" qualifies works of art that are actualized by practice, while its editors also acknowledge the usefulness of the noun form as it exists in French "insofar as the practicable is a potential site of action or performance."[3] Parent used the noun *praticable* as a name for his temporary installations, an appropriate word choice not only because they were manifestly stage-like, but also given that their primary purpose was to test the feasibility of his theoretical ideas. The practicables—as they will be referred to throughout this book, with the added English "c"—were, in other words, a platform for putting into practice a theory of architecture.[4]

This book brings together nine of these installation designs—encompassing the extent to which these works were originally documented—each situated in its own particular context yet part of what is, in effect, an iterative series of objects and interrelated events. The book contributes to the existing scholarship on Parent as the first publication to date entirely dedicated to these projects and constitutes their first full compilation in any format. Also included in this study is the necessary background for understanding the development of the practicables as part of the architect's larger body of work and in relation to the particular conditions that enabled, and at times constrained, their realization. Using archival materials, fieldwork, as well as existing publications as a basis for in-depth documentation, analysis, and interpretation of this work, my research brings overdue attention not only to the practicables as a series of compelling architectural objects but also to the social and spatial contexts within which they came to exist. As part of this research, the practicables were reconstructed digitally, resulting in an original set of architectural representations that enables us to see them in a new way. In addition to archival photographs, drawings, pamphlets, posters, and other graphic materials—many never before published—these new drawings present with increased consistency and precision each of the individual schemes, while also enabling them to be seen as an iterative, and thus comparable, series of design experiments.

The purpose of this book is not to echo the architect's advocacy for life on sloped ground, nor is it—as has already been done elsewhere—to perpetuate any particular predispositions related to architectural form or style. Instead, the intention here is to examine how the sum of this work serves as a model for a particular form of experimental practice that may be useful, as a matter of precedent, to contemporary designers. Written from an architect's perspective, *Oblique Experiments* captures the intersection of visionary speculation and public engagement in Parent's work that resonates with potential and excitement more than fifty years after its realization. By examining these acts of experimental architecture from a contemporary perspective, the book creates a space for two particular themes to unfold throughout its chapters. First is the role of interiority in these experiments, and second is the appropriation of an expanded definition of obliqueness as an approach to practice in and beyond architecture. In sum, therefore, the book treats Parent's practicables as an iterative series of experiments rather than one-off projects; it brings out the underlying condition of interiority and presents it as an essential aspect of Parent's work and a critical part of what makes the practicables experimental; and it considers obliqueness as more than either a formal architectural strategy or a literal prospect of life on slanted ground, whereby Parent's experiments serve as a prompt for imagining and articulating other potential oblique orientations in contemporary practice.

Choreographer Nicole Parent performing on the practicable in Amiens, c.1973.

CLAUDE PARENT AND THE OBLIQUE FUNCTION

An architect whose prolific practice began in the early 1950s and evolved over six decades, yielding numerous buildings, projects, and publications, Claude Parent remains best known for his explorations of inclined planes according to the theory of the oblique function. *La fonction oblique*, as it is referred to in its original French, was initially the result of Parent's productive, albeit relatively brief, collaboration with Paul Virilio, with whom he cofounded the group Architecture Principe in the mid-1960s.[5] Virilio, who later emerged as a leading theorist and philosopher, was a decade younger than Parent and, at that time, in an early stage of what turned out to be an auspicious career. The group—part intellectual think tank and part architecture office—advocated for the use of inclined planes in buildings instead of level floors, a radical proposition with an intended impact on all scales of human habitats, from individual bodies to entire cities. According to Parent and the group, sloped surfaces inspire people's active engagement with the built environment, the anticipated bottom-up effect of which was to be architecture's renewed social relevance.[6] By provocatively proposing to place all of life's activities on oblique substrates, they envisioned the future of architecture free of orthogonal form as well as of strict distinctions between program and circulation, that is, between predetermined uses of space and the necessary movement through it.[7] Architecture Principe's eponymous manifesto-magazine captured a desire to emancipate architecture and its inhabitants from the outdated orthodoxies of modernism, while also projecting an alarming sense of anxiety and doom about the status quo.[8]

The group's principal built work is the Church of St. Bernadette of Banlay in the central French town of Nevers, whose angled design, constructed between 1964 and 1966, was integral to the development of the oblique function as a theory. Parent remained preoccupied with the oblique function even after the group stopped functioning as an entity, producing a series of other related designs and texts. His sole-authored, self-published booklet *Vivre à l'oblique* from 1970, for example, was written as a manifesto in its own right and served as a key theoretical reference for his practice.[9] He continued testing the feasibility of living with oblique architecture by attempting to implement its principles in various projects as well as by engaging with the people for whom they were intended. Temporary architectural installations and public engagement were central to this exploration. In the book's first chapter, "Obliqueness," I provide a detailed account of the trajectory that links Architecture Principe's accomplishments as a group with Parent's subsequent development of the practicables as a series of experiments.

For much of his ambitious career, Parent maintained a reputation as an outsider among the French architecture establishment while remaining relatively unknown outside of his native country.[10] All of his surviving built works are located in France and many of his texts continue to be only available in their original French versions. In 1996, coinciding with the thirtieth anniversary of the Nevers church, the work of Architecture Principe received a burst of international attention prompted by a prominent feature in the exhibition *BLOC: Le monolithe fracturé* at the Venice Biennale of Architecture.[11] Installed at the French Pavilion, the show introduced the Church of St. Bernadette of Banlay to contemporary audiences as an exemplary postwar building, while foregrounding Parent as a key figure in the realm of experimental architecture.[12] Along with the staged "rediscovery" in Venice of the church and its creators, a reissue of the group's complete set of nine magazine issues took place the same year—including an English translation of the original texts.[13] Around the

Church of St. Bernadette of Banlay in Nevers, completed in 1966.

The French Pavilion's front façade augmented by a temporary construction designed by Parent for the 6th Venice Biennale of Architecture in 1996.

same time, another English-language publication, titled *The Function of the Oblique: The Architecture of Claude Parent and Paul Virilio 1963–1969* and released by the Architectural Association in London, also helped make the group's work available to a new generation of architects and students, even though it has long since been out of print.

A handful of other books about Parent have been published in English since then, including a 2010 bilingual French-English monograph focused solely on the church in Nevers;[14] a book on Parent's collaboration with the artist Yves Klein published in 2013;[15] the 2019 *Claude Parent: Visionary Architect*, whose primary focus is his extraordinary drawing practice;[16] as well as the 2020 collection of interviews and sketches titled *Oblique Time with Claude Parent*.[17] Although these publications encompass only some parts of Parent's oeuvre, they do give English readers insight into the oblique function as a theory and its manifestation in projects like the church in Nevers. They also provide useful context for understanding the importance of collaboration in his practice as well as the influence of his experimental work on subsequent generations of like-minded architects. With the exception of *Oblique Time with Claude Parent*, however, none of these texts sufficiently focus on his oblique installations. In many cases, they are not even mentioned.[18]

Two particular publications in the French language that are still in print cover more ground in this regard: the 2010 retrospective monograph *Claude Parent: L'œuvre construite, l'œuvre graphique* and the 2022 *Claude Parent: Les desseins d'un architecte*. Both offer comprehensive considerations of the architect's entire career, including the period between the late 1960s and mid-1970s, when the practicable emerged as an important experimental device. The former is a catalog accompanying a major exhibition of the same name at the Cité de l'architecture et du patrimoine in Paris, a thorough and overdue overview of Parent's entire career published several years after his office closed.[19] The latter, written by the architectural historian and preeminent Parent expert Audrey Jeanroy, is in effect a critical biography in which the architect's creative output serves as the material for understanding his lifelong creative and intellectual evolution.[20] Despite their scope and depth, even these two indispensable pillars of scholarship on Parent's work only partially convey how these experimental installation designs collectively form a cohesive body of work.[21]

PRACTICABLE INSTALLATIONS

Despite the differences that distinguish them from one another, commonalities emerge across all the practicables allowing them to be seen as an interrelated series. One way they are brought together is via the architect's traveling tour across France (including a stop at the country's own pavilion at the Venice Biennale) whose itinerary consisted of sites for which the installations were designed. With some exceptions, the practicables were generally intended to be temporary in nature and made of construction materials like scaffolding and wood planks. Most of them were built inside existing buildings; several occupied the cultural centers that proliferated throughout postwar France known as *maisons de la culture*, which roughly translates as "houses of culture." The establishment of such centers was part of the national effort to decentralize and distribute access to cultural resources away from the capital, thanks to which most of the practicables landed in smaller provincial cities like Amiens, Caen, and Douai. Beyond their inherent functionality as sloped stages or ramps, the installations were often conceived as integral elements of thematically related public programs, including exhibitions, performances, lectures, and workshops. The organization and development of such projects usually involved artists representing different disciplines while, in addition to engaging popular audiences, Parent often realized the practicables with teams of local partners. The installations were in this way both a device for, and a product of, collaboration. In Chapter 2, "The Tour," I examine the itinerary of Parent's travels as well as the conditions that made the practicables possible. This includes the nature of the public institutions that served as hosts and coproducers, along with the underlying politics of the post-1968 era that shaped such institutions and their role in French society.

In a number of the cities that were part of Parent's *Tour de France*, public programs took place even if the practicable intended for that particular site ultimately did not get built. Whether fully realized or not, the apparent role of each design shifted depending on its context. In some cases, the purpose was to help display artifacts such as drawings, photographs, and models as part of an exhibition; in others, it was the installation itself that was on display and whose completion was conceptually contingent upon the presence of people rather than other artworks. Some practicables served as temporary venues tailored to the accompanying cultural programs; in other instances, especially the unbuilt designs, their assigned role was more permanent, a type of corrective measure prompted by the limitations posed by existing architecture.[22] Of the nine installation schemes documented in this book, five were constructed and, prior to their eventual demolition, in some way photographed; none outlived their ephemeral purpose.[23] The designs of the other four schemes—each unrealized for different reasons—are known thanks to surviving drawings, models, and photographs of

Public display of Parent's posters promoting his ideas about architecture, captured along Boulevard Raspail in Paris in August 1972.

discarded models that have been archived at the Kandinsky Library of the Pompidou, the Institut français d'architecture, and the family-managed Claude Parent Archives in Paris, as well as the FRAC Centre-Val de Loire in Orléans.

Since their realization more than half a century ago the practicables have been presented and talked about in different ways but never fully compiled as a series. Some are well known among certain audiences, while others remain obscured by various factors, including their uneven surviving documentation. Individually, each practicable varied in complexity and resolution, with some of the larger and architecturally more elaborate ones simply known as standalone projects. Elsewhere, the practicables have been associated with Parent's public poster campaigns—during which he plastered the streets of Paris with oversized copies of sketches and written provocations about the future of architecture—bringing to light the architect's inventive strategies for engaging the public. However useful a role they play within such narratives, the contribution of such accounts to a more nuanced, detailed, or situated understanding of the practicables is limited. As objects, the installations—whether constructed at full scale or conveyed through drawings and models—capture the specificity of engagement in space, with people, and through architecture that is difficult to convey solely through generalizing narratives. Of interest and value, in other words, is grasping them as situated objects. The third chapter—the book's core—collects them all under the self-evident title "The Practicables." Organized chronologically, the chapter recreates the itinerary of Parent's tour, starting with Le Havre in 1969 and ending in Caen in 1975. By combining detailed narratives with existing photography, drawings, promotional graphics, as well as newly produced drawings, I reconstruct each practicable as an object embedded in a specific context, which in addition to existing architecture and urbanism included various public programs engaging a range of stakeholders and collaborators.

The practicables were experimental devices that are, from a contemporary point of view, easiest to describe as installations. This is how they are referred to throughout the book—starting with the title. On its own, however, the word "installation" fails to convey the practicables' objecthood with enough specificity, individually or as a series. Meanwhile, despite their relative simplicity and raw execution, Parent's experimental installations can be seen as many things at once. Designed by an architect, the floor-mounted assemblies of ramps, platforms, and landings were ephemeral works of architecture. Not unlike buildings, these architectural fragments were situated in specific contexts without which they were incomplete, even if their individual structure, or overall form, could provisionally be extracted as a stand-alone figure. Their partial, temporary, and exploratory character made them akin to improvised full-scale models used for quickly testing an idea or mocking up an architectural condition so that it might be further studied. The practicables were, as such, the working instruments of an ongoing experiment. In some of the iterations, the inclines were painted in bold blocks of color, envisioned by the artist Andrée Bellaguet as large three-dimensional canvases made to be walked on. In this sense, the practicables appeared as devices for the display of art as well as art objects in their own right, although it would ultimately be insufficient to refer to them as either exhibition designs or works of art. Moreover, true to their name and configuration, some appeared as scenic elements or served as performance stages, even if ultimately the objective of such obliquely staged theatrics was to find possible connections with, rather seek separation from, everyday reality.

The practicables were, in effect, site-specific furnishings sized to accommodate both resting in place and moving about, using public institutions as their support. Intended to occupy, augment, or otherwise intervene within existing buildings, they provided adjustment to the architecture that already existed and offered suggestions of what could be. Through the sum of such spatial undertakings, this series of oblique objects functioned as proofs of concept but were also leveraged as professional self-promotional materials wishfully tasked with reinforcing intellectual notoriety as well as attracting new commissions. In relation to each physical site as a container, they were the content, part of a larger composite of interrelated activities and actions—even if some of the practicables were only exhibited as design proposals, while others took place as full-scale constructions. Counting these multifaceted objects as constituent parts of a series is made possible by the overall itinerary of Parent's traveling experiments as well as their oblique form. As an object, each practicable can as such be described as both experimental and oblique. Taking into account the various ways in which they took shape, the roles they played, and the contexts they engaged, however, also enables us to regard them, I argue, as interior objects. The book's fourth chapter, "On Interiority," considers how contemporary notions of the interior as both a spatial and subjective condition help reframe the practicables in relation to the development of Parent's praxis. In this chapter, I explore the architect's earliest period of practice, during which he refurbished quite a few interiors, as well as his writing on the subject of industrial design and decoration, followed by his two domestic interiors designed according to the principles of the oblique function. Considering these pursuits allows us to grasp the significance of the practicables as interior objects that engage the public realm.

EXPERIMENTATION, MANIFESTATION, AND PARTICIPATION

In his long out-of-print monograph *Entrelacs de l'oblique* from 1981, Parent dedicated a section, titled "Expérimenation, manifestation, participation," to the practicables.[24] While only thirteen pages long, it is likely the architect's most complete published account of the installations as a body of work. Nuanced differences in meaning notwithstanding, the French title reads just as easily in English while also providing a useful vocabulary for distinguishing the variously intertwined aspects of the traveling installations from one another. Moreover, Parent's choice of words prompts an explanation of how each term also appears throughout this book.

In architecture, experimentation generally refers to approaches to practice that challenge, and in some cases entirely circumvent, convention. In his 1970 book *Experimental Architecture*, Peter Cook considers experimental work to be driven by "the desire to undermine and explode all rival positions," while also being charged with resisting the widespread "horrific mainstream" of the profession.[25] Not unlike the provocative speculations produced by Cook's avant-garde group Archigram in the 1960s, architectural experiments often come to life through drawing and image making. Such "visionary" or "paper architectures"—experiments in the form of purposely drawn unbuildable propositions—are part of a longstanding disciplinary tradition exemplified by the works of eighteenth-century figures like Giovanni Battista Piranesi and Claude-Nicolas Ledoux.[26] Contemporary discourse on experimentation in architecture continues to evolve in response to a rapidly changing world, yet many of the core values associated with such modes of practice remain intact. Rachel Armstrong, researcher, scholar, and author of the 2019 book *Experimental Architecture: Designing the Unknown*, also considers experimentation as a visionary practice, while situating it as research "capable of developing alternative architectural paradigms by redefining the materials, tools and limits of the field."[27]

Perhaps not surprisingly, Parent's lifelong pursuit of architecture encompassed many of these aspects of experimentation, from his collaborations with Yves Klein in the 1950s (they worked together on the concept of "air architecture") to his prolific drawing practice continuously pursued in lieu of retirement. The creative outcomes of his partnership with Virilio in the 1960s were a perfect match with Cook's characterization of French experimental architecture, which he explains in his book as follows: "In France there is a tradition of utopian prognostications, accompanied by the most demonstrative physical images: these often combine a dramatic structural feat with a radical statement about society."[28] That Architecture Principe actively sought a place in the visionary domain of practice is evident, for example, from the 1965 exhibition *Exploration du futur* shown at Ledoux's Royal Saltworks at Arc-et-Senans. Focusing on architectural *visionnaires* from the eighteenth and twentieth centuries, the exhibition was curated by Parent and Virilio and also featured their own work. In this dual capacity, they placed their own drawings in relation to works by Ledoux and Étienne-Louis Boullée as well as those by a group of chosen contemporaries consisting of Archigram, the Metabolists, and Paolo Soleri—a declaration of their ambition to be considered as part of both the French lineage of visionaries and a new international wave of experimental architects creating new images of the future. In such a context, the medium of drawing provided a shared connection among architects pushing the boundaries of their discipline across different eras and geographies. Even as Parent engaged various other modes of practice throughout his career, he never stopped drawing. In fact, despite all his accomplishments, including numerous built projects, his contemporary reputation continues to grow in large part thanks to his drawings—architectural objects to be contemplated in their own right rather than documents used for constructing buildings—many of which he completed long after the permanent closure of his office.[29]

Practicable installations were distinguished from such drawing experiments in that they sought to engage ordinary conditions—the realities of daily inhabitation, physical sites, relationships with people, material means, and so on—in ways that extraordinary speculations on paper or screen cannot. Space—the interiors of public buildings in particular—replaced paper as the substrate for these equally experimental explorations. Paralleling Armstrong's contemporary perspective on experimentation, Parent's installations were in effect instruments for developing an alternative architectural paradigm, testing along the way the limits of professional practice. Not unlike Armstrong decades later, Parent viewed experimentation as a form of research. Practicables were research tools, and the purpose of these architectural experiments, as he articulated in *Vivre à l'oblique* and elsewhere, was akin to that of science—to test a hypothesis. To reiterate: practicables were a key phyical component, like hardware, of experiments designed to test Parent's hypothesis about living on inclined planes; the ultimate objective was to substantiate the oblique function's theoretical claims and demonstrate the viability of implementing them in practice.

In his 1975 memoir *Architecte: Un homme et son métier*, Parent reflects on the experimental nature of the public encounter between the practicables and people as follows:

> To experiment is to feel something, seen as a broadening or enrichment of knowledge, skills, and abilities. Such is the dictionary definition. Who experiments? People, the population, the crowd, the person who sets foot on these inclined planes. Who makes

Drawing by Archigram in the foreground, and another by Architecture Principe in the back, as part of the exhibition *Exploration du futur*, shown at the Royal Saltworks at Arc-et-Senans in June 1965.

> experimental architecture? The architect who combines these inclined planes into a deliberate strategy of space to enable others to feel. To feel and not to see, to feel and not to say, to feel and not to think, to feel before any action other than that of sensing through the body.[30]

"Experimentation," "experimental," and "experiment" variably refer both to specific aspects of Parent's work and, more broadly, to alternative modes of research and design that have historically challenged the conventional scope of architectural practice and continue to do so today. Uniting all this work, then and now, is its infinite capacity for failure. The trials, errors, misses, messes, omissions, and cancelations all verify that an experiment is an experiment—and that all experiments are neither efficient enterprises nor guaranteed successes.

Parent's experimental installations were a manifestation of the oblique function, different in their means and methods from both his published manifestos and built commissions (or "built manifestoes," as the Parent expert Frédéric Migayrou, for example, regards the church in Nevers).[31] As an action, to manifest means bringing something into reality, view, or—as is true to the definition of the word "manifesto" as a declaration or statement—making it public; and this is how manifestation as a term, along with its variants, occasionally appears throughout this book. The public dimension of these particular actions is typically a reflection of their context, such as the types of institutional spaces where the practicables took place, or the ways in which Parent's self-published booklets, magazines, posters, or pamphlets circulated, often free of charge, in order to reach broader audiences. However, the English use of "manifestation" adopted in the book is not to be confused with its common French meaning, where it also refers to a range of public events from rallies and protests to performances. It is appropriate as such to interpret Parent's use of it in the chapter title "Expérimenation, manifestation, participation" as an

Claude Parent, *Villes satellite 3*, 2006.

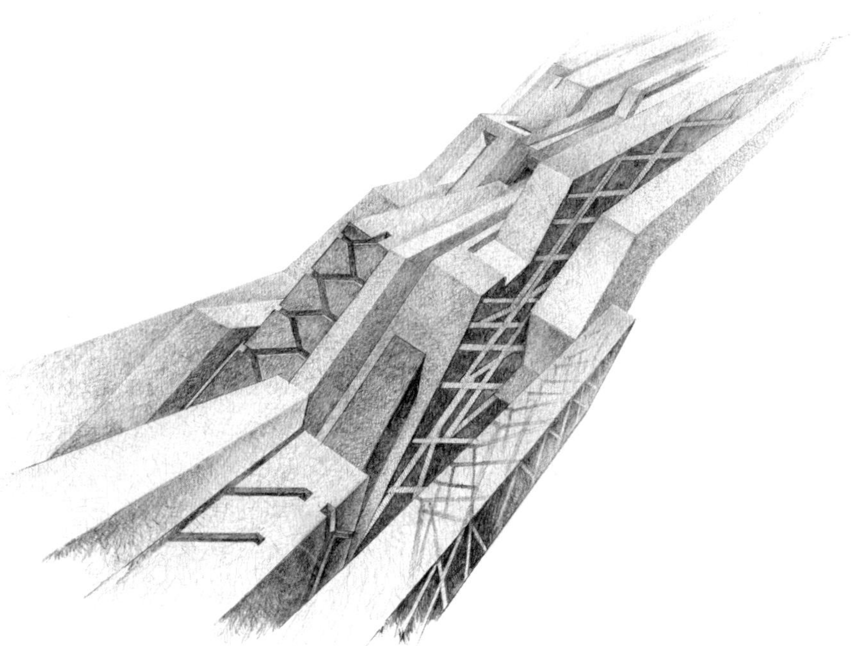

umbrella term that encompasses all the cultural and social activities that he was involved in throughout his tour, including presentations, lectures, debates, discussions, choreographies, demonstrations, and screenings. In this book, such *manifestations* are usually referred to as public programs or events.

Intertwined with experimentation and manifestation is participation as another multivalent aspect of Parent's tour. In a general sense, the term refers to various forms of civic or social engagement, whether emerging through a grassroots process or structured by institutions or organizations. In the context of the venues that hosted the oblique experiments—the *maisons de la culture* and other similarly public institutional spaces charged with providing their communities a range of extracurricular engagements—participation may simply mean citizens showing up and taking part in government-funded programs, such as the "participation of inhabitants in the available facilities such as the library and the social center."[32] As publicly commissioned spatial interventions made for such venues, Parent's practicables are in this sense participatory as a reflection of their assigned role in attracting people, encouraging their involvement, and assisting in forging a sense of social belonging in cities undergoing postwar modernization. On the whole, such forms of organized participation were part of a complex top-down effort to instill a sense of agency and self-determination among people across various layers of daily life.[33] A suite of various participatory programs and activities accompanying Parent's architectural installations and presentations in different cities reflected such institutionally driven objectives. This included self-directed workshops and working groups exploring various topics related to the built environment, from housing and urbanism to craft, prompted by but often seemingly tangential to Parent's oblique endeavors. The difference between these programs and those already covered in the discussion above is increased direct involvement—whether it be a local community member leading a discussion group or getting their hands dirty making pottery—that rendered the participants as more than just passive viewers.

In the context of art, the curator and historian Claire Bishop addresses participation as a social practice that brings art closer to everyday life while "striving to collapse the distinction between

Flyer for Parent's programs at the Maison de la culture André Malraux in Reims from 1972.

MANIFESTATION CLAUDE PARENT
ARCHITECTURE CONTEMPORAINE
exposition du 25 mars au 30 avril

maison
de la culture
andré malraux
reims
direction: rené jauneau

Vendredi	14	21 h	Rencontre avec Claude PARENT et des Architectes ayant travaillé à REIMS «LA VILLE ET L'HABITAT»
Samedi	15	15 h	Visite commentée de l'exposition par Claude PARENT
Dimanche	16	15 h	(Salle de répétition) Rencontre - Débat avec Claude PARENT
Vendredi	28	15 h	Projection au sein de l'exposition d'une enquête réalisée lors de l'exposition : «LA SCULPTURE DANS LA CITÉ»
Vendredi	28	18 h 30	Projection en petite salle d'un film sur la Biennale de Venise Débat avec Claude PARENT
Vendredi	28	21 h	Débat avec Claude PARENT des Architectes, des Sculpteurs, des Critiques, etc... «ANIMATION DANS LE CONTEXTE URBAIN»

performer and audience, professional and amateur, production and reception."[34] From art and architecture to governance and public policy, participation generally involves multiple stakeholders in a decision-making process that shapes matters relevant to the very people engaged in it. Participatory processes across a range of fields bring together people with expertise in a subject or area gained not only through professional credentials or formal education but also life experiences or interests as citizens and members of a community. One version of such a bottom-up crossover in architecture involves "architects eschewing conventional practice and non-architects participating in space," an encounter that is not unlike how Parent engaged the public throughout his tour.[35] Participation in this sense describes Parent's work as an intersection of his alternative approach to architectural practice and people's direct engagement with it, with a twofold objective: From an institutional perspective, his experimental architecture was a tool for getting people to actively take part in their social environment, while the context of the everyday provided a space for Parent to figure out how to get them to care about architecture.

Throughout *Oblique Experiments*, I use engagement and interaction as terms that describe ways of making social contact that are already encompassed by most definitions of participation. If my use of the term participation is as such restrained, it is part of my attempt not to overstate or misrepresent Parent's socially driven motives or rely too heavily on the contemporary significance—and seemingly ubiquitous presence—of the term as it applies to a vast range of practices that are outside this scope. Moreover, the three terms originally brought up by Parent—experimentation, manifestation, participation—are neither stable categories of practice nor are they autonomous in relation to one another. On the contrary, the book shows in different ways how experiments are participatory and public programs can be experimental, and in this way opens up the question of practice as a series of alternative trajectories. In this spirit, the book's fifth chapter, "Other Angles," explores a set of relationships between Parent's practicables and contemporary practice. While the first part of the chapter considers the layers that make up architectural ground as a series of hierarchically organized layers that can be disrupted—not unlike what Parent's installations sought to do in their time—the second part examines how Parent's presence throughout the tour, as an outcome of various modes of manifestation and participation, points toward new possibilities for conceptualizing the transmission of authorship in architecture. I end the chapter, and the book as a whole, with a reflection on obliqueness as a matter of motives, orientations, and approaches to experimental practice. In total, "Other Angles" presents a set of alternative connections between Parent's oblique experiments and contemporary practice, in this way inviting readers to speculate and further build upon two themes that carry throughout the book—namely, interiority as a space of experimentation and obliqueness as an approach to experimental practice.

> Plan view of all nine practicables, including (top left to bottom right) Le Havre, Venice, Nevers, Amiens, Mâcon, Douai, Chalon-sur-Saône, *Praticable no. 7*, and Caen.

1. OBLIQUENESS

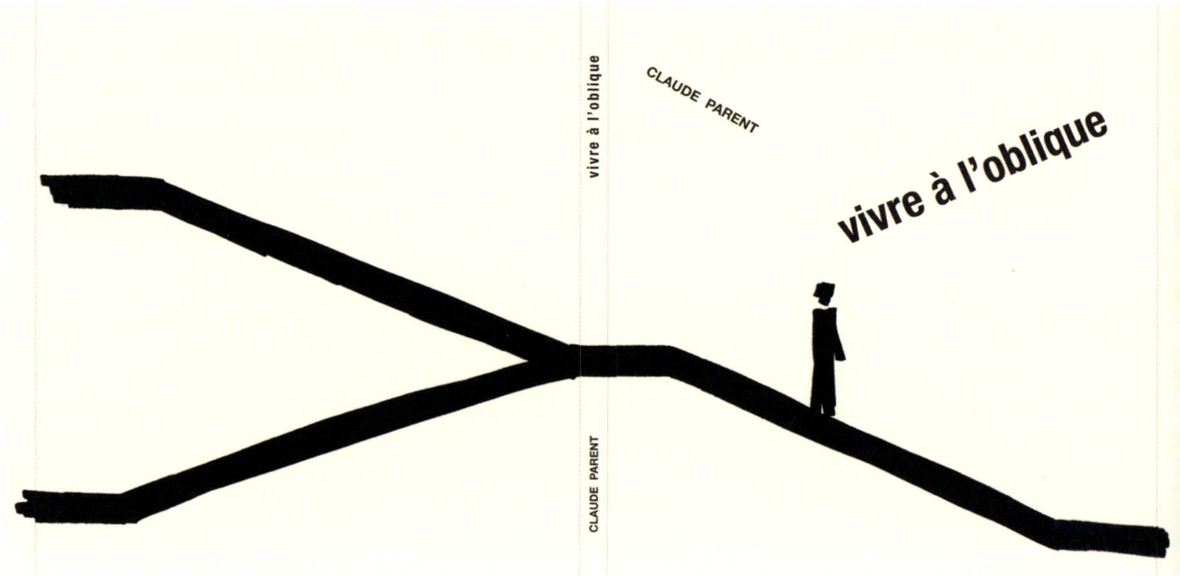

Cover of *Vivre à l'oblique*, front, spine, and back.

"In the new urban age, people will live on inclined planes," writes Claude Parent in his 1970 *Vivre à l'oblique*, summing up in a single sentence the book's theoretical wager.[1] Written from an architect's perspective, the self-published text is less of a premonition than a pitch. Rather than predicting that the world might tilt on its own, the book argues why an architecture built in this way would create preferred conditions for contemporary life. As conceptually comprehensive as any ambitious design proposal, Parent's book makes a provocative, if not unsettling, case for what its French title announces: life on the oblique, or oblique living. Through a combination of diagrammatic sketches and text, *Vivre à l'oblique* frames existing problems to be solved; identifies precedents that imbue the presentation with a sense of viability; considers a whole range of scales, from domestic interiors to cities; presents multiple scenarios for the implementation of Parent's ideas; and speculates on the far-reaching impact of the proposal, if actualized. The book, however, stops short of presenting specific design schemes, focusing instead on a set of broadly applicable strategies. In fact, the architect presents the oblique function—the term he uses for the sum of architectural principles that enable oblique living—as a *hypothesis* that requires experimentation and testing before it can be fully applied in practice.[2]

Before delving into the experiments that Parent carried out according to these principles—encompassing the design of practicables and the production of related public programs delivered as part of a traveling tour—this chapter focuses on the conceptualization of obliqueness in his work. *Vivre à l'oblique* provided a theoretical basis for his use of inclined planes in a series of architectural projects and should therefore be seen as a critical text for understanding Parent's objectives in practice.[3] An overview of Parent's book offers a starting point for considering his experiments formally and conceptually by explaining how the architect imagined using oblique geometries at different scales and what he thought their effects would be on people and the built environment. Just as important, however, is to engage in a certain prehistory—that is, to look back at how obliqueness had already emerged, evolved, and expressed itself in Parent's work prior to the publication of *Vivre à l'oblique* and the start of his experimental tour. For this, the chapter turns to his earlier involvement with Architecture Principe and the group's collaborative pursuit of obliqueness, focusing on three key projects: an independently published magazine, a built church, and the unrealized design for an experimental living duplex. Such a backstory enables a before-and-after comparison between his collaborative and solo pursuits, providing in turn an expanded conceptual and temporal context for situating the practicables as a series of—primarily interior—architectural experiments.

OBLIQUE LIVING

Vivre à l'oblique proposes an architecture of oblique surfaces in lieu of level ground. The modestly sized publication combines a long-form essay with annotated ink sketches, as if Parent were drawing while writing or, one might imagine, using a writing board while giving a public lecture. The book's cover features one such sketch, a thick diagonal line with a simply drawn scale figure on it, branching in two as it wraps around the back. It is a simple diagram of an architecture mostly made up of slopes, an oblique infrastructure for life with a multi-scalar reach, from individual bodies to entire cities.

At the scale of the city, Parent's text describes the oblique morphology as an alternative to conventional patterns of urban growth exemplified by horizontal sprawl and vertical densification. According to Parent—and debated more broadly among his generation of architects concerned with the future of cities—existing models for urbanism no longer produced sufficiently livable environments and were thus obsolete.[4] Their core deficiency, the text argues, is their exacerbation of the separation between circulation and habitation. The former is the space of movement, a navigable public ground typically distributed between and around buildings; the latter, conversely, is the sum of interior spaces contained by building figures, with housing and the private realm a particular focus of Parent's critique.[5] The oblique model of urban organization integrates, in section, public movement and private dwelling such that they are layered onto rather than separated from one another side by side—a folding of continuous surfaces as a means of unmaking the binary relationship between figure and ground.[6] Accompanying drawings show that, among the salient characteristics of the city organized in this way, boundaries between the inside and the outside are no longer defined by vertical building enclosures, but are instead mediated by omnipresent inclines: over/under, rather than front–back. Hypothetically reconfiguring the city in this way, Parent imagined it as a habitat with a revitalized connection between people and their physical surroundings.[7]

The oblique reorganization of urban form is one aspect of achieving such vitality; the other entails the physical and psychological dimensions of life on sloped surfaces. According to *Vivre à l'oblique*, inclined planes increase one's sense of agency. A person inhabiting a slanted floor, the text argues, can do, think, feel, and sense more than if they were on level ground. Their weight, under the influence of gravity, becomes the *moteur interne*, an inner mechanism that moves them and amplifies their sense of engagement, "a permanent energy exchange between the human body and its support."[8] Parent refers to this constructed terrain as an "architecture of effort," whose impact counters the numbing pursuit for comfort.[9] If such an architecture instigates discomfort, its affordances are meant to emancipate: They enable the emergence of multiple possibilities for navigating, inhabiting, and engaging one's living environment, while also providing freedom from unnecessary material possessions. Obliqueness would in this regard have the greatest effect on the domestic interior, where nearly everything would have to shift. The most audacious dimension of such an oblique habitat, ubiquitously askew, is thus not its nonorthogonal form—a single, simple machine multiplied and variably aggregated—but rather its ambition to rewrite the script for human life itself.

Vivre à l'oblique was not Parent's first attempt at articulating the design principles of a life on inclined planes. A few years earlier, as part of the group Architecture Principe, he and Paul Virilio famously coined the term "oblique function" to encompass a range of shared ideas about sloped architecture. Given this history, one may regard the 1970 booklet as a new draft of an old script; or, in the spirit of architectural drawing, as a set of new plans traced from existing ones.[10] Rather than retelling the entire biography of Parent and Virilio's encounter, a story already well told by others, the remainder of the chapter focuses on three specific outcomes

read from *Vivre à l'oblique*, pages 20 and 21.

read from *Vivre à l'oblique*, pages 28 and 29.

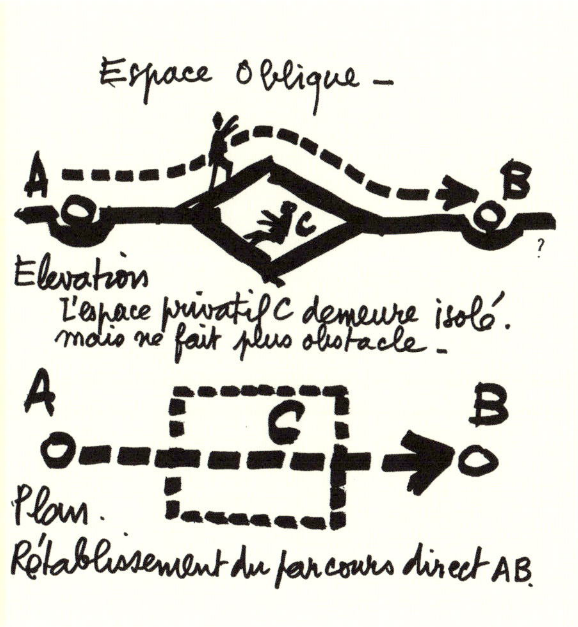

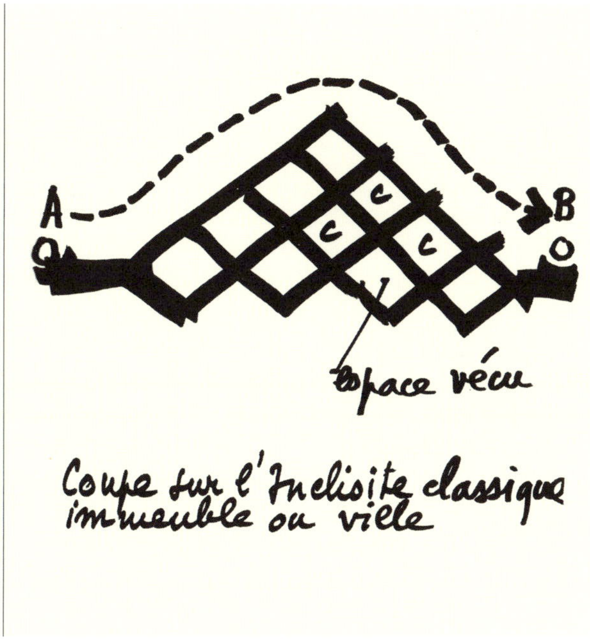

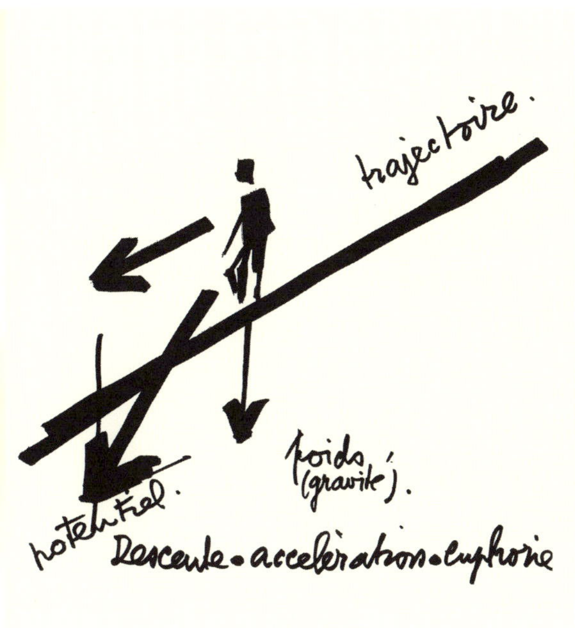

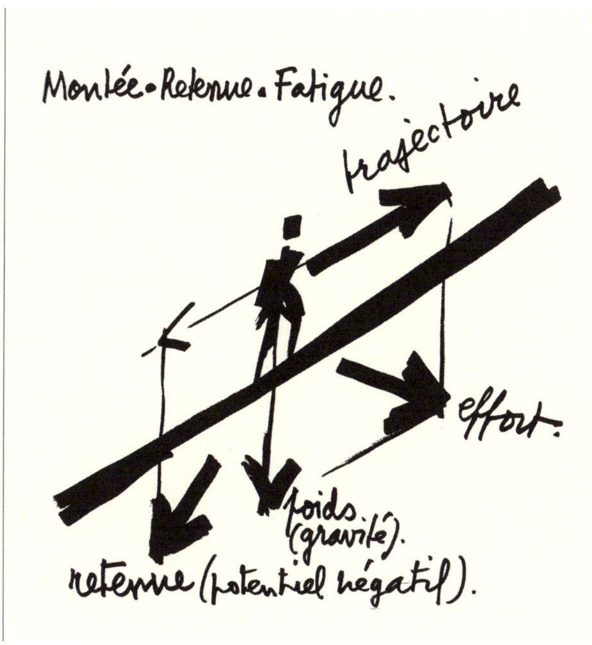

of their collaboration. Together they elucidate the origin and evolution of Parent's ideas about oblique architecture as well as his sustained attempts to realize them in practice.

THE MAGAZINE

Parent's partnership with Virilio lasted no more than a few years, and their group Architecture Principe practically had no other active members.[11] Despite the limited period of activity and small size, they garnered broad attention, back then and decades later, in part thanks to their eponymous magazine. Published throughout 1966, the nine issues of *Architecture Principe* provided a self-made venue for disseminating the group's work—a mixture of theoretical provocations, drawings, and in-progress projects—through which they sought to earn a place in ongoing debates about architecture's role in society.[12] Written in fine print inside the back cover of each issue was the declaration of the journal's purpose as the group's "permanent manifesto,"[13] appearing as if its authors hoped to imbue their evolving ideas with a sense of durability. Like many other intellectually ambitious architects and artists engaged in the production of publications at that time, they used the printed medium as a platform for critiquing the present and asserting their visions of the future.[14] Even though this was his first such manifesto, Parent was no stranger to publishing. He had regularly written for publications such as *L'architecture d'aujourd'hui* since the early 1950s, and also served, just one year prior to the launch of *Architecture Principe*, as a guest editor for *Aujourd'hui: Art et architecture*.[15] For this occasion, Parent produced, alongside the architecture curator and writer Patrice Goulet, a special issue on British architecture prominently featuring the work of Archigram, whose already established approach to publication as a form of avant-garde practice was not unlike what he and Virilio were attempting do with their own magazine.[16]

Selection of *Architecture Principe* magazine issues.

Combining their different backgrounds and overlapping interests in architecture and urbanism, Parent and Virilio set out to articulate a series of preoccupations centered around the inclined plane. For Parent, the significance of oblique surfaces emerged from his various attempts, as a practicing architect, to break away from the constraints of orthogonal form.[17] In the overall massing of buildings like Maison Soultrait (1956–58) and Maison Drusch (1963–66), for example, certain volumes appear as if they were rotated diagonally, resulting in a contrasting orientation between straight and tilted elements. Although designed nearly a decade before slanted surfaces started appearing in Parent's work as fully inhabitable, photographs of the Maison Soultrait were staged in such a way as to already suggest that the building's steeply pitched roof—the formal result of an oblique rotation—could be walked on. Paul Virilio's path to developing an interest in inclined planes was more oblique. Trained as a master stained-glass artisan, his professional position vis-à-vis architecture was at that time relatively peripheral. Prior to meeting Parent, Virilio had developed a fascination with World War II bunkers. In particular, he was drawn to a series of such

Photograph from Paul Virilio's *Bunker Archeology* series taken around 1958.

Maison Drusch, a single-family house in Versailles, designed by Parent for the local industrialist Gaston Drusch and built between 1963 and 1966.

structures that formed the Nazi-built Atlantic Wall and in part stretched along the French coast where he spent his wartime childhood.[18] He discovered the inclined plane as a feature of these brutal concrete forms, but also observed the bunkers' indifference to existing ground, their "not being rooted in the soil," which later also became a salient characteristic of the group's architectural designs.[19] As wartime artifacts, the bunkers inspired Virilio to conceptualize postwar architecture and urbanism in psychological terms, writing how "these primitive works announce a new architecture founded no longer on the physical proportions of man but on his psychic faculties."[20] In the broadest sense, these concrete remnants marked an irreversible shift in human experience as a result of the war, while also rendering obsolete, according to Virilio, any prior principles for ordering the physical world. By adopting the inclined plane as an architectural element capable of effectively engaging postwar subjects, Virilio leaned into his interest in Gestalt principles, which the architectural critic Jacques Lucan interprets in the context of the group's work as a "psychology of form, which promoted continuous, fluid movement and forced the body to adapt to instability."[21] The inclined plane was, as such, a generator of human engagement and an expression of a world whose underlying conditions needed to be rethought, a pair of ideas that Virilio and Parent both embraced and elaborated on in their magazine.

A short paragraph of the first issue's opening essay by Virilio, boldly titled "Warning," summarizes what subsequently unfolded as the group's recurring argument:

> As the static horizontal-vertical position no longer corresponds to man's own dynamic, architecture from now on has to be realized on an incline, situating itself on the new plane of human consciousness; if not, all architectural projects will increasingly become unusable.[22]

The outdated orthogonal orientation in question is that of buildings—the conventional assembly of horizontal floors and vertical walls—but also applies to the morphology of cities, as Parent later reiterated in *Vivre à l'oblique*. As an alternative, Virilio's text proposes obliqueness as a new direction for the necessary realignment between the built environment and people, in line with the specific notion that dynamic life requires a formally equivalent setting but also reflecting a deep belief in the inextricable link between architectural form and human experience.[23] The inclined plane is thus presented as a tool for recalibrating the relationship between architecture and its users as well as, more generally, a weapon for challenging the status quo. The group's boldness is summed up in the closing essay of the same issue, titled "The Oblique Function," as they envision nothing less than "the creation of a new urban order and . . . the total reinvention of architectural vocabulary."[24]

If *Vivre à l'oblique* reads like a lecture accompanied by Parent's quick sketches, the magazine graphically appears more like a serial portfolio. Laid out in an alternating pattern of striking drawings and equally provocative blocks of text, most of the issues are no more than a dozen pages long. Despite the publication's modest zine-like format and short page count, Virilio and Parent's critiques of present conditions pack an unsparing punch. As the epitome of the vertical city, for example, "New

< Maison Soultrait, a single-family house in the commune of Domont, north of Paris, built between 1956 and 1958.

York can die";[25] on the dismal status of his profession, Parent concludes that "every weapon is prepared to wage merciless war on architecture";[26] meanwhile, interiors are nothing more than "micro-ghettos," cluttered with furnishings that are "but remnants of a way of life historically out of date."[27] Such rhetoric provides a foil against which the emancipatory character of the oblique function is intended to unfold. "We shall make our way through all dangers, we shall confront all risks, we shall live on ramps, our body will get used to this new position which for the moment seems unlivable," pledges Virilio.[28] The potential inconvenience and discomfort of oblique architecture is part of the process because ultimately, Parent promises, the inclined plane will enable a person to "recover their freedom and their autonomy as an individual."[29]

As their writing oscillates between what is and what could be—and thus between gloom and optimism—the accompanying drawings equally contribute to the magazine's pattern of mood shifts. Parent and Virilio drew and drafted, much like they wrote, in order to capture a set of evolving ideas rather than documenting fully formed architectural designs. The drawings are imposing in their form and vantage point, their severe appearance amplified by the high contrast that resulted from mechanically reproducing them. They are projections into a possible future, a fictional world in which angular forms—suggestive of buildings large enough to contain populations of entire cities—tilt, cantilever, zigzag, and float "on the surface of an earth that has lost its materiality," while diminutive human figures, when they do appear, reassert an overwhelming sense of monumentality.[30] Contrary to the claims of engagement and connectivity as core tenets of the oblique function, many of the drawings betray a certain sense of alienation and isolation. Intended to teem with life, the oblique world appears, in the most extreme of its images, hauntingly desolate. The oblique forms lack interiority not only in the way that the perspectives through which they are constructed situate the viewer outside of and on top of (rather than inside of) them, but also because Parent and Virilio's representations convey little in the way of intimacy, livability, privacy, or joy associated with what the manifesto refers to as individual freedom and autonomy. The moody remoteness of the drawings—their dark tones and aerial vantage accompanying the apocalyptic tone of the text—shaped the magazine's aesthetic as well as, inevitably, its reception.[31]

If, at first glance, the portfolio-style format gives *Architecture Principe* the appearance of design proposals intended to be built, its true power was in provocation. Taking the magazine at face value would be to tragically misconstrue its purpose, akin to critiquing Archigram's *Plug-in City* (1964) or Superstudio's *Continuous Monument* series (1969) on the basis of life quality or sustainability. That said, while Architecture Principe had the desire to operate like its radical contemporaries in the UK, Italy, and elsewhere—who explicitly chose to draw and write rather than build—the group was also driven by the ambition to convert its provocative pursuits on paper into buildings. The magazine thus appeared as a portfolio representing architects as serious about their speculative fiction as they were intent on engaging material realities of architectural practice. In the second issue of *Architecture Principe*, Virilio writes, "We have not chosen the oblique order through any concern for aesthetics, but because it contains a potential of life for future societies, because it is a solution to actual contemporary problems."[32] By intending

Spread from the magazine *Architecture Principe*, no. 3, "Le troisieme ordre urbain."

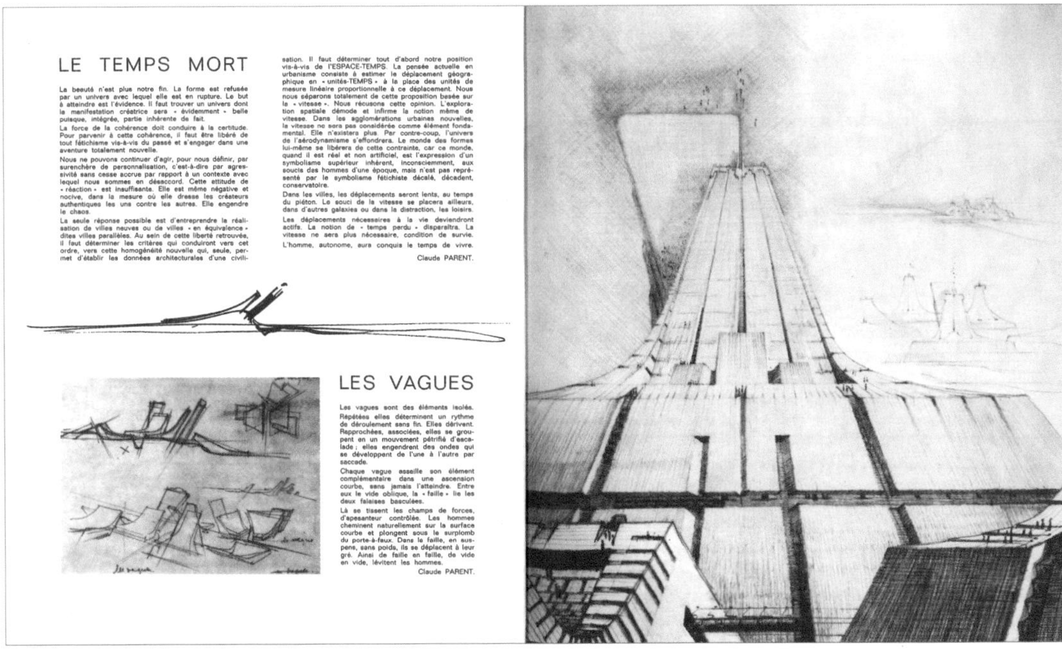

LE TEMPS MORT

La beauté n'est plus notre fin. La forme est refusée par un univers avec lequel elle est en rupture. Le but à atteindre est l'évidence. Il faut trouver un univers dont la manifestation créatrice sera « évidemment » belle puisque, intégrée, partie inhérente de fait.

La force de la cohérence doit conduire à la certitude. Pour parvenir à cette cohérence, il faut être libéré de tout fétichisme vis-à-vis du passé et s'engager dans une aventure totalement nouvelle.

Nous ne pouvons continuer d'agir, pour nous définir, par surenchère de personnalisation, c'est-à-dire par agressivité sans cesse accrue par rapport à un contexte avec lequel nous sommes en désaccord. Cette attitude de « réaction » est insuffisante. Elle est même négative et nocive, dans la mesure où elle dresse les créateurs authentiques les uns contre les autres. Elle engendre le chaos.

La seule réponse possible est d'entreprendre la réalisation de villes neuves ou de villes « en équivalence » dites villes parallèles. Au sein de cette liberté retrouvée, il faut déterminer les critères qui conduiront vers cet ordre, vers cette homogénéité nouvelle qui, seule, permet d'établir les données architecturales d'une civilisation. Il faut déterminer tout d'abord notre position vis-à-vis de l'ESPACE-TEMPS. La pensée actuelle en urbanisme consiste à estimer le déplacement géographique en « unités-TEMPS » à la place des unités de mesure linéaire proportionnelle à ce déplacement. Nous nous séparons totalement de cette proposition basée sur la « vitesse ». Nous récusons cette opinion. L'exploration spatiale démode et infirme la notion même de vitesse. Dans les agglomérations urbaines nouvelles, la vitesse ne sera pas considérée comme élément fondamental. Elle n'existera plus. Par contre-coup, l'univers de l'aérodynamisme s'effondrera. Le monde des formes lui-même se libérera de cette contrainte, car ce monde, quand il est réel et non artificiel, est l'expression d'un symbolisme supérieur inhérent, inconsciemment, aux soucis des hommes d'une époque, mais n'est pas représenté par le symbolisme fétichiste décalé, décadent, conservatoire.

Dans les villes, les déplacements seront lents, au temps du piéton. Le souci de la vitesse se placera ailleurs, dans d'autres galaxies ou dans la distraction, les loisirs.

Les déplacements nécessaires à la vie deviendront actifs. La notion de « temps perdu » disparaîtra. La vitesse ne sera plus nécessaire, condition de survie.

L'homme, autonome, aura conquis le temps de vivre.

Claude PARENT.

LES VAGUES

Les vagues sont des éléments isolés.

Répétées elles déterminent un rythme de déroulement sans fin. Elles dérivent. Rapprochées, associées, elles se groupent en un mouvement pétrifié d'escalade ; elles engendrent des ondes qui se développent de l'une à l'autre par saccade.

Chaque vague assaille son élément complémentaire dans une ascension courbe, sans jamais l'atteindre. Entre eux le vide oblique, la « faille » lie les deux falaises basculées.

Là se tissent les champs de forces, d'apesanteur contrôlée. Les hommes cheminent naturellement sur la surface courbe et plongent sous le surplomb du porte-à-faux. Dans la faille, en suspens, sans poids, ils se déplacent à leur gré. Ainsi de faille en faille, de vide en vide, lévitent les hommes.

Claude PARENT.

to distinguish between appearance and reality—aesthetics versus "real" problems—in order to clarify the group's agenda, Virilio instead articulates the underlying conflict in the publication as a whole—that is, between the use of provocative aesthetics as a way of unsettling ways of thinking about reality from the distance offered by mediated images and text on the one hand, and the desire to reshape reality through built form on the other. The oblique function's aesthetic and social aspects were, in other words, as inextricably intertwined as Architecture Principe's engagement with both theory and practice.

The magazine's three special issues, which interrupt its regular format and flow of fictional graphics and narrative, reflect the authors' interest in directly engaging the physical world. One of the issues, the sixth in the series titled "Bunker Archeology," focuses on World War II blockhouses, the subject of Virilio's individual exploration, which he started in 1958.[33] Virilio's black-and-white photographs capture massive concrete objects in the French landscape along the Atlantic coast, tragic remnants of a then-recent past. Some are partially buried in the ground, while others perch above the horizon or appear adrift, surrounded by sand and sea. Their angular filleted forms are solid with few signs of what is inside, obsolete relics left over, each like "an empty carcass" projecting a haunting sense of permanent ruin.[34] The pictures and two main essays reveal Virilio's source of intellectual inspiration and echo, in their brutal presence, the aesthetic of Architecture Principe's ink and graphite visions of future oblique architectures. The overlap between the group's drawings and Virilio's photographs is deliberate and precise, so much so that he uses the same sentence to describe both his speculative design of a city for two hundred thousand inhabitants in the magazine's first issue and the Nazi-built bunkers in the opening essay of "Bunker Archeology."[35] Once made, such an association—the visual resemblance between wartime bunkers and a housing proposal—is difficult to escape, much like it is impossible to unsee a striking image.

Two other issues, including the final among the series, feature commissioned projects taken up by the group in the role of a professional architecture studio. This last issue features the design for a ten-thousand-square-meter multiuse cultural complex for Charleville, a small town in northeastern France, which is identified as the group's second building commission.[36] A set of models and drawings describe various aspects of a single building in the shape of a tilted trapezoid, including its siting along the Meuse River, the overall exterior massing, as well as the schematic organization in both plan and section. The accompanying essays, while written in the unmistakable tone of their authors, are in comparison to the rest of the magazine decidedly pragmatic, focusing on the particularities of the site strategy and programmatic distribution, as well as including the project engineer's note on the design of the structural concrete shell. A pair of renderings that isolate the building from its urban context and represent it as a floating object are not unlike the group's more theoretical images published elsewhere in the magazine, but this final issue is otherwise sober in tone compared to the authors' punchier provocations. Finally, there is the special issue dedicated to the group's project for the Church of St. Bernadette of Banlay in Nevers, which appears fourth in the series. The building is published in a state of near completion and touted in the introductory text as "the first materialization of our theoretical research."[37] The built church, along with Virilio's bunker studies and the unrealized Charleville scheme, contributes to the magazine's multifaceted exploration of the oblique function through what one may today refer to as blended reality, a mixture of fictional and factual realms.

THE CHURCH

Sited on the outskirts of the small city of Nevers in central France, the Church of St. Bernadette of Banlay was Architecture Principe's first built commission.[38] Constructed from cast-in-place concrete, its exterior is imposing and heavy, not unlike the bunkers that Virilio studied. The upper volumes, with curved transitions between the surface of the roof and the adjacent walls as their distinguishing feature, contain the nave. Inside, this main space is split in half by a pair of floor slabs, elevated from the ground and sloping up like two raked stages facing one another. Light and people enter the nave through the middle zone defined by the meeting of these two inclined planes, resulting in an environment more luminous and inviting than one might imagine from the outside.[39] A number of smaller-scale elements, such as the red stained-glass windows, the volcanic stone altar and baptistry, as well as an unfinished tapestry, are the work of the collaborating artists who were initially counted, along with Parent and Virilio, as members of Architecture Principe but were otherwise absent from the group's subsequent activities.[40] Writing about the building in the special issue of the magazine, Parent describes the church interior as "a cryptic space closed off from the exterior, an enclosed world" with openings, above and below, for visual escape.[41] In his own article about the church, Virilio refers to the floor as "the flying carpet of architecture," made to revolutionize ways of building and living alike.[42] Like a fragmented pebble fallen from the sky, as it has been described, the Church of St. Bernadette of Banlay is a mass estranged from its surroundings. Nesting within is an interior made oblique by its slanting floors and smooth in the way that the transitions between walls and the ceilings are gently rounded rather than sharp. If the sloped interior was meant to physically engage people, the bunker-like exterior served as an aesthetic provocation. In his essay "The Definition of a Critical Architecture," on the work of Architecture Principe, Frédéric Migayrou writes, "The vocabulary of the bunker was intended to create a 'repellent' architecture that would overturn established perceptions and provoke a response from the user."[43]

That the church's publication occurred no sooner than in the fourth issue of *Architecture Principe* gives the impression that its design was preceded by theoretical research in a chronological progression from writing and drawing to building. It is as if the concrete church was made to appear, through such ordering, as proof of an already established theoretical premise, when in fact the development of the oblique function's principles and the building's realization took place simultaneously. The production of the magazine's first issues, in other words, came after the building design was already established—not before. Indeed, the design for St. Bernadette of Banlay Church began in August of 1963 as a response to an invited competition, not long after the group's forming and well before any of the other magazine content (except for Virilio's research on

Church of St. Bernadette of Banlay in Nevers, exterior view.

Church of St. Bernadette of Banlay in Nevers, interior view.

Church of St. Bernadette of Banlay in Nevers, interior view.

World War II bunkers) had been produced. Various accounts of the group's formation support the observation that Architecture Principe coalesced largely in and around the church project.[44]

As the building was approaching its final stages of construction, Parent and Virilio launched the magazine. The timing intimates a sense of anticipation surrounding the church's completion, underscoring the magazine's role in providing the building with a theoretical context while also publicizing it as a professional achievement. Likewise, the building can be seen as an artifact—not unlike many of the drawings and essays appearing in the

pages of *Architecture Principe*—that is made to travel, like a newsworthy message transmitted via print media, from provincial France to its intended cosmopolitan audiences interested in reading architect-designed pamphlets. The incomplete state of the building as it was photographed for the magazine (the formwork and scaffolding were already removed, but the built-in pews inside were not yet installed) reveals certain aspects of the project's construction process, but perhaps even more so indicates Architecture Principe's eagerness to showcase their first built work in a widely sharable format.

If the coordinated timing between the magazine and the church was meant to provide a smooth segue from theory to practice, as well as between drawing and building, the actual outcomes of the strategy were not so tidy. The presence of the church inside the magazine complicated the publication's status as a future-oriented manifesto and likewise compromised the group's posture as a radical practice whose role, by certain definitions, was to produce work virtually impossible to realize.[45] Architecture Principe's demonstrated motivations to not only function as a think tank but also operate as a commercial architecture practice likewise came to light, a challenge to the intellectual purity of radical visionaries and the orthodoxy of the profession alike. A realized building, after all, poses a threat to established conventions that speculative drawings, no matter how assertive or provocative, generally do not. Yet, if the radicality of Parent and Virilio's oblique function lay in the tilting of all substrates that organize human activity, the perceived menace of the church had much less to do with its interior section of sloped floors than it did with its resemblance to war bunkers. The referential exterior, in other words, overshadowed the primary intentions nested within the building, in turn negatively shaping its immediate public reception.[46] All of this, according to Parent and others who have recounted the church's opening, amounted to something of a fiasco.[47] Parent retrospectively referred to the Church of St. Bernadette of Banlay as "the church that everyone mocked and rejected (apart from the local congregation, who like it)."[48] The narrative of misunderstanding and rejection that surrounded the church persisted, even decades later as the work of Architecture Principe received renewed attention and the building itself was awarded, among many overdue distinctions, the status of a protected national monument. One possible explanation for the architects' persistent retelling of such narratives is the enduring emotional toll that negative public reception of a building can have on its authors. Another possibility, however, is that the insistence on misunderstanding and rejection becomes part of a constructed mythology according to which the work and those who produced it are positioned as outsiders in relation to an established system, which can be a desirable privilege of its own.

Grievances, timelines, and publicity strategies aside, the Church of St. Bernadette of Banlay in Nevers was a leap in the exploration of the oblique function, an object conceived along an ambitious trajectory toward the application of an emerging theory. Along with the magazine, the church was an artifact—elsewhere referred to as a built manifesto—through which Parent and Virilio attempted to perform a shift in their own work and its relationship to architecture as a culture.[49] However, even if the building was proof that what they envisioned through drawings and text could be physically constructed, the architects still lacked sufficient evidence that the public reception of their architecture, and the subjective responses of those who experienced it, were in line with their own theoretical expectations. This gap subsequently prompted Parent and Virilio to develop another instrument of research—a temporary oblique dwelling for two.

THE EXPERIMENTAL LIVING DUPLEX

Although never realized beyond drawings and models, *Instabilisateur pendulaire no. 1*, designed by Architecture Principe in 1968, chronologically follows the magazine and the church as a third type of oblique object: a temporary installation. Conceived as an architectural experiment, in which Parent and Virilio were to serve as subjects, the original design consists of two living units—with sloped floors elevated high above the ground—where they were both supposed to live for a month, side by side. Two versions of the design exist, each a pairing of two diagonal tube-like enclosures with tilted floors, approximately thirty degrees steep, spanning between flat landings. Both design schemes gave form to the notion that the two architects would live their lives in parallel and thus independently from one another, except for specific points where they would intersect. In one version, the two adjacent parts of the duplex slope in opposite directions but interlock around a common middle landing, forming an X-shaped profile. The later version is configured as a sideways V-shape, the result of locating the common landing to the side, with each living space ramping up and down respectively. Drawings for this scheme also show a system of diagonally braced scaffolding holding up the units ten meters above the floor level, an expression of oblique architecture's deliberate disassociation from any existing ground condition. While there is no explicit indication of access between the interior of the units and the space below them, the drawings do show that the architects envisioned the top of the installation as an inhabitable roof. A small square shown on the roof plan indicates access to this upper level—referred to as *terrasse*—and two lightly drawn human figures climbing on it also illustrate this intention.

Parent and Virilio planned to make living inside *Instabilisateur pendulaire no. 1* their temporary full-time job, while adhering to relative isolation from the outside world.[50] As a matter of research, they also intended to place themselves under the observation of physicians, psychologists, and sociologists while inhabiting the installation.[51] Their aim was to test on themselves the assumptions that they had made about life on inclined planes, with the installation marking the first organized attempt to explore the potential of the oblique function through a staged event-based experiment. The project sought to further Architecture Principe's engagement with behavioral aspects of architecture, particularly in relation to Virilio's interest in Gestalt psychology, expanding as such the group's view of research methods

Model of the first of two schemes by Architecture Principe for the installation *Instabilisateur pendulaire no. 1* from 1968.

Drawings of the second of two Architecture Principe's design schemes for the installation *Instabilisateur pendulaire no. 1*, dated April 24, 1968.

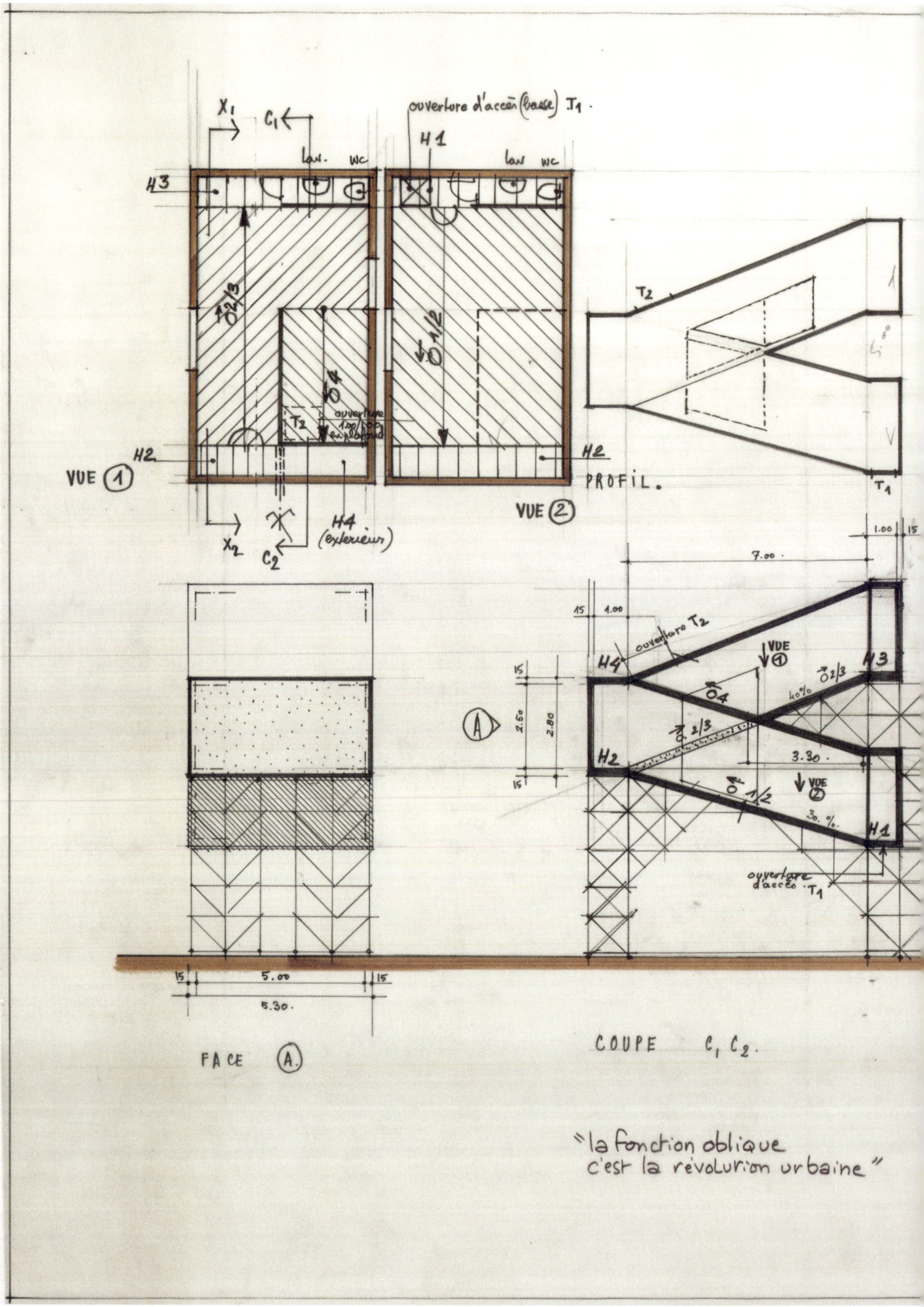

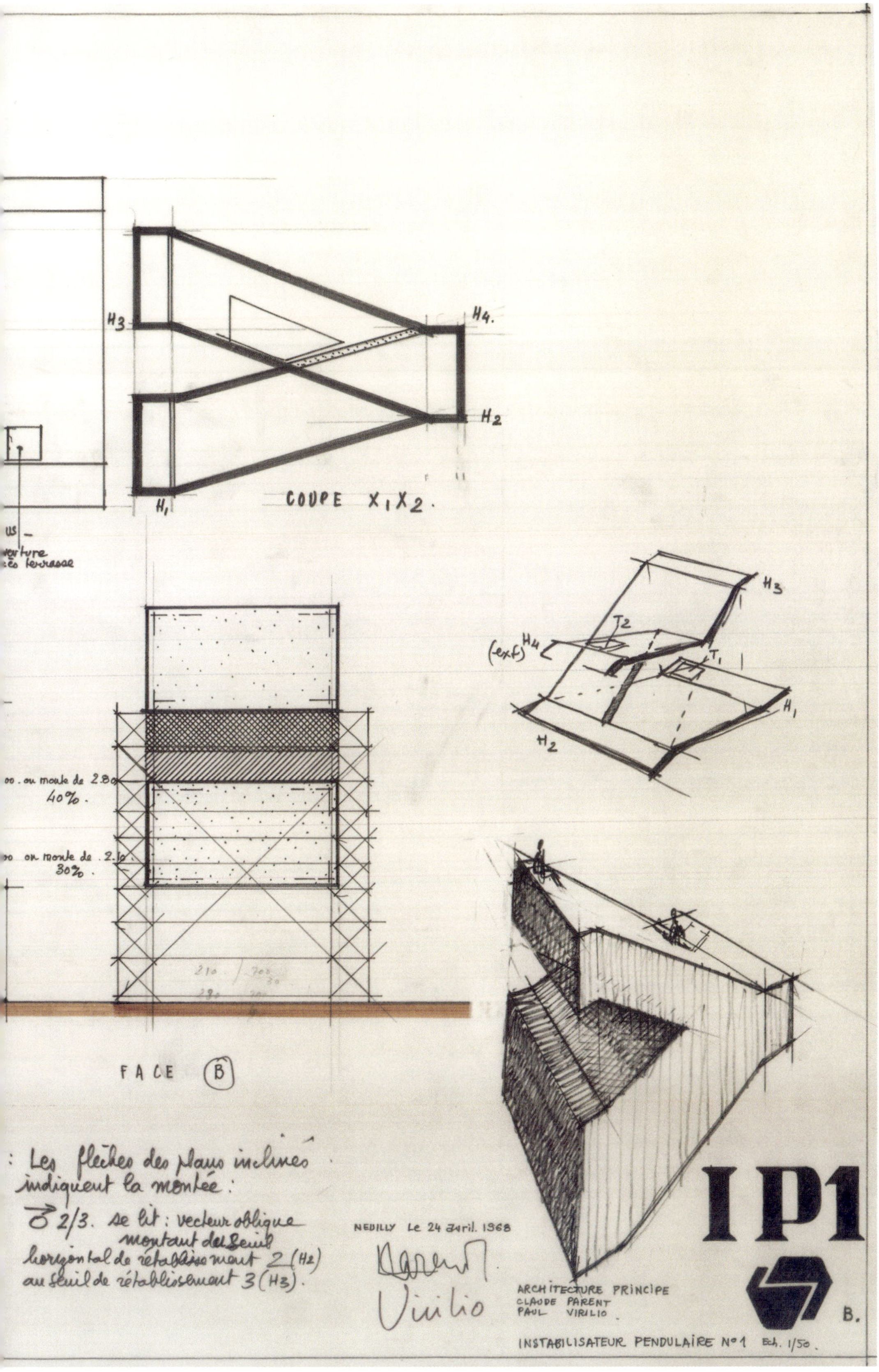

H3
H4.
H2
H1
COUPE X1 X2.
H3
T2
(exf) H4
T1
H1
H2
00. on monte de 2.80
40%.
00 on monte de 2.10
30%.
FACE (B)
: Les flèches des plans inclinés
indiquent la montée :
2/3. se lit : vecteur oblique
montant du seuil
horizontal de rétablissement 2 (H2)
au seuil de rétablissement 3 (H3).
NEUILLY Le 24 avril. 1968
Parent
Virilio
ARCHITECTURE PRINCIPE
CLAUDE PARENT
PAUL VIRILIO.
IP1
B.
INSTABILISATEUR PENDULAIRE N° 1 Ech. 1/50.

capable of accounting for people's subjective experiences.[52] Although Parent articulated this more fully in *Vivre à l'oblique* and elsewhere following his split from Virilio, he expressed the necessity for such an approach as early as the third issue of *Architecture Principe*, published in March of 1966. Following the speculation that being on the oblique plane charges people in a certain way, he concedes that this "needs to be analyzed and studied by successive experiments following the most rigorous scientific methods."[53] The implication was that architectural imagination conveyed through visual representation and visionary rhetoric was not enough. Following the production of the magazine and the construction of the church, the installation was thus an attempt to mitigate the potential presumptuousness, if not arrogance, of architectural representation, or the conviction that once it is resolved on paper a work of architecture must already be worthy of physical manifestation.

As a whole, *Instabilisateur pendulaire no. 1* was meant to combine aspects of architectural installation, durational performance, and evidence-based research, and can therefore be seen as the seed of a hybrid form of practice from which Parent's tour of France would later grow. The plan was to build the installation at the Paris Nanterre University (then Paris X–Nanterre), in the western suburbs of Paris, in June of 1968, and the architects were supposed to live in it for thirty days. Just a month before that, however, the university became the epicenter of student protests that, along with general strikes and widespread antiestablishment revolt, provoked a crisis throughout France and beyond.[54] What started as a clash between students and administrators at one university earlier that year grew into a movement that shook the intellectual foundations of French society and foregrounded the possibility of a revolution in an advanced capitalist society. In his book *Prelude to Revolution: France in May 1968,* the journalist Daniel Singer describes the events as "a mental revolt against the existing industrial state, both against the capitalist structure and the kind of consumer society it created. It was coupled with a striking revulsion against anything coming from above, against centrism, authority, and hierarchical order."[55] Given the circumstances in the city and throughout the country, Parent and Virilio's project—an exercise in questioning the foundations of daily life in its own right—was cancelled. This ultimately brief episode of unrest had a profound impact on French society in the years that followed, not the least of which was recalibrating relationships between citizens and their public institutions.[56] Parent's collaborations with cultural centers discussed in the next chapter are but one particular set of attempts at such recalibration.

Without sufficient evidence, it is impossible to confirm how and why Parent and Virilio chose the university campus as a site for their living experiment, nor is it possible to verify any foresight they may have had in terms of its imminent political significance. The dates marked on the drawings for *Instabilisateur pendulaire no. 1*, however, do help place the development of the installation design onto the same timeline as that of the events leading up to the May crisis. The two design schemes were dated March 18, 1968, and April 24, 1968, respectively. Reports of conflicts at the university first occurred as early as January, and were followed by rounds of student protests and arrests by the police in March. By then, these student-led activities coalesced into a movement, known as the *Mouvement du 22 Mars*.[57] The events further escalated in early May, with the protests moving off-campus and violent clashes between protestors and the police taking place, just days after Parent and Virilio produced the second version of their design. In fact, the design of *Instabilisateur pendulaire no. 1* was developed at the same time as the protests increasingly gained traction. To put it another way, the architects were designing their installation for a site where other challenges to the status quo were already taking place.

Aside from stunting the realization of the oblique living experiment, the events of 1968 had an even broader impact on Parent and Architecture Principe in at least two ways. First is the group's breakup in part due to the partners' diverging ideological stances toward the surrounding political climate. Virilio became active in the movement as a whole, while Parent remained skeptical of what he saw as a prevailing mob mentality, where "those involved in the 'events' merely tore everything apart without proposing any realistic alternative."[58] Unlike Virilio, Parent also insisted that the oblique function had no overt political agenda, which, rather than a denial of its broader transformative potential was an acknowledgment of his commitment to, first and foremost, being an architect.[59] Meanwhile, Virilio, who had no formal training in architecture but was politically engaged and intellectually prolific, dedicated himself to theory and teaching, eventually assuming directorship of the École spéciale d'architecture in Paris. Their professional separation approximated in its appearance the split between theory and practice, even if in actuality Parent stayed committed to both. The other major impact that the turbulence of 1968 had on Parent's work was through the favorable shifts in cultural policies and increased support for public art programs that resulted from widespread revolt. Such state and municipal government efforts enabled the architect, as the next chapter explores, to further experiment with the oblique function on his own and to advance his methods of working collaboratively in the public realm beyond those previously conceptualized with Virilio as part of the design for *Instabilisateur pendulaire no. 1.*

AFTER ARCHITECTURE PRINCIPE

These three works by Architecture Principe are critical markers in the development of the oblique function as a theory, while also capturing distinct forms of its manifestation. Setting them in relation to *Vivre à l'oblique* and the practicables that followed conveys how Parent's conceptualization of obliqueness shifted as he transitioned from working with Virilio to proceeding on his own. The magazine, the church, and the installation design can in this way be regarded as artifacts that Parent rewrote, remade, revised—and thus updated—in his solo work following the dissolution of Architecture Principe.

Vivre à l'oblique is, in this sense, a rewritten version of the magazine, with marked differences. Formatted as a long-form essay written in a single voice—rather than a succession of short magazine articles alternating between the two authors—the book emphasizes the oblique function's role not as a novel provocation, but as a practicable hypothesis. Instead of presenting it as an autonomously conceived vision of an architecture—either ready to be implemented as is, no compromises allowed, or so radical that it is in fact not meant to be built—Parent proposes living on the oblique as a potential outcome dependent upon the participation and feedback of those willing to engage it. By calling for "individual participation in the act of building," for example, he promotes a form of joint authorship between architects and the public, an attitude that he likewise projected throughout his tour of France as he experimented with bridging the distance that conventionally separates those who design the built environment and those who live in it.[60] While *Architecture Principe* portrays the future as a radical departure from the past, *Vivre à l'oblique* uses references to the past as a means of conveying temporal continuity. In lieu of projecting the magazine's sense of alienation and an impending situation "without precedent"—a "fundamental disturbance" requiring "elementary transformation" and "total reinvention"—the book calls for the past to be rediscovered in order to shape the future.[61] Such a narrative shift reads as an attempt to normalize the oblique function by portraying it as already present rather than entirely unprecedented. While Parent refers to the search for precedents as an "archeology of the past," he omits mentioning in this context Virilio's bunker archeology, to which *Architecture Principe* dedicated an entire issue. In fact, bunkers are entirely absent from *Vivre à l'oblique*, not only in name but also visually. The book replaces the magazine's images of concrete surfaces (of wartime bunkers and the Nevers church alike) and imposing bunker-like architectural forms intricately rendered in graphite and ink with simple freehand diagrams describing spatial relationships, patterns of movement, and schematic organizational principles. The absence of severe graphics and explicit architectural forms, in other words, appears deliberate.

Not unlike the before-and-after comparison between these publications, putting the church next to the experimental installations that followed it similarly conveys a departure from the bunker aesthetic. While the church's inclined floors are obscured by a thick concrete shell, the practicables were nothing but slopes framed by the existing buildings that temporarily housed them. The practicables were as such stripped of earlier aesthetic references, and their construction—using lighter materials and reusable components instead of concrete— projected an intentional sense of contingency rather than overstated certainty. The oblique installations were in this sense a more open-ended remake of the church, much like *Vivre à l'oblique* appears to be in relation to the magazine. Moreover, while the practicables were, in their installation format, a continuation of the group's earlier plan for *Instabilisateur pendulaire no. 1*, their purpose by comparison also shifted. Rather than designed as enclosures to be lived in only by their architects, they were opened up to engage the public. From an audience perspective, as I further discuss in later chapters, they were presented not as objects to be looked at but rather as social spaces to inhabit, co-create, and experiment with in the context of the everyday.

A final observation on this work, one that I will build upon in Chapter 4: The three Architecture Principe projects discussed here reveal the increasingly significant role of interiority—both architecturally and psychologically—in these explorations of obliqueness. Such a development can in effect be seen as a chronological progression, or switch, in the means of experimentation from image to space or, more precisely, from drawing to interior. In other words, if the magazine served as a venue for disseminating experimental drawings, *Instabilisateur pendulaire no. 1* marked a reorientation toward experiments that took place not on paper but rather somewhere *inside*. The design of the 1968 oblique installation sought to consider interiority beyond the way that it had been considered in the church design, namely, as a key design consideration from the start, rather than as only an outcome or byproduct of other priorities. Parent and Virilio's theoretical proposition in this way needed to be validated by the necessary alignment of the two forms of interiority that were critical to it: interior space and subjective experience. Or, to put it another way, spatial consequences of oblique form had to be more precisely calibrated to the people it sought to engage.

This trajectory toward and through the interior is inextricably intertwined with the subsequent development of Parent's approach to experimental practice. *Vivre à l'oblique* foregrounds the role of the hypothesis as a starting point of experimentation; much like a hypothesis is the beginning of an experiment and not the end, the text situates the oblique plane as a premise or prompt rather than a conclusion. By articulating a process that spans across the space between theory and application, the text makes room for design experiments. Parent filled this conceptual space with practictables—that is with objects deemed experimental by the virtue of repeatability, adjustability according to given criteria, as well as the potential for failure. In Parent's vision of design experiments, this conceptual space—the space where experiments could occur—found its physical equivalent in the interior of other existing buildings, where his practicables, as the next chapter will explore, were to unfold.

2. THE TOUR

Shopping center in Sens, a commune in north-central France, desig
by Parent and built in 1970, in its recent state as a supermarket.

Office building at 58 rue de Mouzaïa, in the 19th arrondissement of Pa
designed by Claude Parent with André Remondet and built in 1974.
part of a major renovation in 2020 by Canal Architects, the building
converted into housing for students and young workers as well as cowo
ing space.

> Mapping of Parent's traveling programs from 1969 to 1975, indicat
locations of built practicables (magenta), practicables that were desig
but not built (cyan), and those with no practicables (yellow).

Political turbulence in 1968 halted the realization of Parent and Virilio's *Instabilisateur pendulaire no. 1* and effectively marked the end of their collaboration, but Parent held onto the idea of using public installations as a means of further testing the oblique function's practical viability.[1] In the years immediately following the dissolution of Architecture Principe, Parent completed the construction of a number of substantial projects, including the shopping centers in Sens (1970) and Ris-Orangis (1971), the Rue de la Mouzaïa office building in the 19th arrondissement of Paris (1974), and the house in Soual for the painter Michel Carrade (1974), among others. Yet, it was alongside such building commissions that he dedicated a substantial amount of energy and time to the design of temporary installations—practicables—and the development of related public programs through which he experimented with the principles of oblique architecture.[2] These design experiments occurred in towns all over France (with a side trip to Italy[3]) between 1969 and 1975. Venturing out from the French capital, Parent visited over a dozen provincial centers and small cities—*villes étapes* or "stopover towns" as he called them—including Le Havre, Saint-Étienne, Rennes, Nevers, Toulouse, Reims, Amiens, Mâcon, Douai, Chalon-sur-Saône, and Caen. At each destination he collaborated with local organizations on the development of programs generally aimed at audiences with little or no prior experience engaging experimental architecture. In addition to the usual repertoire of visiting lectures and exhibitions often pursued by architects promoting their work while traveling, Parent's productions also included performances, workshops, study groups formed by local residents, various art demonstrations, debates, and other activities. Describing what one of his visits to a town may be like, he said to a magazine writer, "First and foremost, this event is not fixed and rigid like an exhibition. Its form

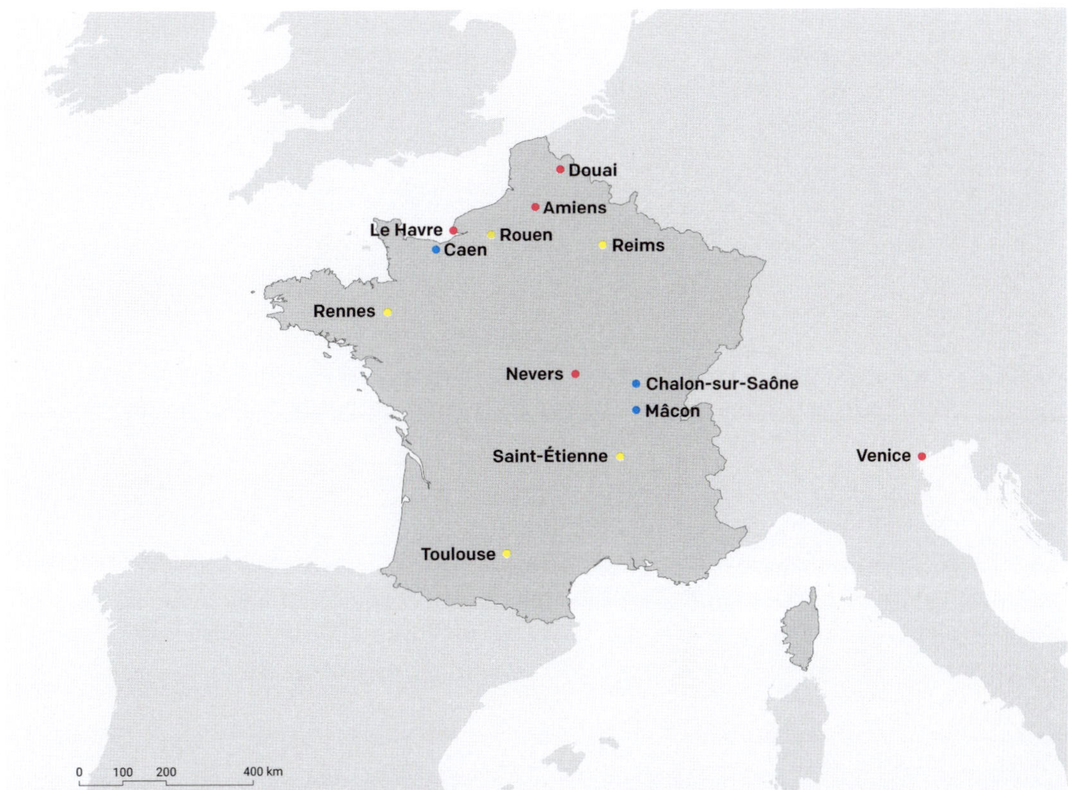

View of Parent's exhibition at the Maison de la culture in Reims in 1972, with a display of photographs of built projects.

Selection of Parent's models exhibited at the Maison de la culture in Reims in 1972.

is determined by the nature of the host structures, their resources, and their contacts with the public. It's never the same!"[4] Wherever Parent went, he also tried, with varying degrees of success, to build a full-scale practicable installation as part of the overall production. He fully succeeded in five of the locations, and designed schemes for four other cities in which his plans advanced as far as drawings and models.[5]

While the practicables expanded upon Parent's ongoing preoccupations with non-orthogonal geometries and their destabilizing effect on people, this series of objects physically exemplified the shifts—already introduced in the previous chapter—in his attitude toward experimental practice. In the broadest sense, the change can be seen as a movement toward direct social engagement, that is, getting people interested in the built environment, while also trying to elicit among them excitement about his own work. Moreover, even though his methods of data collection remained elusive, the objective was to solicit feedback and gather evidence in support of his design hypothesis about oblique living. These productions were, in other words, a sustained exercise in the public reception of his architecture. Working outside of the domain of his design studio, Parent was able to situate the oblique function in the world in ways that exceeded his earlier attempts to do so through writing, drawing, and building. While throughout the mid-1960s Architecture Principe's work undeniably reflected the era's "utopian prognostications" through provocatively rendered representations of imposing structures, Parent's pursuit of a more socially interactive approach to practice can be seen as an attempt to surpass the limitations of what had arguably become inadequate modes of experimentation.[6]

This next phase of Parent's oblique experiments is often referred to as a tour. In the spring of 1973, the popular magazine *Le Point* published the story titled "Le tour de France de Claude Parent," describing the architect's traveling programs as an effort in establishing a dialog about architecture "between those who make it and those who live in it."[7] At the time of the article's publication, Parent was working in Mâcon—a city four hundred kilometers southeast of Paris with a population of approximately thirty thousand inhabitants—where he mounted an exhibition; participated in a series of public workshops with local residents and public officials; staged live events, debates, and discussions with artists representing a variety of creative fields; and designed a sloped practicable as part of the children's reading room in the city's newly constructed library. As was usually the case, the combination of these activities reflected the particular circumstances of the city in question. When reflecting upon this period decades later, Parent continued to refer to it as his "tour of France" and, as if speaking of a theater group or circus—or the famous cycling event—rather than an architecture studio, called the team he worked with "his troupe."[8] These productions were collaborative, with each of the tour stops featuring a different cast of characters, from special appearances by out-of-town figures representing different areas of the arts and culture to local makers, performers, and organizers. There were those with recurring roles: Among this group of ongoing collaborators was the artist and writer André Barey, who joined Parent after the architect's involvement in the 1970 Venice Biennale and served as the producer of the traveling show; the painter Andrée Bellaguet; the sculptor Gérard Mannoni; the choreographer Nicole Parent, the architect's sibling; the photographer Gilles Ehrmann, in the primary role of a documentarian; and the mime performer Alain Hullot, among others.

If the *grand tour* in the history of architecture refers to the tradition of travels to unknown

Parent (left) surrounded by his artist collaborators in the French Pavilion at the 1970 Venice Biennale.

Parent's sister Nicole, a choreographer, in a spread from the book *L'Inclipan,* published by Robert Laffont in 1972. The book documents a gymnastics routine she developed for oblique architecture, which was often performed throughout the tour.

cities as part of one's privileged education, Parent was a *tour*-ist in his own culture, attempting to both learn new perspectives and share his own with others. The notion of a national tour as an exploratory journey likewise brings to mind the ongoing tradition of the Compagnons du Devoir et du Tour de France, an educational program for craftsmen and artisans who travel throughout the country for extended periods of time to apprentice with experts in their respective trades.[9] The student's journey is a key component of the learning process and Parent's tour can analogously be regarded as an experience that not only impacted the communities he visited along the way, but also transformed his own perspective on architecture.

Before elaborating further on how the tour impacted Parent, however, it is helpful to first examine the conditions that shaped it. The architect's ambition and drive notwithstanding, his experiments—including a shift toward a less mediated relationship with the public—were just as much a product of the external factors that made them possible. As such, this chapter examines the institutional context within which Parent's peripatetic experiments took place, as well as the influence of related government policies, social conditions, and cultural shifts. Of particular significance is a network of cultural organizations founded in the first decade of the French Fifth Republic (constitutionally established in 1958) as well as the subsequent changes in how they were locally administered, programmed, and financed in the years immediately following the events of 1968. Known as *maisons de la culture*—cultural centers or houses of culture—these organizations, and their different variants, were tasked with promoting visual and performing arts throughout France and served as Parent's hosts and partners in staging his oblique experiments.[10] To convey how these cultural centers shaped the tour as well as why they were particularly conducive to the kind of experimentation Parent was after, I focus on the geographic affinities and programmatic alignments between the two. I also consider the shared need by both Parent and the *maisons de la culture* to reach new audiences, as well as the ideological resonances between them. Finally, I account for how these organizations supported Parent's experiments financially and otherwise, serving as a composite infrastructure consisting of building architecture, programming, funding, and labor.

GEOGRAPHIC AFFINITIES

The *maisons de la culture* were the result of a statewide effort to distribute cultural resources throughout the country beyond the capital. Their evolution in France can be traced back to the establishment of institutions bearing that same name as early as the 1930s, serving as intellectual and political grassroots centers known to have been frequented by some of the most avant-garde artists and architects of the time.[11] The houses of culture with which Parent collaborated, however, emerged in a later era and are principally associated with the work of France's first Minister of Cultural Affairs André Malraux, appointed to the post by President Charles de Gaulle in 1959. Immediately after taking office, Malraux launched a national plan to establish new cultural centers all over France as a means of decentralizing and democratizing French culture.[12] The rollout was intended to provide accessible cultural experiences to all of the country's administrative regions, consistent with the government's obligation to provide equal access to culture—in addition to education and professional training—to each citizen.[13] In addition to the intended domestic impact, Malraux's policy also had international aspirations: The *maisons* were envisioned as instruments for externally projecting France's influence as the world's most culturally developed nation.[14] In his total vision of public institutions, Malraux differentiated the role of the cultural centers from that of universities. Accordingly, while the academy's assigned objective was the pursuit of knowledge and truth, the cultural centers had a different task. Malraux envisioned houses of culture as places for emotionally enriching experiences available to all.[15] The cultural centers were thus administratively imagined as a system of public places imbued with emotion powerful enough to resonate globally as a salient national feature.

The first such *maison de la culture* opened its doors in 1961 in Le Havre, which was also the site of Parent's first practicable from 1969. Parent subsequently built similar installations in the then-newly constructed houses of culture in Nevers and Amiens, as was also the intention for the practicables designed for Chalon-sur-Saône and Caen.[16] The oblique installation in Douai was likewise made possible by a collaboration with the town's house of culture, even if its unique outdoor siting—the only fully exterior practicable in the series—reflected the fact that as an organization the Maison de la culture de Douai did not have its own standalone building.[17] In these and other locations, including Rennes, Saint-Étienne, Toulouse, and Reims, it was with the support of such organizations that Parent was able to present architecture—and the oblique function—as the content, subject matter, and focus of their public programming. Circulating throughout provincial France, often in cities undergoing postwar rebuilding and a public housing boom, allowed Parent to project the potential of oblique living onto a larger territory and population—beyond Paris, beyond the art and architecture scene, and beyond the scope of any single building commission. Parent's efforts to engage these less urbanized regions, many of them experiencing new waves of construction, was reasonably shrewd for an architect on the lookout for possible future commissions.[18] After all, it was in smaller towns like Nevers and Charleville, not Paris, that he and Virilio had the most

Exterior view of the Musée d'art moderne André Malraux in Le Havre, known as the Nouveau Musée du Havre at the time of the 1969 exhibition *Espace architectural*.

Interior view of the main gallery at the Musée d'art moderne André Malraux in Le Havre, the site of Parent's first built practicable and the first building in France to open as a Malraux-era *maison de la culture*. The building's original name, when it opened in 1961, was the Musée-Maison de la culture du Havre.

Exterior view of the Maison de la culture Nevers agglomération (MCNA), referred to as the Maison de la culture de Nevers et de la Nièvre at the time of Parent's visit.

Interior view of the MCNA, in the area on the ground floor where Parent's 1971 practicable was installed.

Exterior view of the Maison de la culture d'Amiens, shown with modifications to the original building made as part of an extensive renovation from the early 1990s.

Interior view of the Maison de la culture d'Amiens, showing the street-level foyer and the upper-level space, on the right, where Parent's practicable was installed. One of the original glazed openings in the façade that made the 1972 installation visible from the outside has been replaced by a solid wall, as seen on the far right.

Exterior view of the ground-level space originally occupied by the children's reading room at the municipal library in Mâcon, for which Parent designed a practicable. Since 2000, when all library-related facilities were moved to a new location, the building has served as the Archives départementales de Saône-et-Loire.

Interior view of the space formerly occupied by the children's reading room at the municipal library in Mâcon.

luck finding new work just a few years earlier. Meanwhile, his pursuit of opportunities in such regions beyond the capital can also be interpreted as a refusal to further densify the already established metropolis. This is a point that Parent argued both with Virilio and on his own, whereby the diagonality of the oblique function was meant to serve as an alternative to horizonal sprawl and vertical growth of cities alike. His position as such embraced constructing new types of settlements outside of already established urban centers, with the idea that their size and density—and quality of life—could be better managed.[19] Parent's tour as such unfolded across a territory ripe with prospects, crisscrossing a map that Malraux had already established a decade earlier as the expanded ground for the proliferation of culture.[20]

By the time Parent started his tour, Malraux had concluded his decade-long term as minister, part of a larger change in government administration. The state program he established had yielded several *maisons de la culture* housed in newly constructed buildings, with a number of others accommodated in newly renovated structures—plus numerous additional centers that were in various planning and design stages.[21] Although the construction of new houses of culture continued selectively into the 1980s, Parent's tour of France unfolded during a particularly opportune period of their existence, enabling him to experiment with different ways of wedging oblique architecture into everyday reality.[22] The timing was good simply because of their availability as a new type of institution to work with—André

ce d'Armes in Douai, the site of Parent's outdoor practicable.

Exterior view of the Espace des arts, the cultural center known, prior to the 1980s, as the Maison de la culture de Chalon-sur-Saône. The exterior portion of Parent's practicable design was sited under the concrete awning seen on the far right.

Interior view of the Espace des arts in Chalon-sur-Saône, facing the exterior plaza, showing the location of Parent's indoor-outdoor practicable design.

Barey was particularly well connected in this regard[23]—but also working in Parent's favor was the increasing demand, following the events of 1968, for the cultural centers to prioritize community engagement. The effectiveness of Malraux's initial vision, in other words, came into question, particularly in relation to the actual reach of the cultural centers within their respective communities.[24] Likewise, the overall cultural initiative had a number of conceptual and operational conflicts that had by then been identified by its critics, including the dissonant relationship between decentralization as an objective and Malraux's ultimately "conservative definition of culture as artistic genius."[25] An inclusive scheme in terms of geographic access in essence collided with an overly exclusive conception of what counts as culture. Such rifts were at the core of the cultural centers' pressure to evolve as institutions as the state program entered its second decade and as Parent set out to explore oblique living nationwide.

PROGRAMMATIC ALIGNMENTS

Beyond their geographic distribution, it was the mixed programmatic makeup of the *maisons de la culture* that was particularly conducive to the development of Parent's events and installations. From the start, the centers were envisioned as facilities for a variety of art forms, and the need to attract broader audiences later on further intensified their pursuit of diverse programs.[26] The architectural brief written for the construction of Malraux's houses of culture emphasized the need to support all forms of artistic expression, including those not yet imagined, resulting in the design of multiuse complexes and building configurations that sought to promote flexibility, versatility, and polyvalence (in addition to this direct translation from French, *polyvalence* also stands for multivalence or multifunction).[27] A typical complex included theaters, exhibition galleries, workshop spaces, a library, bar, or café, along with room for emergent needs. Ultimately, their purpose was to stage encounters with various forms of art in which the public could potentially be both the audience and the producer. Visitors could, for example, attend a performance or be a part of a local theater group; see an exhibition or take a photography class; and watch a movie or make one. Under one roof, such experiences were to provide a mixture of exposure to requisite cultural content and participation in artistic activities as a part of

Exterior view of the Théâtre de Caen, known as the Théâtre-Maison de la culture prior to 1968 and as the Théâtre municipal de Caen at the time of Parent's 1975 visit.

Interior view of the Théâtre de Caen's multistory foyer, with the stairs and oversized landings to which Parent's practicable design proposed to connect.

aison de la culture de Chalon-sur-Saône's program pamphlet from October 1973.

5, AVENUE NICEPHORE NIEPCE
Téléphone : (16.85) 48. 48. 92

HEURES D'OUVERTURE M.C.C.
mardi au samedi : 11 h à 22 h
dimanche 11 h à 20 h
lundi, la m.c.c. est fermée.

DISCOTHEQUE
mercredi : 15 h à 19 h
jeudi : 12 h à 14 h
samedi : 15 h à 18 h
20 h à 22 h
dimanche : 16 h à 20 h

CINEMA
mardi à 18 heures 30 (prix : 4 F.)

PRIX
SPECTACLES INVITES : consulter la Presse
SPECTACLES M. C. C. : 8,00 F – 5,00 F.
EXPOSITIONS : 2,00 F – 1,00 F

AUCUN CHANGEMENT DE PROGRAMME N'ENGAGE LA RESPONSABILITE DE LA M.C.C.
«Se reporter à la presse locale»

LES MANIFESTATIONS COMMENCENT A HEURE PRECISE.

Une garderie gratuite est assurée pour les enfants de moins de sept ans pendant les spectacles et concerts.

CHALON
SUR SAONE

Atelier Offset MCC

MOIS D'OCTOBRE 1973

MAISON
DE LA
CULTURE

middle-class leisure.[28] The cultural center's hybrid role as part performance hall, part exhibition gallery, and part hobbyist art laboratory was echoed in the entanglement of different activities and presentation formats prepared by Parent, as if each built practicable were an alternative, scaled-down encapsulation of the larger host institution. The versatile programmatic agenda of the houses of culture, or what the architectural historian Richard Klein calls "the beautiful idea of programmatic indetermination," reflected the foundational administrative intention to have the buildings serve as enablers for all forms of artistic production—present and future.[29]

Such a programmatically inclusive schema was well suited to the presentation of architecture as an experimental art form. In general, houses of culture were already relatively open to the promotion of architecture through their public events, an example of which was the posthumous exhibition on Le Corbusier presented as part of the 1968 inauguration of the Maison de la culture de Grenoble.[30] These programs provided an existing baseline for Parent's exhibitions, lectures, and workshops, the experimental nature of which he pushed, more successfully in some cities than others, beyond conventional presentation formats. Incorporating aspects of live performance was particularly in line with the spirit of the cultural centers, whose theatrical inclination generally dominated the intended mixture of represented art forms that they housed. It was appropriate, given the context, that Parent's practicables were designed as multifunctional stages where life and art could blend with one another. The architect in this way positioned architecture not as an object to be looked at, in the manner of fine art or conventional architecture exhibitions, but rather as a device that both enabled the transformation of audiences into performers and of performances becoming part of life. This orientation toward theater was in large part the result of Barey's involvement with the tour from 1971 onward. (A case could also be made that it was thanks to Barey that a few of Parent's early engagements, such as his exhibitions in Le Havre and Venice, were eventually converted into the longer traveling program.) The architecture historian Audrey Jeanroy describes Barey as an impresario and actor, who imagined Parent's public programs as live art shows, resembling experimental theater, based on the oblique function.[31]

REACHING NEW AUDIENCES

Parent and Barey's multifaceted productions—an unusual blend of popular entertainment, interactive activities, and high-concept discourse—helped fulfill the need for a broader appeal and deeper involvement with the audiences that were deemed least likely to set foot in a cultural center, aligning with what local and state administrations classified as *actions culturelles* and *animations*. These terms referred to public programs conceptualized during this era to encourage participation and expand the definition of culture in an effort to better engage local populations.[32] Such shifts reshaped not only event planning but in some instances the organizations themselves. In Mâcon, for example, instead of a *maison de la culture*, the municipality built a similar facility but named it the Centre d'animation culturel. (The building opened in 1975; Parent's programs in Mâcon took place during its construction, making use of different locations throughout the city instead of a single center.) That this was a change from the types of programs people were already familiar with is captured in a local newsletter from November of 1968, in which residents of Mâcon could encounter the article titled "L'action culturelle: Pourqoui?" Through a dozen bullet points, the socialist-governed municipality explained the purpose—why?—of *actions culturelles*. Listed among the aims is forging collaboration among multiple organizations; creating necessary conditions for "the power of leisure" and entertainment; exploring culture as "a perpetual means of liberation"; staging first encounters between new artists and large crowds; linking past cultural heritage and contemporary forms of expression; providing opportunities for every resident to be heard; and making space for each person to "cultivate" themselves in their own authentic way.[33] By promoting a compatible set of values, Parent's programs in Mâcon, as well as in other cities throughout the tour, tapped into a synergy between state and municipal ambitions to "activate" their citizens and the oblique function's use of the slope as a dynamic prompt.

Joining forces with such organizations enabled Parent to frame his theory of architecture as a popular pastime crossing into the quotidian domains of recreation, entertainment, and kitchen-table conversations. His interest in closer contact with the public—as an architect with an established reputation for utopian visions more suited by convention to avant-garde salons than working-class community centers—was shaped by various factors, not the least of which was his ambition to test the oblique function as a hypothesis. His architectural experiments needed human subjects and thus, through interacting with the public, his methodologies expanded, as he had promised they would in *Vivre à l'oblique*, beyond those already part of his repertoire.[34] Through his travels, he attempted to test how people throughout the country would receive his ideas, with the hope of generating feedback from such encounters. As a self-proclaimed people person, he was eager to talk to the public about architecture and urbanism as well as listen, even if being in this role throughout the tour was not without its challenges.[35] If the oblique function were to make a difference in changing architecture and improving people's relationship to it, Parent optimistically explained, he needed to find out whether there was interest in what he imagined.[36] In much the same way that the cultural institutions he collaborated with needed to attract as broad of an audience as possible, Parent's programs aspired to earn mainstream acceptance for his vision of life in a new type of built environment.

CONSUMPTION AND PRODUCTION

If, as others have suggested, establishments like the *maisons de la culture* were the state's instruments for countering the evolving effects of postwar consumerism and mass production,[37] then it is possible to identify another affinity that Parent shared with these institutions—his own anxieties about the same types of prevailing societal tendencies. The state's apprehension about the alienating effects of mass consumption and mass media as expressed through the countering programmatic efforts of houses of culture and cultural actions (some of the cultural centers even had spaces where people could watch TV together, in public, rather than at home) were in line with Parent's views on mass production and its effect on architecture, the built environment, and modern life.[38] Throughout his writing,

Construction of the Amiens practicable.

Construction of the Amiens practicable, 1972.

Parent's visit to the construction site of the Amiens practicable in the fall of 1972.

individually and with Paul Virilio, Parent associated orthogonal geometries in architecture with all that is mass-produced, the alternative counterpoint to which was the oblique slant. The practicables can thus be seen as stages for countering consumerism, aligned with the cultural centers' mandate to promote active participation rather than passive reception of the arts.[39] They served, in effect, as devices for rehearsing in public the kind of evacuation of unnecessary possessions—and the complacency of comfort—that *Vivre à l'oblique* proposed to implement in the domestic realm.

In addition to serving as physical venues with favorable institutional dispositions, houses of culture provided the resources, including funding and labor, for realizing Parent's experiments. Not unlike Architecture Principe's magazine and other self-started projects, Parent's proof-of-concept tour required initiative, not the least of which was having to chase opportunities for public engagement as well as budgets to pay for it.[40] At the time—though in many cases not for long thereafter—most of the *maisons de la culture* he worked with were still state-financed, including Le Havre, Nevers, Amiens, Douai, and Chalon-sur-Saône. State funds generally not only ensured better budgets for cultural projects but also required less dependence on box-office profit than was typically the case for locally run organizations, enabling greater degrees of experimentation and creative risk-taking. The cultural centers' various departments had staff with various skills and expertise, providing Parent with the necessary labor to help realize his plans—including the construction of the practicables—as well

Cover of *5 réflexions sur l'architecture* published by the Maison de la culture de Nevers in 1972.

Cover of *Mobile*, the Maison de la culture d'Amiens's monthly publication in which Parent's work was featured throughout the months of his visit to the city.

as access to local networks of businesses that made contributions in the form of donations and sponsorships.[41] In addition to the staging of live programs, collaborating with houses of culture also yielded a range of printed artifacts—such as newsletters, leaflets, pamphlets, posters, and also entire books—in ways that exceeded the limitations of self-financed publishing of the manifesto-magazine a few years earlier.[42]

While it lasted for only a few years, such financial and creative support sustained Parent's public experiments and resulted in a variety of programs of which those produced for the Maison de la culture d'Amiens from late 1972 to early 1973 are, as the next chapter further conveys, the best example. In addition to the prominently sited practicable, visible from the outside through the oversized glazed openings of the Pierre Sonrel-designed building façade, a robust rollout of programs captured the overarching intention of these productions. It included exhibitions of not only Parent's architectural portfolio but also paintings by the Chilean artist Roberto Matta and Parent's frequent collaborator Andrée Bellaguet, along with various musical performances, discussions, as well as extensive printed matter promoting the architect and the many events on and around the practicable. Once institutional funding cuts started to occur along with shifting state policies and municipal priorities,[43] Parent's practicable designs were no longer getting built, and eventually his tour came to its conclusion.[44] The end coincided with the state's diminishing commitment to the overall initiative, validated by a damning report from 1976 which disclosed the cultural program's ineffectiveness in meeting its objectives.[45]

EXPERIMENTAL ENGAGEMENTS

Situated in the broader context, the development of Parent's tour of France, and the design of the practicables, can be traced in relation to the evolution of houses of culture as public institutions. Such consideration reveals the synergies between the institutional interests of these establishments and the architect's professional and artistic ambitions at that time.[46] Explorations of oblique living shaped their public programs, while their

Invitation to Parent's lectures in Nevers delivered in June 1971, the content of which was subsequently published in the book *5 réflexions sur l'architecture*. On the bottom of the card is Parent's statement about experimental architecture.

mardi 8 : réflexions sur le métier d'architecte
mercredi 9 : réflexions sur l'architecture contemporaine (1)
jeudi 10 : réflexions sur l'architecture contemporaine (2)
vendredi 11 : réflexions sur la situation politique de l'architecture d'aujourd'hui
samedi 12 : réflexions sur une architecture différente

Dans les temps de crises, à l'instant où inopinément se présentent des circonstances favorables, surgit l'architecture expérimentale. Scandaleuse, violente, peu élaborée et balbutiante, l'expérimentation ne doit être appréciée qu'au niveau de l'intention et du germe qu'elle porte. Son échec même serait sa plus grande signification. Sur le cheminement lent et contradictoire de la création, les points d'arrêt de l'architecture expérimentale jalonnent déjà un futur qui reste à découvrir.

social and administrative agendas—as well as the very architecture of their facilities—provided a framework for Parent's practice. Programmatic uses of the practicables, as well as various factors related to the realization of each installation—not the least of which is that some of the proposed schemes did not get built—were the result of the particular circumstances encountered in each city, thereby capturing the site-specific nature of the entire architectural tour. Ultimately, while the architect's long-term impact on the places he visited may have been limited, the sum of these touring experiences profoundly shaped not only Parent's work during this period but also his overall attitude toward practice. In particular, the experience of working directly with people impacted his perspective on the nature of architectural experiments.

Parent's call for a less mediated relationship between the architect and the people they served, as exemplified by the tour, did not mean that he toned down his architectural ambitions. His promotion of life on the incline—and of the value of experimental architecture beyond this particular fixation—persisted regardless of the audience's background. The verso side of the invitation card to his five-part lecture series, held at the cultural center in Nevers during the summer of 1971, bore the following text:

> In times of crisis, when unexpectedly favorable circumstances arise, experimental architecture emerges. Scandalous, violent, undeveloped and in its infancy, experimentation should only be appreciated at the level of the intention and the germ it carries. Its very failure would be its greatest significance. On the slow and contradictory path of creation, the stopping points of experimental architecture already mark out a future yet to be discovered.[47]

In this way, the program challenged the audience to question the state of contemporary architecture—and their living environment—much like the *maison de la culture*'s concurrent screening of French New Wave films that summer (which, for example, included Jean-Luc Godard's *A Woman Is a Woman*, Éric Rohmer's *My Night at Maud's,* and Jacques Doniol-Valcroze's *The Beating Heart*) prompted an exploration of the current state of cinema and, by extension, of the society from which it emerged.

Reflecting upon his travels in support of the oblique function in a memoir published in 1975, which coincided with the tour's conclusion, Parent writes about the power of direct physical engagement with the constructed slopes as it unfolded in these public productions, while also recognizing the need for accountability when it comes to experimenting with people's living environments. Radical changes to architecture and its potential behavioral impact, he writes, require "repeated experimentation over a long period time, with care and through provisional actions."[48] The status of the practicables as experimental instruments was thus meant to be, to echo Parent's chosen word, *fugitive*—fleeting or ephemeral—rather than fixed, much like the live programs that accompanied them. He further writes, "In architecture, at a certain level, you can't play with people according to your own ideas, even if you have the best of intentions."[49] The tour, in this sense, was not only a journey that furthered the tenets of a theory but also one that resulted in embracing empathy as a design factor.

Schedule of events featured at the Maison de la culture de Nevers throughout the summer of 1971, including film screenings and Parent's architecture-related programs.

mercredi 7 juil.
aspects du cinéma contemporain
18 h 30 monsieur ripois
20 h 30 plein soleil

vendredi 9 juil.
exposition claude parent
16 h 30 nevers-nord (film)
18 h 30 la biennale de venise (film)
21 h visite de l'église du banlay

samedi 10 juil.
exposition claude parent
18 h 30 entretien : la fonction oblique dans la vie quotidienne

dimanche 11 juil.
exposition claude parent
18 h 30 l'homme en marche, la biennale de venise et le béton (films)

mardi 13 juil.
exposition claude parent
création d'un espace oblique

mercredi 14 juil.
aspects du cinéma contemporain
18 h 30 les créatures
20 h 30 le bonheur

jeudi 15 juil.
exposition claude parent
18 h 30 le m'zab et nevers-nord (films)

vendredi 16 juil.
exposition claude parent
21 h visite de l'église du banlay

samedi 17 juil.
exposition claude parent
18 h 30 le m'zab et nevers-nord (films)

mercredi 21 juil.
aspects du cinéma contemporain
18 h 30 la mariée était en noir
20 h 30 baisers volés

jeudi 22

mercredi 28 juil.
aspects du cinéma contemporain
18 h 30 la curée
20 h 30 sait-on jamais ?

jeudi 29 juil.
exposition claude parent
18 h 30 le m'zab et nevers-nord (films)

vendredi 30 juil.
exposition claude parent
21 h visite de l'église du banlay

samedi 31 juil.
exposition claude parent
18 h 30 le m'zab et nevers-nord (films)

mercredi 4 août
aspects du cinéma contemporain
18 h 30 la vie à l'envers
20 h 30 jeu de massacre

mercredi 11 août
aspects du cinéma contemporain
18 h 30 ascenseur pour l'échafaud
20 h 30 calcutta

mercredi 18 août
aspects du cinéma contemporain
18 h 30 transeurop-express
20 h 30 l'eden et après

mercredi 25 août
aspects du cinéma contemporain
18 h 30 à double tour
20 h 30 les bonnes femmes

mercredi 1 sept.
aspects du cinéma contemporain
18 h 30 la musica
20 h 30 détruire dit-elle

mercredi 8
aspects du cinéma contemporain
8 h 30 la collectionneuse
0 h 30 ma nuit chez maud

pects du cinéma contemporain
h 30 l'eau à la bouche
h 30 le cœur battant

cts du cinéma contemporain
30 une femme est une femme
30 made in u.s.a.

ts du cinéma contemporain
30 mouchette
30 une femme douce

ar voies d'affiches et de presse.

De 1950 à 1970, comment a-t-on fait le cinéma en France ? Influencés par des prédécesseurs prestigieux, les réalisateurs ont pu chercher à imiter ces modè-

aspects du cinéma français contemporain

les, ou déviants, ils ont tentés de créer une école, celle de "la Nouvelle Vague", bientôt dépassée par une société changeante et qui se cherche, comme son cinéma.
Les aspects du cinéma français contemporain proposés cet été sont pris sous l'angle le plus large, avec des films ayant connus une grande diffusion publique. Projections tous les mercredis à 18 h 30 et 20 h 30 de deux films différents d'un même réalisateur.

Dans le cadre de la manifestation d'urbanisme et d'architecture consacrée à l'architecte Claude Parent: 3 films et 3 entretiens avec Claude Parent et

urbanisme et architecture la fonction oblique

claude parent

un groupe d'artistes sur 3 expériences de la fonction oblique : religieuse, artistique, quotidienne, les 9, 10 et 11 juillet. Une création de la Maison de la Culture "l'espace oblique", du 13 juillet au 31 août. Jusqu'au 31 juillet, exposition ouverte tous les jours sauf le lundi de 11 h à 22 h. 2 films sur l'architecture le M'zab et Nevers-Nord, tous les jeudis et samedis à 18 h 30. Une visite de l'église Sainte-Bernadette du Banlay tous les vendredis à 21 h.

Espace architectural exhibition poster, Le Havre, 1969.

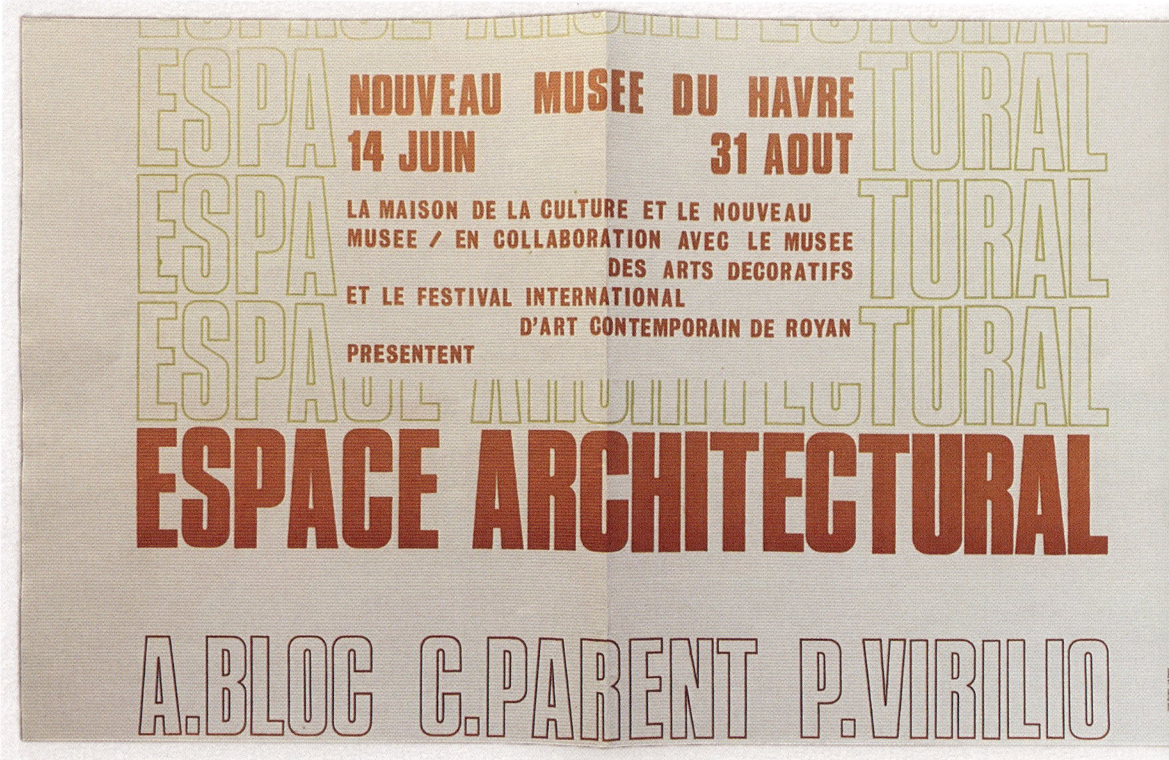

Architecture oblique event poster, Nevers, 1971.

La fonction oblique event poster, Toulouse, 1971–72.

fonction oblique exhibition poster, Nevers, 1971.

Cadre de vie: L'architecture oblique exhibition and event poster, Caen, 1972–73.

Claude Parent exhibition and program poster, Chalon-sur-Saône, 1973.

Claude Parent: Architecture contemporaine exhibition poster, Reims, 1972.

Manifestation Claude Parent: Architecture contemporaine exhibition and event flyer, Reims, 1972.

Cadre de vie: L'architecture oblique poster, Amiens, 1972–73.

Vivre à l'oblique exhibition and event poster, Douai, 1973.

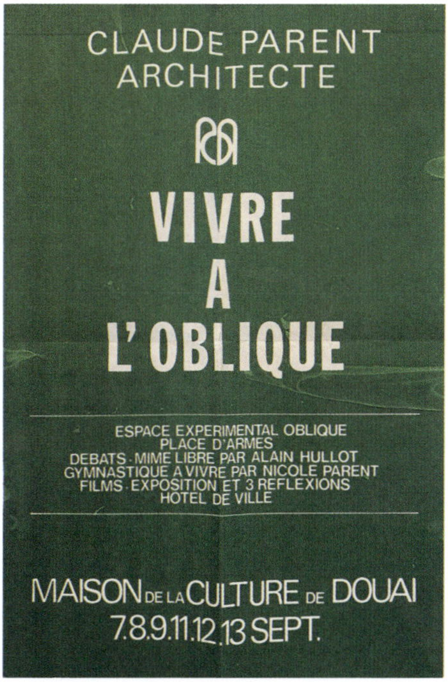

3. THE PRACTI-CABLES

A note about drawings in this chapter

Each subchapter opens with an isometric view of the practicable design in question, produced as an essential part of the book. Together, this new set of drawings intentionally offers visual consistency across all nine schemes in order to compensate for the inconsistency with which the original designs were documented and archived. These reconstructed representations draw from a range of available materials, including Parent's own drawings, surviving images of various physical models that no longer exist, and photographs of the realized installations.

In addition to the practicables' form, also included, when possible, are salient features of the existing buildings within which the installations were sited. This information was gathered from other drawings as well as through visits to each building. The drawings as such seek to convey the practicables as situated objects informed by their immediate context.

First modeled digitally and then captured as two-dimensional isometric images, the drawings use layers of linework and transparency in an attempt to show each practicable as a whole object, while also capturing the existing architectural elements, such as overall massing, structure, and façades that support or frame it. The drawings appear either at the scale of 1:100 or 1:200, as indicated in each case. To give a sense of their relative size in relation to one another, a plan view of all nine schemes shown together is provided at the end of the book's introductory chapter.

As the tour unfolded—from what first seemed like a one-off exhibition in Le Havre, followed by the exceptional appearance at the Venice Biennale, and eventually a succession of coordinated visits throughout France—Parent kept designing one practicable after another. Some were built; others were not. In some cases, dozens of design iterations were produced, testing various configurations, implementing different angles of incline, and incorporating outside feedback as part of the process. At least one installation appears to have been constructed with no preceding drawings or models in sight. There were also tour stops, such as Toulouse and Reims, where Parent delivered various programs related to oblique architecture—sometimes pursuing types of public engagement and social participation that far exceeded conventional roles assumed by architects—without producing any installations. This chapter focuses on nine practicable designs, identified by location and presented in chronological order. It maps out the tour geographically and over time, while also conveying how these architectural objects evolved in relation to one another and in response to their specific surroundings.

The previous two chapters discussed what drove and determined Parent's experiments both internally and externally. By tracking the traveling itinerary from one place to another, this chapter conveys how his intellectual, creative, and professional ambitions manifested themselves as they encountered the opportunities and obstacles posed by each location. As such, the chapter follows the iterative development of his approach to oblique architecture and more broadly to experimental architecture as a socially engaged practice. The practicable designs and the public programs that accompanied them throughout the countrywide journey can be compared to one another, with certain aspects worth noting along the way: morphological variety, site adaptability, means and methods of construction, modes of artistic collaboration, programmatic uses, intended and spontaneous forms of audience engagement, and the incorporation of broader community-building strategies as part of the project. With its multiple layers, this series of experiments yields a composite landscape specific to its time yet in many ways as compelling and provocative today as it was back then.

LE HAVRE (1969)

The first oblique practicable was built in 1969 for a museum exhibition titled *Espace architectural* (Architectural Space). The installation was Parent's first realized attempt at applying principles of the oblique function in practice since the 1966 completion of the church in Nevers, and it marked the start of a focused period of experimentation through the production of ephemeral events and installations.[1] Built inside the Nouveau Musée du Havre, the first home to the city's *maison de la culture*, the practicable had a rectangular footprint of approximately five by thirty meters and appeared as a freestanding object within the building's main exhibition space.[2] Its salient feature was a wide, moderately steep ramp leading up to a landing more than two meters above the existing floor level, while narrower, shorter, and steeper sloped surfaces provided alternative routes for going up and down. A yellow stripe running down the middle gave the main slope a road-like appearance, like a sliver of painted scenography conveying a fictional exterior in which, according to local press, the visitor

Le Havre (1969)

People inhabiting the practicable as part of the exhibition *Espace architectural*.

was "purely and simply transformed into a pedestrian of the year 2000 who sees houses and cities transformed into itineraries full of fantasy and freedom."[3] The generously proportioned gallery interior, enveloped in glass and sparsely punctuated by slender steel columns, provided ample space for the realization of such a structure. Sheathed in hundreds of square meters of plywood, which included the angled railings supported by a series of triangular frames arrayed along the perimeter, the "gigantic and unusual wooden construction" was the exhibition's centerpiece.[4]

The practicable organized the exhibition's three constituent parts into different zones. The first part, subtitled *Espace quotidien* (Everyday Space), featured a selection of models and photographs documenting Parent's professional practice and was laid out in the area between one long side of the practicable and the gallery's vast sea-facing curtain wall. On the other side, accessible by walking underneath or around the installation, was *Espace sculpté* (Sculpted Space), the part of the exhibition dedicated to sculptural works by Parent's longtime mentor and collaborator André Bloc.[5] The curated set of amorphously shaped objects, some shown on pedestals and others in photographs, included Bloc's alluringly cavernous building-sized habitable sculptures known as *habitacles*. The exhibition's third part, *Espace dynamique* (Dynamic Space), focused on Parent's collaboration with Virilio and their exploration of the oblique function. Images related to this part of the show were mounted on transparent screens, suspended from the ceiling at heights corresponding to the angle of the main ramp, and configured in a way that encouraged viewers to climb up the slope in order to see them more closely. Moreover, a number of notebook-sized pages of text, placed directly onto the installation's main ramp, appeared as if sliding down the slope and as such prompting visitors to meander instead of moving in a straight line. In this way, the practicable fulfilled the purpose of laying out the exhibition, choreographing people's movement through it and providing them with firsthand experience of being on a slope.

In the opening paragraph of the accompanying exhibition pamphlet, the show's de facto curatorial statement, Parent defines movement as "the fourth dimension" of architecture, distinguishing it from "the three orthogonal directions in space."[6] What follows is a brief about an architecture

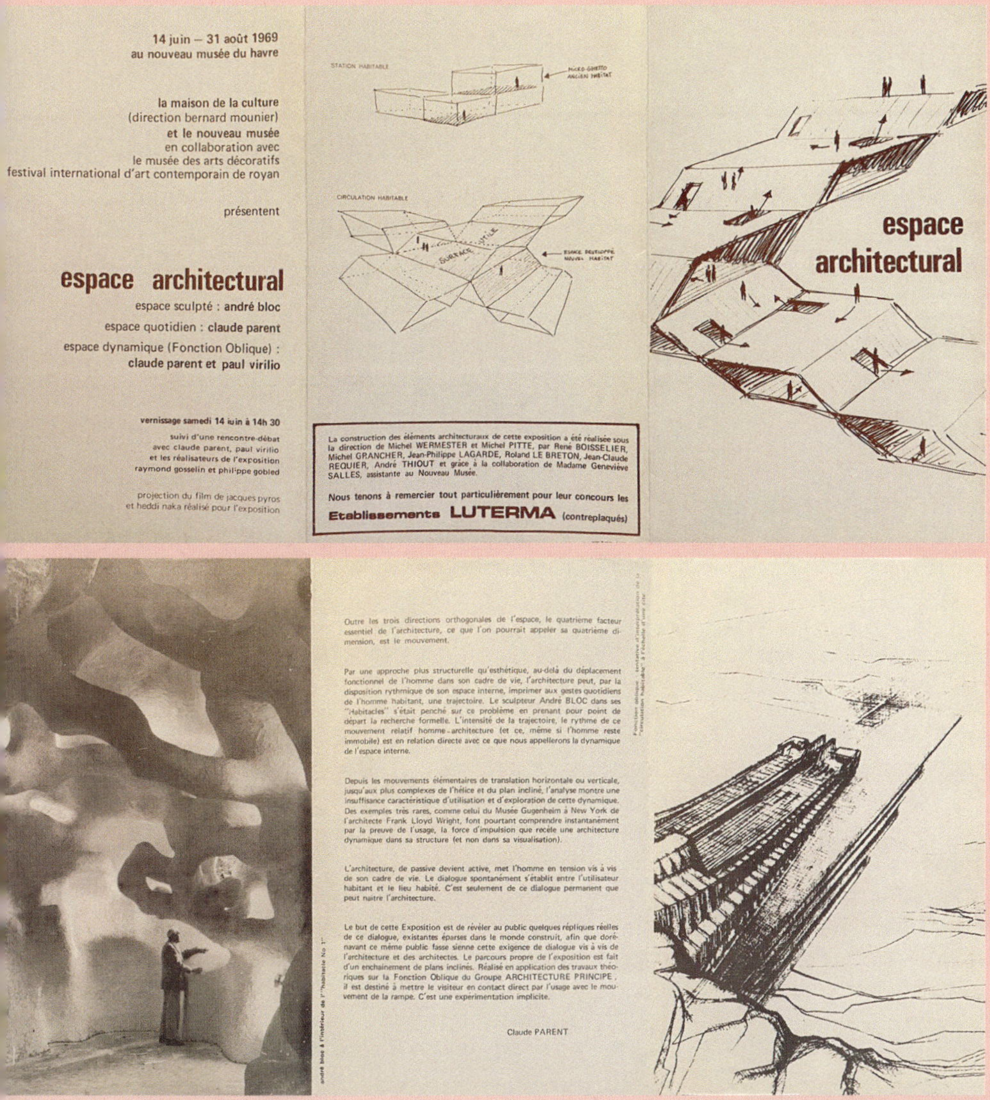

14 juin – 31 août 1969
au nouveau musée du havre

la maison de la culture
(direction bernard mounier)
et le nouveau musée
en collaboration avec
le musée des arts décoratifs
festival international d'art contemporain de royan

présentent

espace architectural

espace sculpté : **andré bloc**

espace quotidien : **claude parent**

espace dynamique (Fonction Oblique) :
claude parent et paul virilio

vernissage samedi 14 juin à 14h 30
suivi d'une rencontre-débat
avec claude parent, paul virilio
et les réalisateurs de l'exposition
raymond gosselin et philippe gobled

projection du film de jacques pyros
et heddi naka réalisé pour l'exposition

La construction des éléments architecturaux de cette exposition a été réalisée sous la direction de Michel WERMESTER et Michel PITTE, par René BOISSELIER, Michel GRANCHER, Jean-Philippe LAGARDE, Roland LE BRETON, Jean-Claude REQUIER, André THIOUT et grâce à la collaboration de Madame Geneviève SALLES, assistante au Nouveau Musée.

Nous tenons à remercier tout particulièrement pour leur concours les **Etablissements LUTERMA** (contreplaqués)

Outre les trois directions orthogonales de l'espace, le quatrième facteur essentiel de l'architecture, ce que l'on pourrait appeler sa quatrième dimension, est le mouvement.

Par une approche plus structurelle qu'esthétique, au-delà du déplacement fonctionnel de l'homme dans son cadre de vie, l'architecture peut, par la disposition rythmique de son espace interne, imprimer aux gestes quotidiens de l'homme habitant, une trajectoire. Le sculpteur André BLOC dans ses "Habitacles" s'était penché sur ce problème en prenant pour point de départ la recherche formelle. L'intensité de la trajectoire, le rythme de ce mouvement relatif homme-architecture (et ce, même si l'homme reste immobile) est en relation directe avec ce que nous appellerons la dynamique de l'espace interne.

Depuis les mouvements élémentaires de translation horizontale ou verticale, jusqu'aux plus complexes de l'hélice et du plan incliné, l'analyse montre une insuffisance caractéristique d'utilisation et d'exploration de cette dynamique. Des exemples très rares, comme celui du Musée Gugenheim à New York de l'architecte Frank Lloyd Wright, font pourtant comprendre instantanément par la preuve de l'usage, la force d'impulsion que recèle une architecture dynamique dans sa structure (et non dans sa visualisation).

L'architecture, de passive devient active, met l'homme en tension vis à vis de son cadre de vie. Le dialogue spontanément s'établit entre l'utilisateur habitant et le lieu habité. C'est seulement de ce dialogue permanent que peut naitre l'architecture.

Le but de cette Exposition est de révéler au public quelques répliques réelles de ce dialogue, existantes éparses dans le monde construit, afin que dorénavant ce même public fasse sienne cette exigence de dialogue vis à vis de l'architecture et des architectes. Le parcours propre de l'exposition est fait d'un enchainement de plans inclinés. Réalisé en application des travaux théoriques sur la Fonction Oblique du Groupe ARCHITECTURE PRINCIPE, il est destiné à mettre le visiteur en contact direct par l'usage avec le mouvement de la rampe. C'est une expérimentation implicite.

Claude PARENT

gram pamphlet for *Espace architectural*, including Parent's introductory text for the exhibition.

Floor plan drawing of the exhibition *Espace architectural*, with an overlay of freehand sketches. Section drawing of the Le Havre practicable shown inside the existing gallery, with handwritten annotations throughout.

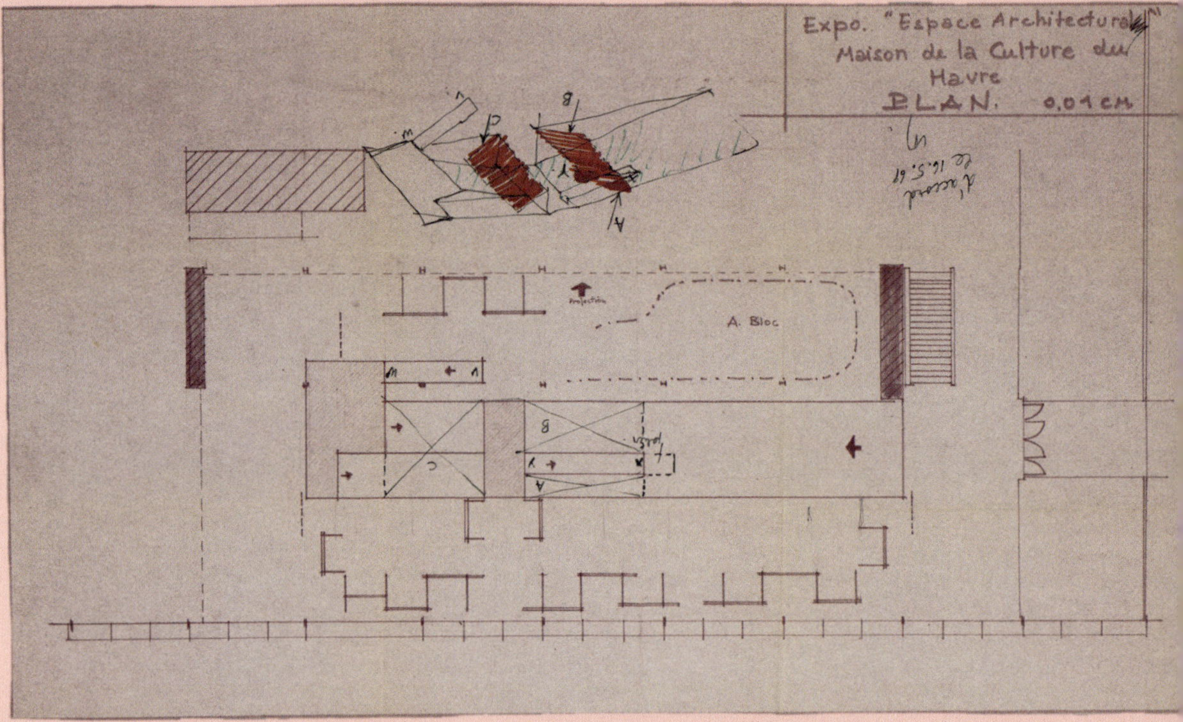

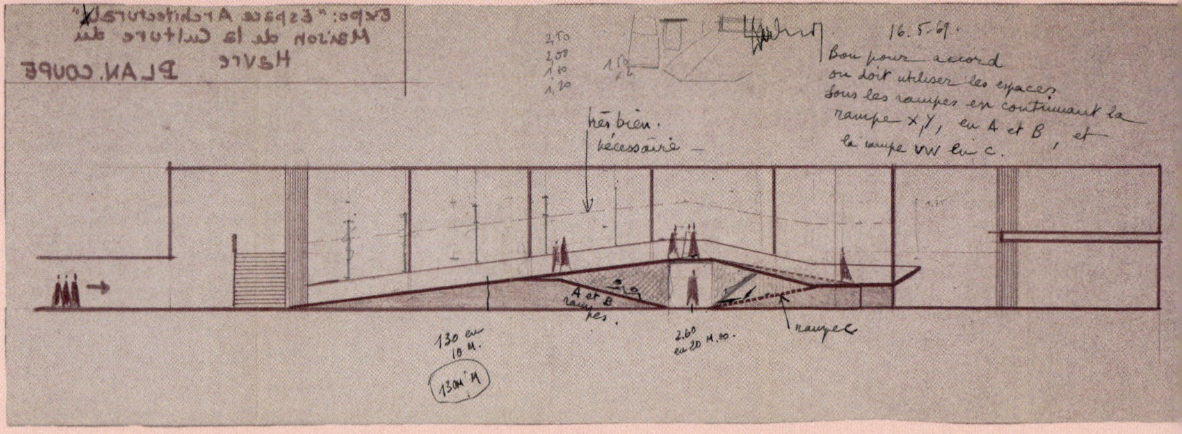

that is dynamic rather than static—a dynamism not of mobile structures but rather of an active exchange between inhabitants and their physical environment. For Parent, this was a "permanent dialog" from which new architecture could emerge.[7] The emphasis on movement served as a prominent conceptual thread that ran through an otherwise eclectic selection of works, ranging from Parent's steel-framed buildings designed in the late 1950s to Bloc's amorphous sculptures, alongside Architecture Principe's explorations of the oblique function. The other connection throughout the exhibition was Parent himself, whose personal and professional relationship with both Bloc and Virilio profoundly impacted the course of his career. In a sense, the exhibition was Parent's farewell to them both as he forged ahead on his own: to his mentor and collaborator Bloc, who unexpectedly died in 1966, leaving behind a body of work that had yet to be exhibited at the scale of a retrospective; and to Virilio, with whom he had just parted ways after several years of a robust partnership. Tied together in this way by movement as a curatorial conceit—and by Parent's personal relationship to all parts of the show—this diverse selection of works filled the entire museum, resulting in a reputation-affirming exhibition by a group of figures mostly unknown to the Norman audience.[8]

While the exhibition text mentions the oblique function just once, its principles dominated the show, the boldest evidence of which was the practicable itself. An accompanying promotional flyer for the exhibition was perforated and scored in such a way as to suggest that even a flat sheet of paper could be transformed into a miniature oblique structure. Referencing the installation at the end of his curatorial statement, Parent calls it *une expérimentation implicite*.[9] The phrase yields multiple, slightly different translations in English, with the word *expérimentation* variably referring to an experiment, experience, or experimentation. Similarly nuanced shifts in meaning are also present in the original French. Accordingly, the meaning shifts depending on one's relationship to the practicable as an object. For the architect who created it, it can be seen as an experiment whose implicit aims have not yet been fully revealed, whereas for the users, it can be an experience whose occurrence is not entirely conscious, like a minor background event. The user's experience, in this sense, is the architect's experiment, a relationship that Parent further articulated in *Vivre à l'oblique*, published the following year. The dynamic of people engaging the ramp and the architect observing the interaction—while also placing movement on display as part of the exhibition—is one of several aspects of what throughout the later tour constituted participation and research;

Side view of the practicable as part of the exhibition *Espace architectural* during a public event.

The Le Havre practicable with photographs and drawing reproductions suspended from the ceiling around it.

Promotional flyer for *Espace architectural*, foldable into an oblique shape.

it was one method, in other words, of producing and gathering evidence in support of the architect's hypothesis.

That Parent found a way to build such a structure in public was itself an achievement in bringing the oblique function to life. Its physical realization was another useful piece of evidence demonstrating the viability of his theoretical claims. The installation's linear form recalled Parent's abstractly rendered visions of oblique cities as elongated monoliths slashing through space.[10] Not unlike these figures, emerging diagonally from otherwise blank sheets of paper, the Le Havre practicable, placed at the center of the luminous gallery, appeared independent of its surroundings. Yet, its design enhanced the existing setting rather than transforming it beyond recognition—an assertive architecture that was also sympathetic to its surroundings. The practicable was as such remarkably site-specific: Rather than ignoring or rejecting its context, it engaged existing architecture in a number of ways. Its length, for example, measured exactly five of the museum's structural bays, with the installation's ends neatly aligned with the building's structural grid. Likewise, the start of its main ramp was placed in front of the main entrance to the gallery, resulting in an overall entry sequence informed by the relationship between the building and the installation. Rising above the gallery floor, the inclined planes took advantage of the available volume of space in a way that not only served the specific interests of the exhibition but also accentuated the verticality, thereby enhancing rather than negating the existing architecture.[11] Finally, by siting the installation parallel to the vast curtain wall overlooking the sea, its oblique slopes were juxtaposed against the flatness of the horizon beyond, putting on display the difference between the normative datum of the ground and the skewed orientation of Parent's oblique architecture. Through this relationship, the practicable exchanged its presumed role as museum scenography with the landscape outside, which appeared like a wallpaper in the background, filtered by the layers of architecture that separated it from the inside. It was, as such, a work of site-specific architecture, made interior by the envelope of the host building and temporary in duration as a function of the ephemeral nature of the exhibition.

VENICE (1970)

For the French Pavilion at the 1970 Venice Biennale, Parent used the practicable as an assertive element capable of transforming existing architecture, unfolding like a "phenomenon of cannibalization of one space by another."[12] Visitors to the pavilion—a 1912 structure designed by the Venetian engineer Fausto Finzi—first encountered the neoclassical building's elliptic front loggia framed by ionic columns, beyond which was the main entry with its threshold modified by a V-shaped wood structure.[13] This introductory reveal of the interior installation framed by the existing entrance appeared as a sign of the imminent shift underfoot—or an obstacle, as some critics remarked—as one moved from the outside in.[14] Inside, a floor consisting of two planes sloping up and away from one another took up half of the front gallery's depth, with a crease running along the center like the gutter of an open book. Upon negotiating the entry, visitors came upon a flat landing ahead of which the floor split again along the center, except here the pair of planes sloped toward the back rather than sideways. The left plane ascended, while the right one descended. Landing at two different levels,

Venice (1970)

Drawing sheet, dated May 5, 1970, documenting the third and final iteration of the design scheme for the Venice installation.

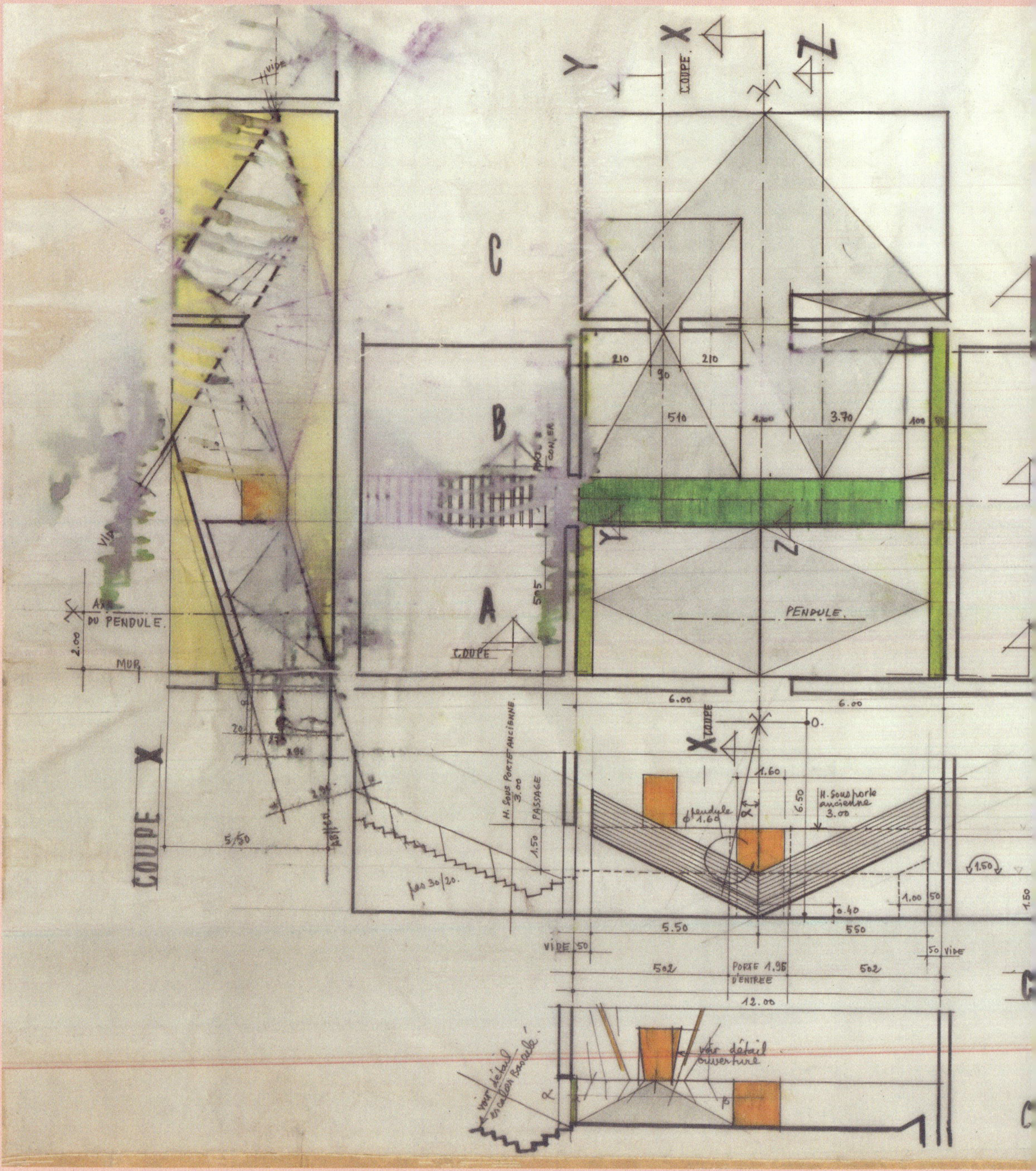

both ramps nonetheless ended up in the pavilion's back gallery where the built-up floor was also tilted. Visitors walked on slopes that ranged from fifteen to thirty degrees in steepness, without a strictly prescribed path. Smaller-scale built-ins jutted out of the sloped floor in some areas, creating places for perching, gathering, and resting. Such elements contributed to the installation's capacity to support both movement and stasis, in this way realizing one of the core tenets of the oblique function.[15] Additional

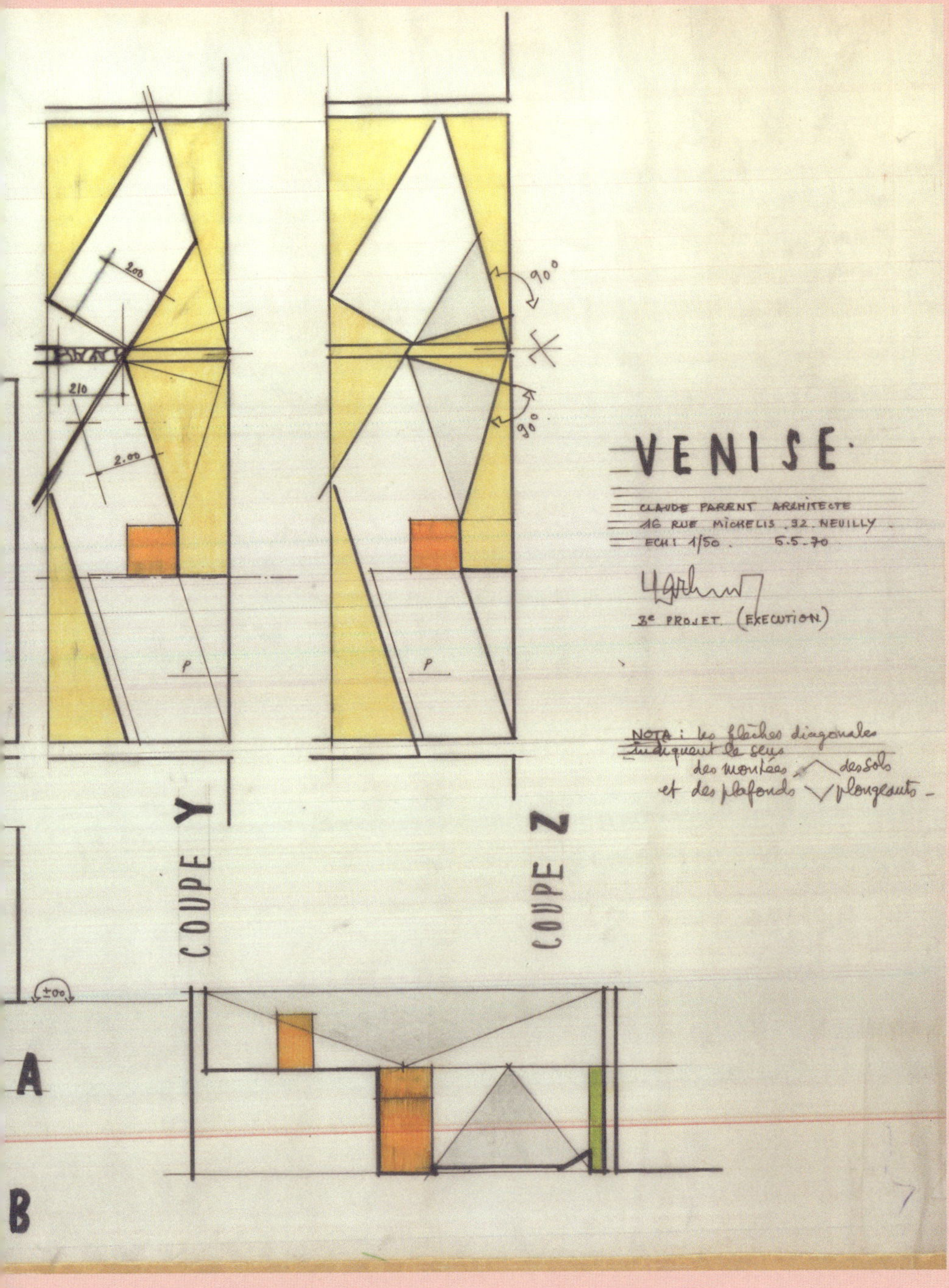

non-orthogonal surfaces concealed the existing brick wall separating the two galleries—and further blurred the visible distinction between horizontal and vertical surfaces—while similar geometries also defined the dropped ceiling throughout. The overhead construction further obscured the building shell, including the conventional shape of an oversized skylight, while also serving as a device for modulating daylight and integrating artificial lighting. Everything was made of wood, like formwork used for casting concrete or

Parent and his collaborators making a scaled model of the oblique installation for the Venice Biennale.

a piece of handmade furniture the size of two large rooms.

The interior reflected the aesthetic attributes of the scale models that Parent used to design it. The photographer Gilles Ehrmann documented the development of the installation from the early design studies to its final realization, capturing in his images a succession of working models, from volumetric studies of the overall form to larger mockups exploring the assembly of wood planks and framing.[16] Ehrmann's photographs also show Parent using an adjustable floor-mounted incline as a means of testing slopes of different angles, a full-scale tool that helped the design work in the studio approximate the results of on-site construction. In the most detailed parts of the models, as well as inside the French Pavilion, the design leveraged the capacity of standard wood members to articulate lines, planes, and volume in different ways, resulting in a diverse, if not idiosyncratic, range of surface effects, tessellation patterns, and edge conditions in spite of the overall material homogeneity. The direction of wood planks, for example, shifted from one part of the floor to another to create a patchwork of ruled patterns: In some places, the surface of the floor appeared to separate itself from the underlying structure, undermining the overall volumetric form, while in others, platform edges were cut in a zigzag pattern or left intentionally frayed rather than neatly trimmed. The wood object in this way produced an interior environment that was immersive, but not totalizing—an architectural insert as adjustable as it was assertive. This is because the Venice practicable was first and foremost a curatorial strategy, intended as an opening statement rather than the final word.

Study model of the installation scheme for the French Pavilion at the 1970 Venice Biennale.

Parent was appointed as the curator of the French Pavilion at a time of widespread debate over the international exhibition's legacy and boycotts linked to broader political conditions worldwide.[17] Such circumstances presented a mixture of opportunities and challenges for Parent, who assumed the role after others had allegedly refused it.[18] He was cognizant of his unusual position as a curator of an art exhibition (the 1970 biennale was primarily an art event, with the first Venice Biennale dedicated solely to architecture not launched until 1980), admitting that "an architect is not, in fact, prepared to choose artists according to qualitative criteria."[19] In lieu of a conventional selection of artists and artworks, Parent conceptualized the curation of the exhibition as a development of a creative action "closely linked to the notion of space."[20] He recalled presenting the wood model to a group of artists as the condition given by the architect, telling them: "Transform it as you wish, according to your sensibility. Work together,

Interior of the French Pavilion in Venice under construction. Structural framing at the front entrance is shown before it was covered by wood planks, with Parent in the background, left, and Gérard Mannoni, right.

one with the other, one against the other, appreciating or hating each other, in order to humanize this purely geometric form."[21] The design of the practicable was, in other words, the curatorial brief delivered in the form of an architectural object; a spatial framework for artists to respond to in relational and site-specific terms. The resulting exhibition, titled *La ligne de plus grande pente* (The Line of Greatest Slope), featured seven artists, some of whom Parent had worked with before, and others with whom he was collaborating for the first time. The group consisted of the sculptors Gérard Mannoni and Charles Maussion; the painters Andrée Bellaguet and Samuel Buri; the filmmaker and light artist François Morellet; and the photographers Jean-Pierre Cousin and Gilles Ehrmann.

How each artist contributed to the exhibition was an expression of their attitudes toward the proposed architecture and their willingness to collaborate with one another. Mannoni and Maussion took charge of the practicable's overall buildout, which was completed with the help of a local contractor.[22] For the ceiling above the V-shaped slopes at the entrance, Morellet made a large neon diagrid emanating a variable mixture of red, white, and blue light depending on how visitors interacted with it.[23] On the ascending ramp ahead, Mannoni placed a large sculpture made from the same unfinished wood as the rest of the installation, a bundle of carefully balanced protrusions at home in their oblique surroundings. Around the sculpture, Bellaguet painted a composition of white, red, and blue triangulated shapes, sympathetic to the geometry of Parent's architectural form, whose surface she used as a canvas. By obscuring the difference between three-dimensional edges formed by wood surfaces and those created with the change of applied color, Bellaguet's painting intensified the appearance

View of the Venice installation from the front entrance looking left toward the back, where Bellaguet's painted intervention reinforced the installation's angled geometries. Morellet's neon grid provided an ambient glow of colored light.

of the interior as a continuously faceted tessellation. To the left of the front gallery, within one of the two unused wings of the pavilion, Buri created an appendage to the oblique installation containing a dead-end staircase. He painted the side walls and plastered them with silk-screened prints of cows in a rainbow of colors; a decorative pattern was applied to the stairs in the style of kitschy carpeting or tile; and an array of illuminated frames completed the tunnel-like space so that it appeared like an immersive environment in its own right, a solo sideshow next to the collaborative group environment of the practicable. Cousin and Ehrmann's joint intervention was more subtle, as they installed a rarely mentioned and easy-to-miss pendulum from the ceiling, an ostensible reference to gravity as a key factor in the theory of the oblique function.[24] Distorting mirrored foil inserted between ramps and a stretched banner that reads *ESPACE PINCE* (PINCHED SPACE) in cutout letters, along with dozens of white balloons released inside of the pavilion, projected an air of a popular event rather than a highbrow affair.

View of the Venice installation with the front entrance in the background.

View of the Venice installation with changing colors of Morellet's neon ceiling grid, and balloons throughout.

View of the Venice installation, with Bellaguet's mirrored surface in the foreground, Mannoni's wood sculpture above, as well as the entry to Buri's stair intervention in the center and Morellet's neon ceiling grid in the upper left.

View of the Venice installation showing how angled surfaces blurred differences between floors, walls, and ceiling.

ESPACE

If the practicable's curatorial role was to prompt artistic response, its ultimate purpose—as an exhibition and an architectural experiment deployed in public—was to engage people. Much as its physical form was completed by the artists, so the installation was made to come to life as a social environment by those who visited it. The installation and its interactions with the existing shell, along with the artists' interventions, offered the public a stage-like setting in which everyone was both performer and audience. Likewise, in spite of its assertive geometry, the practicable was not an autonomous object whose form could be grasped or seen in its entirety but was instead to be discovered by moving through it. As an architectural intervention, it was as inseparable from the art it hosted as it was conditioned by its site. Its form was cropped by the existing architecture, like a small sample of an expansive territory of possibilities—the continuity of which would eventually no longer be constrained by conventional enclosures.[25] In this way, *La ligne de plus grande pente* was an experiment contained by the pavilion as an opaque petri dish.

In the absence of a substantial record of what it was like to be there as a visitor, Parent offered his own perspective. He recounted the pavilion's invasion by delighted schoolchildren and other repeat-visitors, noting people's irrepressible joy upon encountering the sloped interior.[26] Such reflections can perhaps only be taken as the architect's projected aspirations, rather than actual feedback, but they nonetheless elucidate Parent's optimistic attitude about the exhibition, which he referred to on one occasion as the first successfully realized oblique space.[27] One part of the success was the evolved integration of circulation and program—the oblique function's holy grail[28]—since the realization of both the church in Nevers and the Le Havre installation. The other part, however, may have stemmed from Parent's perception of joy and the oblique architecture's

People exploring the pavilion's "pinched spaces."

capacity to elicit it—a sense of confirmation of the public's interest in the proposition of life on the slope. The success of the project in Venice, in other words, was the perspective it gave on oblique architecture as a vehicle for the discovery of delight through physical in-the-moment engagement. Stripped of references to bunkers and crypts, the practicable offered an invitation rather than posing a threat; it had the disposition of a device that attracts rather than repels.[29]

Like in Le Havre, the pavilion was an experiment in that it enabled the architect to observe how people—set in motion by the slopes—inhabited, reacted to, and interacted with their surroundings. Rather than serving as a container for encountering other objects, the interior environment itself was the main event. Its intended takeaway was the sensing of oneself engaging the slope and having this experience in relation to other people. *La ligne de plus grande pente* was in this way interactive and socially engaging, and given everyone involved in its creative realization, the project was also collaborative. Outside of the French Pavilion, various notions of participation permeated the biennale as a whole. A significant portion of its main exhibition, titled *Proposal for an Experimental Exhibition*, for example, was dedicated to participatory artistic practices, where hands-on opportunities, such as the lithography workshop offered at the American Pavilion, were also available to the public.[30] While not out of place in this context, Parent's exhibition had not yet incorporated similar types of scheduled programs and activities that later became an integral participatory aspect of the tour.

As a curatorial assignment and an opportunity to further test the oblique function, the exhibition continued to be reexhibited afterward through other media, having been extensively photographed and filmed by Parent's main documentarian in Venice, Gilles Ehrmann. The exhibition served as a precedent for Parent's further public explorations of oblique architecture, and it gave credibility to similar experiments that followed back in France.[31] Later that same year, Parent self-published *Vivre à l'oblique*, in which he refers to the installation at the Venice Biennale as "embryonic" and "a seed that will open up a whole world."[32]

NEVERS (1971)

After his post-Venice appearances at the houses of culture in Saint-Étienne and Rennes, and an unsuccessful attempt to build a practicable in Rouen, Parent spent the summer of 1971 involved in a series of interrelated public programs in Nevers, which included the construction of a new oblique installation. The occasion marked Parent's return to the provincial city in central France where five years earlier he completed, in collaboration with Virilio, the Church of St. Bernadette of Banlay. Hosted by the newly opened Maison de la culture de Nevers et de la Nièvre, the programs centered around the exhibition *Architecture Oblique* (Oblique Architecture) and included seminar-style lectures, film screenings, as well as architect-guided evening visits to the church.[33] Such a range of programs was typical for the tour as it later also landed in other cities, in part reflecting the involvement of André Barey as a coproducer starting in 1971. Parent was proud of the attendance in Nevers; even at the height of summer holidays, each of his lectures had an average of eighty participants.[34]

Nevers (1971)

View of the Nevers practicable from the top of the slope toward the bottom.

As an exhibition sideshow, the oblique practicable occupied the northeast side of the cultural center's multistory foyer and was wedged between an orthogonal party wall and the curved volume of the main theater. The general direction of its incline led people from the street-facing foyer toward the back, where they landed one level above the existing floor. The ramped installation consisted of two adjacent paths, intertwined and touching at a common landing, like two abstracted bodies reclining side by side. In addition to incorporating prerequisite oblique geometries, its overall form also responded to existing building conditions. The gently curved split down the middle of the structure, for instance, was the result of a metal railing demarcating the edge of an opening in the foyer's floor to the level below. One half of the practicable was built over this void, dipping down to a low landing before its ascent to the top. The other half, with a longer and wider ramp of a gentler slope, was tailored to fit around an existing stair, its contours echoing the non-orthogonal orientation of the theater next to it. A structure rigged from standard scaffolding supported the entire assembly of sloped wood-plank platforms and landings and also doubled as new railings along the perimeter. The entire wood surface was painted in a composition of black, yellow, and white shapes in dialog with the practicable's geometry. Designed by Andrée Bellaguet, who similarly contributed to the installation in Venice, the abstract painting revealed itself gradually for those walking on it or could be seen in its entirety from the foyer's mezzanine level, like an enormous obliquely shaped canvas facing the skylighted ceiling above.

hildren lingering along the Nevers practicable.

Overall view of the Nevers practicable from above, with furnishings and a TV.

The Nevers practicable was made from simple reusable materials by the cultural center's technical staff.

Side view of the Nevers practicable, with people walking on it.

Bellaguet's color composition painted on the practicable using nonslip paint.

While the installations in Le Havre and Venice were physically embedded within larger exhibitions and provided necessary circulatory paths through them, the Nevers practicable had more autonomy in both function and placement. Neither a scenography nor the main part of the curatorial strategy, it was installed in an area adjacent to the exhibition but without immediate physical or visual interaction with it. Rather than providing a path toward or through something else—the raked platforms dead-ended into the foyer's back wall—the installation was a destination of its own, offering a combination of diagonal movement and rest in a space that programmatically resembled something of a lounge. Contributing to the lounge-like quality was the unusual presence of furniture throughout, including multiple sections of sofa-style seating, movable stools, and a TV. The placement of these objects was antithetical to Parent's attitude toward furniture, as expressed in *Vivre à l'oblique* and elsewhere, as well as redundant given the flexibility with which oblique surfaces could, in theory, account for a range of ergonomic needs.[35] Yet their presence is less contradictory if it is considered as a legible marker of habitation, an attempt to publicly present the oblique floor not only as an itinerant space of circulation but also as a surface where all of life's activities could take place. Furnished like a living room, the Nevers practicable effectively put leisure, an essential part of middle-class existence, on a slant, an effort that reflected the aspiration of the oblique function to ubiquitously merge circulation with program both at home and out in public.

The installation's conceptual ambition was paired with a modesty of execution and an ad hoc sensibility. The existing building interior informed the design as much as available means and methods impacted its realization, reflecting in this way the practicable's—and through it the architect's—adaptability to given conditions. Despite the clearly stated distinction between the work of the architect who designed it and the in-house technical staff who built it, the site-specific installation appeared as if its overall geometry was determined directly in the field rather than first having been drawn on paper, an intervention shaped through mutual collaboration rather than compartmentalized authorship.[36] The assembly of metal pipes and roughly cut wood planks—a reusable kit of parts borrowed from construction scaffolding—yielded a seemingly makeshift structure, a quickly erected spatial experiment whose improvised qualities bypassed the usual precision and refinement of architectural projects and formal exhibitions alike.[37] The presence of a handwritten sign, containing the title, authorship credits, and dates pinned to a portable easel, underscored the informality of the whole production. Such aesthetics reflected limited material resources but also imbued the oblique installation with a sense of possibility offered by the present moment. Instead of conveying an image of a distant future, the practicable served as a prompt for taking possession of public space through immediate engagement. As such, it presented a quotidian possibility rather than an unattainable, utopian dream—an architectural realization no less real than Architecture Principe's concrete church two kilometers north.[38]

The juxtaposition of the church and the practicable in the same city demonstrated a shift in Parent's approach to the development of the oblique function since his days of collaboration with Virilio. The two works reveal a number of striking contrasts when considered side by side. One is made from heavy cast-in-place concrete, the other from

Invitation to Parent's lectures in Nevers, the content of which later became the book *5 réflexions sur l'architecture.*

la maison de la culture de nevers et la nièvre vous invite à assister à :

5

cinq réflexions sur l'architecture par claude parent les 8, 9, 10, 11 et 12 juin à 18 h 30 salle des réunions

boulevard pierre de coubertin - tél. 61-52-46 - entrée libre
exposition ouverte tous les jours de 11 h à 22 h, sauf le lundi

materials used for construction formwork and reusable scaffolding; one is thus permanent, the other temporary. The church serves as an instrument for preestablished rituals, while the practicable invited improvisation. One emerged monumentally on a vacant lot at the outer edges of Nevers, the other unassumingly embedded itself within another building. If the bunker aesthetic of St. Bernadette was meant to repel, the purpose of the practicable's informal aesthetic was to attract people.[39] If the presumed disconnect between people and architecture served as a prompt for Architecture Principe's theoretical explorations, then Parent's return to Nevers provided another opportunity for exploring how to mend the situation through a more direct, bottom-up approach. The practicable was thus a device for connecting with people, part of a larger suite of programs designed to introduce Parent's ideas about the future of architecture, urbanism, and life at large to general audiences. Speaking to local press at that time and clearly conscious of his reputation, Parent declared: "I am not an avant-garde architect."[40] In this light, the practicable was also, decidedly, not a work of avant-garde architecture. On the contrary, building it with little more than some scaffolding, wood planks, and paint convincingly placed it, despite its unconventional form, into the realm of the ordinary.

By organizing direct encounters with locals, Parent made himself available in ways that reflected his interest in bringing architecture, and the figure of the architect, closer to people and their daily lives. The social aspect of the Nevers repertoire—which included secular, architect-led Friday-night church visits as well as weekly film screenings[41]—was echoed in *5 réflexions sur l'architecture*, the published result of a five-part seminar that Parent conducted there in June of 1971. The introduction states: "This is the path that architecture must take if it is to exist, rather than through schools: the path of concrete dialogue between architecture and those for whom it is created."[42] This proposal was in effect an appeal for an alternative mode of architectural education based on experimental public participation rather than conventional disciplinary training.[43] If at its origin the rhetoric of the oblique function lamented the disconnect between people and architecture, in this context the aim was to forge new connections outside of the rarified milieu of elite institutions—in line with the state cultural centers' ambitions to be perceived as inclusive places open to everyone.

AMIENS (1972–1973)

Parent's retrospective exhibition of oblique architecture and the accompanying bill of public events traveled south to Toulouse in early 1972 and then to the northeast of France where it was on view at the Maison de la culture de Reims throughout the month of April.[44] Despite its otherwise complete programmatic assortment—talks, film screenings, and other iterations of previously rehearsed offerings from Nevers and elsewhere—neither of these stops along the oblique tour yielded designs for a practicable. The next one would appear at the Maison de la culture d'Amiens at the end of that year, remaining in use throughout the spring of 1973 as a part of the program titled *Cadre de vie: L'architecture oblique*, where *Cadre de vie* roughly translates into English as "Living Environment."[45]

Located in northern France, the city of Amiens is perhaps best known for its Gothic cathedral, the subject of John Ruskin's 1885 *The Bible of Amiens*. While the cathedral itself was not bombed during World War II, other parts of the city suffered significant damage. The cultural center was built in 1965 according to a design by the architect Pierre Sonrel, as part of the final stages of postwar reconstruction.[46] Although chronologically the Maison de la culture d'Amiens opened after those in Le Havre, Caen, and Bourges, it was the first venue designed from the outset specifically for the purpose of fulfilling—and concretely representing through its architecture—the objectives of Malraux's program. The original building had a square footprint divided into four structural bays on each side and was two stories in height, except for the taller vertical volume of the fly tower along its southern edge.[47] The internal volumetric arrangement of its program initially dictated by the Ministry of Culture guidelines—including two enclosed auditoriums, a cinema, exhibition spaces, workshops, meeting rooms as well as, at the time, a library, a discotheque, and TV and reading rooms—broke away, in some places, from the orthogonal geometry of the exterior.[48] Such a layout resulted in a sequence of irregularly shaped interior spaces connected to one another in different ways horizontally and vertically, such as the double-height entry foyer on the ground floor and the open bar area adjacent to theater entrances at the upper level.

Parent's large practicable was installed in the space between the front façade and the enclosure of the large theater on the second floor, overlooking on one side the foyer below. Not unlike the oblique installations before it, the design of the Amiens practicable responded to the architecture that contained it. The oblique form demonstrated compliance with the geometry of the existing interior by aligning with it as well as echoing it in certain places.[49] Its polygonal shape in plan, for example, was produced by tracing the existing boundaries adjacent to it, while its flat landing was precisely centered on the solid segment of the exterior wall between two large glazed openings facing the city, effectively dividing the practicable

Amiens (1972–1973)

Drawing sheet, dated September 29, 1972, documenting the final design scheme for the Amiens practicable.

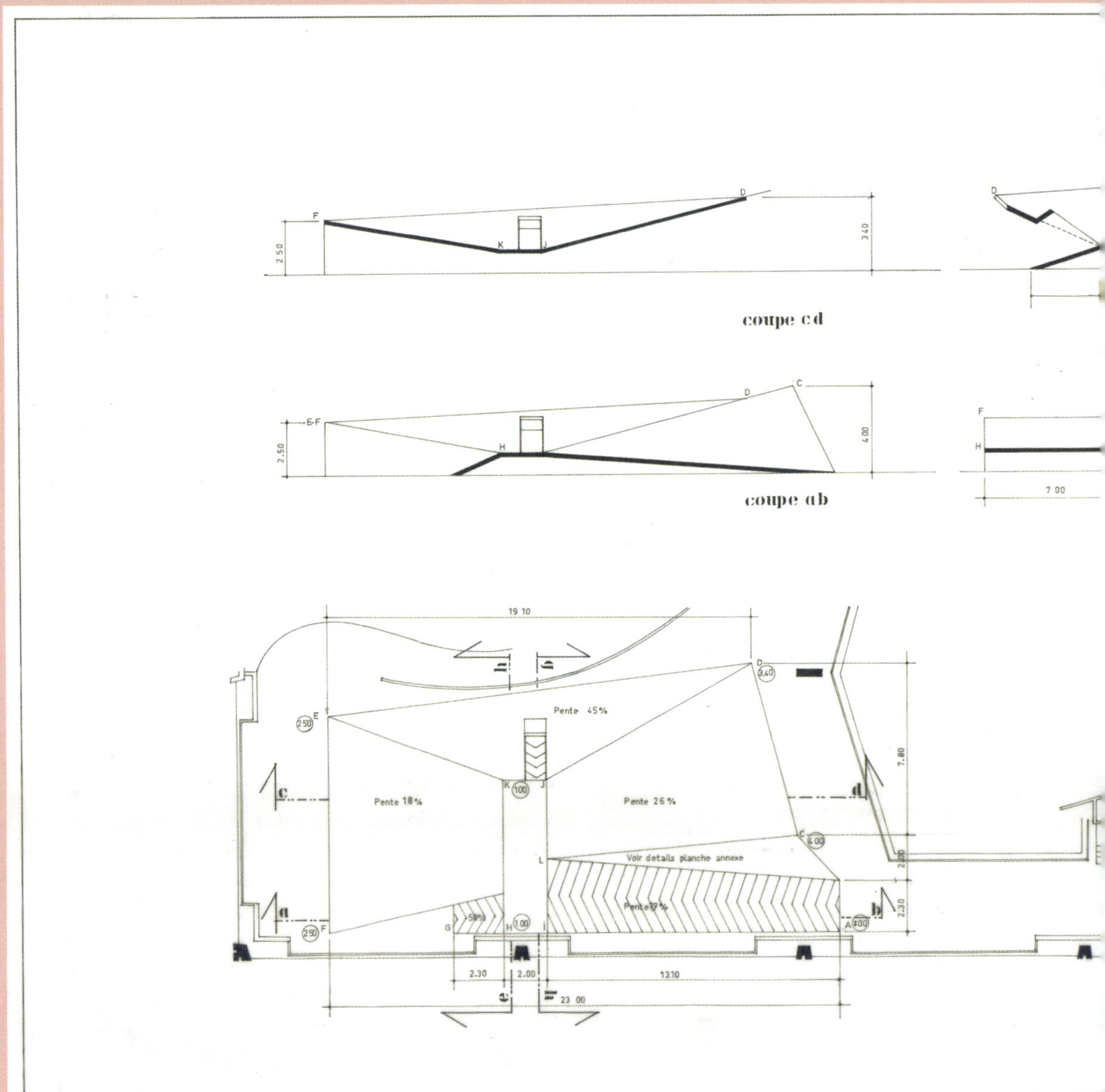

into a framed diptych when viewed from outside. Parent referred to this space as a balcony overlooking the city.[50]

As an evolving exploration of the oblique function, the installation further advanced the use of the inclined plane as a tool for synthesizing program and circulation, offering possible uses beyond those afforded by earlier practicables. The sloped platforms needed little accessorizing; they were both *immeuble* and *meuble*, equally building and furniture. People didn't simply surf along from one place to another; they gathered on it. Such a concentration of activity was in part enabled by the amphitheater-like configuration. Radiating from the single flat landing at the center was a series of interconnected sloped surfaces, some of which connected the existing floor level to the landing above, while others ascended from the

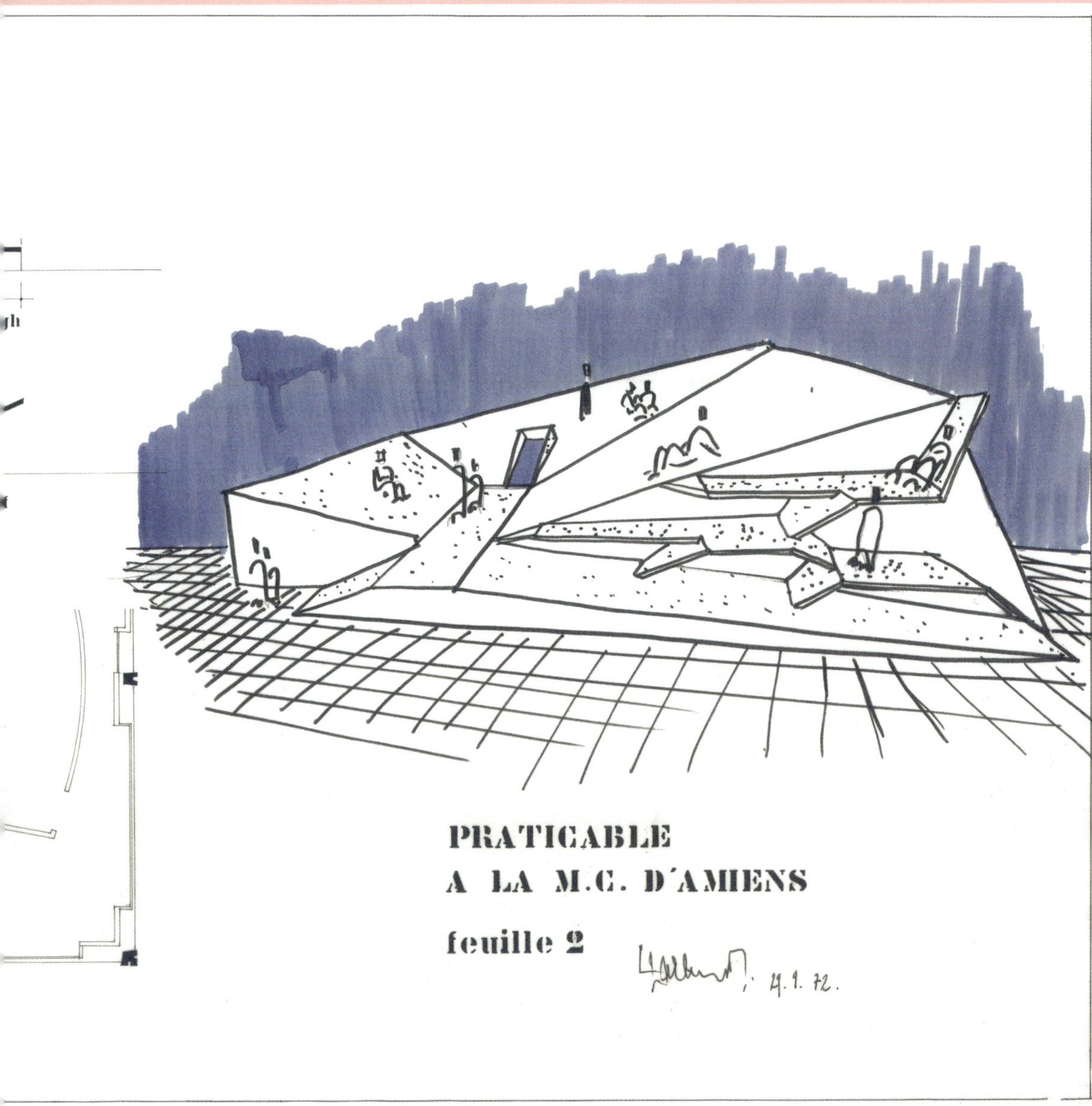

landing up, enveloping it on three sides like raked seating surrounding a stage. Forming a faceted half-funnel, these three slopes—angled at ten, fifteen, and twenty-five degrees respectively—accounted for most of the installation's floor area and provided abundant room flexible enough to accommodate both scheduled events and informal socialization. A secondary network of landings and ramps in the configuration of a branching structure—like a practicable within a practicable[51]—was attached to one of the other sloped surfaces, its proportions suited to individual bodies and inclines steeper than fifty degrees. Like in Nevers, the Amiens practicable was modestly constructed from off-the-shelf metal scaffolding and cut-to-measure wood planks, its surface likewise painted using nonslip paint according to another design conceived by Andrée Bellaguet.[52] A composition of subtly differentiated analogous shades of red and orange, with smaller elements painted in dark gray and muted yellow, imbued the interior topography with a luxuriously incandescent glow. In contrast, the practicable's underside—accessible to the public and used as part of the program rather than utility storage, as was the case in Venice and Nevers—remained unfinished, an assembly of metal posts, cross-bracing, and exposed framing, like the verso of a painting. All aspects of the installation were publicly accessible and on full display, including its ongoing construction during the first weeks of Parent's residency at the cultural center.[53] People could see how the work progressed through the large glass façade openings framing the installation, as if it were a performance in its own right. Parent was particularly captivated by the practicable's incrementally changing appearance, from its initial raw wood state to it being painted according to Bellaguet's design and, finally, to it having art installed around it.[54]

The practicable could be used whether there was a special event happening or not. Photographs show groups of schoolchildren congregating on it, and Parent recalled visually impaired people successfully navigating the slopes, an anecdote which he took as evidence of the intuitive and tactile, rather than visual, nature of oblique inhabitation.[55] At peak times, according to Parent's writing, attendance reached the full capacity of

Exterior view of the Maison de la culture d'Amiens, with the practicable visible inside.

four hundred people.[56] The exhibition of project photographs and models, speculative drawings, a projection of hundreds of slides as well as several films, including Eric Rohmer's *Le Béton*, were shown in a separate space. Between November and January, Parent delivered five talks with titles not unlike those in Nevers, except that in Amiens the presentations also included other presenters. André Barey's role in these productions became increasingly more visible as both public speaker and author of texts that appeared in the cultural center's monthly magazine *Mobile* and elsewhere. The architect's sister, Nicole Parent, performed her gymnastics routine called *Inclipan*, developed as a method of working on an oblique floor and documented in her book of the same name published that year.[57] Also among the participants was Francoise Séjourné, a public health expert with whom Parent and Barey worked, as well as Bellaguet who, in addition to being an artistic collaborator, was also a client as the first person living in a home designed according the principles of the oblique function.[58]

Bellaguet's multifaceted role as a collaborator was reflected in the curated program. In addition to designing the color composition painted on the practicable, her series of paintings titled *Profils*—produced while living and working in her Parent-designed oblique apartment—surrounded the installation. Six of these paintings were hung along the curved wall enclosing the adjacent auditorium and another five suspended from the ceiling in the perpendicular direction by the side window.[59] Bringing together the paintings, the practicable, and the artist herself served, in a sense, as a reconstruction of the intimacy of the private apartment—within the interior of the *maison de la culture*—for the purpose of public demonstration. Press articles covering Bellaguet's participation, including thise appearing in the cultural center's magazine, were as interested in the art as they were in learning how the oblique architecture of her apartment inspired her daily life. The opening of Bellaguet's exhibition occurred in late January of 1973, accompanied by the installation of a sculpture by Gérard Mannoni on the practicable (he was a collaborator

The Amiens practicable used as a conversion pit for a public program, c. winter 1972–73.

The Amiens practicable framed by oversized openings in the building façade.

Invitation to Andrée Bellaguet's exhibition of paintings, part of a series of programs engaging the practicable.

Public programming taking place on the Amiens practicable, with Bellaguet's paintings mounted along the perimeter.

already known from Venice), as well as by various thematically related discussions and other forms of entertainment, such as performances of Andean music by the group Los Pachayachachic that took place *dans le cadre de l'espace expérimental* (as part of the experimental space).[60] While Parent continued showing Bellaguet's apartment as an example of an oblique living environment over the years, this turned out to be, after Venice and Nevers, the artist's final appearance on the oblique tour.[61]

According to the variously published posters and event schedules, these January events were intended to mark the culmination of Parent's work in Amiens, but the practicable nevertheless remained in place for an additional month, serving as a setting for an exhibition of paintings by the Chilean surrealist artist Roberto Matta (whose son Gordon Matta-Clark's architecture-focused work was also gaining prominence around that time).[62] The intricate world of distorted figures, structures, and landscapes in Matta's large canvases contrasted with the nearly monochromatic surfaces of Parent's temporary architecture. Unlike Bellaguet's *Profils*, however, which shared with Parent's installation a like-minded formal language but were relatively independent from it in terms of how they were installed in the space, Matta's paintings were mounted in such a way that their arrangement responded to the form of the oblique environment. Photographs of the installation show paintings suspended from the ceiling at irregular angles; and a group of paintings were installed in such a way as to appear like a continuous surface, not unlike the practicable beneath them, unfolding in different directions. In addition to canvases hovering on and

Interior view of the practicable during a public event in January 1973.

above the installation, there were also those that were placed underneath it, drawing one's attention to the practicable's underbelly. Thanks to such placement of the artwork, Matta's large paintings and Parent's painted platforms worked well together both visually and spatially.

The artistic programming in Amiens was matched by activities pursued by working groups whose task was to explore questions raised by Parent's programs beyond the duration of the curated events. The cultural center in part framed *Cadre de vie: L'architecture oblique* in relation to questions of freedom and choice in the lived environment, continuing a program that in the previous season featured exhibitions about urban streets.[63] Consisting of Amiens residents, including, for example, students from a nearby technical university, the loosely organized groups were to be formed with the idea that curated cultural programs would instigate longer-term engagement among local populations.[64] The range of activities related to Parent's residency at the cultural center—installations, exhibitions, performances, discussions, demonstrations, debates, projections, and so on—reflected the programmatically diverse nature of *maisons de la culture* as defined by their original mission, with the added duty to also address the institution's evolving need to be more approachable than it may have been in its earlier years. In this way, the practicable may be seen as an informal theater facing the city, an alternative to the two other enclosed auditoriums in the building. On this oblique stage, different creative endeavors were able to mix with one another as could visiting

Matta's paintings above the practicable, with the artist below, left.

Matta, left, and Parent, right, in conversation while being filmed.

Matta's paintings surrounding the practicable.

Foldable brochure, with schedule of events related to Parent's residency in Amiens printed on the outside. On the inside, a drawing by Parent, with a written reflection on architecture's relationship to earth, vegetation, and the sea.

Multipage booklet with essays, inserted into the red foldable sleeve.

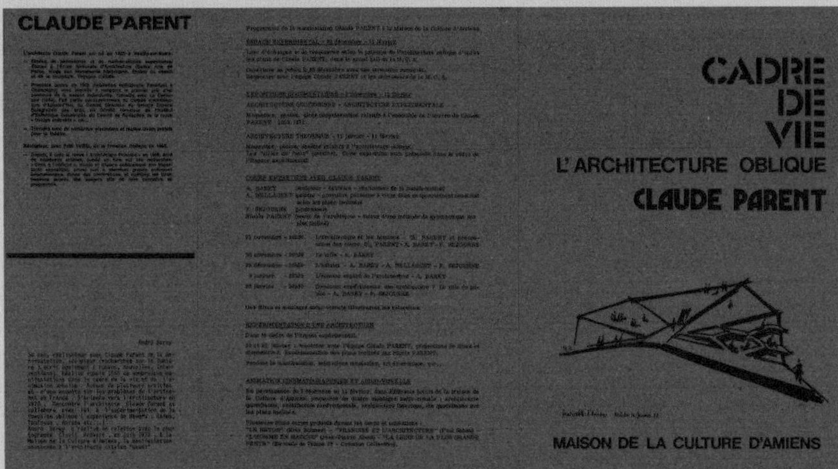

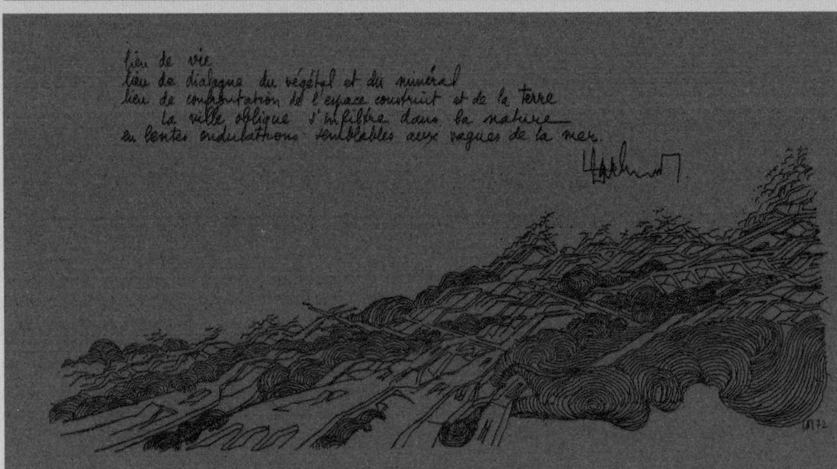

artists and local audiences by virtue of occupying the same structure.

In terms of both architecture and overall programming, the work produced during Parent's nearly four-month residency in Amiens—including all that happened on, around, and under it—was emblematic of the tour of France, not only because it was best documented (and thus best known), but also because of the production's overall scope and resolution.[65] It was the tour's peak, which Parent wished could have been sustained longer as an experiment, and stands out as a breakthrough in Parent's grasp of the power of an architectural experiment—even if his search for an effective research methodology was far from complete.[66]

Invitation to the exhibition of paintings by Roberto Matta taking place between February 15 and Mach 11, 1973.

MAISON DE LA CULTURE D'AMIENS

Dans le « Praticable oblique » de Claude PARENT,
« L'Espace de l'Espèce » polyptyque 1959/1967
« Grimau - Les puissances du Désordre » (3 m×10 m) 1964/1965
« Watchman what of the night » (3 m×10 m) 1968
de MATTA

à la Maison de la Culture d'Amiens, place Léon-Gontier
du 15 février au 11 mars 1973

Rencontre avec *MATTA* et *Claude PARENT*
jeudi 15 février à 18 h 30

Trains :
Gare du Nord
D. 17h05 A. 18h05
Amiens
D. 20h41 A. 21h50
21h20 22h27

MÂCON (1973)

Following his extensive engagement in Amiens, Parent's next stop was Mâcon in Burgundy. His exhibition at the municipal library opened on February 3, 1973, the first of several activities he pursued there throughout the spring of that year. On the opening night, he gave two public talks accompanied by a projected slideshow, or *le mur d'images* (the wall of images) as the press called it, the exhibition's key element. Consistent with the overarching ambition to instigate public participation at the local level, the opening also marked the establishment of work groups for further explorations of the exhibition content and to address broader questions related to architecture and urbanism. The idea was, not unlike in Amiens, that Mâcon residents would work together in these groups throughout the duration of the show, eventually reconvening with the architect to share their insights upon his return to the city a month later.[67]

During this era, the city's administration projected a decidedly non-elitist image of Mâcon, prioritizing the wellbeing of its working-class residents as its population approached nearly forty thousand people, the largest count even compared to today. At the time, Mâcon had already been governed for two decades by Louis Escande, the socialist mayor after whom the city's main cultural center was later named. The municipal monthly magazine regularly featured Mâcon's various accomplishments in the realm of new public facilities, services, and programs. In 1970, for example, it touted the near-completion of more than six hundred units of public housing in the new Gautriats neighborhood.[68] At the start of the municipal library's construction in 1968, the same publication referred to the project as their city's own version of the *maison de la culture*, a snide reference to the state's Malraux-era initiative, implying that Mâcon chose combating illiteracy over promoting high art as a matter of national culture.[69] Instead of a *maison de la culture*, the city chose to build the Centre d'animation culturel financed by the municipality, presumably with a more inclusive program in line with the city's already existing cultural endeavors. The building, designed by the architect Robert Levasseur, broke ground in 1971 and was completed two years after Parent's visit to the city.[70]

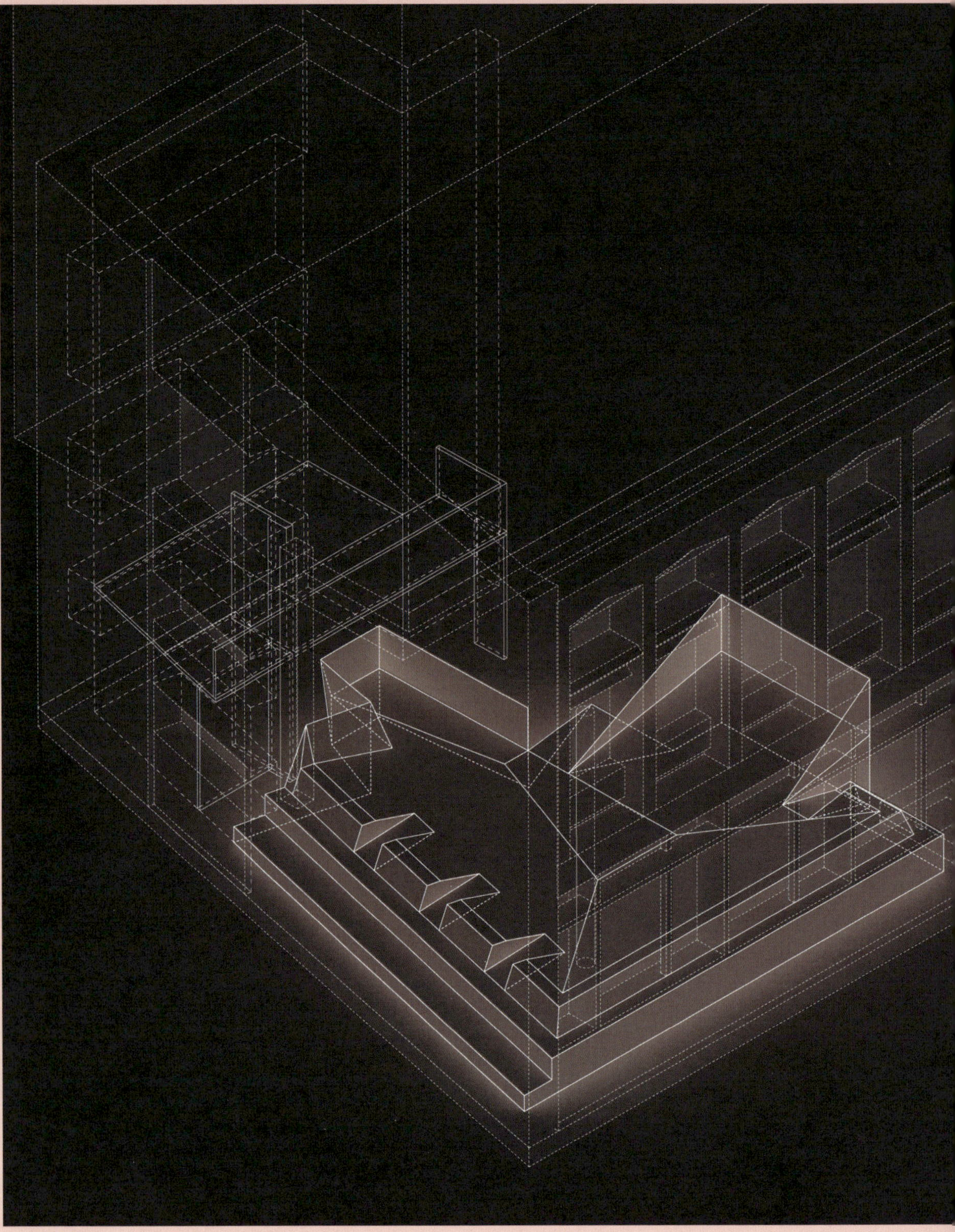

Mâcon (1973)

0 1 2 4

Article from the newspaper *Le-Progrès* from May 20, 1973, reporting on the staged debate about oblique architecture in Mâcon, in the presence of numerous artists.

MACON

Débat sur l'architecture oblique en présence de nombreux artistes du C.R.E.P.S.

La semaine d'animation sur l'architecture oblique se termiuait samedi au C.R.E.P.S. par un grand débat sur le thème de cette nouvelle conception. De nombreuses personnalités avaient été invitées par M. Chalosse directeur de l'action culturelle : notons MM. Claude Parent architecte et instigateur de la conception oblique, André Barey, Michel Parent, inspecteur des monuments historiques Samuel Bur, peintre participant à la biennale de Venise, Nicole Parent créatrice de l'inclipan, Alain Hullot mime, Michel Humbert directeur du théâtre de Bourgogne, Maxime Decombin, de nombdeux animateurs culturels de la région.

L'après-midi débuta par une démonstration de Nicole Parent sur l'inclipan. Directrice d'une école de gymnastique celle-ci montra les mouvements qu'il est possible de faire sur un plan incliné. « Le corps prend, dit-elle une autre dimension il devient un moteur, On ne subit pas une telle gymnastique on la vit » ; le mime Alain Hullot, parla ensuite de l'intégration du spectateur dans le lieu théâtral. Il faut selon lui supprimer la scène. Ceci inviterait le public à participer pleinement au jeu des acteurs.

L'assistance se rendit à la salle de projection où un film sur le pavillon français à la biennale de Venise fut présenté. La réalisation de Claude Parent et des artistes qui participèrent n'a aucune fonction. Elle est seulement provoquante et la réaction du public fut selon l'architecte très intéressante.

Après cette projection Michel Parent s'explique « je m'intéresse au passé, dit-il, dans la mesure où il m'éclaire sur l'avenir. Il st nécessaire de rompre avec le passé le plus récent et de mettre en question l'ensemble de nos conceptions architecturales. Nous arrivons au bout du rouleau et il va fallol trouver autre chose ».

Autour de ces différents sujets la discussion s'anima mais elle fut surtout entretenue par les initiés et le public eut sans doute à certains moments du mal à suivre.

Les exposés de Claude Parent se terminent donc et l'on ne peut que souhaiter un prolongement mâconnais à ses idées. Cela permettrait de juger sur pièce.

The city's politics and the administration's approach to urbanization and public infrastructure formed the backdrop against which Parent's work in Mâcon unfolded. Such factors help explain the variety and multivenue organization of the programs that he and Barey produced throughout the city. They also provide some context for understanding the specific siting of the proposed practicable. Given the availability of public facilities and based on feedback from locals, Parent used the children's reading room at the municipal library as a site for which a practicable was designed.[71] In his narrative recollections of the tour, as well as in photographs, children frequently—usually full of delight—appeared on the practicables, yet this was the first instance where an oblique installation would be designed specifically for them. It was also the first time that a practicable was conceived not in relation to exhibitions or performances but rather in order to fulfill a distinct programmatic use. The only remaining record of the design is a set of photographs documenting Parent's three-dimensional model of the proposed scheme. Yet its overall geometry and references to the existing structure, such as column locations and the shape of the building footprint, provide enough detail to accurately situate the design within the larger municipal complex, which, in addition to the library, also included archives for the entire Saône-et-Loire department.

Partial model of the Mâcon municipal library's existing building façade, with the practicable behind it.

Mâcon practicable model, top view.

Built in 1970, the complex consists of a large low-rise Z-shaped base and a tall tower containing the archives emerging from it.[72] Compared to the exterior's monumental presence, Parent's proposed interior intervention appeared like a tiny jewel nested within it.

Although Parent's site for the practicable—a ground-floor room in the shape of a trapezoid—was modest in size, it had a ceiling generous enough in height to accommodate a mezzanine, making it suitable for raising and sloping the floor. The proposed practicable's center landing was elevated about half a meter from the existing level. The entrance ramp, leading from the interior lobby and sloping up to the landing, ramped up at about seventeen degrees, while the surrounding slopes made for seating were angled up from it at approximately eleven degrees. The result is a funneled, amphitheater-like configuration, designed to encourage gathering, which recalled the form of the Amiens practicable but was smaller in size. The height of existing windowsills along the main glazed wall made it difficult for children to see out; Parent's scheme was an improvement to the original architecture by providing an incline toward the level of the window and an uninterrupted view of the outdoors. On the two sides adjacent to the exterior, Parent provided a narrow gap between the practicable and the existing walls, a reveal wide enough for a child to comfortably sit facing away from the center of the room, and toward the windows, for a more solitary experience.

This scheme was among the most specifically fitted practicables in relation to the building envelope as well as in function, where static inhabitation was prioritized over circulation. It is not certain whether the installation was to be a temporary experiment or permanent alternative to the child-sized Alvar Aalto chairs and tables that instead populated the reading room. In any case, it was designed to function as a room-sized built-in fabrication whose affordances were to make all other furniture obsolete. From an ergonomic standpoint, the practicable

Maĉon practicable model, side view.

Maĉon model with cutout scale figures, and a sketch in the background.

View of the Maĉon model showing the sloped entrance to the children's reading room.

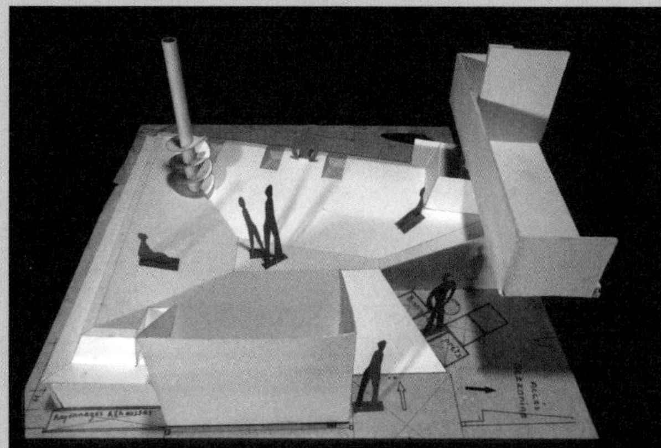

Photograph of the children's reading room, in Maĉon, as it existed.

Promotional material for Maĉon's municipal library, showing an image of the children's reading room and provocatively declaring it "neither a temple of culture nor a drugstore."

proposed a range of informal postures—possibly inspired by the enthusiasm with which children appropriated the other sloped installations—which challenged the conventional behaviors, reinforced by typical furniture of a standard learning environment. The design of this practicable was unfortunately never realized, and with that the potential of oblique architecture in Mâcon could only be explored in other, less direct, ways.

A series of public programs under the title *Architecture du possible: L'oblique* (Architecture of the Possible: The Oblique) took place across various venues in Mâcon from May 14 to 19, 1973. In the Gautriats quarter, André Barey conducted evening craft workshops as well as an event featuring the Greek-born artist Costas Coulentianos, whose triangulated sculptures cast in metal are reminiscent of Parent's own formal predispositions. At night, images related to oblique architecture were projected outdoors throughout the neighborhood, animating the repetitive pattern of midrise apartment buildings and their prefabricated concrete façades. These events were part of longer-term efforts by the city administration to provide the residents of the newly constructed public housing development with a range of weekly artistic and socially engaged programs. In this way, rather than strictly adhering to the tenets of oblique architecture, these workshops, discussions, and presentations engaged people's relationship to their broader living environment. Another example of such engagement was the encounter that Barey organized as a part of the weeklong program with students and faculty from the nearby nursing school to explore connections between urbanism and health.

The week culminated with events at the regional physical education center (CREPS–Centre regional d'éducation physique et sportive), starting with a Friday night conversation between Barey and Parent. Afterward, the projection of film footage and slides shot in Venice and Amiens enabled the practicables from those cities to appear virtually in Mâcon, as if to compensate for not having one built there for the event. The following day, Parent and Barey were joined by a whole cast of participants for the final public presentation. The program opened with another version of Nicole Parent's gymnastics routine, this time performed on a portable stage inclined at forty-two degrees, with its athleticism registering as a nod to the hosting sports venue. The mime artist Alain Hullot also participated, offering another perspective on engaging oblique architecture through the lens of performance. His presentation included a preview of a program he was developing for Parent's upcoming deployment of a practicable in Douai later that year.[73] If the inclusion of such art forms appears frivolous at first, it is worth pointing out that the dissolution of physical boundaries between the performer and the audience specific to mime routines is not entirely unlike the removal of barriers that Parent pursued between the architect and the public. The discussion that followed included other frequent collaborators, friends, and relatives of the architect as well as regional and municipal cultural administrators, artists, artisans, and members of the working groups. Among them, according to the press, were the Swiss artist Samuel Buri, who took part in the 1970 Venice Biennale; Michel Parent, inspector general of historic monuments from the Ministry of Culture; the art and architecture critic Marc Gaillard; director of the Théâtre de Bourgogne Michel Humbert; the sculptor Maxime Descombin, and others. Local newspapers reporting on the event described Parent as a prophetic figure with the desire to communicate with as many people as possible, while the long discussion was deemed animated and provocative but at times hard for the general audience to follow.[74] The sum of these programs nevertheless leaned into the participatory formats that encouraged people to come out and partake in shared activities.

It is difficult to speculate upon the impact that Parent's program may have ultimately had on Mâcon. Perhaps its value was in its demonstration of architecture's capacity to prompt a public reimagining of reality. From today's perspective, the further the discussion or activity veered away from the literal implications of life on inclined surfaces, the more convincing it becomes that the oblique function was an open-ended provocation rather than a finite solution.

DOUAI (1973)

In September of 1973, Parent brought the traveling exhibition to Douai, a city in northern France near Lille. His work was presented by the *maison de la culture* housed within Douai's city hall. This is also where the exhibition was mounted, while the site for the practicable was Place d'Armes, the main public square a block away.[75] This placement distinguished the Douai practicable as the only one in the series designed to be entirely outdoors. The installation expanded the public institution's footprint by using the outdoor plaza as its extension—like an interior space defined by a floor rather than walls.

Various design drawings show the practicable's overall form as a faceted sectional profile composed of straight segments extruded horizontally to create a platform six meters in depth. A narrow landing elevated no more than a meter off the ground was the only entirely level part of the installation, while on each side of it the floor sloped up at different angles. The resulting asymmetrical arrangement—a steeper and longer incline vis-à-vis a shallower and more gently sloped one—recalls the traditional theatrical arrangement of raked seating facing the stage, even if the practicable's actual use was far less formal in how performers and the audience related to one another. Drawings and models of the project include a railing-height wall along one side of the platform, which appears to be omitted from the

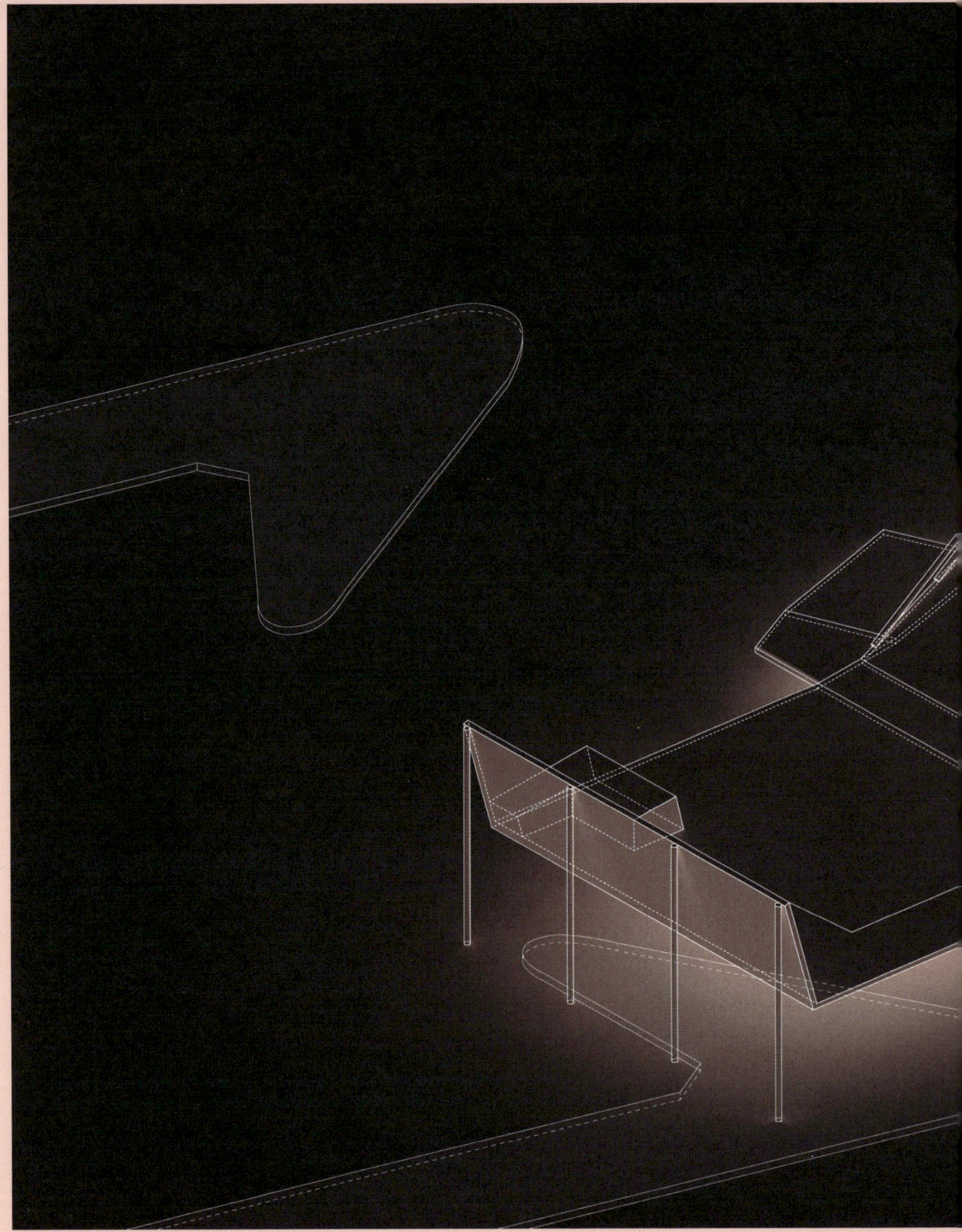

Douai (1973)

0
1
2
4

Drawing sheet, documenting the design scheme for the Douai practicable.

Model of the design scheme for the Douai practicable.

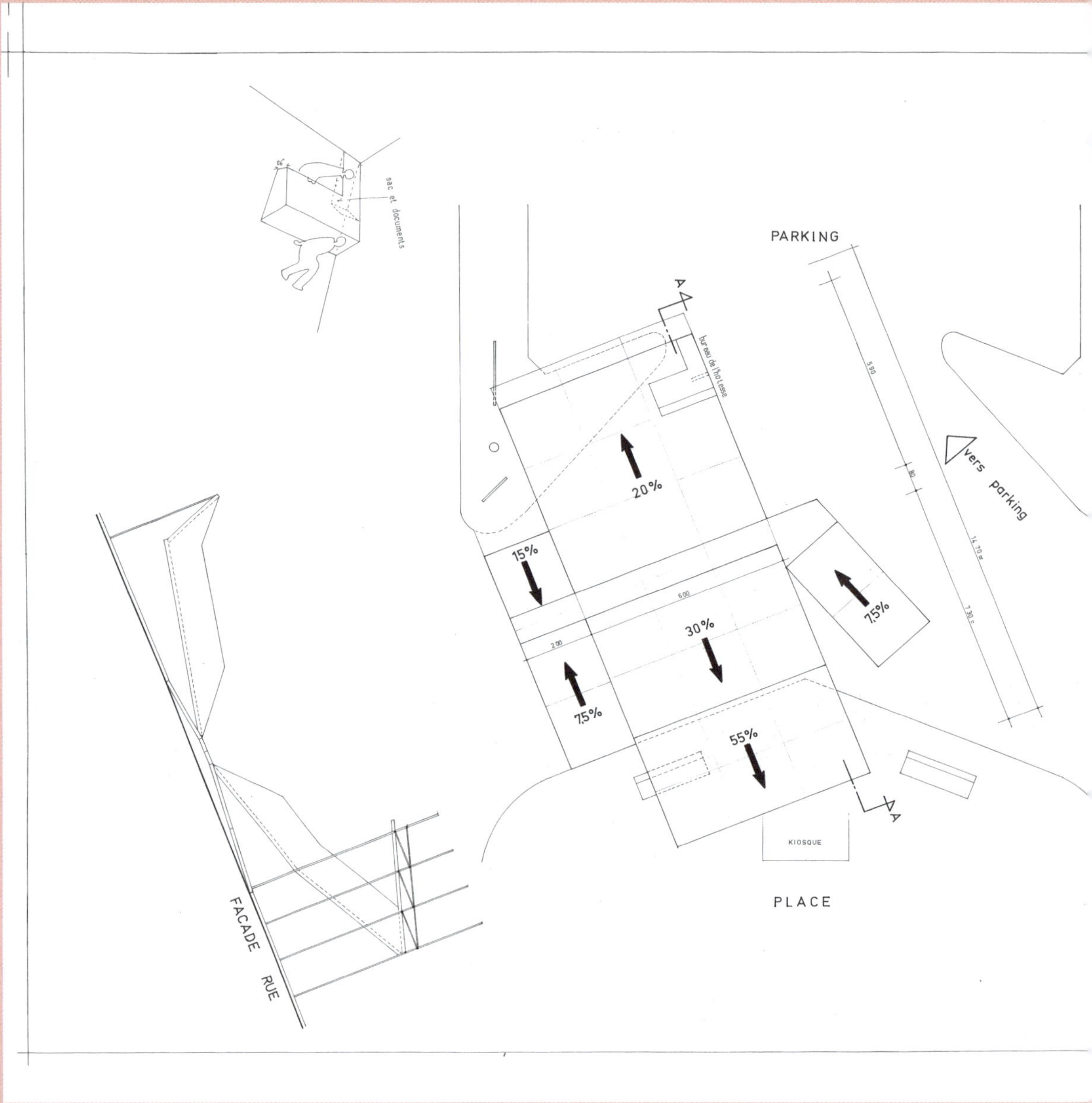

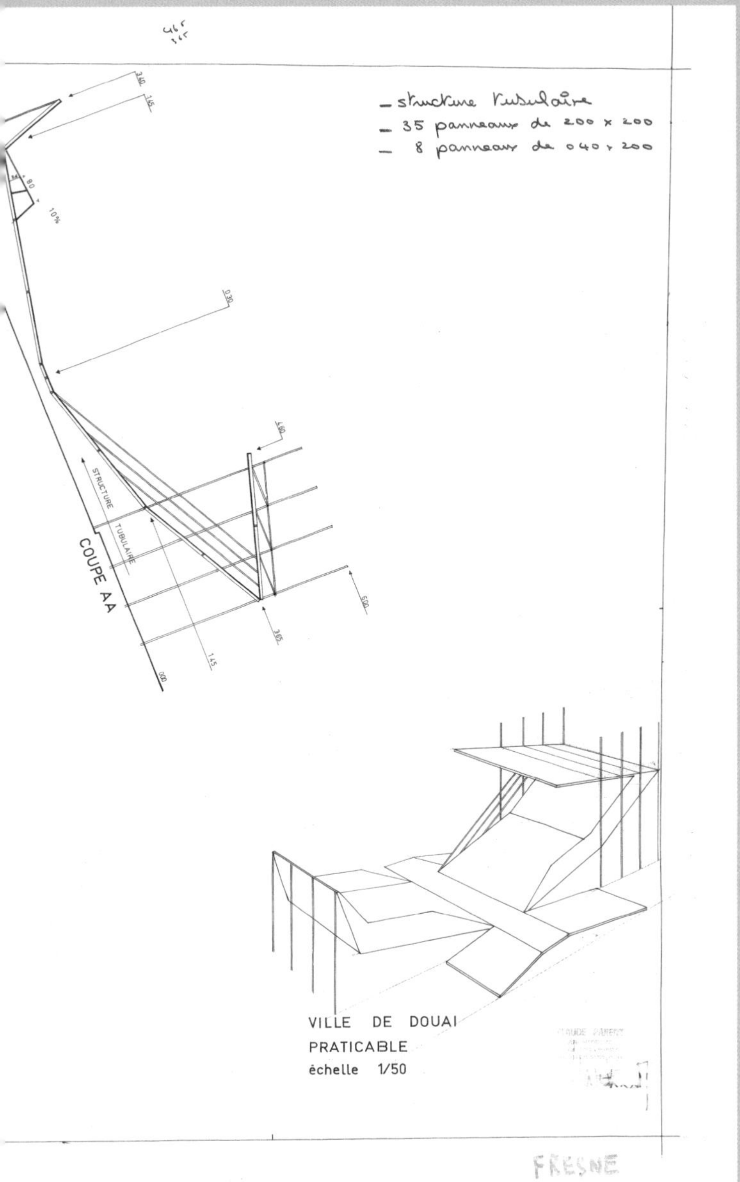

realized version of the design, as were smaller side ramps leading from the street level to the main flat landing. Not unlike earlier iterations in other cities, the practicable was built by city workers according to Parent's design and supported on scaffolding furnished by a local company.[76] In this particular iteration, the raised floor was assembled from sections of flooring used for stage and dance floor construction.[77]

Exhibition opening events featuring Parent and Barey, as well as three evenings of Parent's seminars, took place at the city hall at the beginning and the end, respectively, of the weeklong program.[78] The main focus, however, was the public events that took place throughout the weekend on and around the exterior practicable—referred to as *espace expérimental*

Parent, with André Barey to his right, and Nicole Parent in a green bodysuit.

Nicole Parent performing the *Inclipan* routine on the Douai practicable, with the local architect Patrick Wattel's multistory metal scaffolding, made in collaboration with the Groupe Synthèses et Confrontations, in the background on the right.

> Alain Hullot performing *L'amour même* while interacting with children on stage.

oblique—scheduled as a part of the Foire de Douai, the town's autumn fair. The experimental space served as a stage for what was in effect a free variety show titled *Vivre à l'oblique* and hosted by Parent. The mime artist Alain Hullot, who had already made an appearance in Mâcon, performed *L'amour même* (Love Itself), a piece commissioned specifically for the occasion, using movement, poetry, music, and costumes to enact inhabiting the oblique environment.[79] Nicole Parent also returned with another version of her *Inclipan* choreography, using the oblique structure rather than a portable inclined plane, as she had previously done in Reims and Mâcon.[80] These staged performances offered two alternate versions of the body in space. The mime's body was in a way an instrument for externalizing one's interiority through their physical gestures, while the gymnast made use of the external environment as a device for harnessing their vitality and strength. One projected out into the environment, while the other absorbed it. Beyond entertainment, these choreographed routines can be seen as artistic prompts for imagining ways of living with new forms of architecture.

Parallel to staged performances on the practicable were interventions by invited artists under the theme *Occuper la rue* (Occupy the Street), whose collective takeover of the street manifested itself in multiple ways. Patrick Wattel, a regional architect, built a multistory trellis from metal scaffolding next to the practicable in collaboration with the Groupe Synthèses et Confrontations, whose members placed printed text, images, and people inside the structure as an exploration of a freely inhabitable space. Another collaborative named Textruction, who were interested in visual blurring between images and text, also took part in *Occuper la rue*, as did a team of artists who hung colorful canvases onto adjacent building façades.[81] Midway through the weekend, the two parallel programs—*Vivre à l'oblique* and *Occuper la rue*—converged in a procession to a nearby tavern for a joint discussion between participating artists and locals.[82]

chedule of programs in Douai, September 7–9, 1973.

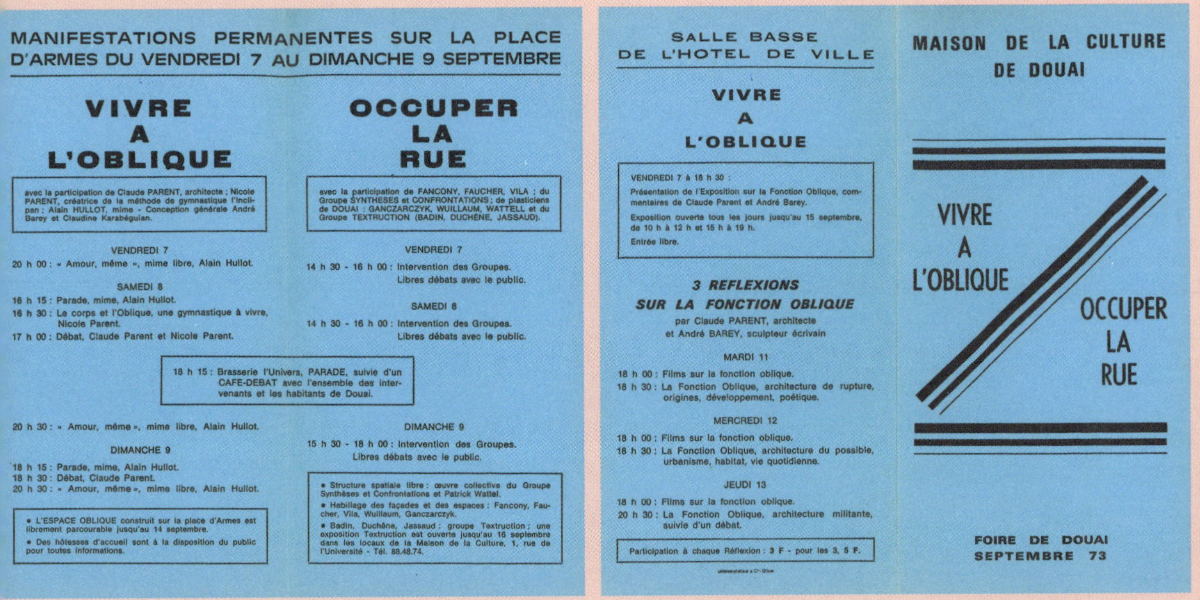

MANIFESTATIONS PERMANENTES SUR LA PLACE D'ARMES DU VENDREDI 7 AU DIMANCHE 9 SEPTEMBRE

VIVRE A L'OBLIQUE

avec la participation de Claude PARENT, architecte ; Nicole PARENT, créatrice de la méthode de gymnastique l'Inclipan ; Alain HULLOT, mime - Conception générale André Barey et Claudine Karabéguian.

VENDREDI 7

20 h 00 : « Amour, même », mime libre, Alain Hullot.

SAMEDI 8

16 h 15 : Parade, mime, Alain Hullot.
16 h 30 : Le corps et l'Oblique, une gymnastique à vivre, Nicole Parent.
17 h 00 : Débat, Claude Parent et Nicole Parent.

18 h 15 : Brasserie l'Univers, PARADE, suivie d'un CAFE-DEBAT avec l'ensemble des intervenants et les habitants de Douai.

20 h 30 : « Amour, même », mime libre, Alain Hullot.

DIMANCHE 9

18 h 15 : Parade, mime, Alain Hullot.
18 h 30 : Débat, Claude Parent.
20 h 30 : « Amour, même », mime libre, Alain Hullot.

• L'ESPACE OBLIQUE construit sur la place d'Armes est librement parcourable jusqu'au 14 septembre.
• Des hôtesses d'accueil sont à la disposition du public pour toutes informations.

OCCUPER LA RUE

avec la participation de FANCONY, FAUCHER, VILA ; du Groupe SYNTHESES et CONFRONTATIONS ; de plasticiens de DOUAI : GANCZARCZYK, WUILLAUM, WATTELL et du Groupe TEXTRUCTION (BADIN, DUCHÊNE, JASSAUD).

VENDREDI 7

14 h 30 - 16 h 00 : Intervention des Groupes. Libres débats avec le public.

SAMEDI 8

14 h 30 - 16 h 00 : Intervention des Groupes. Libres débats avec le public.

DIMANCHE 9

15 h 30 - 18 h 00 : Intervention des Groupes. Libres débats avec le public.

• Structure spatiale libre : œuvre collective du Groupe Synthèses et Confrontations et Patrick Wattel.
• Habillage des façades et des espaces : Fancony, Faucher, Vila, Wuillaum, Ganczarczyk.
• Badin, Duchêne, Jassaud : groupe Textruction ; une exposition Textruction est ouverte jusqu'au 16 septembre dans les locaux de la Maison de la Culture, 1, rue de l'Université - Tél. 88.48.74.

SALLE BASSE DE L'HOTEL DE VILLE

VIVRE A L'OBLIQUE

VENDREDI 7 à 18 h 30 :
Présentation de l'Exposition sur la Fonction Oblique, commentaires de Claude Parent et André Barey.
Exposition ouverte tous les jours jusqu'au 15 septembre, de 10 h à 12 h et 15 h à 19 h.
Entrée libre.

3 REFLEXIONS SUR LA FONCTION OBLIQUE

par Claude PARENT, architecte et André BAREY, sculpteur écrivain

MARDI 11

18 h 00 : Films sur la fonction oblique.
18 h 30 : La Fonction Oblique, architecture de rupture, origines, développement, poétique.

MERCREDI 12

18 h 00 : Films sur la fonction oblique.
18 h 30 : La Fonction Oblique, architecture du possible, urbanisme, habitat, vie quotidienne.

JEUDI 13

18 h 00 : Films sur la fonction oblique.
20 h 30 : La Fonction Oblique, architecture militante, suivie d'un débat.

Participation à chaque Réflexion : 3 F - pour les 3, 5 F.

MAISON DE LA CULTURE DE DOUAI

VIVRE A L'OBLIQUE

OCCUPER LA RUE

FOIRE DE DOUAI SEPTEMBRE 73

Parent on the practicable in Douai, surrounded by people.

Nicole Parent on the practicable in Douai.

The front page of the local publication *Présences* announcing the construction of Parent's oblique experimental space, "a place to explore, a floor to discover."

PRÉSENCES
A LA FOIRE DE DOUAI

N° 11 DU 7 AU 13 SEPTEMBRE 1973 - EDITION SPECIALE
PLACE D'ARMES ET SALLE BASSE DE L'HOTEL DE VILLE

CENTRE D'ANIMATION CULTURELLE
MAISON DE LA CULTURE DE DOUAI
1, RUE DE L'UNIVERSITÉ - TEL. 88.48

l'architecte claude parent construit un espace expérimental oblique

UN LIEU A INVESTIR, UN SOL A DÉCOUVRIR

TROIS GROUPES DE PLASTICIENS OCCUPENT LA PLACE D'ARMES

Pendant les trois journées de Foire, du vendredi 7, du samedi 8 et du dimanche 9, la fête bat son plein place d'Armes.

Les façades des maisons sont couvertes de banderoles, de rubans, l'espace des rues est envahi par les calicots, le sol devient miroir d'une joie soudaine de formes, de matière, de couleurs qui pénètrent la ville et la rendent pour quelques jours insolite, exotique, carnavalesque, imaginée, heureuse, libérée, lieu à découvrir, rendu à l'homme à pied.

Au centre de la place d'Armes, face à l'espace expérimental oblique construit par l'architecte Claude Parent, un treillis métallique, circuit-labyrinthe de nos pulsions secrètes, diffuse les propositions d'artistes.

Cette réalisation est l'œuvre de trois groupes de plasticiens qui se proposent sous forme d'une intervention collective, d'occuper la rue, chacun d'eux avec sa créativité propre.

maquette de l'espace expérimental oblique

architecture poésie mime, proposition spectaculaire de alain hullot : l'amour, même

avec des textes de : André Breton, l'Union Libre - Joyce Mansour, l'appel amer d'un sanglot - Henri Michaux, Magie et avis aux jeunes ménages - Philippe Soupault, Poèmes et poésies - et quelques autres citations tirées des Diaconales, « manuel à l'usage des confesseurs » de Mgr Bouvier,
et des musiques de : David Bedford, 2 poèmes pour chœur ; Pink Floyd, Ummagumma ; Aphrodite's Child-666.
Costumes, masques et projections de Jacqueline Labrot.

Je vous construirai une ville avec des loques, moi !
Je vous construirai sans plan et sans ciment
Un édifice que vous ne détruirez pas,
Et qu'une espèce d'évidence écumante
Soutiendra et gonflera, qui viendra vous braire au nez,
Et au nez gelé de tous vos Panthéons, vos arts arabes, et de vos Mings.

Avec de la fumée, avec de la dilution de brouillard
Et du son de peau de tambour,
Je vous assoirai des forteresses écrasantes et superbes,
Des forteresses faites exclusivement de remous et de secousses,
Contre lesquelles votre ordre multimillénaire et votre géométrie
Tomberont en fadaises et galimatias et poussière de sable sans raison.

Henri MICHAUX.

Notre manifestation, particulièrement l'expérimentation quotidienne d'un espace oblique, veut briser les blocages psychologiques, ouvrir l'espérance de l'homme vers son avenir urbain, et réconcilier, du moins dans leur vision du futur, l'homme et la ville.

Elle n'a d'autre motivation et d'autre intérêt que de permettre de reprendre un dialogue entre population et architecte en direct, se targuant d'établir la communication à un niveau élevé, car elle aura auparavant libéré les esprits de tous les vetos, de tous les quiproquos.

Claude Parent.

Manifestation conçue par Claude Parent, André Barey et Claudine Karabégulan, réalisée par la Maison de la Culture avec le concours des services techniques de la Ville de Douai et de l'entreprise Entrepose-Lille.

éditorial

Mettant à profit l'animation exceptionnelle qui règne dans la ville à l'occasion de la Foire, la Maison de la Culture a décidé de porter témoignage de sa présence créatrice en organisant, au cœur même de la Cité, un vaste rassemblement de forces vives — architectes, plasticiens, musiciens, mimes — venues des quatre coins de France : Marseille, Paris, Saint-Etienne, Lille, Limoges, Douai...

Nous remercions tout particulièrement Monsieur le Maire de Douai d'avoir adhéré d'emblée à ce projet et de l'avoir soutenu en mettant les Services Techniques de la Ville à notre disposition. Nos remerciements vont également aux Associations et aux Commerçants dont la participation nous sera précieuse.

Douai, lieu de rencontre des poètes ? Pourquoi pas ?

Roland POQUET.

While diverse in style and method, these artists, including Parent's group, had an apparently shared objective of engaging public space as a creative territory that enabled the questioning of common assumptions about each of their respective fields. Parent's work fundamentally challenged the nature of flat ground in architecture, not unlike how the other artists questioned the status of images in painting, text in poetry, movement in dance, and so on. Furthermore, they sought to diminish boundaries between life and art, or, in Parent's case, life and architecture. If the entire tour of France was prompted by Parent's desire to eliminate the separation between the architect and people, in Douai he may have pushed this idea as far as he possibly could. His daily talks on the practicable took place in broad daylight, surrounded by people and distractingly loud vehicular traffic. In photographs of the event, he appears strikingly dressed in a black shirt, yellow wide-legged trousers, and matching neckerchief and socks, holding a microphone while seated on the edge of the angled stage and addressing a crowd around him—a performer in his own right. The absence of building enclosure made this practicable different from the others; Parent compared the vulnerability of appearing on the Douai stage to being naked.[83] Yet, the whole endeavor was worth it—"a beautiful memory"[84]—as he concluded in his reflections on the visit:

> When the miracle happens, when the children stop bawling and running up and down the slopes, when we forget about the noise of the cars and when those who are laughing decide to get up on the platform and ask a question or listen to a little old man explain his case, then we tell ourselves that it's not wrong to be there, that it's even a duty, an architect's duty among many others.[85]

Hence, among the realized practicables, the installation in Douai was perhaps the most theatrical in its use as a stage embedded in daily life. It was accessible to people who, according to Parent, would have perhaps never entered a museum or cultural center, the passers-by for whom architecture may yet matter.[86] Outside of scheduled events, the practicable stayed open for people to explore as they pleased, even if, overall, it remained in place for no more than ten days. Unbeknownst at the time, this was also Parent's last constructed practicable during his tour. Today, Place d'Armes is less noisy and easier to navigate, having been cleared of car parking and traffic in favor of pedestrian circulation. In place of Parent's practicable, the city built an elaborate fountain.

CHALON-SUR-SAÔNE (1973)

After Douai, Parent immediately moved on to pursuing another set of *maison de la culture*-sponsored programs in Burgundy, this time in Chalon-sur-Saône, located less than sixty kilometers north of Mâcon. His activities there included a series of presentations throughout the city, a six-week exhibition at the cultural center, as well as another unrealized proposal for a practicable.[87] At the time of his visit to Chalon-sur-Saône, the city had welcomed the opening of its cultural center, the work of the architect Daniel Petit just two years earlier.[88] The building—the site for the proposed practicable as well as the venue for Parent's exhibition—is part of a mixed-use complex occupying an entire block, including a sports hall that is still in use today.[89] In addition to the large auditorium, articulated as a rounded volume disrupting the otherwise orthogonal building massing, the *maison de la culture* consists of spaces that at the time contained typical community programs including a library, exhibition spaces, meeting rooms, a cinema, as well as a discotheque, all organized around an interior courtyard. Adjacent to the courtyard is the main foyer, a tall luminous volume of space one level above the street, defined by a field of concrete columns and accessible by a set of wide stairs located on the exterior of the front glass façade.[90] The resulting circulation sequence leads one from the ground level up to the glazed entrance, framed by a concrete awning overhead, beyond which one encounters the ticketing area and, another few steps up, an interior space overlooking the courtyard on the other side of the transparent glass wall. The foyer is in this way sandwiched between two glazed sources of daylight, one at the front façade and the other at the inner courtyard, a play of transitions between inside and outside that one experiences moving through the otherwise massive concrete structure.[91] It is for this particular part of the building, the main circulatory thoroughfare, that Parent proposed a practicable, the only one in the series of oblique installations that was envisioned as both indoor and outdoor.

Chalon-sur-Saône (1973)

Drawing sheet, dated September 19, 1973, documenting the design scheme for the Chalon-sur-Saône practicable.

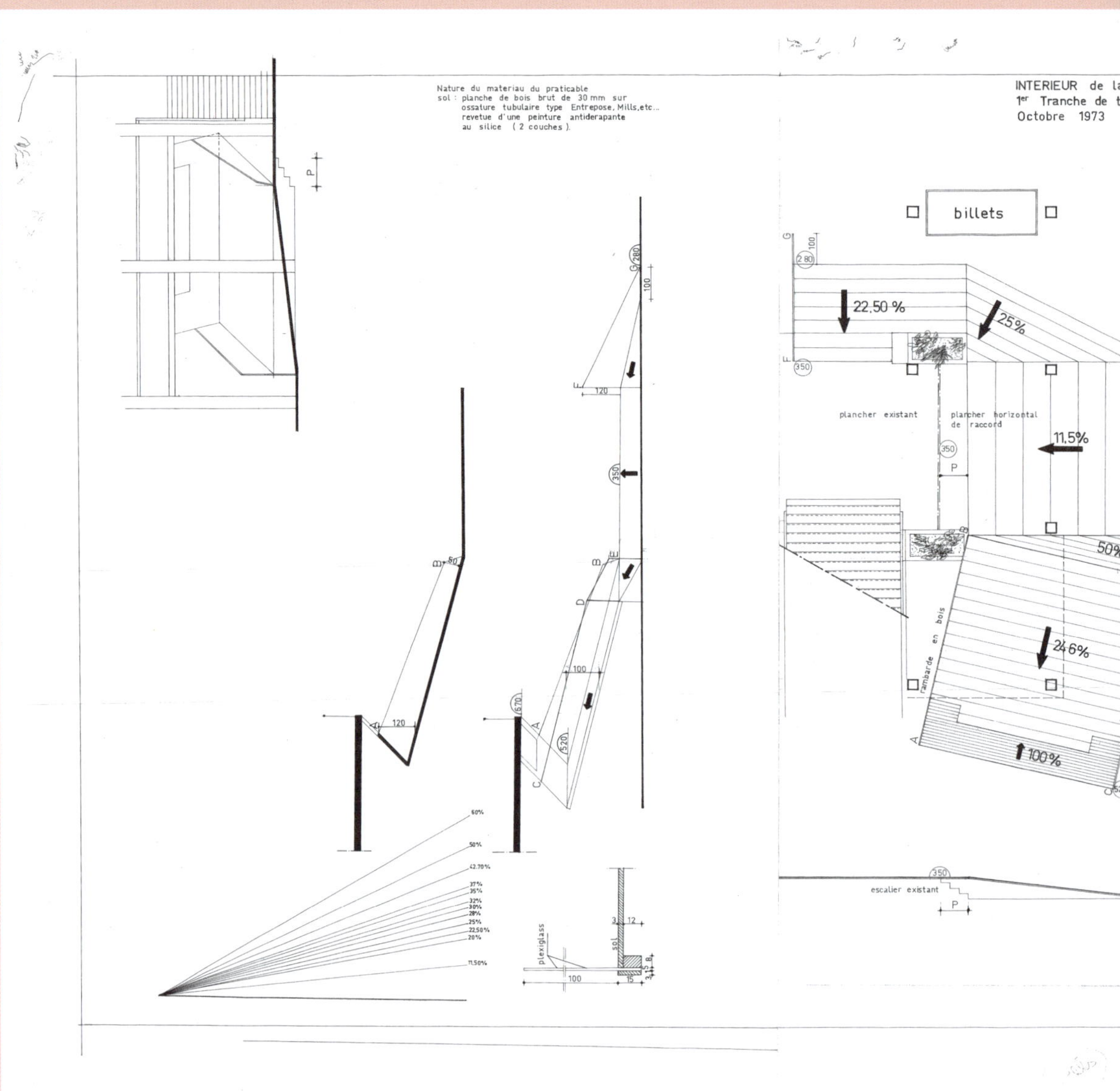

While he for the most part accepted the existing flow of circulation in and out of the building, Parent transformed other aspects of the existing architecture by layering continuously folding surfaces on top of it. On the exterior, the proposed installation—represented in a white paper model and a set of orthographic drawings—appears as an oversized surface draped over the monumental stair, offering a variably navigable inclined field in lieu of a formal entrance. In doing so, the practicable functions as a space of circulation but also affords the possibility of other forms of occupation. At a smaller scale, two bridge-like parts are integrated into the larger surface, another version of his strategy, already applied in Amiens, to nest a practicable within a practicable. These parts are inhabitable from both above and below, like two modules that Parent used in an earlier set of projects, titled *Inclisite,* exploring the Architecture

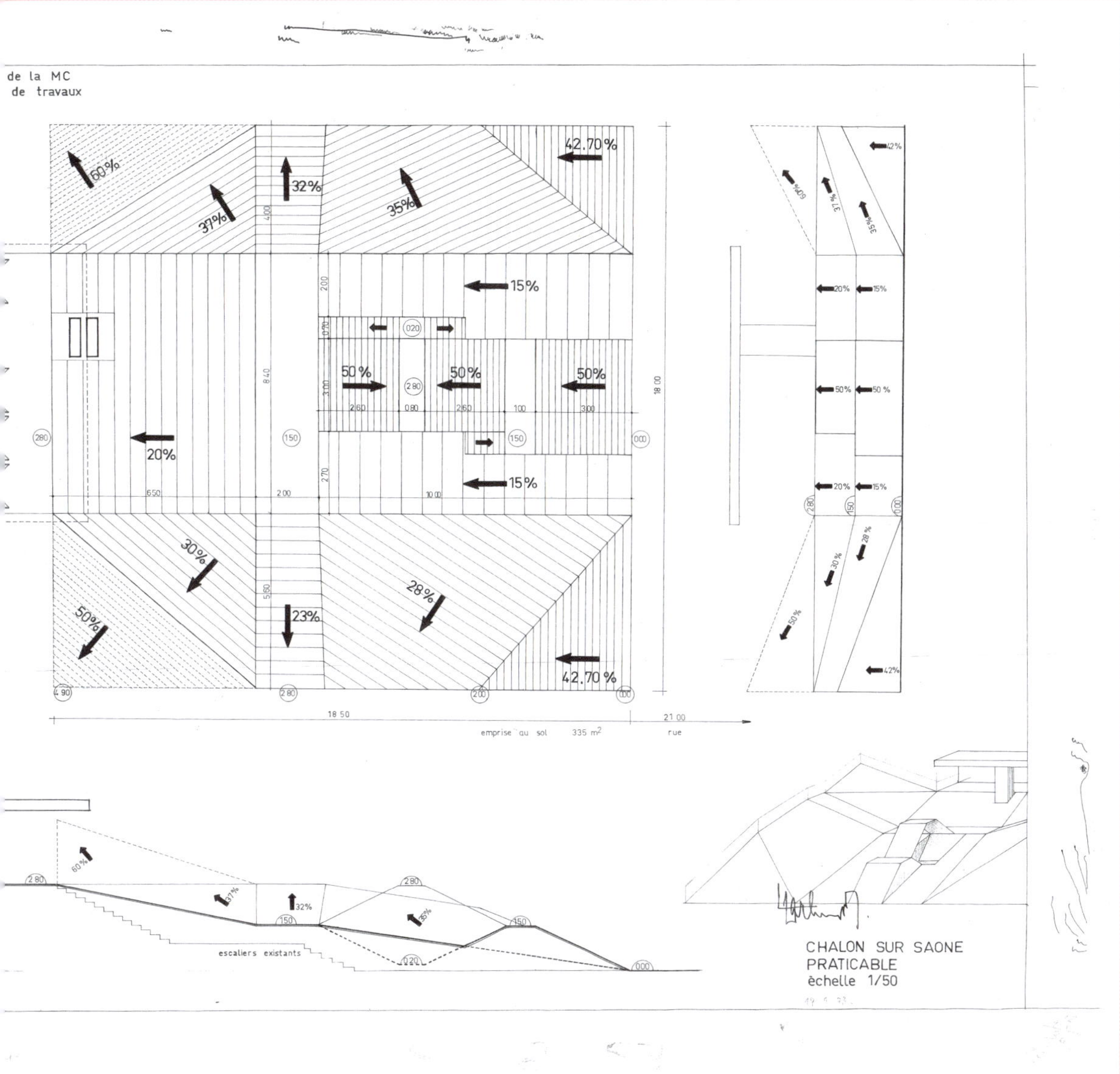

Principe-era concept of cellular private spaces crossed, from above, by public circulation.[92] Inside the building, the floor continues to slope up, smoothing out the foyer's split floor, where the two levels were four steps apart. (The split level has since been flattened, the result of a recent building renovation.) Then, to the left of the entrance, next to the existing stair leading to the lobby's mezzanine, the practicable slopes up at a steeper angle to create a sitting perch. Compared to the outside, the interior intervention is less extensive; yet the few components that are introduced to the space effectively disrupt the orthogonal order of the existing building. In fact, the importance of the interior portion of the design was that, according to Parent's annotated drawings, it was intended to be constructed first, while the exterior was to follow in June of the following year.

Model of the Chalon-sur-Saône practicable, with the building façade removed to show both interior and exterior parts of the proposed design scheme.

Like a theatrical stage that sits on top of an existing floor slab, the proposed practicable is structurally redundant but essential as an element that affords multiple uses. The formal continuity of the design expressed in the study model recalls the Le Havre installation in the way that railings and floor surfaces merge together rather than being separated into platforms and framing as was done in other designs—even if material specifications for the project indicate the typical combination of raw wood planks, metal scaffolding, and nonslip paint. The overall geometry of the surface has a complexity perhaps only matched by the Venice installation. Rather than using a one-directional extrusion as was done in Douai, an elongated ramp—such as in Le Havre and to some degree Nevers—or an amphitheater-like funnel shape found in both Amiens and Mâcon, the Chalon-sur-Saône design consists of a plane that folds in multiple directions, with many of the folds and creases occurring diagonally, like a fabric creased on the bias. The incline follows the path of movement from lower to upper levels, yet beyond facilitating vertical circulation in this direction, surfaces also slope up toward the sides, as if trying to contain rather than disperse people. As designed, the practicable produces a new façade for the entrance, one not made of enclosure but rather a sculpted floor that enables connection instead of separation. It is a study of the floor in elevation; an interior that not only spills outside but becomes the building's dominant exterior appearance—an advanced iteration of the idea already introduced in Amiens.

Although Parent's exhibition was on view inside the *maison de la culture*, most of his scheduled public appearances happened elsewhere. During a four-day period in mid-October, Parent met with and spoke to different audiences throughout the city—not unlike what he had previously done in Mâcon—with oblique architecture as a prompt for instigating an open dialog about living conditions and the future of the built environment.[93] His Wednesday night presentation, for example, took place at a youth

Model of the Chalon-sur-Saône practicable ramping up to the exterior building entrance.

Detail of the Chalon-sur-Saône practicable, showing a smaller ramp nested within the larger inclined platform.

Exhibition and lecture flyer, September–October, 1973, Chalon-sur-Saône.

Event flyer, October 10–13, 1973, Chalon-sur-Saône.

A flyer announcing Parent's presentation to a working group at a community center, October 11, 1973, Chalon-sur-Saône.

CLAUDE PARENT

EXPOSITION
15 septembre 31 octobre

ANIMATIONS.
CONFERENCES
10. 11. 12. 13. octobre

CHALON SUR SAONE
MAISON DE LA CULTURE

CLAUDE PARENT
ARCHITECTURE OBLIQUE
CONFERENCES
10. 11. 12. octobre *(20h 30)*
13. octobre *(17h)*

10. charreaux. club de jeunes
11. zup. centre social
12. centre ville. skblllz
13. maison de la culture

CHALON SUR SAONE
MAISON DE LA CULTURE

La Maison de la Culture de Chalon-sur-Saône
et le Groupe de Travail Urbanisme du Conseil Culturel

vous invitent à une rencontre avec l'Architecte
Claude PARENT

le Jeudi 11 Octobre à 20 heures 30
CENTRE SOCIAL DE LA Z. U. P.

La démarche de Claude Parent recherche en priorité le dialogue permanent avec tous ceux qui sont prêts à expérimenter avec lui un mode de vie du futur.

Le débat prévu après chaque exposé sera orienté sur les principales préoccupations des habitants du quartier auxquels elles s'adressent et permettra ainsi une approche plus immédiate de la Fonction Oblique.

Projections de diapositives.

center, the Club de jeunes des Charreaux, on the western edge of the city—interrupted by a jazz rehearsal and rounds of foosball—while the following evening he appeared at a social club in the Prés-Saint-Jean district as part of an event organized by an urbanist working group.[94] These appearances were orchestrated by the cultural center's administration, with Parent feeling a sense of being "parachuted" into these locations under less than ideal circumstances, often having to quickly adapt to social situations as they emerged. On the third day of these roaming appearances, for instance, Parent was dispatched to the city center, where he was unexpectedly confronted by dozens of local shopkeepers more eager to share their grievances with the municipal administration than discussing the oblique function.[95]

His final public talk took place at the *maison de la culture* on a Saturday afternoon—unlike the other appearances throughout the week, this was a ticketed event with the admission price of five French francs, or about three euros in today's currency. A local newspaper reported was an audience of some fifty people, including city officials.[96] Parent recalled a patient mayor, engaged, supportive, and willing to sit through a three-hour architecture lecture.[97] The sampling of different populations, neighborhoods, and organizations helped fulfill Parent's aspirations to broaden his audience, and he described the total sum of such experiences as transformative. Reflecting on his encounters in Chalon, he writes: "Little by little, I got into the habit of better understanding, of more quickly defining what people came to ask me, what was important to them."[98] Likewise, he noted that his presence was equally critical to city officials—particularly the *maison de la culture* leadership—who were seeking new ways to engage people that such institutions otherwise failed to attract; he saw himself in the role of a catalyst, "a powerfully ionized intermediary."[99]

The design for the unbuilt practicable represented through its architecture the same intermediary role that Parent performed socially. To put it another way, Parent and the practicable were both tasked with connecting the institution and the people outside of it. The practicable made visible the institution's imperative to attract visitors, to create a connection between the city and the building interior. If Parent was used as a liaison between the cultural center and the local population, the proposed installation would have done the same as a connection between the interior of the *maison de la culture* and the city. Depending on one's position, the Chalon practicable can be seen as an interior that gushes out of the building as much as it is the urban ground ascending like a flying carpet finding its way in.

PRATICABLE NO. 7 (1974)

A set of architectural drawings from Parent's office, dated March 23, 1974, describe the design of a room-sized installation consisting of a series of interconnected ramps and titled *Praticable no. 7*. It is the sole scheme among the archived practicables not explicitly identified according to a specific city or venue, nor does it appear to be an alternate version of any of the other site-specific designs.

Without disclosing the exact location of the site, the drawings provide useful information about the existing architecture that was to contain the oblique installation. According to the floor plan, the overall space is about six by nine meters in area, split asymmetrically in the middle by two pairs

Praticable no. 7 (1974)

0
1
2
4

of slender columns in line with the load-bearing walls along the perimeter. The ceiling height was drawn at four meters in height, barely enough for a conventionally sized mezzanine but with enough flexibility for sloping the floor, as the scheme does, following a set of steep angles. To the left of the entrance, a small ramp slopes up toward a flat landing that extends the entire width of the room. From it, a large ramp with an incline of approximately twenty degrees slopes up toward the other end of the room. Another similarly angled and sized ramp stretches in the opposite direction, with

Practicable no.7, isometric drawing.

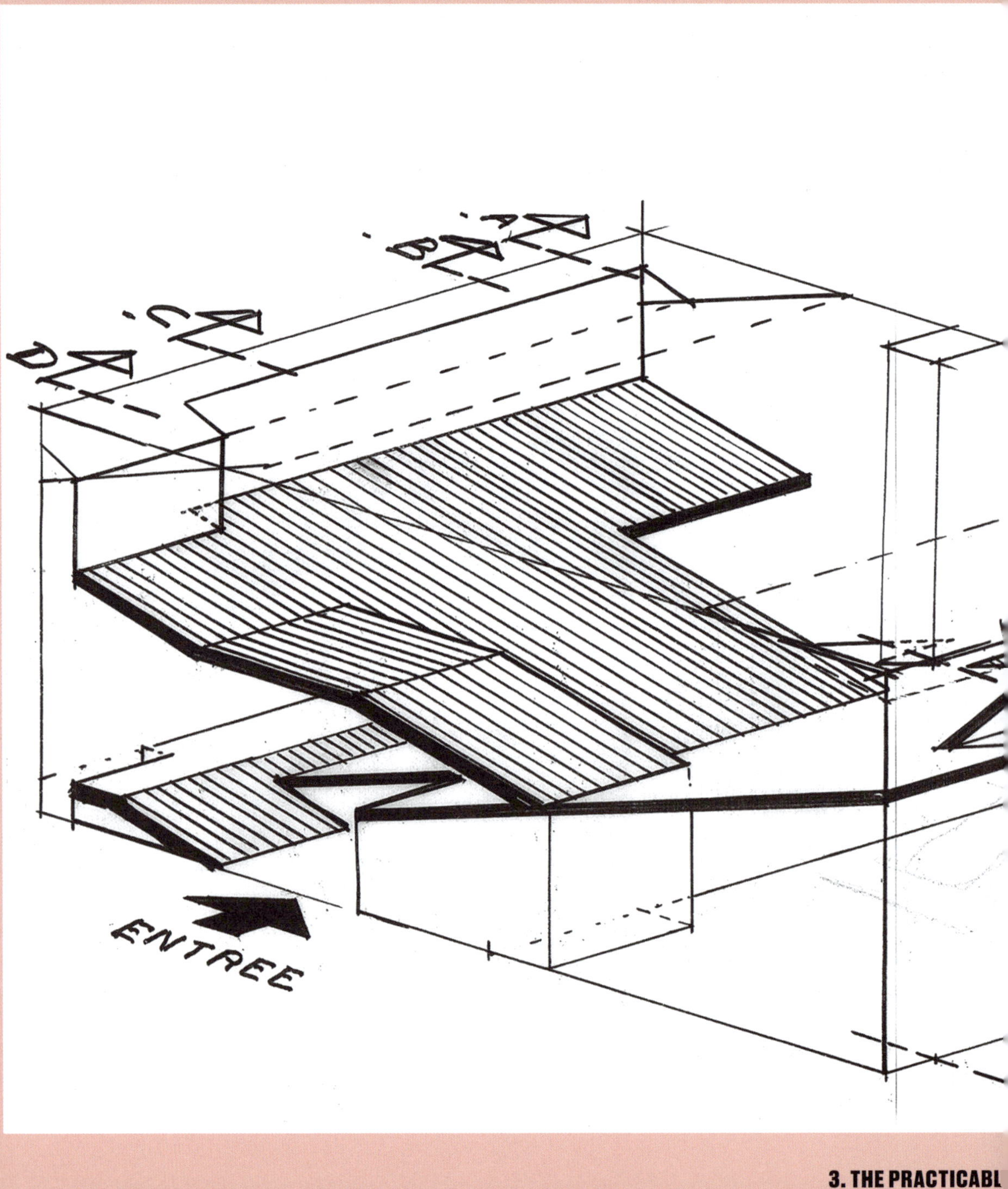

the two intersecting inclines forming an X-shaped configuration. Smaller sloping planes provide additional paths of movement throughout as well as a sense of enclosure in areas where they create a dropped ceiling above.

Sectional drawings of the design include loosely sketched figures of human bodies, inhabiting the slopes in a range of standing and seating postures. One such drawing shows multiple rows of seated figures on one slope, facing a single upright figure—drawn as if performing in a dance-like manner rather than standing still—on the opposite side. Meanwhile, the spaces underneath each incline are also populated by outlines of bodies, conveying a sense of simultaneity among the activities occurring within a single space. Other sectional drawings likewise show figures walking along the inclined paths as well as sitting inside various cocoon-like nooks. Even though it is relatively compact, the presence of multiple figures suggests that this interior was intended to be used for a range of group activities. Dimensional notations imply that, unlike the sloped interior of the children's library in Mâcon, this space was sized for adult bodies.

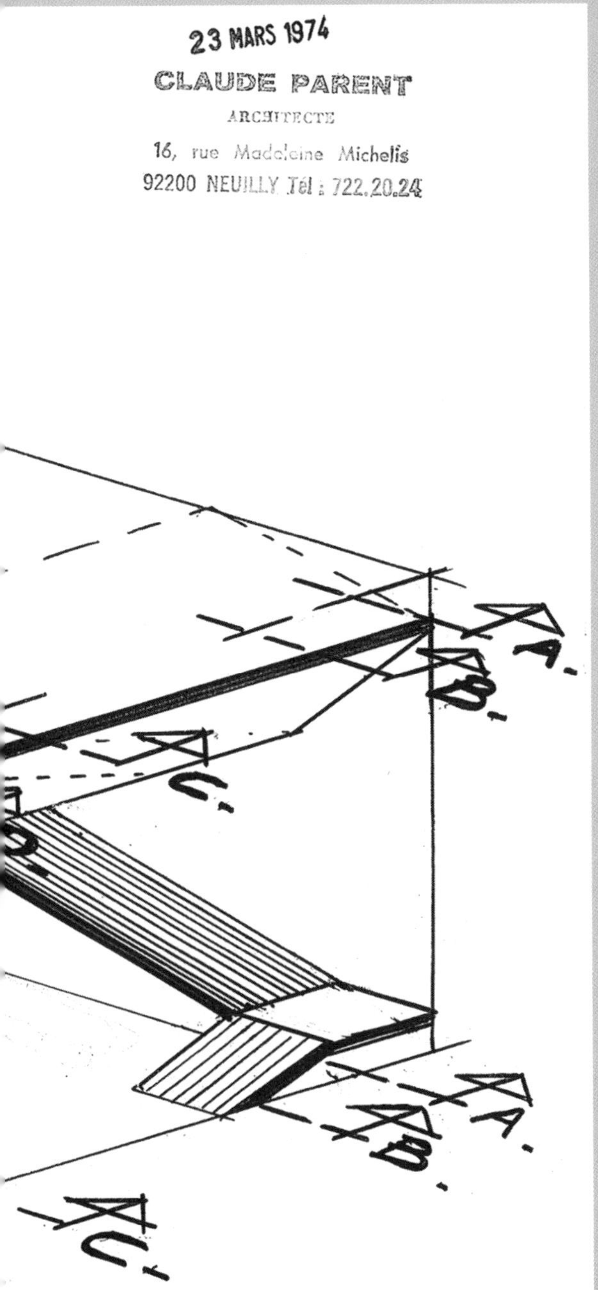

The numbering of the project brings into question how Parent counted these installations. Given the date written on the drawings, *Praticable no. 7* was designed after his visit to Chalon-sur-Saône but before the completion of the first design scheme for Caen, which he publicly presented in June of 1974.[100] However, placing this scheme along the chronological timeline starting with Le Havre—as this book does—makes it the eighth in the series rather than seventh. To make it seventh requires excluding one of the earlier installations, such as either Le Havre or Venice, as part of the series, for which there could be multiple justifications. Only counting installation designs that were part of Parent's tour of France with André Barey starting in 1971—and thus including some of the nondocumented proposals (for places such as Rouen),

Practicable no. 7, section drawings.

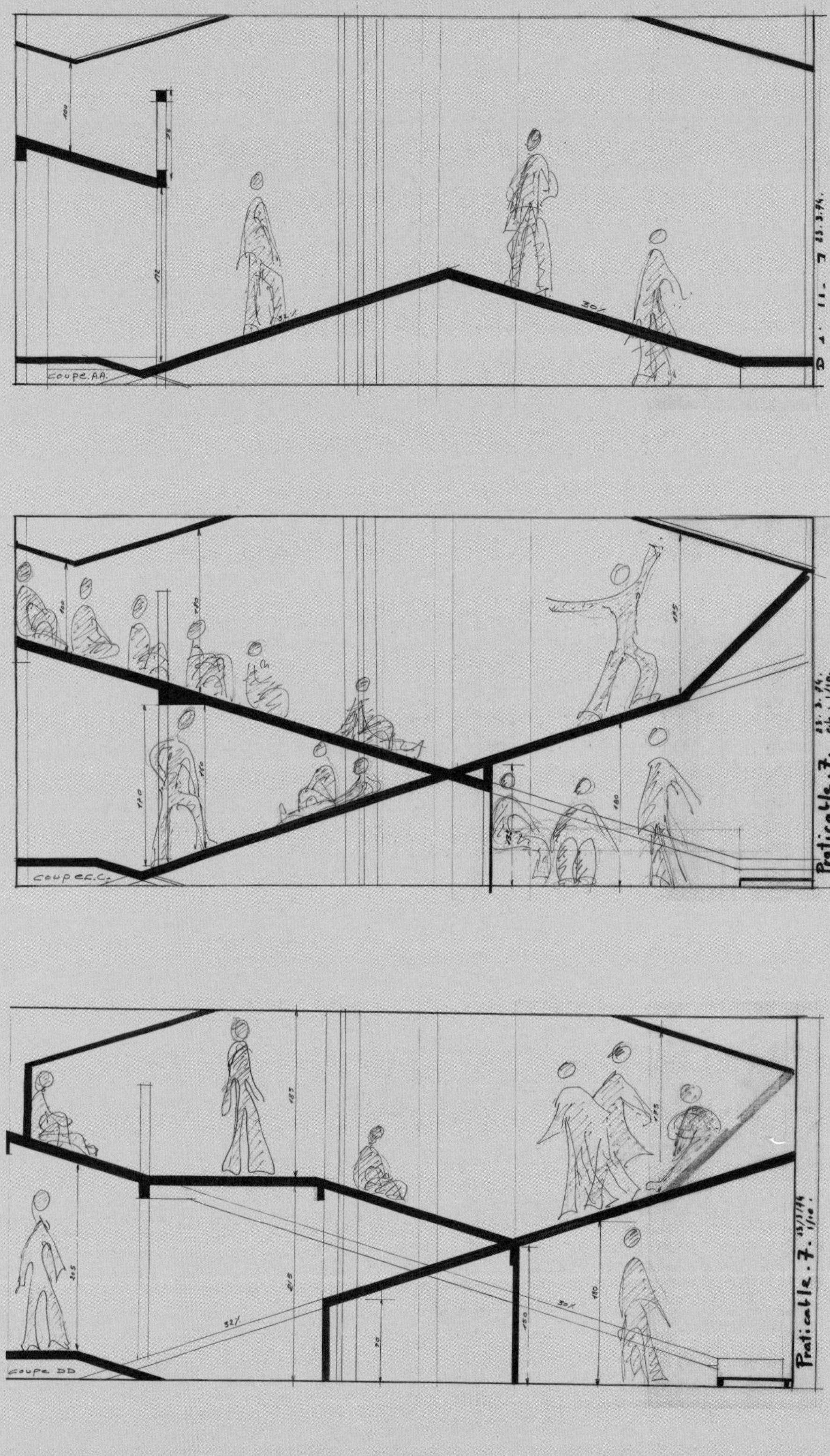

which are mentioned but otherwise without a trace of a tangible design—could achieve a similarly numbered sequence.

As a strategy for an interior installation, *Praticable no. 7* is not unlike the schemes for Venice or Mâcon in the way that it fills up the entire available footprint defined by the existing architectural envelope. The design emphasizes gathering and rest, even if circulation is an inextricable part of it. The resulting space lends itself to multiple uses and can be imagined as enabling a range of nondomestic daily activities. A magazine article published during Parent's stay in Mâcon reported on a request made by the staff of a local teachers college to have him transform one of their classrooms according to the principles of the oblique function.[101] Had the request been honored, the result would have been the second Mâcon practicable. It was nonetheless likely never fulfilled given that there is no other record of such a project. Yet it is reasonable to speculate that, had it been pursued, the design for an oblique classroom could have resembled the *Praticable no. 7* scheme, given the presence of an existing room and the ramps inserted into it.

CAEN (1975)

Parent's multiyear tour of French cultural centers concluded in Normandy, the same region where he started with the 1969 installation in Le Havre, but this time in Caen. For this visit, he and Barey worked with city officials on preparations for a variety of programs to take place at the municipal theater, the building that had earlier also served as Caen's *maison de la culture*.[102] Their planned repertoire included another iteration of the traveling exhibition, a mixture of live events previously staged in other cities and those created with local organizations specifically for the occasion, as well as the construction of a site-specific practicable. The proposed installation

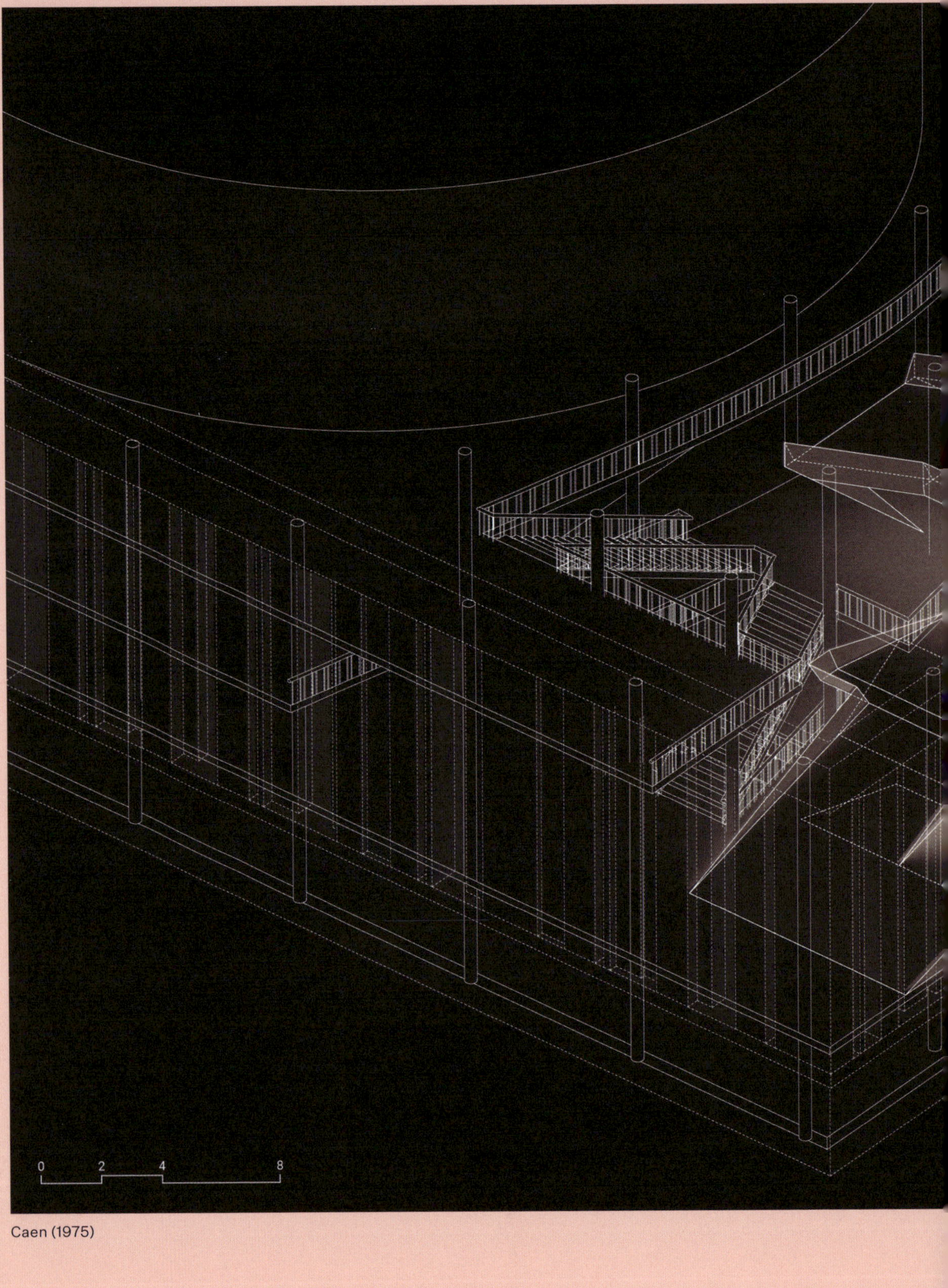

Caen (1975)

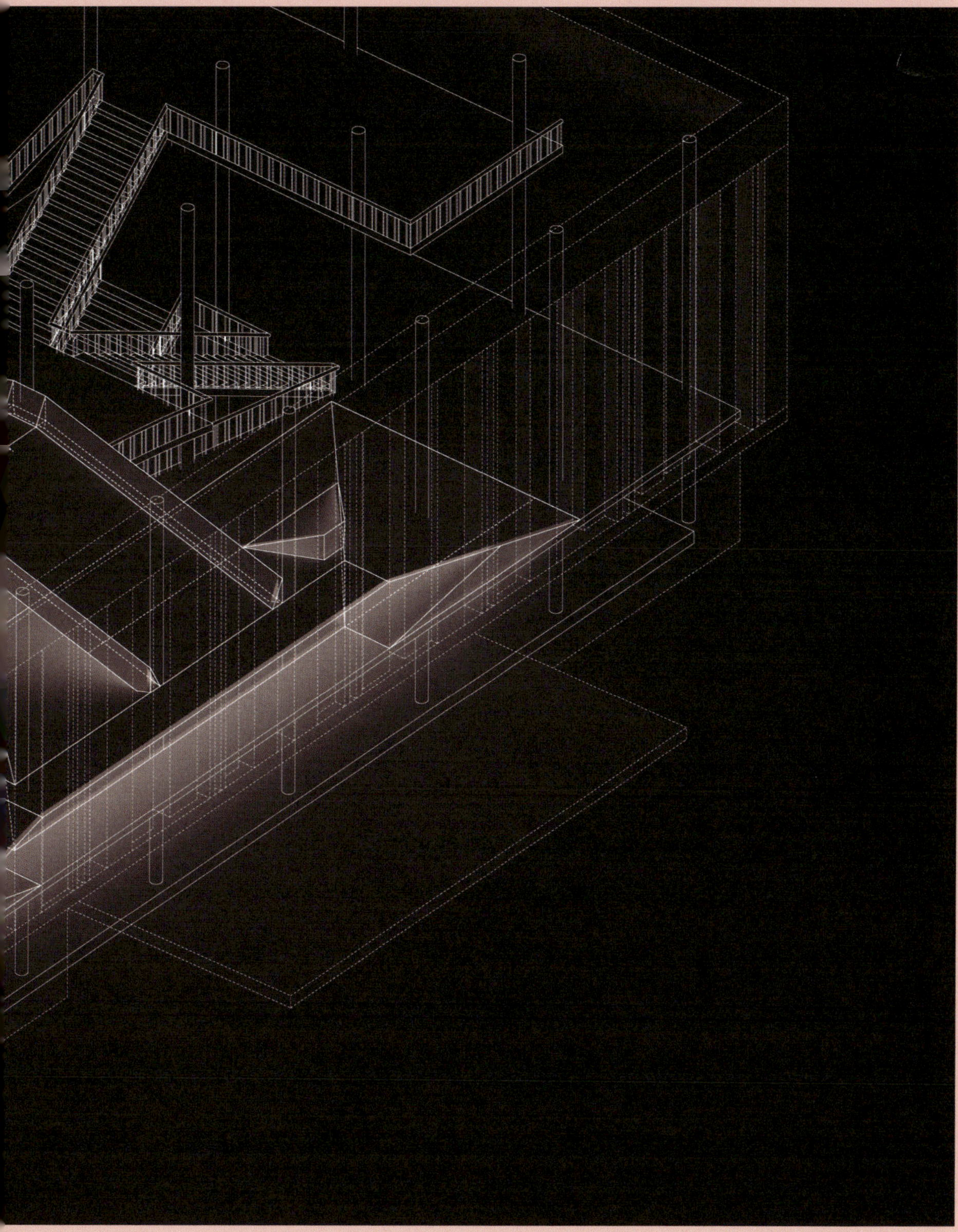

Drawing sheet, dated November 6, 1974, documenting a modification to the initial design scheme for the Caen practicable.

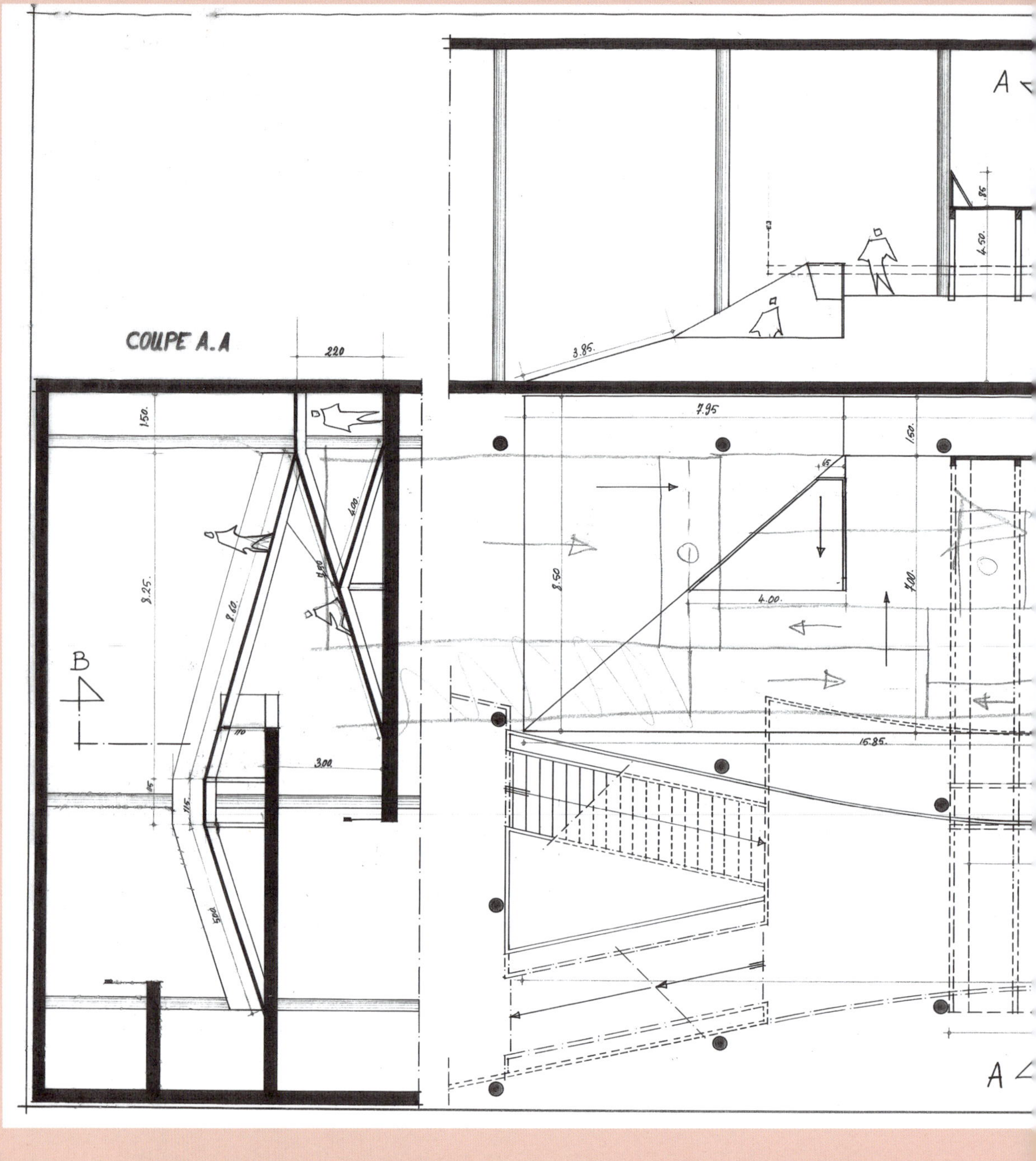

design was exceptional among the practicables for its verticality as well as for how it engaged existing interior circulation.

The venue for the practicable and the accompanying programs, the Théâtre municipal de Caen, was built in 1963 as part of the city's final phase of postwar reconstruction. From the outside, the building is a rectangular prism raised above street level—the visual effect of material changes in the façade from the ground level to its upper portions. It is composed of vertically oriented concrete and glass stripes whose variation in width and

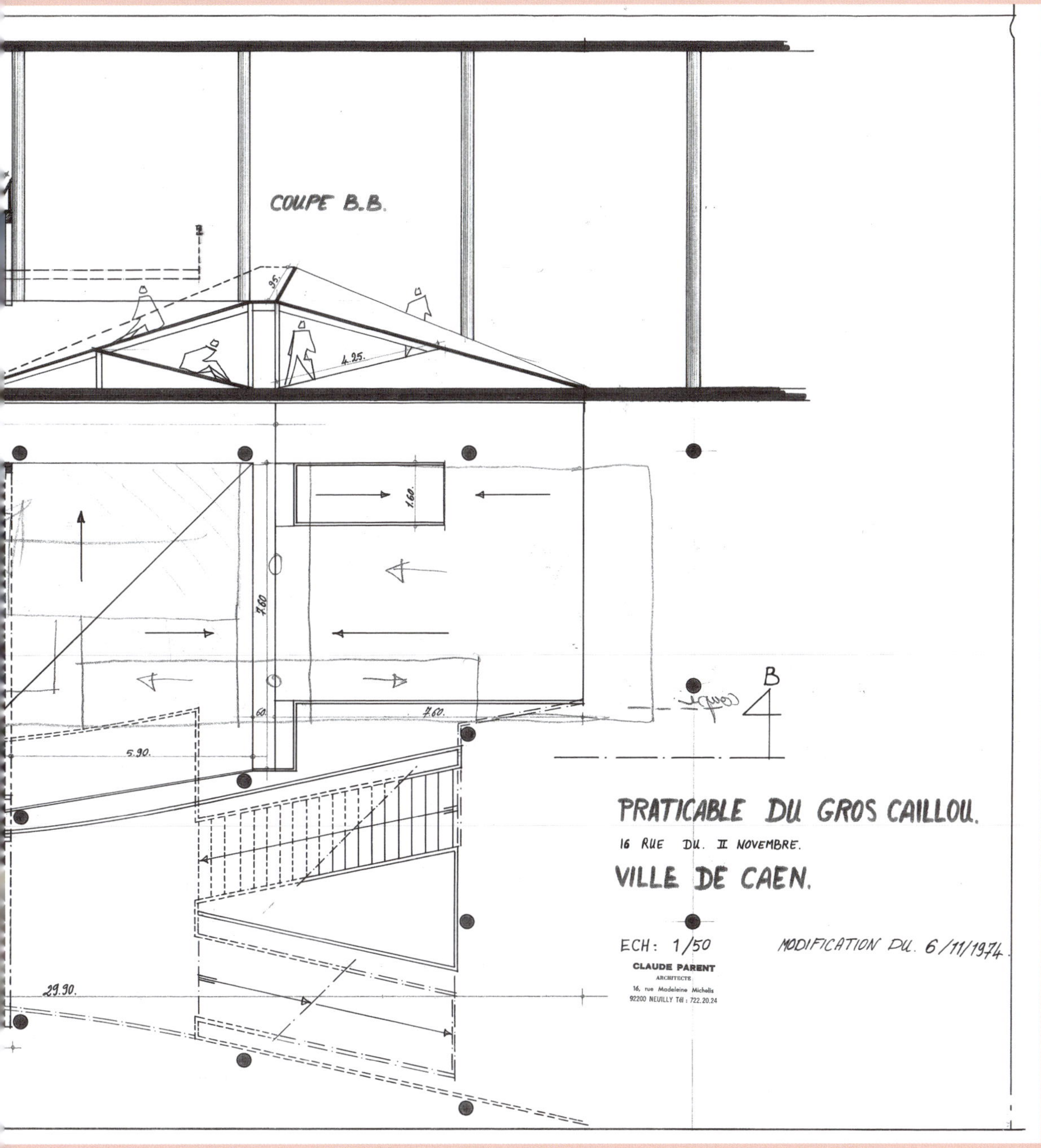

depth yields a seemingly randomized pattern. The relatively opaque façade is the work of the architect François Carpentier, while the rest, including the interior, was designed by another architect, Alain Bourbonnais.[103] Centered along a short side of the rectangular footprint, facing the pedestrian square, is the main entrance beyond which a low-ceiling vestibule leads to a stair that finally delivers people to the large foyer on the upper level. This generously proportioned space unfolds between the interior face of the striped façade overlooking the square on one side and the curvature of the round

Overall views of the Caen model.

auditorium on the other. The geometry of a branching staircase connecting oversized landings at multiple levels, along with the pattern of metallic columns arrayed throughout, serves as a transition between the orthogonal form of the building perimeter and the auditorium's curved volume. The result is a cascading arrangement of sinuous circulation paths set against the verticality of the foyer. This is where Parent intended to place his oblique intervention.[104]

Local newspapers reported on Parent and Barey's visit to Caen in June of 1974 to reveal the first version of the practicable. The pair's presentation was part of a meeting whose agenda included discussions with local organizations involved in developing programs for its use, with the anticipated realization of the installation scheduled for January of the following year.[105] Parent's design scheme was represented in a scaled model made of wood, one of the only surviving and archived three-dimensional artifacts from the entire series of practicables.[106] Emerging from the model's rectangular plank base are vertical

Detail views of the Caen model.

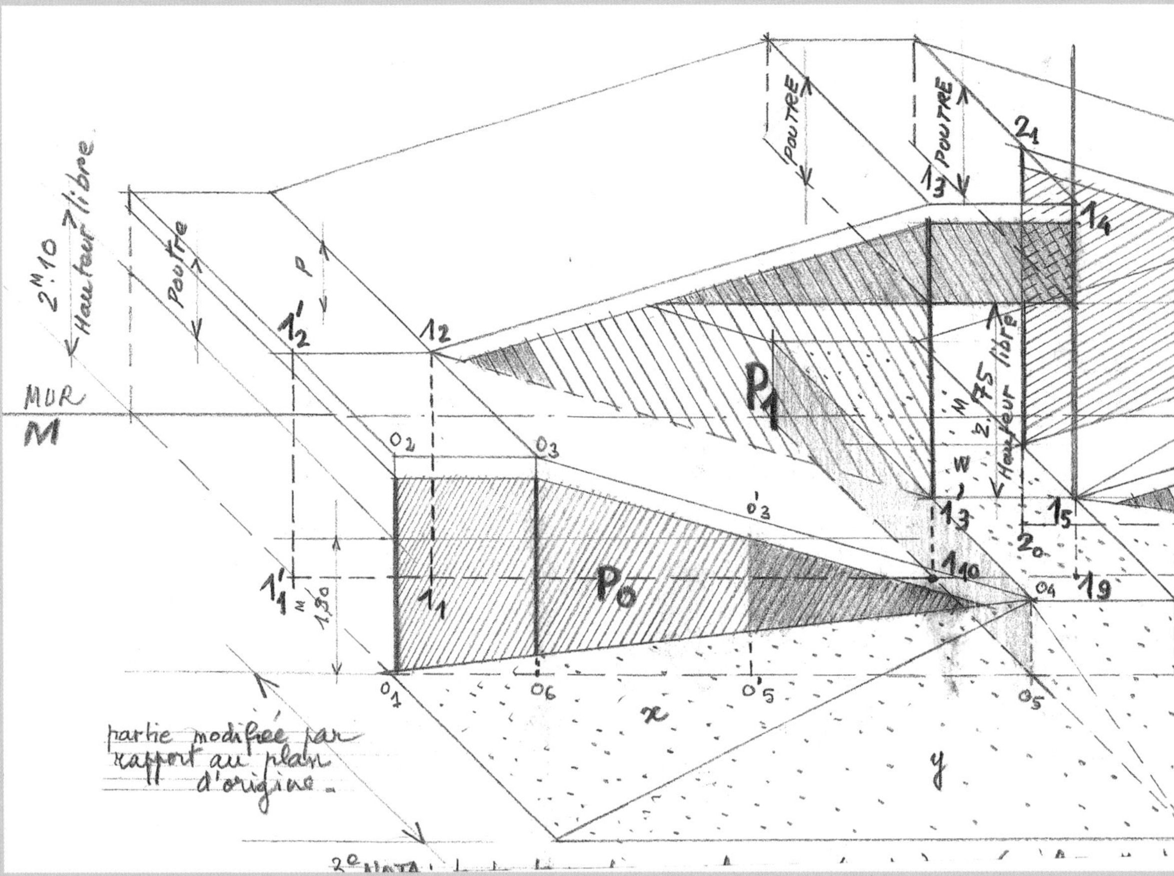

Paraline drawing, dated August 8, 1975, of an alternate scheme for the Caen practicable.

wood dowels representing existing structural columns populating the foyer; also included are two levels of intermediate landings leading to various tiers of the auditorium, as well as double stairs connecting the different levels but shown more simply as ramps rather than steps. Within these abstracted existing conditions, the inserted practicable was modeled as having two main parts. The first part emerges from the floor, stretching from one side of the foyer to the other, like a faceted mound reaching up, at the center, toward the exterior wall. With such placement, the form acknowledges the existing foyer's symmetry but is itself asymmetrical, offering in this way different paths for movement and usable spaces on each side.

Like some of the other schemes, this practicable was designed to be inhabited from both above and below. The outer surfaces appear conducive to more extroverted uses, with larger areas suitable for groups of people, while the spaces below are smaller and more secluded. The second part of the practicable is bridge-like and laid out perpendicularly to the other part. It connects the highest level of the faceted mound-like platform resting on the foyer floor with the existing mezzanine platform above it. This part of the design resembles, albeit with its proportions significantly adjusted, the form of the installation in Le Havre. Starting in the back of the mezzanine, the bridge slopes up in the direction of the building's front façade and rises high enough to land above an existing banister before descending again to meet a flat landing at the top of the practicable below.

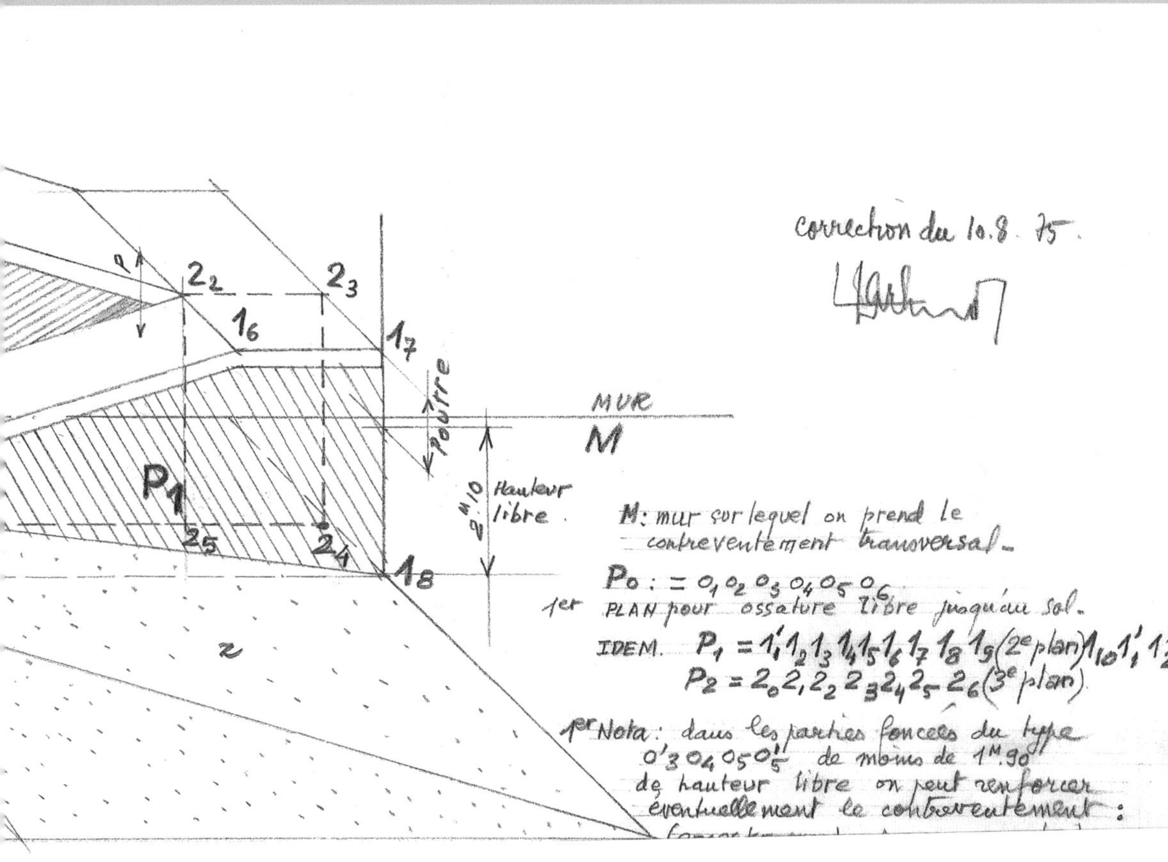

Its overall width, determined by the spacing of existing columns, equals the combined dimensions of the stairs on each side of the foyer, not only creating a platform conducive to socialization but also accounting for the same circulation capacity as the sum of the existing means of egress. By engaging existing stairs and landings, the scheme offers a choice between traditional and oblique circulation. Doing so was part of Parent's architectural experiment, a method of tracking people's interest in one versus the other.[107]

Rather than in January of 1975, as was previously announced, Parent's programs partially opened at the end of March. The exhibition, bearing the title *Cadre de vie: La fonction oblique* (Living Environment: The Oblique Function) and consisting of architectural models and photographs, was on view in the foyer of the municipal theater for approximately three weeks. Parent appeared, along with Barey and Nicole Parent, in a set of evening discussions occurring during the exhibition's final week. The program was visibly scaled back from its earlier planned version and less extensive than what they presented in other cities. There was also no practicable. The press surmised the reasons for what some referred to as the program's overall *demi-échec* (half-failure), listing among the possible culprits a lack of interest from municipal technical staff, safety concerns, and even resistance from some city administrators.[108] The member of the municipal council for cultural affairs responsible for

Model of an alternative scheme for the Caen practicable, with the design correlating with drawings for "Caen projet no. 3," from June 1975.

Drawings of an alternative scheme for the Caen practicable, dated June 1975.

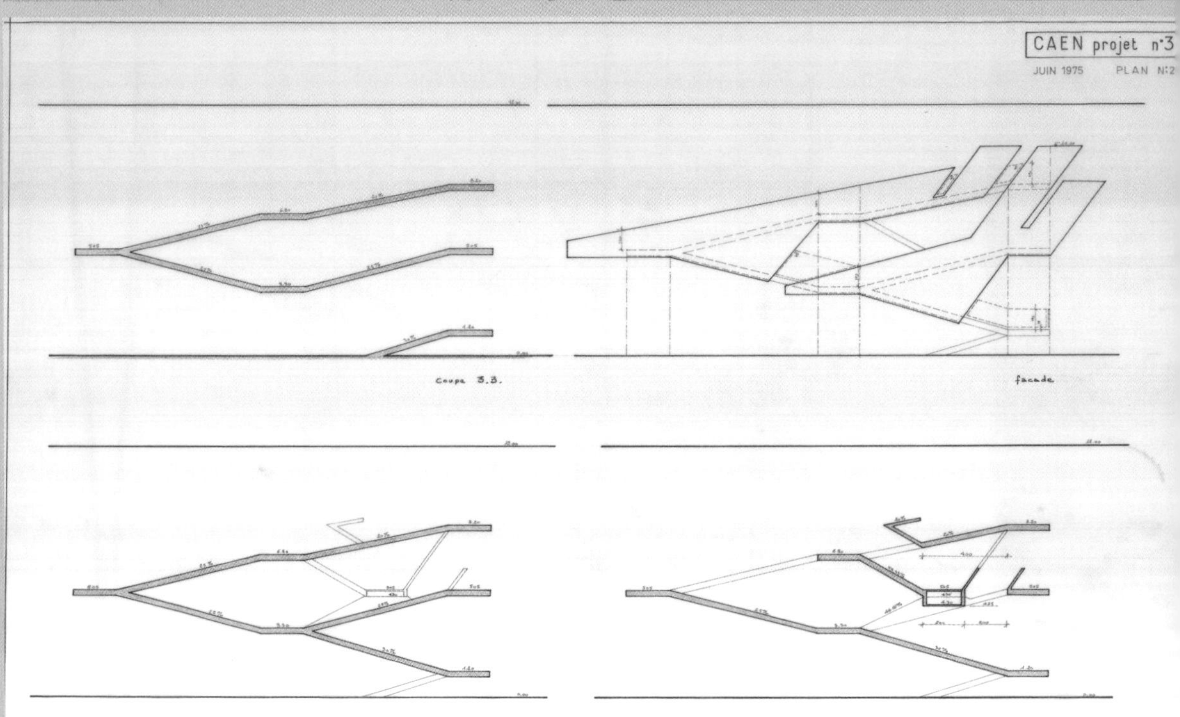

the event, quoted in the same article, explained that the status of the practicable was one of delay rather than cancellation. The installation was to be built the following September as a part of the city's annual autumn fair—though still in the theater foyer—several months after Parent's exhibition at the municipal theater ended. The reported plan was to have the installation engage the fair's theme, while also delivering previously postponed programs made in collaboration with various local and out-of-town participants.[109] These changes apparently also necessitated the reevaluation of Parent's original design to consider the need for furnishings in the foyer in other ways.

A series of designs produced by Parent as late as August of 1975 confirms that the exploration of alternate schemes continued well after the exhibition closed. Based on existing drawings, and the numbering system that Parent's office used to document various projects, there were at least four different practicable designs developed throughout that summer. Each of these versions focuses on the part of the practicable resting on the floor, while the other part resembling a bridge appears to have been eliminated. Also not included are explicit references to the existing architecture of the foyer, making these subsequent schemes appear as if, rather than being tailor-made for a specific site, they could be installed anywhere. The first such scheme consists of a stack of multiple ramped floors, like a more intricate version of *Praticable no. 7*. The second scheme has one half of the previous design removed, yielding a yet more asymmetrical configuration. The following version, another evolution of the previous iterations, introduces a vertical panel partially covering one side of the ramped installation, the first such element to be introduced in a practicable. While it may superficially appear as an attempt at constructing an applied façade, it is in fact an exercise in integrating railings along the elevated portions of the ramp within the formal logic of oblique geometries. The fourth and presumably final version is less complex but likewise deals with railing design and introduces plexiglass, in addition to wood and metal tubing, as an optional material. These follow-up schemes captured a new sense of possibility—like a burst of inspiration that propelled the potential of the practicable beyond what had already been actualized over the years in its previous iterations—but they also effectively marked the end of this series of experiments.

4. ON INTERIORITY

As both a quality and condition, interiority is evident in all of Claude Parent's practicables, like a thread that strings them together and prevents their scatter. In the most elemental sense, an object is interior if it belongs to, goes into, or comes from within a space defined as interior. Each practicable was tailored to the institutional interior of its host, which in all but one case simply meant the inside of a building.[1] The practicables were thus interior as a reflection of the spaces for which they were designed. Working with the existing architecture as support and enclosure, the installations generated the kinds of environments that neither they nor the existing buildings could produce on their own. "The interior is that space that architecture makes," writes Mark Pimlott in the book *The Public Interior as Idea and Project*.[2] Taking Pimlott's definition of the interior into account places the practicables in a collaborative and complex relationship with the existing architecture, such that the space that they participate in making can be described as a series of twists: an interior made by existing architecture and remade by Parent's architecture playing the role of interior objects defined by the existing interior. If that last sentence needs to be reread, it is because tracing how interiority is spatially folded into the architecture of the practicables may require it.

Beyond considering their interiority in relation to spatial boundaries, the practicables were also interior because they served as instruments for exploring subjectivity. Subjective perspectives based on one's personal encounters with one's surroundings—part of the individual's interiority or inner self—were among Parent's most challenging and persistent preoccupations. This was the case in the initial stages of developing the oblique function as a theory with Virilio, and even more so later on, as he attempted to gather feedback about his hypothesis throughout the tour. The practicables were thus interior objects because they engaged interiority as a spatial but also subjective condition.[3] While placing an object within a fixed boundary is by definition an act of limitation, designating the practicables as interior by no means narrows one's perspective on their inventiveness, ambition, or relevance. On the contrary, considering them as interior objects opens up the possibility of multiple new readings, expanding upon their already established significance both within Parent's decades-long career and as a precedent for contemporary practice.

Approaching the practicables through the lens of interiority places them in a context in which multiple elements—different layers of architecture, but also art, performances, exhibitions, screenings, graphics, publications, audience, various participants, as well as the architect himself—register as part of the overall work. Such positioning also links the practicables with other parts of Parent's creative output, including those that preceded the establishment of Architecture Principe, yielding new insights. In this chapter, I first investigate Parent's conceptualization of and positioning toward interiority through his published writings, followed by an examination of realized projects selected from the period between the early 1950s and the mid-1970s. This discussion shows how such spaces and texts help situate the practicables as interior objects, part of the architect's broader engagement with questions related to interiority in both theory and practice. The chapter concludes with a focus on the public nature of the practicables and of the interior as a productive space for architectural experimentation. By unfolding in public interiors, these objects model a significant departure from the overlap between interior space and subjective interiority that is typically thought of as taking place in private.

OBLIQUE HOME IN THEORY

Interior space played a key, if at times understated, role in Architecture Principe's articulation of the oblique function as a theory. According to Parent, it was the interior that differentiated the St. Bernadette du Banlay Church from the solid concrete bunkers that inspired it and which, from the outside, it resembled.[4] Virilio referred to the church as "the model of a future home."[5] In one of the early issues of the magazine, he mused: "We are able to live in a state of disequilibrium. Why then have we never used instability in the interior of our dwellings?"[6] Indeed, as earlier chapters already began pointing out, the domestic interior appeared throughout Parent's subsequent work on oblique architecture and, more generally, his pursuit of fundamentally rethinking how people live. In *Vivre à l'oblique*—where the word *intérieur* appears no less than thirty times—he challenges comfort as a priority in the domestic realm, believing that it stifled people's sense of agency and encouraged complacency. In this regard, he writes: "The oblique function is the architecture of effort that awakens and catalyzes man; it is opposed to the lenient comfort that puts him to sleep and leads his mind to death."[7] Likewise, Parent imagines an alternate future in which "the notion of comfort, which is currently all-powerful, fades away."[8] He reiterated this vision in other texts, including the essay "L'habitat" in the book *5 relaxions sur l'architecture,* in which he explains that the home need not only provide protection from the outside world but also propel the user outward. The home should in this way be a "springboard" rather than a "cocoon," instigating social engagement instead of seclusion.[9] If the domestic realm is historically regarded as a site of self-definition where interior space and individual interiority overlap, the terms of such a process, according to Parent's theory, required revision.[10]

In his rhetoric, Parent rejected domestic décor defined by the arrangement of collected objects whose role, beyond utility, was to reflect inhabitants' identities, aspirations, and taste. The inclined plane thus also served as an instrument for clearing the domestic interior of, in his view, superfluously accumulated belongings. He observes that "the living space is cluttered with furniture that is an obstacle to the journey inside the home. The proliferation of these furniture-objects creates a museum. Our apartments are small museums where the isolated contemplation of each piece of furniture allows all the decorative nonsense."[11] The process of acquiring things transforms the home, Parent argues, from a space for living to an environment in service of appearance; not unlike cities with their own alienating effects, homes too are thus places made, in effect, "not to be inhabited."[12] His depictions of private homes in question evoke the nineteenth-century "phantasmagorias of the interior" famously captured by Walter Benjamin in the 1930s, which describe the dweller as a subject who "needs the domestic interior to sustain him in his illusions."[13] Envisioning the domestic interior reformed according to the principles of the oblique function, Parent writes: "The definition of habitable spaces is no longer made by the decorator's accumulation of anachronistic furniture which replaces the expression of interior architecture until it completely disappears."[14] The decorator was as such regarded as a figure, professional or amateur, who propagates the very accumulation of goods that need to be expulsed from the interior, not only because objects stand in the way of living life fully but also because their existence threatens to erase the presence—and relevance—of architecture.

As already discussed, *Vivre à l'oblique* served as a theoretical script for Parent's tour of France and a playbook according to which the practicables came to be. Although the installations took place outside of the domestic realm, they demonstrated, in a public context, their capacity to reorder interior space similarly to what Parent had imagined for the private realm. As prototypes of a ubiquitous and multi-scalar oblique system, the practicables were interior objects used to displace other objects from the interior. Much in the same way that inclined planes were intended to eliminate outdated and unnecessary objects in the home, the installations commissioned by the *maisons de la culture* more generally sought to replace public consumption of mass-produced goods and media with cultural production and social engagement. The mirroring, reciprocity, and reversibility of private and public realms in Parent's engagement with interiority—from domestic floors to the practicables and, therefore, from homes to houses of culture—was not particularly unique. On the contrary, it reflected broader cultural and professional attitudes about the character and role of interior spaces in the twentieth century, neither uncommon among architects of Parent's generation nor those that preceded them. In her essay "Taste and the Interior Designer," the historian Penny Sparke identifies a shift in the development of interiors that occurred in the 1920s—from serving as instruments for shaping social status to facilitating social engagement—nearly half a century before Parent's theoretical texts prioritized similar values. Sparke notes that these modernist domestic interiors borrowed elements and spatial strategies "from the public sphere in order to minimize the relationship of the home with trade, consumption, bourgeois domesticity, and, most importantly, the concept of taste."[15] In this regard, the practicables, not unlike what Virilio believed the church had done, modeled a way of living in the public sphere that could, theoretically, be imported back into private homes.

Neither in theory nor in practice—whether in public or private—were Parent's inclined planes entirely without other objects. In *Vivre à l'oblique*, he speculated upon ways in which the oblique function would inspire furniture designers to innovate in response to the new way of life. Projecting himself into the future that he envisioned, Parent, for example, optimistically promises, "Adventure abounds for the creators who are concerned with furniture."[16] In *5 réflexions sur l'architecture*, he follows his own critique of the current state of the domestic interior, and the role of furnishings in it, with several suggestions for further consideration. One set of ideas called for increased customization based on personal needs as well as for users to exert pressure on furniture manufacturers to offer better products. Another suggestion was to conceptualize interior architecture in such a way that it allows users to make personalized adjustments to products and even create opportunities for completing some of the construction work on their own.[17] As interior objects, the practicables began fulfilling some of those principles, while also demonstrating that their intended role was not to entirely replace all other objects but rather to condition their presence and character.

ARCHITECTURE AGAINST DESIGN

Parent's perspective on interior objects predated the conception of the oblique function and his use of practicables. In fact, he expressed an interest in product design and interiors from the very early stages of his career, not only in professional practice but also through his writing for various magazines. In 1961, for example, he wrote a review of the 42nd edition of the Salon des artistes décorateurs—the prestigious annual design fair in Paris—published in *Aujourd'hui: Art et architecture* in which he expressed a preference for "materials without falsehood" and the evolution of design beyond "decorator-style."[18] He praised the work of the designer Jacques Dumond, calling it "beautiful in proportions, functional in its use, detached from the ground despite its mass,"[19] as well as showed admiration for exhibited artifacts by Roger Fatus and the designer duo Janine Abraham and Dirk Jan Rol. These designers explored new materials and methods of fabrication, using a formal vocabulary that privileged abstract forms in lieu of overt historical references. Parent concludes the review with a sense of optimism: "Soon, we hope, thanks to the multiplication of this kind, decorators, architects, and artists will find a community of thoughts; a pejorative vocabulary will no longer separate them."[20] His professionally inclusive sentiment, however, was not without its caveats. Although he had a sustained interest in design innovation, was deeply connected to artists with whom he often collaborated, and regularly engaged with interiors as sites for his work, his attitude toward designers—as distinct from architects—was at times unfairly harsh. Acknowledging this is one way of grasping how his perspective was both shaped and limited by the culture within which he operated, while also elucidating the terms and conditions under which his many collaborations, including the multidisciplinary programs related to the practicables, occurred.

Jacques Dumond's Meuble Universel from 1952.

The magazine *L'architecture d'aujourd'hui* published a special issue in 1971, titled "Le design," to which Parent contributed his essay "Face à face: Architecture et design." The cover of "Le design" is a color drawing of a stylized question mark set against a horizon approximating the earth's curvature, the work of the Belgian artist and illustrator Jean-Michel Folon. The oversized punctuation mark is assembled from cubes, as if it were a modular structure, with a figure of a person holding up the character's upper hook while standing on the lower dot. The special issue was devoted to the topic of design as an emerging field—focusing to a large extent on furniture, prefabricated assemblies, and other serially produced objects—with the cover posing a question as if to convey a sense of uncertainty or doubt as a precondition for the discussion. Featured inside were the likes of Olivier Mourgue, Joe Colombo, Quasar Khanh (identified by the mononym Quasar), and Barbara Stauffacher Solomon, each of whose pioneering work made a convincing case for design as an accomplished field in its own right, increasingly distinguished and independent from other allied professions. The magazine's agenda, however, as captured in the introduction by the editor Marc Emery, was to compare it to architecture rather than exploring it on its own terms. The essay positions designers and architects side by side in each of their quests for command of the built environment, while also identifying uncertainties about their respective roles in a changing society.[21] Parent's essay echoes a similar, architecture-centered, sentiment as if to amplify the already established editorial bias of the magazine. His article's title reinforces a confrontational stance between the two professions—a power struggle of sorts. In the text's first paragraph Parent vocally rejects what he refers to as the Anglo-Saxon definition of design as a generalized activity applicable to all aspects of the constructed environment, claiming that such terminology distorted the significant distinctions among different fields, especially that of architecture in relation to the others.[22] Beyond offering semantic clarifications, the article portrays designers and their work as complicit with the dominating forces of industry and as an existential threat to architects and architecture. Running through the text is the sentiment that design owed something to architecture, recounting how architecture ennobled this young field—"a child of industry"[23]—only for designers to subsequently dominate the built environment by becoming "*imperialist* and *universal*."[24] If decorators were to carry the blame for encouraging frivolous consumption of industrially made products, designers in this way bore responsibility for their very existence.[25] Having framed the relationship between design and architecture in confrontational and binary terms, Parent subsequently claims a position of neutrality and proposes a truce:

> The designer will fit into the natural hierarchy of disciplines that contribute to the act of building if they no longer tie their ambition to the imperialist action of industry. Let it be understood that, in this text, it is not the designer that I am attacking, nor am I trying to protect architects, but that I am stigmatizing any action of architect, designer or decorator that tends to submit architecture to marketing and, through it, to a decadent technology that is nothing but the nostalgia of the 19th century.[26]

Reflective of his overarching values, his expectations are thus threefold: first is the demand for a critical position toward industry; second is the

Gae Aulenti's prototype for the living environment Grandi Conaminazioni, produced by Kartell and shown at the Museum of Modern Art in New York as part of the exhibition *Italy: The New Domestic Landscape*, 1972.

imperative not to reproduce the material culture of the previous century; and third is the expectation that architecture remain at the center (or top, depending on one's view) of all creative fields.

Regardless of how reasonable some of the proposed terms may appear, Parent's perspective was not without serious problems. As the design historian and curator Alexandra Midal argues in her book *Design by Accident: For a New History of Design*, Parent's essay betrayed a lack of understanding of—or willingness to acknowledge—the progress that designers had achieved by that time in forging both intellectual autonomy from industry and the capacity to challenge the status quo on their own terms, independently of architecture or art.[27] For example, in Italy, as the work published in "Le design" demonstrated, a new generation of designers including Joe Colombo and Gaetano Pesce, but also Enzo Mari, Gae Aulenti, and others, used the design of interior objects as a vehicle for questioning consumption, labor, industry, and the relationship between the domestic realm and the city, devising their own conditions for engaging architecture. Aulenti—whose reconfigurable interior living unit produced by the furniture manufacturer Kartell in 1972 included, incidentally, a ramped element resembling a practicable—had a perspective on personal belongings not unlike Parent's own. In a 1970s interview, for example, she gives the following advice to readers of a popular magazine: "Whoever asks me how to make a home is to not have anything, just a few shelves for books, some pillows to sit on. And then, to take a stand against the ephemeral, against passing trends . . . and to return to lasting values."[28] Likewise, Colombo had adopted an unambiguously critical perspective toward the economic system that supported design production, which Midal describes as follows:

> [Colombo] denounced the dominant model of furniture design and production as complicit with the capitalist system, to which he refused to subscribe. He condemned the proliferation of objects, not as a phenomenon in and of itself, but rather as a vector for the alienation of the working class to which design was originally addressed, and as a means for increasing the wealth of the bourgeoisie at the expense of workers.[29]

The accumulation of such examples undermine Parent's generalization about designers' complicity with industry to the point where they appear blatantly unfounded and outdated. His denial over the kind of independence and agency that designers had achieved by then also registers as an indicator of threat; it suggests an anxiety around architecture's vulnerability in relation to the emerging agency of design.[30] Figures like Aulenti and Colombo—whose work was presented to American audiences in the Emilio Ambasz-curated exhibition *Italy: The New Domestic Landscape* at the Museum of Modern Art in 1972[31]—used the design of objects as a vehicle for reconceptualizing modern life in new ways. One particular tendency of their work, as well as that by Ettore Sottsass, Alberto Rosselli, Ugo La Pietra, and others included in the New York show (but also more broadly including designers like Verner Panton), was the scaling up of the interior object to create its own environment, indicative of what Midal refers to as a means of exerting influence over domestic space.[32] Arguably, such approaches to design were meant to address consumption trends and the problem of accumulating unnecessary "stuff," just as Aulenti had articulated, through a variable mixture of criticism, speculation, and problem-solving. In this way, such efforts were not unlike the practicables and, vice versa, Parent's installations were not unlike these design objects. While the practicables were neither prefabricated nor produced in factories, they shared with such objects the slippery status as either (or both) micro-architecture or macro-design.[33]

EARLY INTERIOR PROJECTS

Parent's engagement with interior spaces and furnishings also played out in his professional practice. Examining his early-career work and following it through the conclusion of the tour of France expands the context for considering the practicables in relation to the interior. Two interiors—one realized at the start of Parent's tour and the other at the end—served as opportunities for implementing the oblique function in the domestic realm. Before focusing on these two projects, however, I want to first turn to the very beginning of Parent's professional trajectory, a period during which he completed several other interior renovations. Taking this earlier professional work into account helps not only contextualize the theoretical positions he embraced at that time, but also foregrounds the development of his practice leading up to the establishment of Architecture Principe.

His use of furniture throughout the 1950s, for example, provides a useful background for interpreting his later writing on the subject. Likewise, his involvement with artists during the same era can be read as informing his subsequent approach to the realization of the practicables in the 1970s. This includes how he accounted not only for exhibiting standalone works of art but also embedding the use of painted color as a spatial element and integrating collaboration as a way of working. While the discussion in this chapter thus far has primarily centered on Parent's treatment of interior objects in his writing, how he populated interior spaces with objects in his practice—and what kind of objects they were—is no less insightful.

Even though Parent's architecture career began in earnest with Maison Gosselin—a house built in 1953 and realized, in partnership with the architect and schoolmate Ionel Schein, as a winning entry in a competition sponsored by the magazine *La maison française*—his early portfolio also featured several small-scale interior commissions, including a studio-sized apartment for his sister, Nicole Parent, in Neuilly-sur-Seine on the outskirts of Paris.[34] The modest but nonetheless photogenic project occupied the upper level of a garage, a building that later became the architect's own family residence. A suite of photographs, published in the magazine *Maison et jardin* in 1958, shows a compact interior spatially defined by the relationship between thin linear elements—black trim, slender stair railing, and metal door frames—and planes of applied color that at times meet one another at right angles to imply three-dimensional volume.[35] A selection of modern furnishings, fixtures, and accessories—including a large record player as well as carefully placed tableware—conveys a sense of occupation the way a theatrical stage set might, while a pair of open glass doors leading to a stone-paved patio with a miniature pool is suggestive of an indoor-outdoor lifestyle. The combination of 1920s de Stijl and mid-century American Case Study aesthetic references was in line with Parent's interests at the time.[36] This studio and other similar commissions, limited in scope to interiors of existing buildings, are representative of the type of work often pursued by young architects—both then and now—for the purpose of gaining practical experience, sustaining their small businesses, developing portfolios, and establishing useful social and professional connections while often asserting their identity as architects rather than interior designers.[37] In Parent's case, these interiors happened alongside other types of projects, including single-family houses, which are perhaps better known examples of his early realizations.

Most of Parent's photographically documented interiors from this era appear as neither overly elaborate nor exceedingly experimental in comparison with his later work.[38] Yet his use of elements like paint and furnishings—part of interior design's essential repertoire—was neither incidental nor was it outside the scope of Parent's creative aspirations. Rather, it played a critical role in the development and application of his theoretical framework. In these projects, paint delivered color to the interior but also had a more conceptually profound role of enabling the integration of architecture with art.[39] The introduction of painterly abstraction into living environments was, in other words, a recurring pursuit found in much of Parent's work from that period and a reflection of his association with his mentor André Bloc and the influence of the Groupe Espace.[40] Conceptually, the topical application of paint was the domain of art—in most cases the color compositions in these projects were developed by his artist collaborators including Bloc, Maximilien Herzèle, and others—while the supporting surfaces played the role of architecture. The relationship between art and architecture was thus negotiated in terms of precedence as well as how their simultaneous presence balanced out. This means that sometimes color reinforced architectural form and in other instances it had the freedom to introduce new geometries to a space. Parent saw the potential of paint to expand architecture's repertoire for overcoming its own limitations, but also, as he later reflected, to enable "the destruction of the architecture itself."[41] Paint, in this sense, could be used as a tool for emancipating architecture from its existing ordering principles based on geometry, structure, and part-to-whole relationships, much like the oblique plane would attempt to do later in his work.

Like paint, ready-made furniture was often prominent in these commissions.[42] In photographs of a Parisian apartment renovation from 1954, for example, a black Butterfly chair designed by Jorge Ferrari-Hardoy in 1938, sits prominently in the foreground. (Two such chairs also appeared on his sister's outdoor terrace.) For a small dining room in the same apartment, Parent designed a round custom table surrounded by a set of Charlotte Perriand stools. Another residence from the same year appears furnished with an assortment of freestanding interior objects, including Eero Saarinen's Womb chair and ottoman, designed in 1948, and a pair of large Harry Bertoia Diamond chairs. Florence Knoll's Hairpin side tables made an appearance in more than one project. The interior of Café du Rond-Point on the Champs-Élysées, designed with Bloc, included a field of Arne Jacobsen's then-recently issued stackable Series 7 chairs, a part of the restaurant's overall mix of seating arrangements. A magazine article from 1961 compared Parent's

Interior of the apartment designed by Parent for his sister Nicole in the early 1950s at Villa des Peupliers in Neuilly-sur-Seine, in the same building that later became the architect's family home.

Parent's renovation of the apartment for the editor Jean Baillais, c. 1954, designed in collaboration with Ionel Schein, c. 1954.

Living room of the Bourgeois apartment, c. 1954.

Café du Rond-Point des Champs-Élysées in Paris, designed around 1957 by Parent working in collaboration with André Bloc. In addition to the use of site-specific artwork throughout the space, furnishings played a key role in the overall design strategy.

own domestic interior from this era to a museum[43]—the general notion of which he categorically rejected in *Vivre à l'oblique*—thanks to the arrangement of furnishings and artworks; others interpreted it as evidence of his personal commitment to the synthesis of the arts "under the auspices of architecture."[44]

The presence of and relationship among furnishings, applied color, art objects, built-ins, and building elements in these interior projects echoed the ordering principles already established by Le Corbusier in his Pavillon de l'Esprit Nouveau from 1925. The temporary building, installed during the International Exhibition of Modern Decorative and Industrial Arts in Paris, concretized Le Corbusier's stance against decoration, his conditional embrace of industrial objects, and inclusion of art—as both standalone object and as color applied directly to building surfaces—in the domestic interior and beyond. Comparing Parent's early work with the pavilion in particular helps further clarify his position toward industry and the embrace of certain kinds of objects over others. Le Corbusier, in theory, embraced the lack of authorship in such objects, explaining in *The Decorative Art of Today* that "this art without decoration is made not by artists but by anonymous industry."[45] If, contrary to his later provocations, interior objects figured prominently in some of Parent's work, it is because they were exemplary of the kind of quality and ethos that he demanded of contemporary designers.

Yet, Parent's ready-made selections seem to have been made by consciously considering their background beyond manufacturing—authorship, in other words, mattered. He curated his objects not unlike the way Bloc handpicked members of the Groupe Espace, which among its mix of some of the most established artists and architects of the time included Jacobsen, Jean Prouvé, Victor Vasarely, Richard Neutra, and others. As such, the interior served not only as a living space but also a stage for enacting a series of artistic affiliations. In addition to the artists that he worked with directly on these projects, the curated objects themselves appeared as aspirational markers of engagement with other figures from various creative fields, as if collecting certain objects in a room simulated a social gathering of their authors. Such intentionally implied relationships among people and objects were a preview of how Parent later used practicables as stages for collaboration. In these early projects, each object acted as a time stamp, a chronological marker meant to furnish the space with a sense of contemporaneity. With their inward orientation, these spaces, at least in pictures, rarely revealed their broader architectural or urban context in terms of place; instead, it was to a large extent through furnishings that these interiors occupied their proper moment in time. In this way, the arrangement of furniture, a key interior design strategy, was used for the purpose of imbuing the architecture—and the architect—with a sense of time-specificity and thus contemporary relevance.

OBLIQUE HOME IN PRACTICE

If the interior environments from the 1950s sought to place their subjects into the present, mid-century moment, in the early 1970s Parent's attention was focused on the future. The domestic interior was thus used as a space for experimenting with and prototyping a different way of living that could subsequently be applied elsewhere. Two apartment renovations from this

Interior of the Bellaguet apartment in Neuilly-sur-Seine, featuring the artist's own artwork throughout.

period—one created for Andrée Bellaguet in 1970 and another, his own family residence, from around 1974—were attempts to bring the oblique function into daily life, at the intimate scale of the body, and within the private milieu of the home. These interior interventions were, along with the practicables, part of Parent's larger project of establishing the slope as a viable substrate for living.

A written document signed by the architect—resembling a certificate of authenticity that may typically accompany an artwork rather than an architecture project—identifies the Bellaguet apartment as the first realized example of an oblique living space, the first test of a new way of life according to the hypothesis presented in *Vivre à l'oblique.*[46] A 1972 article in *Journal de la maison*, a popular French home décor magazine, provided an overall description of the space. It declares: "No wall is vertical. No floor is straight. Everything has been rebuilt, in lacquered wood. The bed, which blends in with the black carpeting, is tilted. The table is in laminate and goes up three steps. One chooses their level, sits on the raised floor and leans on the backrests provided for this purpose."[47] The overall composition of black and white surfaces, angled at either ten or forty degrees in relation to the ground, resulted in an immersive environment prescient of the formal ambitions that later preoccupied many architects emerging in the

1980s and 1990s, but was in its autonomy as an object also not unlike the domestic devices envisioned by designers in the 1970s who, as has already been discussed, Parent fought against.

Contributing to the spatial reading of the apartment—an otherwise typical postwar one-bedroom unit, within which it is mostly the open-living area that served as a testing ground for Parent's hypothesis—was the placement of paintings throughout that Bellaguet made during this period, using the apartment as both a residence and an art studio.[48] Each square-format canvas, a part of the *Profils* series exhibited in Amiens, has a tapered frame that slightly skews the painting's surface away from frontal view while also accentuating its presence as a volume rather than a flat picture.[49] Abstract compositions of angular planes and diagonal lines appeared as extensions of the apartment's tilting geometries, but also infused the otherwise mostly achromatic environment with punches of saturated color. Widely published photographs of the apartment show an interior that is rich in geometry and graphics, visually depicting a continuum between the physical space and the painted images, but also between life and work. In one staged photograph accompanying the *Journal de la maison* article, Bellaguet is working on one of her paintings; in another, the camera captures a gathering around the dining table as framed by an aperture that connects living and work areas. Such photographs fulfill their role as evidence of the synthetic relationship between architecture and art, and of the viability and versatility of life on

Built-in inclines of the Bellaguet apartment obscured distinctions between walls, floors, and furnishings, but also introduced an unexpected play of hard and soft surfaces.

Dining area of Parent's family residence in Neuilly-sur-Seine, renovated to include inclined floors with built-ins replacing conventional furniture, including a table around which guests ate facing each other at different levels.

angled surfaces to which Parent and Bellaguet were both committed.[50] Images of the apartment later provided, as was already discussed in Chapter 3, the content to be disseminated along Parent's tour of France—a case study of private life on the oblique gone public.

A few years later, Parent radically transformed his own house by introducing two oblique objects to its interior. In a rectangular volume of space one story above the street level—the same building, originally a garage, that he renovated for his sister some two decades earlier—were two domestic practicables, one to be used for dining and another as a living area. The dining side had a white, two-tier table placed perpendicular to the direction of the slope, including the built-in seating. The lounge-like living area, formed as a composite of multiple sectional profiles through which Parent tested various degrees of slope, encouraged a range of physical postures and was also partially inhabitable from below. As in the living area of the painter's apartment, this interior landscape was covered in black carpeting, yielding a sense of continuity and, at times, serving unexpected tactile effects underfoot. In an interview with Rem Koolhaas, Parent explains: "In some areas there was foam underneath, so it felt like a cushion . . . without any sort of signal [laughs]. Suddenly people would feel it, and be completely surprised—but most didn't like this unexpected feeling."[51]

The appeal of these installations is their hybrid quality, part wall-to-wall carpeting and part oversized multifunctional furniture, appearing in such a domestic context as both familiar and entirely unexpected. As objects inserted into homes, these interior objects can be seen as architecture's reaction to the emerging ambitions in product design, by the likes of Colombo, to annex the domestic interior as part of its domain. In Parent's home, aside from the two floor-mounted structures—and a

Claude and Naad Parent surrounded by students in their oblique living room, c. 1974.

few shaggy throw pillows and some displayed art notwithstanding—these areas appear free of other furnishings with photographs as evidence that the inclined planes succeeded in banishing most freestanding furniture from the environment. A portfolio of such pictures show Parent, his wife Naad, and a group of students in colorful outfits informally populating the sloped floor in various poses as if reenacting an animated outdoor gathering indoors—a staged interior picnic. If the Bellaguet apartment served as an early example of home life on the slope promoted by the tour, Parent's own house demonstrated the commitment to his principles even after the traveling programs came to an end. (He did eventually give up on oblique life when, around 1996, he had the house fully refurbished inside and out, making the floors once again level.)

Implemented in spaces that, unlike the practicables, were intensively loaded with daily uses as well as more permanent, these domestic interior objects demonstrated their potential for future implementation but also confirmed certain limitations. One obvious challenge, for example, was incorporating programs like kitchens and bathrooms into oblique geometries. Rather than finding a way to replace them altogether, they are pushed to the side so as to minimize their overall visibility—both from the viewpoint of the inhabitants and the photographer converting the living interior into images. As opposed as Parent seemed to be to the domestic interior as a stage for self-expression in the way that decorators traditionally treated it, these two realized projects conveyed their own sense of theatricality and social aspiration, a bond they also shared with the practicables.

GOING PUBLIC

Designating the practicables as interior objects—a move that is at once straightforward and slightly oblique—conceptually connects them to the domestic realm in and beyond Parent's work, even if their presence was profoundly public. In this capacity, they can be understood as publicly implemented devices used for practicing, exercising, and experimenting with new modes of domestic occupation. Positioned this way, they are also brought into proximity with other creative disciplines—particularly those whose claims over the domestic sphere may compete with architecture's—which yields new insights about disciplinary crossovers and collaboration in Parent's work as well as the conditions under which they were either welcomed or refused. In addition to being formally and behaviorally motivated, regarding the practicables as interior objects elucidates their aspiring role as instruments for regulating the reach of industry and mass consumption into daily life's many crevices. As such, the simply assembled handmade installations manifested the drive to resist the emergence of design as a competitive practice capable of taking over architecture's lead in certain domains, such as the interior. Yet, if these oblique objects colonized the interior on behalf of architecture—like the nesting of architecture inside architecture—they also inadvertently underlined some of the ways in which other spatial practices can potentially occupy architecture using their own motives, means, and methods.

Parent's practicables draw attention to the interior both as a space for experimentation and as public space. The installations' siting, in other words, foregrounds the interior's prevalent but critically understated role in architectural experimentation, while also demonstrating the value of directing questions about interiority, as they relate to the design of living environments, toward the public. Unfolding in public interiors, these objects model by example a significant departure from the limiting notion that overlaps between interior space and subjective interiority only take place in private.[52] In this way, the practicables contribute to the increasingly relevant (although by no means new) discussions about architecture's capacity and readiness to engage subjectivity in the public sphere, whether it be indoors or out.

Finally, whether at a *maison de la culture* or the architect's home, the enclosed interior made the oblique function—and the inhabited inclined plane—extraordinary. Outside, in the city or in the countryside, on a street or on top of a building, an incline is nothing more than an unnoticed slope in the road, a shallow rise of a hill, or an ordinary surface engineered to move water from one place to another. Inside, however, even the slightest tilt underfoot is as disruptive as it can be spectacular. The interior, in other words, amplifies the radicality of the slope (as well as its less convenient aspects), and by doing so limits—like a system of checks and balances—the ultimate extent to which the oblique function can inflect all facets of the built environment.

Exterior view of Parent's family home in Neuilly-sur-Seine, redesigned by the architect in the late 1990s.

5. OTHER ANGLES

In an attempt to ground the oblique function in reality, Parent reached back in time. *Vivre à l'oblique*, as I noted earlier in the book, opens with a call to discover the future by reading the past—or, *ON DOIT LIRE LE PASSE COMME UN FUTUR A DECOUVRIR*, as he wrote in all caps for emphasis—a process subsequently referred to as an "archeology of the future."[1] The same book ends with a resume-style list which, in addition to the architect's published texts, exhibitions, conferences, and appearances in films, includes the section "The Archeology of the Oblique Function." Under this title, Parent rolls out an eclectic variety of appropriated references: natural reliefs, shorelines, dikes, and dams; Çatalhöyük, the nine-thousand-year-old settlement in southern Anatolia, Turkey, where roofs were used for public circulation in lieu of streets; Monte Albán, the ancient Zapotec complex of stepped terraces and pyramids in Oaxaca, Mexico; the Great Mosque of Samarra in Iraq, built in the ninth century, with a minaret encircled by a spiral ramp; eighteenth-century astronomical observatories in India built by Jai Singh; highways and parking garages; as well as Frank Lloyd Wright's Guggenheim Museum and Frederick Kiesler's 1950 design for the Endless House.[2] By sampling from a range of geographies and eras, Parent's list takes stock of available references—forms, structures, settlements, patterns, images, and phenomena reminiscent of oblique architecture—so that they can be drawn from, built upon, and in this way become part of what may be best described as a retroactive genealogy or lineage.[3]

More recently, Parent himself became the subject of similar "archeologies," or inclusions in various narratives that linked his work to the works of more recent generations of architects. Among the examples already mentioned in the book's introductory chapter is the 1996 Venice Biennale exhibition *BLOC: Le monolithe fracturé*, which presented him as a pivotal figure in the postwar development of French experimental architecture, while also effectively positioning architects like Jean Nouvel and Odile Decq as his contemporary successors. A similar sense of continuity between the past and the future—forged by like-minded theoretical interests as well as overlapping formal sensibilities—is captured in the reissue of the entire magazine *Architecture Principe* as a book, also in 1996. In addition to the original nine issues from 1966, the publication includes a tenth issue, titled "Disorientation or Dislocation." Featuring new texts by not only Parent and Virilio but also the era's next-generation architects like Daniel Libeskind, Wolf Prix, and Bernard Tschumi, this additional issue connects more recent voices in architecture to this past body of work, while also reinserting Architecture Principe into contemporary discourse. The construction of such intergenerational links also drives the essay "Claude Parent, Present in Posterity," in which the writer and curator Béatrice Simonot identifies various contemporary practitioners "who fall in part within the lineage of theory of the oblique function."[4] This particular account maps out a constellation of works produced in the late 1990s around Parent, including projects by Zaha Hadid, Lars Spuybroek, and Foreign Office Architects. As an architect who rarely appeared or worked outside of his native France, and whose writing has only partially been translated in English, the extent of Parent's presumed influence internationally, including in North America, is nothing short of remarkable. In relation to his approach as proto-digital, that is, prescient of the emergent turn-of-the-century formalism enabled by computation, the architect Greg Lynn notes of Parent: "With his sloped floors and inclined walls, he was there first—he was a key figure for my

Arakawa + Gins, Bioscleave House (Lifespan Extending Villa), East Hampton, New York, 2008.

Sara Hendren, *Slope: Intercept*, 2013–present.

generation."[5] Even Frank Gehry praises the late Parent for his impact on the present:

> His influence abounds in contemporary architecture. Like many great ideas, his ideas would have to wait to be embraced, and they have been. The legacy of Claude Parent is in front of us today: cities of fluidity and continual movement, blurred boundaries between public and private space, and interconnected structures resembling landscapes more than singular buildings.[6]

For many creative practitioners, makers, designers, and certainly architects, the principal purpose of engaging past figures, artifacts, events, and ideas and bringing them into the present moment is never simply to give an account or render a genealogy.[7] The aim of such engagement is instead to motivate, inspire, and make sense of a design process, its approaches and aspirations as well as outcomes. It is the work that architects are always already doing in one way or another, an untidy accumulation of precedent, inspiration, and alibi as productive, generative, and creatively nonlinear as any other attempt to articulate an idea or approach through practice.

In line with such attempts, I approach Parent's work as a predecessor of another set of contemporary explorations. By doing so, I depart from the strict realm of buildings by architects, opening the field up to other creative practices and spatial constructs. Along this expanded horizon, one may expeditiously encounter works such as the artists' Shusaku Arakawa and Madeline Gins's Bioscleave House (2008), the design researcher Sara Hendren's ongoing project *Slope: Intercept*, and other experiments incorporating similarly sloped forms. Both Arakawa and Gins's house (also known as Lifespan Extending Villa) and Hendren's portable ramps made for skaters, wheelchair users, and disability artists have already been in one way or another linked to Parent and Virilio's oblique function in part thanks to the prominence of inclined planes in their work.[8] While the geometry of the ground is a useful common denominator for setting off this oblique journey, in this chapter I expand beyond it in order to continue prioritizing those aspects of Parent's site-specific experiments that may not be as evident or present in other parts of his oeuvre. As such, I further examine the practicables' status as interior objects vis-à-vis existing architecture; their role in framing the architect's relationship to his audience; as well as the ways in which they captured an ethos about practice informed by a certain combination of agility and openness.

Research and experiment-driven architectural installations are perhaps even more ubiquitous now than they were in the 1970s. Likewise, many of the socially engaged strategies deployed throughout Parent's tour of France would not be out of place in the myriad architecture-oriented public programs that continue to pop up worldwide. In other ways, needless to say, as products of a particular time, place, and culture, the practicables belong to the past. As old experiments, they are as flawed, incomplete, and limited by their own circumstances as any contemporary perspective of them might be. Engaging them today, however—and reimagining our relationship to them as a matter of design—provides a productive point of departure for articulating multiple trajectories for experimental practice beyond those solely preoccupied with the prospect of life on sloped floors. Doing so, in turn, helps recognize other, more recent, spatial practices that have since appeared along similarly experimental trajectories and which contribute to establishing alternative connections between the past, present, and future.

With their original purpose and context in mind—as theoretically driven architectural experiments latching onto existing structures—I approach Parent's temporary productions from three angles. The first engages the ground as a composite construct, bringing attention to its material layers and by doing so questioning the nature of the floor as a topical architectural element. The second angle considers Parent's public role, framing his involvement throughout the tour as performance and participation but also in relation to questions of authorship. Each of these first two angles relates certain aspects of Parent's exploration of obliqueness to a series of contemporary works by identifying and comparing their salient features to one another. The third angle traces a series of connections between Parent's experiments and other practices based on their shared engagement with obliqueness as a term, concept, or condition, prompted by a range of diverse objectives. In this final part of the chapter, I take a broader view of obliqueness as a practice. Together, these three of an array of possible angles extend through the present with the intention of pointing to possible future directions. As a trajectory of an alternative lineage, each angle challenges existing ordering principles, from the hierarchies embedded in the layered construction of the ground to the composite of conventions against which divergent forms of experimentation emerge.

LAYER AFTER LAYER

There is no shortage of sloped floors in contemporary architecture. But what would be our time's equivalent of a practicable—a temporary installation framed by existing architecture that questions the nature of the ground we inhabit? Despite the perennial proliferations of installations by architects, some of the most provocative encounters with the ground have over the last decades been produced by artists working across other fields. As a fraction of the most compelling examples, this includes widely known artworks such as Olafur Eliasson's *Riverbed* installed at the Louisiana Museum of Modern Art in Denmark in 2014; the artist Pierre Huyghe's site-specific intervention *After ALife Ahead* produced for the 2017 Skulptur Projekte exhibition in Münster, Germany; as well as the scenery for the opera *Sun & Sea (Marina)* by Rugilė Barzdžiukaitė, Vaiva Grainytė, and Lina Lapelytė, produced for the Venice Biennale in 2019 and on a world tour ever since. Each of these works uses the floor as an element that introduces a radical shift to an interior space, while also— not unlike the practicables—expressing distinct attitudes about human experience. Like the oblique installations, they serve as devices for speculating about the future of the living environment, while departing from Parent's anthropocentric perspective by explicitly prioritizing, for instance, questions related to ecology, climate change, and the agency of nonhuman species.[9] The floor in both *Riverbed* and *After ALife Ahead* is sloped, yet more significant than the particular geometry of each construction is its materiality. Along with *Sun & Sea (Marina),* these installations bring to life Parent's notion of "the culture of tactility," or the use of different materials on the floor as a way of eliciting various reactions from people, an idea that remained largely unrealized in his own work given that, as he admitted with some disappointment, "nobody was ever interested in it."[10] The layering of materials in these contemporary installations is akin to the placement of practicables on top of already existing floors, while their material choices play a critical part in experimenting with the ground specifically indoors—and looking, in effect, at the living environment from the inside out.

In *Riverbed*, Eliasson explored the destabilizing effect of the ground on people's perception of reality and their sense of orientation within an enclosed interior space. The temporary site-specific installation consisted of a walkable terrain distributed across four adjacent galleries that make up the Louisiana Museum's South Wing. A combination of Icelandic rock, pebbles, and running water funneled into a stream is what visitors encountered as they climbed through the installation's varied topography framed by a succession of white walls. As such, *Riverbed* formed part of the artist's ongoing series of "installations that in various ways stage natural materials in isolated presentations."[11] Hidden underneath the rugged surface, an elevated wood structure reminiscent of Parent's practicables provided the floor with its sloping form. The wood substrate's faceted geometry was then softened by subsequent layers of moisture sheeting, sand, gravel, and larger rocks. Visitors traversed the installation in the general direction of

Olafur Eliasson, *Riverbed*, installed at the Louisiana Museum of Modern Art, Humlebæk, Denmark, 2014.

the incline and against the flow of water but were otherwise free to meander at will. This variable act of walking on and through the rocky terrain is what, for Eliasson, completed the work.[12] The use of soil indoors makes *Riverbed* comparable to Walter De Maria's 1977 *The New York Earth Room*, in which the late artist famously filled an entire white-walled gallery with a mixture of earth, peat, and bark, taking over the space like a dark wall-to-wall carpet twenty-two inches thick. De Maria referred to this work as "an interior earth sculpture."[13] The same term can also be used to describe not only Eliasson's installation but also that of other contemporary artists, such as Delcy Morelos, whose floor-mounted installations made of soil and clay ask the viewer to consider earth as a living ecosystem rather than an inert object.[14]

What distinguishes *Riverbed* from these other materially similar works, however, is that it was made to be inhabited rather than looked at from a distance. In this particular way—as a physically interactive space rather than a contemplative object—Eliasson's installation brings another seminal 1970s reference to mind, the scenography for the choreographer

Rugilė Barzdžiukaitė, Vaiva Grainytė, and Lina Lapelytė, *Sun & Sea (Marina)*, performed in the Lithuanian Pavilion at the Venice Biennale, 2019.

Pina Bausch's *The Rite of Spring*. Here, a layer of peat raked across the stage for performers to dance on, a staging still used in contemporary versions of the piece.[15] Like Bausch's performance, Eliasson's interiorized landscape was unambiguously presented as a synthetic construction, the authenticity of which was produced through one's physical engagement with its materiality. Potential narratives surrounding the ground (where it comes from, what it might represent, how it was constructed) and one's interaction with it (how hard is it to walk on, which way do I go, is it wet, can I touch it, will I trip and fall?) could in this way unfold as both fiction and fact. Within the space of the installation, reality was established not by the binary distinction between the two—is this really a riverbed?—but rather as an outcome of one's particular relationship to the environment.

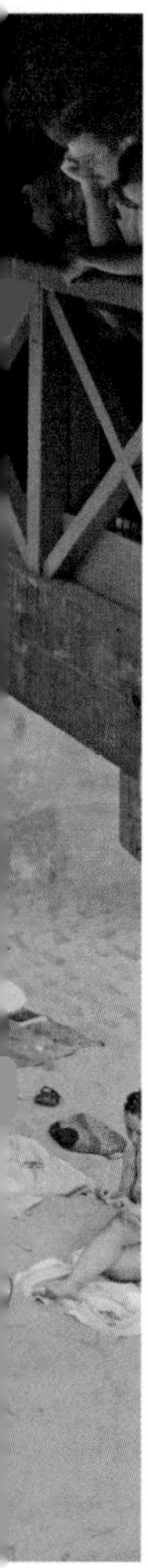

By using the floor as an instrument for interrogating what is perceived as reality, Eliasson's installation shares with Parent's practicables more than just the geometry of is underlying inclined structure. *Riverbed* was in this sense a next-generation practicable in line with Parent's intentions—beyond general shared affinities, interests, and references, it is also known that Eliasson read *Vivre à l'oblique*[16]—in two particular ways. First, it challenged the notion that the ground, and people's relationship to it, is a natural and thus neutral condition. Much like the various ramps that Parent installed throughout France, Eliasson's rocky floor prompted questioning the ground that one inhabits rather than taking it for granted. Second, like Parent, Eliasson used the floor as a tool for building trust between institutions and people. By asking, "Do you really feel comfortable destabilizing yourself on purpose?" Eliasson interrogated not only trust as a factor in the relationship between the floor and those walking on it, but also—much like Parent did in the context of French *maisons de la culture*—the mutual risk-taking that is required in order to build connections between the museum and the public.[17]

As an enclosed terrain, *Riverbed* engaged various ideas relating to boundaries, while its image as an interiorized landscape inspires further reflection about climate, a theme also pursued by the indoor-beach opera *Sun & Sea (Marina)*. The performance of the fictional beach scene takes place on an indoor stage covered in a typically outdoor material, not unlike Bausch's *The Rite of Spring*, except in this case it consists of several tons of silica sand. The all-over composition of sand serves as both floor and backdrop, since the performance is always viewed from above. Although it is in the background, the granular material is a protagonist alongside the opera performers: "13 vocalists and 10 tons of sand" is how promotional materials for one version of the show put it.[18] The performers lie down on towels, beach blankets, and lounge chairs nested in the sand—applying sunscreen on their bodies, reading books, snacking, playing with inflatable toys, and staring at their phones—and in this seemingly relaxed state collectively tell a story of leisure emulsified with boredom, complacency, fatigue, and fear for the planet's future.

A key part of the narrative, the sand transports the audience to an imaginary seashore, but also brings to mind existing synthetic environments like the Seagaia Ocean Dome in Japan or the sprawling indoor beach in Brandenburg, Germany. In this sense, the scenography not only functions as a fictional representation of an external environment but is also a model of an actual habitat—as artificially constructed as it

Pierre Huyghe, *After ALife Ahead*, installed at Skulptur Projekte Münster, 2017. Ice rink concrete floor, sand, clay, phreatic water, bacteria, algae, bee colonies, chimera peacock, aquarium, black switchable glass, Conus textile, incubator, human cancer cells, genetic algorithm, Augmented Reality, automated ceiling structure, rain, ammoniac, and logic game.

may be—in its own right. Given the malaise of the opera's narrative, its existence, however, is more alarming than affirming. In a sense, the sand indoors is a marker of crisis, perhaps not entirely unlike the oblique plane's role in some of Architecture Principe's early and eerie visions of the future. If Parent and Virilio intended for the tilted plane to inspire movement and thus progress toward a better version of reality, however, the ground in *Sun & Sea (Marina)* instigates a sense of inertia. The indoor sand keeps people in place; it physically grounds them. Instead of setting things in motion, the ground produces the sluggishness reminiscent of a hot day on a heating planet.

Another way to appropriate Parent's practicable as a contemporary device would be to attune it to nonhuman agency, including other species, technologies, objects, materials, and phenomena; in other words, to conceive it not only in relation to human experience but rather as a diverse ecosystem. Considered in this way, one can imagine a version of it unfolding as something akin to Pierre Huyghe's excavated environment for *After ALife Ahead*.[19] While the design of both *Riverbed* and *Sun & Sea (Marina)* relies on the addition of new material layers to existing architecture as a way of transforming spaces, experiences, and narratives, for this work Huyghe deployed demolition. Removal as a strategy for revealing hidden aspects of architecture has an artistic lineage that includes Gordon Matta-Clark's site-specific experiments from the 1970s as well as more recent works such as Urs Fischer's *You* (2007). For the latter, the artist jackhammered a nearly three-meter-deep crater inside an otherwise pristine white gallery, accompanied by a sign at the entrance that read: "The installation is physically dangerous and inherently involves the risk of serious injury or death."[20] Instead of a conventional art gallery, Huyghe worked with an abandoned ice-skating rink. He had the building's existing concrete slab cut into angular fragments whose straight edges contrasted the raw state of partially removed layers of gravel, rocks, and soil below. Visitors descended into the resulting void as if occupying an inverted practicable. Navigating a combination of circulatory spaces and moments of pause, they encountered puddles of water green from algae, a smart-glass tank containing venomous sea snails, an incubator holding cancer cells, along with peacocks, bees, and other living organisms. Automated apertures built into the old, tiled ceiling above moved in sync with the shifting opacity of the glass tank—opening up the enclosed environment to the weather outside at certain times—while an overlay of algorithmically animated objects, viewable on individual mobile devices, digitally augmented the physical experience of each participant.[21] These seemingly unrelated elements were in fact folded into a synthetic ecosystem of biotic and abiotic factors engaging one another. Huyghe's interior topography was in this sense an evolution of Parent's practicable in that rather than serving as an exclusively anthropocentric device, its aspirations were forcefully inclusive. Whereas Parent's modulation of the ground was meant to mobilize people, Huyghe's mineral terrain instead set into motion a system of relationships of which humans are only a fraction of the story.[22]

Like practicables, each of these three installations used the ground as a tool for raising awareness of, and instigating engagement with, one's surroundings. Instead of prioritizing the ground's geometry, as Parent's angled installations did, the three works foregrounded the use of specific materials for this purpose. On account of their materiality—with soil, rocks, sand, and rubble among the ingredients—these works can rightfully be regarded as acts of reversal between inside and outside; an interior space becoming an image of an exterior landscape or, alternatively, a sample of exterior ground brought indoors. Yet if audiences engaging with these works were to suspend their personal material expectations based on enclosure (such that raw soil, for example, has no place inside completed buildings), they might also grasp the relationship between the ground and the interior differently. Such a shift in perspective may, for instance, underscore the fact that underlying any interior space there is ground—so long as it is under the influence of gravity—and that ground is a constituent part of any habitat regardless of how architectural enclosures may otherwise define it. Moreover, such a view makes the distinction between *ground* and *floor* all the less relevant. These installations in effect model the behavior of the floor as an architectural element that does not stand in opposition to the ground as a found or natural condition. Instead, the floor is one of many layers that make the ground, whether it be inside, outside, intentionally constructed, or a residue of another process, as captured by the French word *sol*—which stands for both floor and soil. It was a term that Parent used throughout *Vivre à l'oblique* to refer to substrates for living, or, in his original words, *le sol à vivre.*[23] In this spirit, the planet's inhabitable crust is a composite condition that the writer and architect Keller Easterling describes as "thick with layer after layer of floors."[24] Similarly, in their eight-part project *Unconformities* (2016–20), the artists and filmmakers Joana Hadjithomas and Khalil Joreige visually capture how traces of construction, destruction, and reconstruction are sedimented underground, a succession of layers that result from what they refer to as "ecological and planetary perturbations."[25] Core samples extracted from the ground reveal layers of rubble, soil, and trash as an excitable part of geology unfolding over time, a process that renders all ground as floors and vice versa.

Beyond dismantling the notion that the ground is either monolithic (poché) or binary (inside/outside; natural/synthetic), both Parent's practicables and their contemporary counterparts

Joana Hadjithomas and Khalil Joreige, Time Capsules, from the Unconformities series, installed at the Marcel Duchamp Prize exhibition, Centre Pompidou, 2017.

inspire us to imagine how the layers may be reshuffled as a design strategy capable of disrupting conventions and instigating change. What if, in other words, a sectional drawing cut through a typical building did not start with rock or soil on the bottom, a floor slab or other structural element above it, and finished flooring on top? What happens when such layers are out of order? In architecture, modern precedents like Dan Kiley's verdant atrium, part of Kevin Roche and John Dinkeloo's Ford Foundation in New York (1968), and Peter Zumthor's Shelter for Roman Ruins in Chur, Switzerland (1986) contribute to the longer lineage of buildings that begin to challenge the expectations placed on the nature of interior floors. Further reshuffling of the layers from the inside today, however, brings into question myriad other issues, among them: what it means for architecture to be complete; how the ground, rather than enclosure, produces interiority; how the materiality of the ground, as well as the means and methods of its construction, reflects and in turn shapes the distinctions and interactions among the various design disciplines that shape living environments; who takes care of the ground; and how curiosity, interest, and speculation about these layers open up new trajectories for architectural experimentation. Connecting the practicables and their contemporary descendants, in other words, provides an alternative path to further interrogations of material substrates for living.

Vito Acconci, *Seedbed*, 1972.

Lucy McRae, *Delicate Spells of Mind*, 2022.

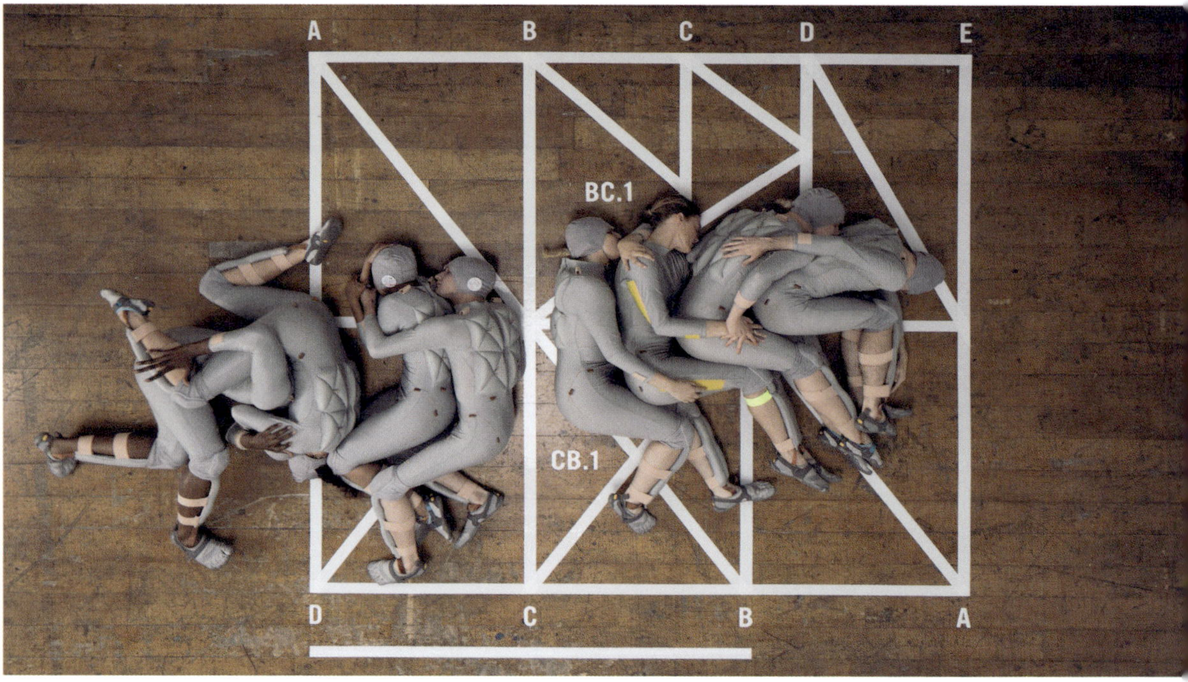

Architects lecture, teach, debate, exhibit, travel, organize, plan, research, promote, and advocate on behalf of others' work as well as their own—not to mention design and build. The multifaceted nature of the architect's skill, interests, responsibilities, and labor is a hallmark of our generalist profession. For Parent, the tour of France was a multitasking affair. What made it a remarkable endeavor in this regard is the multiple roles that he assumed simultaneously; even more so, what made it exceptional is how he expanded upon the conventional extent of the architect's direct engagement with the public.[26] Evidence of sustained attempts to engage people directly, with as little mediation as possible, talking to them about architecture and listening to their perspectives, and observing them interact with his installations have already appeared throughout this book. The sometimes-blurred distinctions between engagement, interaction, and participation as modes of connectivity throughout the tour have also already been captured by various examples and anecdotes. Perhaps the most unusual and intriguing aspect of the tour in this sense, however, was Parent's repeated presence in his own work, as if the practicables were stages on which he—along with the public and his collaborators—performed. Using performance as a form of public engagement, I wish to identify a lineage that connects Parent's live appearances with contemporary perspectives on broadening the range of all the different ways that one can be an architect. Such an exercise reveals the potential of redefining not only the architect's own agency but also that of their audience.

In January of 1972, in the midst of Parent's tour of France, another sloped floor—in a different part of the world, made by a different artist—took over a space: *Seedbed* by Vito Acconci, installed at the Sonnabend Gallery in New York. A simple incline made of wood framing and plywood extended from the middle of the room to the back wall, like a single-slope practicable. The slanted platform created just enough clearance underneath for Acconci to hide, lying down. While people wandered around the gallery, he was pleasuring himself. As he narrated the experience out loud, his voice, amplified by a set of speakers, filled the space. The artist could be heard but not seen. Regardless, he was part of the work by participating in a situation that was simultaneously intimate and shared; a man behind the ramp whispering his most intimate thoughts. The oblique floor mediated the relationship between visitors and the artist, like a slash between two words—such as in public/private—that both connects and separates them.[27]

Acconci's physical presence was deliberately augmented; his voice was amplified while his body remained invisible. Likewise, he could hear but not see what was happening on the other side of the sloped floor. Parent's appearances were less controlled and—partly as a function of the practicables not being a single artifact but rather a series of objects inserted in different situations—more varied. Obvious differences between them notwithstanding, *Seedbed* and Parent's practicables shared with one another more than just the ramp as an architectural element. In addition to showing up in their own work, both the artist and the architect counted on the audience to complete their work. Acconci's fantasies were, for example, dependent on the presence of strangers and, similarly, Parent needed people to activate the oblique. Referring to the 1970 Venice installation, the architectural historian Audrey Jeanroy interprets Parent's interior design for the French Pavilion as a space that "transforms the spectator into a work of art."[28]

The chronological and formal convergence of the work produced by these two figures, however coincidental, is one entry point into the larger field of artistic production that integrates performance in areas traditionally dominated by inanimate objects. Of particular interest in this respect are other artists who are physically present in their own art. The field occupied by such practices serves as a context for placing Parent's event-based projects into, in order to identify specific affinities but also acknowledge considerable differences between them. Joseph Beuys, Allan Kaprow, Yoko Ono, Adrian Piper, Rebecca Horn, Marina Abramović, Joan Jonas, Rirkrit Tiravanija, Wu Tsang, and Brendan Fernandes represent a small intergenerational sliver of such an artistic lineage, which had experienced a particularly robust surge at the time of Acconci's and Parent's respective ramps and continues to thrive today. However, if certain aspects of Parent's work resembled such practices, his intention was not to morph into an artist but rather expand the role of the architect to which he was unambiguously committed.[29]

Although not as extensive as it is in art, the presence of architects in their own work and, more broadly, the engagement of performance in architectural design, has a track record of its own.[30] The claim made by the book *Bodybuilding: Architecture and Performance*, edited by Charles Aubin and Carlos Minguez Carrasco and published in 2019, that

Alex Schweder and Ward Shelley, *ReActor*, installed at Architecture Field, Art Omi, Ghent, New York, 2016.

it is the first comprehensive history of performance by architects, reflects the emerging nature of the field, and similarly the 2024 publication of *Architecture and Choreography: Collaborations in Dance, Space and Time* by Beth Weinstein addresses another knowledge gap related to architecture's overlap with staged performance.[31] In her book *The New Curator: Exhibiting Architecture and Design*, the curator Fleur Watson traces the use of performance as a methodology in architecture and design to the early days of the Bauhaus School in Weimar, noting the artist, designer, and choreographer Oskar Schlemmer's contribution to the development of the school's compulsory curriculum. Schlemmer's theater workshop, offered to students in the early 1920s, focused on performance as a means of exploring the relationship between bodies and space.[32] More than a century later, traces of such an approach are still present in design education, and in practice as well there is a thread that connects multiple generations of architects exploring performance—and their own physical presence—in their work.

In the late 1960s, for example, Hans Hollein, the members of Coop Himmelb(l)au, as well as the group Hans-Rucker-Co, experimented with designing, fabricating, and then inhabiting clear plastic bubbles, with plenty of photographs to prove it.[33] These young Austrian architects explored the potential of pneumatic construction, while also experimenting with ways in which bodies interfaced with media in the age of urban mobility. In the United States, the group Ant Farm went on a performance tour of their own, promoting inflatable architecture and their how-to zine *Inflatocookbook,* first published in 1971. A self-described "body architect," Lucy McRae engages her body as a site and subject of technological fictions reminiscent of 1960s wearable architecture as played out in her gallery installations, narrative-driven images, and videos produced since the early 2010s. Likewise, Alex Schweder, who was educated as an architect and currently practices what he refers to as "Performance Architecture," often works with inflatables and appears in his installations as a performer, inhabitant, or installation operator, depending on the situation.

One such work, titled *ReActor* (2016), was a rectangular glass pavilion built in a rural field to be used as an experimental living unit for two people. Supported by only one center column, the structure hovered above the ground with Schweder occupying one side of it and his partner, the artist Ward Shelley, the other. Depending on how the two people moved in relation to one another, the pavilion tilted back and forth like a seesaw. *ReActor* can be compared to Parent and Virilio's unbuilt gallery installation *Instabilisateur pendulaire no. 1* in the way that it put the two artists on an elevated slope in relation to one another as part of a live-in experiment. Schweder and Shelley collaborated on other projects exploring similar balancing acts, which probe the intimate and codependent nature of one-on-one relationships. In another performance-based installation, *My Turn* (2018), the artists' experimental habitat was a vertically oriented spinning wheel placed inside a gallery; an earlier version of it, *Your Turn* (2017) played out a similarly reciprocal dynamic along a two-sided climbing wall. However, it is perhaps Schweder's ongoing solo series *Performative Renovations* that pushes his presence so close to the conceptual center of the work that the architect is not *in* but rather *is* the architecture itself, to paraphrase a term formulated by the architectural critic Germano Celant for referring to the radical architecture of the early

1970s.[34] In this series of interventions, Schweder renovates people's living spaces not by altering them architecturally but rather through behavioral adjustments. For each commission, he occupies the existing space, usually an apartment or house, by assuming the client's identity and performing the proposed transformation.

Along those lines, other examples come to mind of architects developing alternative approaches to professional practice or using architecture as a subject that is open to other disciplinary references. Allan Wexler's interest in the architecture of daily rituals has often placed him at the center of his own constructions in a role approximating an architectural actor or model. As part of a lifelong exploration of how the relationship of bodies and space is mediated by objects, Wexler produced two works that address inhabiting oblique conditions as if he were in a humorous dialog with Parent. In *Slanting Table–Reslanting China* (1993), a dining table sits on an incline, which in turn prompted the artist to shim each piece of tableware on it back to a level position using tapered wedges of wood. Wexler's *Hypar Room* (1999) performs a similar adjustment of furniture arrayed in a larger space, with table and chairs propped up as needed to account for the shifts in the unlevel floor.[35] In this installation and across much of his body of work, prosthetic devices negotiate how people,

Allan Wexler, *Hypar Room*, installed at the Contemporary Arts Center in Cincinnati, Ohio, 1999.

objects, and space relate to one another, undermining—or disabling altogether—conventional function in order to expose their interdependence.

As the curator of the French Pavilion for the 2006 Venice Architecture Biennale, the architect Patrick Bouchain and his team redesigned and then, over a period of three months, lived, worked, and slept inside the same building where, in 1970, Parent realized one of his first oblique installations. Throughout the 1980s and 1990s, architects like Diller + Scofidio also engaged in performance-based work, exploring the architectural potential of theatricality in relation to both the spectacular and the banal, and an interest in experimental modes of practice that involve live events continues to exist and evolve today. Commenting on the rise of architects exploring the intersection of buildings and performance in an article published in the *Los Angeles Times* in 2017, the architectural critic Christopher Hawthorne identifies a number of contemporary architects—including Schweder, but also Bryony Roberts and Andrés Jaque—as examples. He characterizes their engagement with performance as follows: "The appeal of these efforts, for their creators as well as audiences and critics, has a good deal to do with their impermanence and often their informality. They come and go. They're proudly unprofessional. This puts them in clear opposition to the pricey monuments, the immovable, perfectly polished temples to form-making."[36] It is a way of working, not unlike Parent's tour decades ago, that opens architecture up to new possibilities and, as Hawthorne suggests, "makes room for perspectives that come from other fields."[37]

In these examples and others, how architects appear in their own work varies. In some cases, such as Coop Himmelb(l)au, Wexler, and McRae, the body is simultaneously the architecture's site and inhabitant, often staged in a particular way with the intention of yielding an image or other documentary evidence, like in fashion or product design. In such cases, the dissemination of the evidence can surpass the importance of the actual event or even the physical artifact. In other instances, such as Schweder and Shelley's durational performances, the purpose is to stage an experience for others to watch live. In addition to being presented to in-person audiences and possibly recorded, such events can also be staged in order for the participating architect or artist to have a particular kind of experience within their own work, whether it be to gain insight or experience, or perhaps to elicit some other type of fulfillment. One can imagine, for example, that in addition to testing their patience and endurance, Schweder and Shelley's projects may also yield a sense of trust or empathy between the artists as an outcome of their joint endeavor. Another motive for placing oneself into one's own work may not be the production of one-sided spectatorship, but rather of interaction. This mode of working makes the architect or artist available to the audience in different ways, expanding the opportunities for interaction between them while inhabiting the same environment. With such engagement, what is remarkable in the context of architecture is not the notion of the audience completing the work—since, unlike art, buildings always already anticipate being inhabited, occupied, and used by people rather than solely fulfilling the role of a visual object—but rather that the architect is present. The architect's availability, in other words, to engage people and places without additional layers of mediation (such as, but not limited to, drawings, models, as well as the buildings themselves) is exceptional. While such public interactions can be documented in various ways—and this documentation can play an important part in fulfilling other overarching objectives—the live aspect of the event, such as Bouchain's intervention in Venice, is often the priority.

Throughout his tour of France, Parent generally placed himself into the work not so that he would be looked at but rather so he could talk and listen. In this way, he belongs to the latter category of architects and artists interested in staging social encounters. It was through such activities, after all, that the architect hoped to gather evidence in support of his hypothesis about life on tilted ground. His role was researcher, but also teacher—an important point to note given that, unlike many of his contemporaries, Parent never held an academic post and was thus not directly involved in teaching architecture or working with students in an official capacity. These public events, often delivered as seminar-style presentations and discussions, gave him a platform for disseminating his ideas in formats resembling academic instruction but outside the highly formalized domain of architecture schools. In that sense, the programs were an exercise in the development of an alternative pedagogy. While documenting such appearances was important—multiple photographers and filmmakers appeared as part of his team in Venice, Amiens, and elsewhere, and the gathered footage was subsequently exhibited and screened at other parts of the tour—such materials existed in parallel with the live events rather than as their replacement. Throughout his tour, he was an actor surrounded by his own work, while also gathering around himself other actors and performers—painters, gymnasts, sculptors, mimes, city officials, other architects, sociologists, and so on. In this sense, he was also a curator, a title that he officially held at the 1970 Venice Biennale but also assumed more generally in other iterations of the traveling show.

In *The New Curator,* Watson describes such a role in relation to the integration of performance as a way of "mediating and translating architecture and design ideas in active exchange with an audience."[38] Defined in this way, Parent performed the dual role of the curator and the producer of ideas about architecture presented to the public. By engaging performance, the curator, according to Watson, serves a role similar to that of a dramaturg whose task in theater is to interpret a text so that other participants can actively engage it.[39] Watson identifies the underlying motives of such endeavors as they relate to the institutional context of museums, which one can also relate to the hybrid nature of Parent's programs at the *maisons de la culture* in the 1970s:

> This move is driven by a desire to subvert the traditional museum structure that generally separates out the experience of the exhibition space from its associated programs—curator talks in lecture theatres, workshops in education rooms, and so on—and to compress together these aspects, both in space and duration, to produce an experience that sits somewhere between installation, exhibition and debate. The content is driven by the activity in that space and is curated with an open framework—rather than a didactic structure—for performance, spatial encounter, provocation, and debate.[40]

Dramaturgy in this context establishes conditions for a series of interactions rather than a fixed choreography, and through such a framework, participants—whether a cast of actors or an engaged audience—make the work in question their own.[41] How people make architecture their own was a key question explored by Parent's tour. One may argue that he inserted himself into the work not to underscore his sole authorship or physical presence, but rather to broker an exchange with the public—handing his architecture over to others in order to ensure its further realization. This follows the assumption that popular acceptance would keep him in the business of oblique architecture beyond the tour's itinerary, resulting in a paradox: that the architect's ubiquitous presence from one town to another was in fact intended to dissolve him as the author—the less it was about him, the more successful the work would be.

According to a certain worldview, everything an architect pursues can be seen as architecture, and similarly anything an artist does in their studio must be art.[42] Parent himself claimed, "Everything is architecture."[43] What if the opposite was true? What if, instead of everything architects and artists touched becoming architecture and art, anyone encountering architecture or art became an architect or artist? Parent's presence on the practicables as a user of his own work—perhaps not as relentless as his 24/7 plans for *Instabilisateur pendulaire no. 1* had been, but in a similar spirit—can be seen as a performance of inhabitation, a role that can be appropriated by the public so they can in turn become active authors of their own environment. Taken one step further, such a performance can be seen as a model for how to be an architect, seemingly suggesting that anyone involved in inhabiting architecture can also lean into their role in shaping it. The architect's performance is, in effect, a form of reproducible roleplay.

If such a leap from *everything is architecture* to *everyone is an architect* seems improbable, it is hardly news to fields like art or interior design. Anyone, regardless of their professional credentials or affiliation, is entitled to find their own inner artist. Likewise, the design of interiors is a domain claimed by amateurs and experts alike, exacerbated by contemporary media and do-it-yourself culture.[44] In some corners of architecture, however—not without valuable exceptions—such a notion radically destabilizes the discipline's longstanding self-image, of which Parent's refusal to count non-architect designers as his equals is but a single anecdote in a vast professional complex that has over the decades shifted but not disappeared. The performative conversion of ownership (and, to a degree, authorship) between Parent and his audience was in effect enabled by the art context within which it took place—as part of the *maisons de la cultures'* programming repertoire—with art becoming life and vice versa. Furthermore, transferring such agency from the practicable's architect to its proto-users was enabled by the interior nature of the sites. Anyone, after all, can ostensibly shape the interior through their inhabitation regardless of their vocation. The particular nature of the institutional interiors in which Parent's practicables were installed—public but inside, indoors but not domestic—provides a preliminary sense of direction when searching for potential spaces where similar forms of roleplay may be performed today. Beyond museums, schools, municipal buildings, and other usual institutional suspects where experimental architecture is often accessible to public audiences, such a search may reveal other spatial domains in which the subjective and the public come together in ways that destabilize the conventional dynamics between those who dream up architecture and those meant to be dreaming in it.

DIVERGENCE

So far in this chapter I have drawn connections between the outcomes of Parent's exploration of obliqueness—the practicables and the tour—and works by other practitioners that variably embody, exemplify, or resemble certain aspects of those outcomes. Such an approach is modeled after Parent's own use of references from the past as well as other contemporary attempts to convey the resonance of the architect's work in the present. In this final section, I am interested in linking obliqueness as it is manifested in Parent's practice to other possible expressions of it; in other words, I follow obliqueness as a stated term, concept, and condition that appears across an expanded field of cultural production. Parent's experiments thus intersect with a range of other practices that consider obliqueness as a detour or deviation from certain norms, ranging from matters of motive and process to those regarding orientation, posture, identity, and so on. In some cases, the shared terminology between otherwise seemingly unrelated practices reveals unexpected affinities, while others yield new openings through which Parent's work can be seen from new perspectives, certainly beyond what the architect may have himself imagined or endorsed.

A good place to start: July of 1975—just as Parent's tour was coming to an end with his last efforts to build a practicable in Caen—the musician, record producer, and artist Brian Eno entered Island Studios in London to record the seminal album *Another Green World* without any written material. In lieu of a musical score, he used *Oblique Strategies: Over One Hundred Worthwhile Dilemmas* as his main reference.[45] Designed by Eno with the artist Peter Schmidt, and published earlier that year, *Oblique Strategies* is a deck of cards containing written suggestions, statements, or questions to be drawn at random and followed as a guide in one's creative work "even if its appropriateness is quite unclear."[46] For Eno, who is often credited with inventing the ambient genre of music, the use of the now legendary cards enabled creative discoveries in situations where preconceived expectations may have otherwise diminished them.[47] *Oblique Strategies* can be described as a set of specific how-to instructions for approaching nonspecific objectives.[48] Inspired by chance-based operations explored by John Cage and other mid-century avant-garde figures, Eno and Schmidt devised each card as a prompt for confronting any problem at hand through a seemingly random approach.[49] By deliberately misaligning the relationship between the problem and the method of solving it, the cards inspire the user to act in a way that increases the likelihood of generating new creative responses. The cards, in other words, instigate a process akin to what the writer and philosopher Edward de Bono defined in the late 1960s as lateral thinking—a term that has since become a staple crop of corporate design thinking—with the idea that it would free the user from preconceived ideas or outcome-centered expectations.[50]

Following a similar angle in his 2010 book *Obliquity: Why Our Goals Are Best Achieved Indirectly*, the economist John Kay explores how oblique strategies are applicable more broadly as an approach to dealing with complex problems, uncertain situations, and the pursuit of high-level objectives. For Kay, such accomplishments include "personal flourishing and fulfillment, the sustenance of a great society, the creation of a fine business," all of which "are best achieved by constantly balancing their incompatible and incommensurable components—through obliquity."[51] Throughout the book, architecture, cities, and geography help Kay spatialize his argument. The Panama Canal is an example of an effective solution that is oblique not only in terms of its routing, but also because, rather than connecting the oceans, its discovery was motivated by a search for silver and gold.[52] He interprets Jane Jacobs's explanation for the quality of urban life, an outcome of numerous factors rather than the expression of one particular intention, as "the product of obliquity, not design."[53] Le Corbusier makes several appearances for his singular, and thus reductive, perspectives on complex systems, from individual homes to entire cities, an advocate for starting anew—or reengineering, as Kay refers to it—in lieu of working with existing or competing realities.[54] Kay's perspective privileges on-the-ground engagement and the agility that comes with such experience rather than the presumptuous inflexibility of blank-slate and one-size-fits-all schemes. Addressing a certain type of popular audience, reminiscent of a TED Talk in book form, *Obliquity* presents a late-capitalist theory of the relationship between intentions and outcomes and its wide-ranging implications. Yet its overarching message is familiar to anyone pursuing a serious artistic endeavor: The path that connects the labor that one invests up front and the aspired achievement that it is hoped will follow is messy, nonlinear, unpredictable, and comes with few guarantees.

Parent probably never crossed paths with Eno, nor is he mentioned in Kay's book. Bringing *Oblique Strategies* and *Obliquity* into proximity with oblique architecture is nonetheless a way to foreground—or find yet another way to talk about—acts of doing, acting, and practicing in Parent's work both in terms of approach and aspiration. Eno and Schmidt's cards, for instance, instigate an approach—a path that is open to a change of tack—while Kay's theory defines the relationship between aspiration and finding ways to move toward it. Both promote the efficacy of detours in lieu of direct routes. Despite sharing their terminology, Parent's oblique architecture may in a certain way seem at odds with both. After all, Parent's overarching desire to put the whole world on a new datum was not unlike the modernist attitudes toward new beginnings that defined the generation of architects that came before him, including Le Corbusier, for whom he briefly worked. Parent's answer to the world's complexities was a singular and simple yet seemingly totalizing machine, the inclined plane, which placed him, according to Kay's framework, in the milieu of direct approaches and reductive solutions to complex situations. His insistence on implementing the oblique plane, and the challenges he faced along the way, is comparable to what the theorist Lauren Berlant defines as cruel optimism, or "when something you desire is actually an obstacle to your own flourishing."[55] Parent's persistent pursuit of the oblique—years after even Virilio abandoned the idea—can be seen as the antithesis to both the nimbleness of *Oblique Strategies* and to the fox behavior that Kay admires (as opposed to that of the less agile hedgehog, a distinction made popular by the political theorist Isaiah Berlin[56]). His stubborn optimism is perhaps most soberingly captured by Rem Koolhaas, who declared: "He worked for more than 60 years on The Oblique Function [*sic*]: a life's work for the establishment of a new architecture and urbanism dedicated to living at grade, which has had little impact on architecture."[57]

Considered from another angle, however, Parent's tour took off in part thanks to his recognition of such limitations. Rather than solely designing buildings, he went on the road, like the ringmaster of what some may see as an architecture circus. Parent realized that he could advance the implementation of his concepts more effectively by taking advantage of the ephemeral opportunities offered by the *maisons de la culture* than through new ground-up construction. Staging the occupation of existing buildings, in other words, supplemented his existing design practice in a new and productive way. Beyond their form, the practicables were as such also oblique in how they came to be, the result of a change of course made by the architect to leverage shifting currents. Such a change in the developmental trajectory of oblique architecture—to also pursue the tour—demonstrated a reciprocity between the architectural object (the practicable) and the experimental process (Parent's live events engaging the public). The process shaped the object, in other words, as much as the object shaped the process.

The tour of France is a useful precedent for modeling one's receptiveness to the loose fit between intentions and outcomes, a way for architectural practice to productively engage—or make friends with—uncertainty.[58] Regarding his travels, Parent said, "I would tell myself that there are always surprises with architecture. I just rolled with it. . . . So, surprises were always welcome, and I considered them to be a part of the process, as something that was meant to happen."[59] Being open to surprises is evidence of one's capacity to engage obliqueness. One such surprise is that, despite the obstacles posed by his insistence to build things on a slant, it is the sum of these challenging and at times frustrating efforts that ultimately cemented his stature as a notable twentieth-century architect. Perhaps even more astonishing is that the significant posthumous growth of his reputation can be attributed in large part to the drawings he passionately pursued making—many of which were produced after he retired from professional practice—rather than his numerous building designs.

Such a trajectory exemplifies the importance of not what kinds of objects an architect can make but rather how they can practice. Similar shifts in priority appear in Keller Easterling's book *Medium Design: Knowing How to Work on the World* in which she refers to as the difference between "knowing that" and "knowing how."Inheriting the distinction from the philosopher Gilbert Ryle, Easterling describes it as "something like the difference between knowing the right answer and exercising experienced reactions unfolding over time."[60] While Easterling is largely preoccupied with systems, including political regimes, real estate, and global trade, the practice-over-object attitude transfers to other practicable domains. In the context of architectural experimentation, the shift from the former to the latter amounts to knowing how to experiment rather than using the experiment to arrive at one specific answer—or object. Knowing how, according to Easterling, is akin to muscle memory, improvisational comedy, or cooking without a recipe. Parent wished to imbue a similar kind of responsiveness among people through his architecture, and his oblique tour expanded his ability to think on his feet.

In a public lecture at The University of Texas at Austin some years ago, the architectural engineer Cecil Balmond reflected on the role of research in his practice: "The beautiful thing about research—pure research, like art—is that at the beginning it's useless. You just do it because you feel compelled, or you have an intuition. . . . Some of it turns out to be useful and some, in a strange way, *obliquely*, kicks off something else."[61] Without resorting to romanticization or self-indulgence by taking

Balmond's notion of pure art as a fantasy of unconstrained creative freedom, and thus missing the actual value of his insight, the emphasis on doing—"just do it"—is in tune with Easterling's reminder that "design work in space need not wait for either the revolution or the client commission."[62] "Practiced obliquity routinely wins against disciplined directness," as Kay puts it, which is not unlike the view that *knowing how* takes precedence over *knowing that*.[63] All these ways of working, including Parent's tour, suggest leaning into what one might imperfectly call soft skills—while searching for a more appropriate term for knowing how to live in the world.

Oblique shifts in direction can affect forms, behaviors, and processes. One of Eno and Schmidt's cards reads "Gardening, not architecture" as an instigator of one such shift, a jolt toward lateral thinking; "Question the heroic approach," written on another card, is likewise an instruction for a modification in one's attitude toward something. A change of an angle always produces a vertex, much in the same way that an associational leap can be a pivot in a conversation. In researching the changing role of punctuation, the linguist Anne Curzan noted how the slash mark—the most oblique of characters—started appearing in her students' text messages in an unexpected way. While it could still take the place of a conjunction (such as "and/or") the slash had also become an indicator of a follow-up to a thought or a topic shift.[64] Focusing on the character "/" brings attention to the ways in which Parent's practicables have in this last part of the chapter been placed in relation to texts rather than images, objects, or spaces—a perhaps unanticipated aspect of a reflection centered on architectural practice. The character "/" is a geometry—an appropriate shorthand for the oblique function—that takes the space between words or parts of sentences; it has a name, "slash," like a spurt of aggression, but is otherwise silent in its punctuating role. Obliqueness is a form as well as a behavior—and can also be an approach, action, strategy, attitude, and process—and what brings them all together, or what has made bringing Eno and Schmidt, Kay, and others to join Parent in this space possible, is language: *Oblique Function*, *Oblique Strategies*, *Obliquity*.

One potential liability to such an assembly, of course, is delving too far into metaphors; not necessarily a helpful turn. Yet language, and writing as a primary mode of representation, is already architectural in ways that are also explored, for example, in the theorist Jane Rendell's 2010 book *Site-Writing: The Architecture of Art Criticism*.[65] Thanks to the production of text as a viable mode of architectural practice, one can read Parent's writing just like they can experience his graphic and built works. Speaking and writing about oblique architecture was, after all, as vital to his practice as drawing and building. Engaging speech and text is one more available means of changing a conversation about architecture, something Parent and Virilio were well aware of when they set out to publish their magazine. Likewise, revisiting such texts in order to transform and make new use of them is not unlike renovating a building so as to better suit its current inhabitants or provide more equitable access to it. Or, to return to the milieu of architectural manifestos, as the theorist Beatriz Colomina puts it, "A new manifesto is produced by rewriting an old one."[66] While we may no longer find ourselves in an age of manifestos or what Colomina refers to as the era of "print and pavilions as vehicles of polemic," architects still write, practice, and seek ways to

Vaginal Davis, *HAG–small, contemporary, haggard*, part of the exhibition *Vaginal Davis: Magnificent Product*, Moderna Museet, Stockholm, 2024.

provoke and make the world more livable. She likewise suspects that we might already be "swimming inside a new age of manifesto architecture," but not yet be able to recognize it.[67] Life is still spatial, and the built environment poses both opportunities and challenges for those that inhabit it. Architects, like everyone else in their own way, continue to trace what has existed before them in order to imagine what is yet to be.

The feminist writer Sara Ahmed has, for example, taken on a certain tradition in philosophy in order to reshape it, namely by working to "queer" the field of phenomenology.[68] In doing so, Ahmed engages the French philosopher Maurice Merleau-Ponty's seminal 1945 book *Phenomenology of Perception* in which the term "oblique" describes the relationship between a subject and their environment, particularly noting the subject's capacity to adjust or straighten themselves. In her work on queer phenomenology, she takes on these moments of obliqueness as "queer," a word also used by Merleau-Ponty, albeit in a different sense, in an attempt to redefine the terms of such orientation. She asks: "What happens if we consider the queer potential of the oblique?"[69] Taking this question posed in the context of philosophy and redirecting it toward architecture brings to my mind works that already seem to flow along such a trajectory, including, for instance, the performance artists Gerard & Kelly's *Modern Living*, a sensuous takeover of Le Corbusier's Villa Savoye from 2019, and the interdisciplinary artist Vaginal Davis's *HAG – small, contemporary, haggard*, a compact exhibition pavilion with

Gerard & Kelly, *Modern Living*, 2019. Performance view: Villa Savoye, Poissy, France. Matthieu Barbin, Julia Eichten, Damontae Hack, Kehari Hutchinson, Emara Neymour-Jackson, Jasmine Sugar.

a sloping floor, modeled after the artist's house gallery from the 1980s, first constructed at Participant, Inc. in New York in 2012 and reconstructed in 2024 at Moderna Museet in Stockholm. What comes to your mind when contemplating Ahmed's question?

The experiment of putting various pursuits of obliqueness into contact with one another based on a shared vocabulary pulls Parent's architecture toward music, economics, linguistics, and philosophy and in this way places his practicables into an expanded field of words, images, structures, concepts, processes, intentions, bodies, spaces, and strategies. By surveying and starting to dig into this diverse field, obliqueness emerges as a form of divergence, a common trait that runs through Eno's instructional prompts, Kay's pursuit of higher-level objectives, Curzan's punctuation, Balmond's research, Easterling's know-how, Ahmed's embodied identities, as well as Parent's architectural form. As a departure from a given order—norm, convention, standard, procedure, or posture—divergence instigates ways of working, thinking, making, sensing, and living in the world, of which the practices introduced in this part of the chapter are just the beginning. Furthermore, divergence enables one to make connections across a field from any given point, like a nervous system in which one neuron can communicate with many other neurons. Considered from such an angle, obliqueness is not only a property based on orientation but also describes the capacity to forge connections that have not yet been made.

I once devised an experiment based on this very premise. For a symposium dealing with "rarely mentioned ideas in spatial theory and practice," I designed a deck of cards inspired by Eno and Schmidt's *Oblique Strategies* and called them *Oblique/Interior*.[70] The cards were used as part of an interactive public lecture that I gave with the goal of having each person in the audience generate a new idea, interest, or question related to the interiors that could in turn instigate a new line of research or creative pursuit. Each card contained a word or phrase describing something one might find in an interior space: chalk, cobweb, map of the world, vending machine, gas leak. Based on a single draw and relying on free association, each person made a quick map connecting the item from the card with the new words that immediately came to mind. One association led to the next, branching out in multiple directions. A participant started with "remote control" and ended up with "fragility." Another began with "spare tire" and arrived at "cloning," clinging to the tip of one of the outer branches. Individual participants were to evaluate how far the process took them from the initial object. Players were then instructed to choose a term appearing along the map's edges, far from where they started, and pair it with "interior." The objective was to construct a path connecting a seemingly unrelated object, phenomenon, thought, or idea back to interiors, provisionally yielding far-fetched (in the etymological sense of being brought from afar) results such as "interior fragility" or "cloned interiors" as potential topics of inquiry. Such an exercise would work the same if we had mapped new angles of connectivity for, say, "architecture" or "practice."[71]

PRACTICING OBLIQUENESS NOW

Each of the angles explored in this chapter is an experiment in making new connections, not unlike how Parent thought of practicables as devices capable of generating new continuities.[72] Together, these alternative "archeologies" foreground the distinction between obliqueness as a form of deliberate disruption and as a means of navigating a world full or obstacles—or, to put it another way, the difference between instigating instability and dealing with it. Parent was vocal about the importance of challenging, questioning, and breaking apart assumptions about architecture, which, in the spirit of continuity, also extended into a way of life. (Living in an oblique home with his family over a period of two decades is certainly an example of such commitment!) In his 2001 book *Errer dans l'illusion*, published close to retirement from professional practice, he lists a series of personal reflections on architecture under the title of "Thirteen Subversive Acts against the System."[73] The final among them is "Vivre l'obliquité" (a subtle but meaningful variation on the title of the 1970 book *Vivre à l'oblique*) with which he proposes to "live the obliqueness" as an ethos that extends far beyond sloped floors. To live and work in this way, he wrote, means internally integrating a process of questioning why things are the way they are, deliberately introducing doubt, and thwarting overconfidence.[74] While the pursuit of such a path can be construed as a deliberate choice, for Parent it was one made in part as a survival response to what he describes as having been "beaten down in the field of reality," by which he meant exhausted from professional practice.[75] He tried, in other words, to counter the turbulence, uncertainty, and obstacles presented by his profession with a practice fueled by self-driven disruption. Modeled in this way, the relationship between choice and necessity—that is, between actively destabilizing something and navigating an unstable environment or situation—appears inextricable, like two faces of a surface twisted into a Möbius loop.

A new theory of obliqueness may not be as preoccupied by the inclined plane that inspired it. Obliqueness today is better suited to its function as a theory of experimental practice. What might it mean for experimental architects and designers to work with—and "live"—obliqueness today? We work and live at a time when disruption is not only an overused corporate trope, but also a mode of instigating change increasingly more effective for those intent on dismantling social infrastructure than building it; on a planet burdened by wicked problems for which the virtue of good intentions yields far too little; and in contexts where rule-breaking happens in the midst of everything already being in flux. The baseline for any experimental practice today is the recognition that the vectors that link objectives and outcomes are as uncontrollable as the relationships between motives, means, and methods of work are up for negotiation. An oblique practice inspired in part by Parent's itinerant experiments is not only driven by one's affinities toward alternative angles of approach, but is also recognized for the capacity to make good use of ending up somewhere unexpected—and for leveraging any such journey as an occasion for exploring and experimenting with the same question that preoccupied the architect of the oblique function: How are we to live?

One way to begin addressing the question is to remember that when things seem nearly impossible, divergent vectors of obliqueness may offer life to a nearly dead end.

NOTES

PROLOGUE

1. Sigurður Guðmundsson showed the photograph in the 1980 solo exhibition titled *Situaties/Situations* at the Stedelijk Museum in Amsterdam. See the exhibition catalog: Sigurður Guðmundsson, *Situaties/Situations* (Amsterdam: Stedelijk Museum, 1980).
2. The small reproduction of Guðmundsson's photograph appears in the center of an otherwise blank page of the monograph immediately preceding the chapter titled "La fonction oblique." The caption reads, in French, "Participation d'un artiste à la Biennale de Venise." See Claude Parent, *Entrelacs de l'oblique* (Paris: Éditions du Moniteur, 1981), 44. Given that the original artwork is from 1975 and Parent's monograph was published in 1981, the mention of the artist's participation in the Venice Biennale refers to either the 1976 or 1978 editions of the international exhibition. Guðmundsson represented Iceland in both; at the International Pavilion and the Nordic Pavilion, respectively.
3. See, for example, Igor Siddiqui, "Oblique Interior," *Interiors: Design/Architecture/Culture* 8, nos. 1–2 (2017): 8–15.

INTRODUCTION: COLLECTED OBJECTS AS MODELS OF A PRACTICE

1. *Larousse Dictionnaire Français*, "praticable," accessed March 5, 2023, https://www.larousse.fr/dictionnaires/francais/praticable/63249.
2. Martin Harrison, *The Language of Theatre* (New York: Routledge, 1998), 203–4.
3. Samuel Bianchini and Erik Verhagen, "Introduction: Practicable—Art in the Conditional," in *Practicable: From Participation to Interaction in Contemporary Art*, ed. Samuel Bianchini and Erik Verhagen (Cambridge: MIT Press, 2016), 14.
4. Given the generally slanted—and oblique—form of Parent's practicables, one may also refer to them as "rakes" in English. In theater, a rake is the slope of a stage as well as the incline of auditorium seating. See Harrison, *The Language of Theatre*, 215. For the purpose of staying as close to their original naming as possible, the word "practicable" is used instead as a noun. Alternatively, the surface of Parent's practicables are also at times, and interchangeably, referred to as inclines, ramps, slopes, slants, and diagonals.
5. For Parent's recounting of his meeting with Paul Virilio and the formation of the Architecture Principe group, see Irénée Scalbert and Mohsen Mostafavi, "Interview with Claude Parent," in *The Function of the Oblique: The Architecture of Claude Parent and Paul Virilio, 1963–1969*, ed. Pamela Johnston (London: AA Publications, 1996), 49–57.
6. Claude Parent, "Le potentialisme," *Architecture Principe*, no. 3, April 1966, 3. See the English translation in Paul Virilio and Claude Parent, *Architecture Principe 1966 and 1996*, trans. George Collins (Besançon: Les Éditions de l'Imprimeur, 1997), xi.
7. Paul Virilio, "Circulation habitable," *Architecture Principe*, no. 3, April 1966, 9. See the English translation in Virilio and Parent, *Architecture Principe 1966 and 1996*, ix.
8. This is alluded to throughout the group's magazine in different ways, often as a caution with a catastrophic tone. In the essay "Manhattan out," for example, Virilio writes: "If we do not reinvent profound motivations for architectural creation, the price will be destruction of society." Paul Virilio, "Manhattan Out," *Architecture Principe*, no. 2, March 1966, 1. See the English translation in Virilio and Parent, *Architecture Principe 1966 and 1996*, vi.
9. The title translates to "Oblique Living," or "Living Obliquely" in English, even if such a translation remains unpublished. The book has not been translated to English, although Italian (1978), Japanese (2008), and Spanish (2009) versions do exist. In French, the book was republished in 2004 and agair in 2023.
10. In an obituary upon Parent's passing in 2016, the architect Bernard Tschumi stated, "He was not a mar ginal figure, but a figure who worke in the margins, in an avant-garde outside the mainstream genealogy of the Modern movement." Joseph Giovannini, "Claude Paren Visionary Architect of the Oblique, Dies at 93," *New York Times*, February 26, 2016, https://www.nytimes.com/2016/03/01/arts/design/claude-parent-architect-o -the-oblique-dies-at-93.html.
11. The title of the exhibition and the accompanying catalog refers to "t fractured monolith" as a "block," which is a play on words that also references André Bloc, the artist, engineer, and founding editor of th influential magazine *L'architecture d'aujourd'hui* who was instrumental in promoting postwar French architecture and was also Parent's mentor and collaborator. Bloc's sculptural works, modeling a form break with modernism, were part c the exhibition.
12. In addition to its curatorial narrative, which situates Parent as a link between the past (as exemplified b André Bloc's work) and the presen (as conveyed by the inclusion of th more recent generation of architec like Jean Nouvel, Bernard Tschum Odile Decq, Frédéric Borel, and François Roche), the exhibition literally foregrounds Parent by placir a monolithically sculpted installation of his design on the façade of the French Pavilion. His work is the "face" of the exhibition, a foreground and a structure that visitor must pass through in order to get t the exhibition within. See the exhibition catalog: *BLOC: Le monolithe fracturé*, ed. Frédéric Migayrou, ec *BLOC: Le monolithe fracturé* (Paris Éditions HYX, 1996).
13. In the preface to the 2010 monograph dedicated to the Church of St. Bernadette in Nevers, the 1996 exhibition is referred to as a "rediscovery" of the 1966 building Jean-Marie Panazol, "Préface/Foreword," in *Nevers: Architectur*

Principe—Claude Parent, Paul Virilio, ed. Frédéric Migayrou (Paris: Éditions HYX, 2010), 7.

For the compilation of the magazine into a book, and its accompanying English translation, see Virilio and Parent, *Architecture Principe 1966 and 1996*.

Frédéric Migayrou, ed., *Nevers: Architecture Principe—Claude Parent, Paul Virilio* (Paris: Éditions HYX, 2010).

Yves Klein et al., *Yves Klein, Claude Parent: The Memorial, an Architectural Project* (Paris: Éditions Dilecta, 2013). Parent and Klein collaborated on a number of artistic projects following their 1959 meeting. Just a few years later, after Klein's untimely death in 1962, Parent designed a memorial, as per the artist's family's request, to be built in Saint-Paul de Vence. The book documents both their collaboration and Parent's design for the memorial, which was never realized.

Chloé Parent, ed., *Claude Parent: Visionary Architect* (New York: Rizzoli, 2019).

Mai Abu ElDahab and Benjamin Seror, *Oblique Time with Claude Parent* (Bom Dia Books, 2019). The interviews collected in *Oblique Time with Claude Parent* and conducted by ElDahab, who is a curator, as well as Seror, a visual and sound artist, focus on Parent's life experience and personal insight rather than the strictly architectural considerations of his work. The following chapters in the book discuss the practicables: "Living on the Oblique," 47–54; "Tour de France," 75–90; and "First Venice, Then Liverpool," 137–44.

In the catalog introduction, President of the Cité de l'architecture et du patrimoine François de Mazières writes: "Such recognition confirms the growing influence of the man who was at first an almost 'marginal' figure avant-gardist and whom current events have placed back at the heart of the architectural debates of the moment." My own translation. Claude Parent, "Passant considerable," in *Claude Parent: L'œuvre construite, l'œuvre graphique*, ed. Frédéric Migayrou (Paris: Éditions HYX, 2010), 7. The narrative of Parent's status as previously marginal and reemerging captured in this text echoes other narratives starting with the 1996 exhibition in Venice. It is also worth noting that this is in many ways the culmination of Frédéric Migayrou's efforts to promote Parent's legacy as the exhibition's chief curator. Migayrou also curated the 1996 Venice exhibition and both wrote and edited many, if not most, of the publications through which Parent's work was disseminated internationally—and associated with contemporary experimental architectural practice—between 1996 and 2010.

20. Audrey Jeanroy, *Claude Parent: Les desseins d'un architecte* (Marseille: Parenthèses Éditions, 2022).
21. An older monograph, Parent's out-of-print *Entrelacs de l'oblique* (1980), also includes several of these installation designs, both those that were built and others that were not. They are featured in a thirteen-page section titled "Expérimentation, manifestation, participation," with the exception of the Venice Biennale installation, which is separated into a standalone project. The images, image captions, and short project descriptions included in the monograph are useful but do not provide comprehensive coverage.
22. The prescient nature of some of the practicables came into focus decades later as some of the houses of culture underwent renovations, often attempting to improve existing architecture. The building in Le Havre, for example, now includes a long ramp that connects the main gallery to its upper level in a spirit not unlike that of the 1969 practicable. Recent building renovations in Chalon-sur-Saône changed how people enter the building by eliminating the original monumental staircase that Parent tried to undermine by covering up with his 1973 practicable design.
23. A few other practicables have been built since 1975, especially in more recent years. Among them is a scheme designed by Parent and installed at Tate Liverpool's Wolfson Gallery for the 2014 Liverpool Biennial. A sloped ramp based on the architect's home was built by Rem Koolhaas's firm OMA/AMO for the 2014 Venice Biennale, with the installation eventually moving to Piacé, France, where it has been permanently installed as part of the Piacé le radieux art center. Another temporary installation based on the architect's own home was constructed as part of the *Visionary Architect* exhibition at SCI-Arc in Los Angeles in 2019.
24. Parent, *Entrelacs de l'oblique*, 91–103.
25. Peter Cook, *Experimental Architecture* (New York: Universe Books, 1970), 7. The book provided a survey of experimental practices from Europe, the United States, and Japan, including Cook's own group Archigram. Despite Parent and Virilio's various encounters with Archigram throughout the 1960s, Architecture Principe was not included in the book. Representing France instead were the group Utopie, Jean Prouvé, and the Hungarian-born Yona Friedman.
26. Neil Spiller, *Visionary Architecture: Blueprints of the Modern Imagination* (New York: Thames & Hudson, 2007), 11.
27. Rachel Armstrong, *Experimental Architecture: Designing the Unknown* (London: Routledge, 2019), 39–43.
28. Cook, *Experimental Architecture*, 28.
29. See, for example, a review that I wrote of his 2022 exhibition *Oblique Narratives no. 1* at the gallery a83 in New York: Igor Siddiqui, "An exhibition of Claude Parent's drawings offers a close look at his angular architectures," *The Architect's Newspaper*, June 20, 2022, https://www.archpaper.com/2022/06/exhibition-claude-parent-drawings-offers-close-look-angular-architecture/.
30. Claude Parent, *Architecte: Un homme et son métier* (Paris: Éditions Robert Laffont, 1975), 181. Unless otherwise noted, all English translations of this French text are my own.
31. Frédéric Migayrou, "The Definition of a Critical Architecture," in *The Function of the Oblique: The Architecture of Claude Parent and Paul Virilio 1963–1969*, ed. Pamela Johnston (London: AA Publications, 1996), 62.
32. Kenny Cupers, *The Social Project: Housing Postwar France* (Minneapolis: University of Minnesota Press, 2014), 156.
33. See Chapter 4, "The Expertise of Participation," in Cupers, *The Social Project*, 137–82.
34. Claire Bishop, "Introduction: Viewers as Producers," in *Participation*, ed. Claire Bishop (London: Whitechapel Gallery, 2006), 10.
35. Markus Miessen and Shumon Basar, "Introduction: Did We Mean Participate of Did We Mean Something Else?" in *Did Someone Say Participate: An Atlas of Spatial Practice*, ed. Markus Miessen and Shumon Basar (Cambridge, MA: MIT Press, 2006), 23.

1. OBLIQUENESS

1. Claude Parent, *Vivre à l'oblique* (Paris: Pub. by the author, 1970), 25.

Unless otherwise noted, all English translations of this French text are my own.

2. As Parent explains, the oblique function appropriates "the scientific process of hypothesis, experimentation, and application." Parent, *Vivre à l'oblique*, 25.
3. The design for the renovation of the artist Andrée Bellaguet's apartment from 1970, for example, is accompanied by a letter written and signed by Parent in which he notes the book's use as a reference for the project. Claude Parent, *Lettre tapuscrite, présentation du projet* (Paris: Centre Pompidou Collection, 1970).
4. Parent writes: "Horizontal cities suffocate by the expansion of their structure outside the proper limits, vertical cities perish by the disintegration of the urban fabric." Parent, *Vivre à l'oblique*, 16.
5. According to Parent, "There is a divorce between the private spaces intended for habitation and the community spaces of access from one private space to another, or of crossing the assembly of these spaces." Parent, *Vivre à l'oblique*, 11.
6. Parent's principles of oblique organizations are in this way prescient of similar preoccupations of the next generations of architects. For example, see Peter Eisenman, "Unfolding Events," in *Incorporations*, ed. Jonathan Crary and Sanford Kwinter (New York: Zone Books, 1992), 423–26.
7. Organizational principles of oblique structures also serve to constrain infinite growth, given that they can neither easily merge with existing urban morphologies nor is their own capacity for growth unlimited. As such, the text argues, they will produce smaller clusters of human habitats more livable than existing cities. Parent, *Vivre à l'oblique*, 65.
8. Parent, *Vivre à l'oblique*, 31.
9. Parent, *Vivre à l'oblique*, 47.
10. The historian Audrey Jeanroy refers to this post–Architecture Principe period as Parent's "reappropriation phase" of the initial ideas about obliqueness, during which, as she notes, the architect never failed to credit Virilio for his contributions. Jeanroy, *Claude Parent*, 172.
11. The painter Michel Carrade, Parent's close friend, and the sculptor Morice Lipsi were members of the group, but their contribution to the group's activities was limited. Scalbert and Mostafavi, "Interview with Claude Parent," 54.
12. For one account of the magazine's origin story, see Scalbert and Mostafavi, "Interview with Claude Parent," 54.
13. See any of the nine issues of the magazine *Architecture Principe*.
14. See Beatriz Colomina, *Manifesto Architecture: The Ghost of Mies* (Berlin: Sternberg Press, 2014), 22.
15. Both magazines were founded by the artist, engineer, and publisher André Bloc, who was also Parent's mentor.
16. *Aujourd'hui: Art et architecture*, no. 50 (July 1965); see also Beatriz Colomina and Craig Buckley, eds., *Clip, Stamp, Fold: The Radical Architecture of Little Magazines 196X to 197X* (Barcelona: Actar, 2011), 95.
17. Meanwhile, Parent's interest in utopian ideas was in part shaped by frequent collaborations with artists like Yves Klein and exposure to Parisian intellectual circles. Audrey Jeanroy, "Body and Spirit: The Metaphysics of an Encounter," in Yves Klein et al, *Yves Klein, Claude Parent: The Memorial, an Architectural Project* (Paris: Éditions Dilecta, 2013), 12.
18. Paul Virilio, *Bunker Archeology* (New York: Princeton Architectural Press, 1994).
19. Paul Virilio, "Bunker archéologie," *Architecture Principe*, no. 6, November 1966, 2. See the English translation in *Architecture Principe 1966 and 1996,* xviii.
20. Virilio, "Bunker archéologie," 2.
21. Jacques Lucan, "Introduction," in *The Function of the Oblique*, ed. Pamela Johnston (London: AA Publications, 1996), 5.
22. Paul Virilio, "Avertissement," *Architecture Principe*, no. 1, February 1966, 2. See the English translation in Virilio and Parent, *Architecture Principe 1966 and 1996,* i.
23. Virilio writes that "habitat can finally unite with the secret possibilities of individuals." Virilio, "Bunker archéologie," 2.
24. Paul Virilio, "La fonction oblique," *Architecture Principe*, no. 1, February 1966, 9. See the English translation in Virilio and Parent, *Architecture Principe 1966 and 1996,* v.
25. Virilio, "Manhattan out," 2.
26. Claude Parent, "L'homme déraciné," *Architecture Principe*, no. 3, April 1966, 2. See the English translation in Virilio and Parent, *Architecture Principe 1966 and 1996,* viii.
27. Paul Virilio, "Circulation habitable (2)," *Architecture Principe*, no. 5, July 1966, 9–10. See the English translation in Virilio and Parent, *Architecture Principe 1966 and 1996,* xv.
28. Paul Virilio, "Instabilisation," *Architecture Principe*, no. 3, April 1966, 6. See the English translation in Virilio and Parent, *Architecture Principe 1966 and 1996,* x.
29. Parent, "Le potentialisme," 10. My own translation considers gender neutrality, replacing the existing translation used elsewhere.
30. One example is "a project for an urban unit of 200,000 souls." See Paul Virilio, "Nautacité," *Architecture Principe*, no. 1, February 1966, 7. See the English translation in Virilio and Parent, *Architecture Principe 1966 and 1996,* iv.
31. The apocalyptic tone is easy to detect and has been described as such by others. See, for example, Craig Buckley, "21. Architecture Principe, no. 1, February, Paris," in Colomina and Buckley, *Clip, Stamp Fold*, 98.
32. Paul Virilio, "Le troisieme ordre urbain," *Architecture Principe*, no. 2, March 1966, 10. See the English translation in Virilio and Parent, *Architecture Principe 1966 and 1996,* viii.
33. This was the basis of Virilio's 1975 book *Bunker archéologie*, first pub lished in English in 1994 as *Bunker Archeology*.
34. The description of bunkers as emp carcasses appears in Virilio, "Bunk archéologie," 2.
35. Virilio describes bunkers as follows: "The architecture floats on the surface of the earth which has lost its materiality." Virilio, "Bunke archéologie," 2; he describes the housing project: "The urban plan 'floats' therefore on the surface of the earth that has lost its materiality." Virilio,"Nautacité," 7.
36. See project credits in the special issue of the magazine dedicated to the Charleville project, *Architectu Principe*, no. 9, December 1966, 15
37. Paul Virilio, "Nevers chantier," *Architecture Principe*, no. 4, May-June 1966, 2. See the English translation in Virilio and Parent, *Architecture Principe 1966 and 1996,* xi. The issue was published the summer of 1966, while the buil ing opened in December.
38. Together as Architecture Principe Parent and Virilio designed a serie of other projects that included the Thomson–Houston factory and research center, built in 1969. Tha particular building has, however, since been demolished.
39. This spatial zone, abstracted as a zigzagging line in plan, is captured in the group's logo, which also appears on the cover of the magazine.

. The painter Michel Carrade and the sculptor Morice Lipsi, the absent members of Architecture Principe whose names were printed in the magazine but to which they made no other contribution, were a part of the church's artistic team. Lipsi created five functional elements for the building, sculpted from stone, including the main alter. Carrade designed, but never completed, a tapestry. In addition to these objects, the church's red stained glass windows, the building's only chromatic elements, were the work of the artist Odette Ducarre. Christophe Joly, *Église Sainte-Bernadette à Nevers* (Paris: Éditions Jean-Michel Place, 2004), 58. From the standpoint of collaboration, the building achieved through its construction what the magazine did not in print.

Claude Parent, "Nevers chantier," *Architecture Principe*, no. 4, May-June 1966, 6. See the English translation in Virilio and Parent, *Architecture Principe 1966 and 1996*, xii.

. Virilio, "Nevers chantier," 2.

. Migayrou, "The Definition of a Critical Architecture," 62.

. In one account of the group's origin (and there are several somewhat different versions of this narrative), Virilio says, "Not being an architect, I thought of Claude Parent since I had just moved into one of his apartments!" Marie-Ange Brayer, "Interview with Paul Virilio," in *Nevers: Architecture Principe—Claude Parent, Paul Virilio*, ed. Frédéric Migayrou (Paris: Éditions HYX, 2010), 19.

. In the 1960s, visionary architecture was associated with utopian visions of the future, deemed "too radical to be built" according to Arthur Drexler, who curated the 1960 exhibition *Visionary Architecture* at the Museum of Modern Art in New York. In the press release for the exhibition, Drexler further describes visionary architecture as one that "usually combines a criticism of society with a strong personal preference for certain forms." See the digitized press release, Museum of Modern Art, "Visionary Architecture," September 28, 1960, https://www.moma.org/calendar/exhibitions/2554.

"While for the architects it was only a 'supplementary' intention, the bunker hence crystallized the negative reception of the building, to the point of making inaudible the very essence of the project, its conceptual and operational heart: experimentation through the oblique of a new use of liturgy." Aurelien Vernant, "Saint Bernadette, the Hardship of a Crossing," in Migayrou, *Nevers: Architecture Principe*, 157.

47. Vernant, "Saint Bernadette," 154–61.
48. Claude Parent, "Church of Sainte-Bernadette du Banlay," in *First Works: Emerging Architectural Experimentation of the 1960s and 1970s*, ed. Brett Steele and Francisco González de Canales (London: Architectural Association, 2009), 104.
49. In this regard, Migayrou notes: "In promoting the oblique—a plane lacking both stability and external references—they were making a radical stand against an architectural culture of geometrical volumes firmly inscribed in space." Migayrou, "Critical Architecture," 62.
50. Parent recalls: "To prove that it was possible to inhabit the oblique, we designed The Pendular Destabilizer, an experimental structure that was raised twelve metres above the ground to isolate it from the outside world. There was no telephone, no post, no means of communication, except for a little hole in the wall that we could talk to each other through. It was a bit like those followers of Saint Simon who used to climb up columns and never come down again." Scalbert and Mostafavi, "Interview with Claude Parent," 55.
51. Nadine Labedade, "*Instabilisateur pendulaire no. 1*," in *Claude Parent: L'œuvre construite, l'œuvre graphique*, ed. Frédéric Migayrou (Paris: Éditions HYX, 2010), 194.
52. Marie-Ange Brayer, "The Scandal of Saint-Bernadette of Banlay," in *Nevers: Architecture Principe—Claude Parent, Paul Virilio*, ed. Frédéric Migayrou (Paris: Éditions HYX, 2010), 10; Lucan, "Introduction," 5.
53. Claude Parent, "Structure," *Architecture Principe*, no. 3, April 1966, 8. See the English translation in Virilio and Parent, *Architecture Principe 1966 and 1996*, xi.
54. In the US, for example, the same period was marked by widespread demonstrations against the Vietnam War as well as critical developments in the civil rights movement.
55. Daniel Singer, *Prelude to Revolution: France in May 1968* (New York: Hill & Wang, 1970), 21.
56. For a discussion on architecture's role in these broader shifts related to the events of May 1968, see Caroline Maniaque, Éléonore Marantz, and Jean-Louis Violeau, *Mai 68: L'architecture aussi!* (Paris: Éditions B2, 2018).
57. Singer, *Prelude to Revolution*, 62.
58. Scalbert and Mostafavi, "Interview with Claude Parent," 55.
59. Scalbert and Mostafavi, "Interview with Claude Parent," 55.
60. Parent, *Vivre à l'oblique*, 67.
61. Virilio, "Avertissement," 2 ; Virilio, "Manhattan out," 2.

2. THE TOUR

1. An earlier version of this chapter was published as a peer-reviewed journal article. See Igor Siddiqui, "Claude Parent's Oblique Travels: From Architectural Form to Social Participation," *The Plan Journal: Research in Architecture Design and Urbanism* 9, no.1 (2024): 79–101.
2. In her assessment of Parent's practice during the six-year period following the split from Virilio, Jeanroy notes the strangeness of the architect's predicament: On the one hand, his public reputation was experiencing an upward swing; on the other, despite all his significant accomplishments, new project commissions were scarce. The heart attack he suffered in 1971 only further contributed to his business struggles. This in part explains his availability and eagerness to pursue other modes of practice. Jeanroy, *Claude Parent*, 171. See also Audrey Jeanroy, "Pratiquez l'architecture! Les actions culturelles de Claude Parent, 1969–1975," in *Claude Parent: L'œuvre construite, l'œuvre graphique*, ed. Frédéric Migayrou (Paris: Éditions HYX, 2010), 163.
3. In 1970, Parent served as the curator of the French Pavilion at the Venice Biennale. For the occasion, he designed a practicable not unlike those made for other sites in France. It is the only such installation included in the book outside of the country. Despite being an outlier geographically, it falls in line with the other practicables chronologically. Its inclusion is also a necessary part of the overall narrative of the practicable and of understanding their development and evolution over time. For more information about the Venice installation, see Chapter 3.
4. Claude Parent, as told to Josiane Marié, "La fonction oblique en voyage," *Journal de la maison*, March 1974, 171.
5. Practicables were designed for most but not all the cities that Parent visited. In cities like Toulouse and Reims, for example, he mounted

exhibitions and gave lectures, but these programs were not accompanied by a practicable. Of the cities where he traveled, the book identifies eight as practicable sites, including Venice. The book's ninth practicable was numbered by Parent as no. 7, but its exact location is unspecified.

6. This tendency, referred to here as "utopian prognostication," was noted by Archigram's founding member Peter Cook and already mentioned in the book's introduction. Cook, *Experimental Architecture*, 28.
7. Hélène Demoriane, "Le tour de France de Claude Parent," *Le Point*, March 19, 1973, 58–59; my translation.
8. ElDahab and Sorer, *Oblique Time with Claude Parent*, 78.
9. "Compagnons du Devoir et du Tour de France," accessed May 2, 2024, https://compagnons-du-devoir.com.
10. As noted in the introductory chapter, the French term *maison de la culture* also variably translates to "palace of culture," especially as applied to similar institutions in other countries. Along with the original term in French, this book uses "house of culture" and "cultural center" as acceptable translations, depending on the context.
11. Danilo Udovički-Selb, for example, writes about the convergence of political and artistic activities in the 1930s *maisons de la culture* in the life and work of Charlotte Perriand. Danilo Udovički-Selb, "C'était dans l'air du temps: Charlotte Perriand and the Popular Front," in *Charlotte Perriand: An Art of Living*, ed. Mary McLeod (New York: Harry N. Abrams, 2003), 68–89.
12. Richard Klein, *Les maisons de la culture en France* (Paris: Éditions du patrimoine, Centre des monuments nationaux, 2017), 34.
13. The policy was in place since the adoption of the 1946 preamble to the French constitution. See Préambule de la constitution du 27 octobre 1946. "La Nation garantit l'égal accès de l'enfant et de l'adulte à l'instruction, à la formation professionnelle et à la culture." (The Nation guarantees equal access for children and adults to instruction, vocational training and culture.) https://www.conseil-constitutionnel.fr/en/preamble-to-the-constitution-of-october-27th-1946.
14. Klein, *Les maisons de la culture en France*, 34.
15. Malraux's speech, given at an art festival in Dakar, Senegal, is quoted in Éric Lengereau, "Malraux ministre de l'architecture," in *André Malraux et l'architecture*, ed. Dominique Hervier (Paris: Éditions du Moniteur, 2008), 83.
16. Given the ultimately complex evolution of these establishments, some of the buildings that were used as sites for the practicables had changed their status and modified their name by the time Parent arrived there. In Le Havre, as also noted elsewhere, the *maison de la culture* had become a museum even though the city's house of culture still acted as copresenter of his exhibition. In Caen, where the establishment of the state-funded *maison de la culture* led to a contentious relationship with the municipality, the cultural center was eventually renamed the Théâtre municipal de Caen as its management shifted from state to local administration.
17. The Maison de la culture de Douai had a space for its operations at the city hall, located in the town's historic center a block away from the practicable's outdoor site.
18. Cities like Le Havre, Amiens, and Caen were destroyed by Allied bombing and became major sites of reconstruction; other cities were in the process of building new public housing on their outskirts, such as the Gautriats neighborhood in Mâcon where Parent worked with the residents.
19. In their magazine, Architecture Principe argued against both horizontal sprawl and excessive vertical densification. The oblique diagonal was in a sense the more reasonable middle. Virilio, "Le troisieme ordre urbain," 9; see also Parent's views on the optimal size and scope of an oblique city in Claude Parent, *5 réflexions sur l'architecture* (Nevers: Maison de la culture de Nevers, 1972), 32–33.
20. Decades later, Parent acknowledged, "We were lucky enough that André Malraux had launched *maisons de la culture* around that time!," ElDahab and Sorer, *Oblique Time*, 140.
21. Klein, *Les maisons de la culture*, 42.
22. For example, the architect Oscar Niemeyer's building in Le Havre, the city's second *maison de la culture*, opened to the public in 1982; Mario Botta's design for the center in Chambéry, named after Malraux, was completed in 1987.
23. See the biographical note in André Barey, *Réflexions sur l'artisanat, suivi d'une intervention de Claude Parent* (Mâcon: Action culturelle mâconnaise, 1973). From various local press coverage and publications promoting these local events, it is evident tha Barey was instrumental in linking Parent's practice with the cultural centers' cultural programs. In othe words, it was in large part thanks to Barey that Parent's work was presented as a form of participato practice in these venues.
24. Klein cites the sociologist Pierre Bourdieu as a prominent critic of educational initiatives like the *maisons de la culture*. Bourdieu targeted such institutions' shared belief that the main barrier to publ engagement with art was physical inaccessibility, rather than encour aging people to seek out the works themselves. In other words, the issue, according to Bourdieu, was not how to bring art to people but rather how to get people to activel engage in approaching it. Klein, *Le maisons de la culture*, 42.
25. Kenny Cupers, *The Social Project: Housing Postwar France* (Minneapolis: University of Minnesota Press, 2014), 119.
26. Kenny Cupers, "The Cultural Cent Architecture as Cultural Policy in Postwar Europe," *Journal of the Society of Architectural Historians* 74, no. 4 (December 2015): 470.
27. Klein, *Les maisons de la culture*, 3 Cupers, "The Cultural Center," 47
28. Cupers explains: "Cultural institutions—went the argument, especially on the political Left—should become sites of participatory production and not just passive co sumption." Cupers, "The Cultural Center," 469.
29. Klein, *Les maisons de la culture*, 5
30. Richard Klein, "Des maisons du peuple aux maisons de la culture," *André Malraux et l'architecture*, e Dominique Hervier (Paris: Édition du Moniteur, 2008), 121.
31. Jeanroy, "Pratiquez l'architecture 166. While according to Jeanroy's account, Parent and Barey's initia encounter took place in Venice during the 1970 Biennale, an alternate account exists as well. Paren recounts, "Director of the Maison de la culture, Mr. Philippe Bonzon, sent one of his delegates, Mr. And Barey, to Saint-Étienne, and on his advice, we put together an event." See Marié, "La fonction oblique," 171. My translation. Following the chronology of either account, Barey's involvement started after 1970; Parent's exhibition in Saint-Étienne was in 1971, as was his vis to Nevers, where he built the first practicable after Venice.

This is especially true in cities that experienced a large increase of new public housing. In such areas, the *animations* can be seen as part of a sociological strategy for managing new communities. See chapter "*Animation* to the Rescue" in Cupers, *The Social Project*, 91–135.

"L'action culturelle: Pourqoui?" *Mâcon: Revue municipale* no. 2 (November 1968): 23.

It is important to note that while Parent compares his process with a scientific experiment—and during various stages of this exploration he invited a number of physicians, psychologists, and sociologists to join him—this methodology is not to be confused with the evidence-based research that emerged in the mid-twentieth century and which continues to be part of various design fields today. Nor did Parent's process involve data-collecting in the way that may be more relevant to a scientific study. For Parent, the question of methodology remained open, not an unusual position for a creative practice. As he later wrote, throughout the tour he was seeking direct feedback as much as he was still in search of a methodology. Parent, *Architecte*, 185.

On his eagerness to talk to people, see ElDahab and Sorer, *Oblique Time with Claude Parent*, 78; in his memoir from 1975, Parent wrote about various challenges along the tour, such as occasions in which he was unknowingly pushed by local organizers into encounters with people who were more eager to discuss their grievances concerning the city's administration than exploring architecture. Parent, *Architecte*, 176–77.

See, for example, Parent, *5 réflexions sur l'architecture*, 39–42.

Cupers, *The Social Project*, 122.

For examples, see Claude Parent, "Préfabrication," *Architecture Principe*, no. 2, March 1966, 7. See the English translation in Virilio and Parent, *Architecture Principe 1966 and 1996*, xxii. See also Claude Parent, "Face à face: Architecture et design," *L'architecture d'aujourd'hui*, no. 155 (April–May 1971): 19–23.

Broader engagement with questions of consumption and consumerism in France and internationally appeared in the work of many of Parent's contemporaries across a range of disciplines, particularly sociology, including that of Pierre Bourdieu whose research directly addressed the role of institutions such as the *maisons de la culture*. Jean Baudrillard's book *The Consumer Society: Myths and Structures* was also published in 1970.

40. ElDahab and Sorer, *Oblique Time*, 78.
41. In Nevers, for example, it was the house of culture's technical crew that constructed the practicable; in Amiens, a local construction firm; the planned practicable in Caen was supposed to be built by a contractor from Rouen; in Le Havre, it was a plywood company's material donation that made the construction of the installation possible.
42. This includes the publication of books in Nevers, Mâcon, as well as numerous essays published in newsletters. Amiens, for example, was particularly well funded.
43. Cupers, "The Cultural Center," 472.
44. ElDahab and Sorer, *Oblique Time*, 78.
45. Klein, *Les maisons de la culture*, 43.
46. Jeanroy, "Pratiquez l'architecture!," 168.
47. "5 Réflexions sur l'architecture par Claude Parent." Maison de la culture de Nevers et de la Nièvre, 1972. Printed invitation.
48. Parent, *Architecte*, 183.
49. Parent, *Architecte*, 183.

3. THE PRACTICABLES

1. The architectural historian Audrey Jeanroy notes that the Le Havre installation was realized before Parent started using the term practicable to describe such constructions, giving it, in my own reading, the status of a practicable before the practicables. Jeanroy, "Pratiquez l'architecture!" 169. By the time Parent published *Vivre à l'oblique* the following year, however, he did refer to the Le Havre installation as a practicable. Parent, *Vivre à l'oblique*, 25–31.
2. The building, originally called the Musée-maison de la culture du Havre, was the first French cultural center to open following André Malraux's 1959 establishment of the state program under which such institutions were to be built all over France. It was originally designed as a museum in 1955 by architects Guy Lagneau, Michel Weill, and Jean Dimitrijevic, in collaboration with Jean Prouvé, and it opened to the public in its modified and expanded role in 1961. See Klein, *Les maisons de la culture*, 36. By 1969, the year that *Espace architectural* took place in it, the building once again became primarily a museum and was renamed the Nouveau Musée du Havre, while the operations of the cultural center moved to the Théâtre de l'hôtel de ville. See "Découvrez le MuMa: Une histoire," Musée d'art moderne André Malraux, accessed May 22, 2023, https://www.muma-lehavre.fr/fr/musee/muma/une-histoire. The city's *maison de la culture* was nonetheless one of the institutional partners responsible for the production and presentation of the 1969 exhibition as reflected in accompanying pamphlets, posters, and local press. In 1999, the museum was renamed after André Malraux.
3. "Espace architectural: L'une des plus importantes expositions de ces dernières années, " *Paris Normandie*, June 19, 1969, my translation.
4. "Espace architectural."
5. In addition to his work as the publisher and editor of *L'architecture d'aujourd'hui*—and a frequent collaborator on various endeavors with other artists and architects, including Parent—Bloc, who was educated as an engineer, also had an active studio practice with a focus on sculpture. This is especially true in the final stages of his life preceding his accidental death in 1966. See "André Bloc, Artiste (1896–1966)," FRAC Centre –Val de Loire, accessed June 1, 2024, https://collections.frac-centre.fr/collection/collection-art-architecture/index-des-auteurs/auteurs-58.html?authID=25.
6. "Espace architectural." La maison de la culture et le nouveau musée du Havre, 1969. Exhibition pamphlet. My translation of the curatorial text.
7. "Espace architectural," exhibition pamphlet.
8. The general public, according to local press, knew Bloc no more than they did Parent or Virilio. See the newspaper article "Espace architectural."
9. "Espace architectural," exhibition pamphlet.
10. This includes drawings such as the series *Turbosites* and *Vagues* from the 1960s, some of which also appeared in the magazine *Architecture Principe*, but also various other works on paper from later decades of practice.
11. Introducing a ramp to the museum's main gallery turned out to be an idea that would later appear as part of the building's 1999 renovation. Architects Sandra Barclay and Jean Pierre Crousse, in collaboration with Laurent and Emmanuelle Beaudouin, introduced a ramp, running in the direction perpendicular

to that of Parent's, as a means of accessing the gallery's mezzanine level. See "Malraux Museum," Barclay Crousse, accessed June 20, 2024, http://www.barclaycrousse.com/museum-malraux; see also "Musée Malraux," Beaudouin Architectes, accessed June 20, 2024, http://www.beaudouin-architectes.fr/1999/02/musee-andre-malraux.

12. "Participation Française à la 35e biennale de Venise," *L'architecture d'aujourd'hui* 151 (August 1970): xv.
13. For more information about the building, see Jean-Louis Cohen, "A Beaux-Arts Exercise in the Giardini," in *Common Pavilions: The National Pavilions in the Giardini of the Venice Biennale in Essays and Photographs*, ed. Diener and Diener Architects with Gabriele Basilico (Zurich: Verlag Scheidegger and Spiess, 2013), 59–62.
14. René de Solier, "La biennale de Venise," *Vie des arts* 60 (Fall 1970): 46.
15. Virilio, "Circulation habitable (2)," *Architecture Principe*, no. 5, July 1966, 9–10.
16. See *La ligne de la plus grande pente*, Projet pour le pavillon français de la biennale de Venise, 1970. Photographies de Gilles Ehrmann, 285 ektachromes numérisés, collection Frac Centre-Val de Loire, dépôt Sabine Ehrmann, SAIF, 2015, https://www.frac-centre.fr/collection/hommage/claude-parent/claude-parent-748.html.
17. In Italy, the political Left demanded an update to the biennale's 1938 organizational statute, seeking a more inclusive approach to administering the exhibition. Italy's most influential cultural figures threatened to boycott the biennale in support of the demands. See "Organizers of Venice Biennale Plan Wide Innovations for '70," *New York Times*, February 27, 1970. At the American Pavilion, twenty-four of the forty-seven artists boycotted the show in opposition to wars in Vietnam and Cambodia, among them Roy Lichtenstein, Robert Rauschenberg, Jim Dine, Claus Oldenburg, Robert Motherwell, Robert Morris, Frank Stella, and Andy Warhol. See Paul Hoffman, "35th Art Biennale Beset by Problems at Venice Opening," *New York Times*, June 24, 1970, 32.
18. Among the disadvantages, for example, was that French media had very little interest in the project, resulting in virtually no coverage in the press at the time of the exhibition. On the other hand, Parent had the freedom to do what he wanted with the exhibition, an artistic carte blanche. See Hans Ulrich Obrist, *Conversation avec Claude Parent* (Paris: Manuella Éditions, 2012), 91.
19. Claude Parent, "El Pabellón de Francia en la Bienal de Venecia," *Arquitectura* 144 (1970): 34.
20. Parent, "El Pabellón de Francia," 34.
21. Obrist, *Conversation avec Claude Parent*, 91–92.
22. Jeanroy, "Pratiquez l'architecture!," 169.
23. Images of the installation show the neon grid in different colors but not specific evidence of physical activity that caused the color change to occur. Parent referred to the light installation as interactive, whereby its design allowed visitors to play a role in how its colors changed. He referred to the device allowing for such interaction as a *punching bag*. See Obrist, *Conversation avec Claude Parent*, 92, my translation. By this time Morellet had started incorporating switches and levers as interactive features in his neon-based works, further explaining how the lighting system may have worked. See Alfred Pacquement, *François Morellet: Réinstallations* (Paris: Éditions du Centre Pompidou, 2011), 56.
24. Claude Parent, "Biennale de Venise," *Nueva Forma* 63 (April 1971): 67.
25. I am grateful to the architect Odile Decq for helping me clarify this point through her feedback following my lecture on this research at the Confluence Institute in Paris on April 11, 2023.
26. Parent, "Biennale de Venise," 67.
27. Jeanroy, "Pratiquez l'architecture!," 164.
28. Searching for a fully manifested oblique architecture was a lifelong quest and one that was never fully fulfilled. In an interview, Parent says, in reference to the ramped exterior of Snøhetta's Oslo Opera House "Yes, at the Oslo Opera House . . . it's great, but it is a building access, there is functionality to the ramps, which isn't the same as living on the oblique. Living on the oblique means that every step of your life is oblique, all the important moments have to happen on the oblique." See ElDahab and Sorer, *Oblique Time*, 50.
29. This is in contrast to some of the other works of oblique architecture. Repulsion was, for example, part of the effect elicited by the St. Bernadette Church, which Virilio describes as follows: "When you see the façade, it is a bunker, repulsive architecture. It does not seek to seduce but is hideous while inside it is a heart." Brayer, "Interview with Paul Virilio 20.
30. Hoffman, "35th Art Biennale," 38.
31. In an interview, Parent recalled saying, while pursuing new opportunities upon his return from Venic to France, "Here's what I do. Here' what I did at the Biennale." ElDaha and Sorer, *Oblique Time*, 78.
32. Parent, *Vivre à l'oblique*, 39.
33. Maison de la culture de Nevers et de la Nièvre, later renamed Maisor de la culture Nevers Agglomératio (MCNA), was a part of a larger mul tiuse complex, also consisting of t Maison du travail and the Maison des sports, inaugurated in 1970. The building was designed by the architects Max Guillaume and Hen Veuzelle, with the designer Camill Demangeat. Klein, *Les maisons de culture*, 40.
34. Marié, "La fonction oblique en voy age," 171.
35. For his position on furniture, see Parent, *Vivre à l'oblique*, 39–45.
36. Captured in photographs, a handwritten sign placed by the installa tion reads: "Creation of an oblique circulation realized by the technic service staff of the Maison de la cu ture de Nevers according to Claud Parent's plans and the instruction by the painter Andrée Bellauguet." My translation. The practicable in Nevers is amon the only known practicables with r archived or published drawings or models, suggesting that the desig process may have unfolded informally, quickly, and possibly direct in field as it was getting built.
37. The timeline of Parent's activities in Nevers during the summer of 1971 was as follows: The originally listed dates for the exhibition were June 8 to July 31, 1971 during whic period accompanying weekly film screenings and church visits took place in the evenings; Parent gave his five lectures, the basis for the book *5 réflexions sur l'architectur* from June 8 to 12; separately, the dates for the display of the practic ble were July 13 to August 31. Give these dates, it seems that the desi and construction of the practicabl took place parallel to, and possibl exceeded, the duration of the mor formal exhibition and the accompa nying events.
38. Parent, *5 réflexions sur l'architecture*, 7.
39. On the repellant aspects of the church, see, for example, Migayro "Critical Architecture," 62.

Baudouin Dervault, "Un entretien avec Claude Parent," *La montagne,* 24 June, 1971.

The film repertoire included short films *Nevers-Nord* by Jean-Pierre Prévost and Mireille Bouillé (1967), *Le beton* by Éric Rohmer (1969), *L'homme en marche* by Jean-Pierre About (n.d), along with footage from the Venice Biennale and a film titled *Le m'zab*, referring to the Algerian settlement in the Sahara Desert whose monolithically continuous urban and architectural morphology is reminiscent of the oblique function.

Parent, *5 réflexions sur l'architecture*, 7.

Parent was in some ways an outsider to architecture academia, having formally studied but not receiving the full title of an architect, on the basis of professional achievements rather than a completed degree, until 1966. Jeanroy, "Pratiquez l'architecture!," 166. Unlike most influential architects of his generation, in France and elsewhere, Parent did not hold an academic post as a part of his career in architecture.

The exhibition in Toulouse was mounted at the Centre culturel de la ville, a retrofitted storefront in the old city center, taking over not only the exhibition space but also the adjacent library and the foyer-bar. Parent delivered talks in the foyer, while film screenings took place in the lecture hall as well as at the nearby Theatre Sorano. See "Claude Parent Architecte," Centre culturel de Toulouse, 1971. Printed program.

The program was initially scheduled to run from November 21, 1972 to February 11, 1973; however, it was extended by a month during which an exhibition of the Chilean artist Roberto Matta was mounted.

Architects Jean Duthilleul and Marcel Gogois are credited as Sonrel's main collaborators on the project. Sonrel—who was an authority on theater design and the author of the seminal 1943 book *Traité de scénographie: Évolution du matériel scénique* on the subject—was also a professor at the Beaux-Arts in Paris with whom Parent studied. Parent entered Sonrel's studio at the school in 1953, an experience that is said to have inspired his interest in theater. Marie-Ange Brayer, "L'aventure créatrice: Les collaborations artistiques de Claude Parent," in *Claude Parent: L'œuvre construite, l'œuvre graphique*, ed. Frédéric Migayrou (Paris: Éditions HYX, 2010), 51.

The building was renovated and added to around 1990 and its outside appearance was thus partially altered—an additional footprint in the shape of a quarter-circle was joined to the original massing, along with other alterations and adjustments—but the original parts of the structure and the same number of stories remain.

48. Klein, *Les maisons de la culture*, 37.
49. Earlier schemes of the practicable suggest an interest in echoing the existing building's interior geometries in other ways too, such as the ramp of a rounded footprint following the curvature of the auditorium that was initially proposed.
50. Parent, *Entrelacs de l'oblique,* 93.
51. Existing design drawings of the installation support this interpretation. This smaller part of the practicable was drawn separately on its own sheet, indeed as if it were an installation in its own right within the larger oblique structure.
52. Parent, *Architecte*, 185.
53. The first scheduled events started in November, while the official opening of the installation took place in late December of 1972.
54. Parent mentions the visibility of the construction process from the outside. See Parent, *Entrelacs de l'oblique,* 93. In this paragraph he also mentions how the image of the practicable changed from its raw wood state to the painted version according to Bellaguet's design, and finally transformed by the presence of art exhibited in it.
55. Parent, *Architecte*, 181–86.
56. Parent, *Entrelacs de l'oblique,* 93–94.
57. The book was developed with the assistance of a physiotherapist, with its content centered on photographs in which Nicole Parent performs a series of interconnected postures on a plank propped up by a Swedish ladder. The exercise method was developed according to the principles described in the book *Vivre à l'oblique* and includes a chapter written by Claude Parent, along with an essay by a physician explaining the exercise routine's health benefits. The book is curious in its simultaneous promotion of a novel exercise routine offered by Nicole Parent's gymnastics studio and her brother's architectural theory, a merging of health advice and avant-garde architecture. See Nicole Parent, *L'inclipan* (Paris: Robert Laffont, 1972). Prior to Amiens, Nicole Parent performed the *Inclipan* routine and participated in her brother's oblique tour in Reims and was later also a part of programs in Mâcon, Douai, and Caen.
58. See Chapter 4 for a discussion on Bellaguet's Parent-designed oblique apartment.
59. The paintings, of which there were thirty-seven in total, were exhibited at the Maison de la culture et des loisirs de Saint-Étienne just weeks before Amiens, from November 17 to December 11, 1972. See "Bellaguet: Peintures" Maison de la culture et des loisirs, Saint-Étienne. Exhibition brochure.
60. *Mobile* 10, December 1972.
61. Likewise, subsequent versions of the practicable were no longer being painted.
62. Parent thought of Matta's interest in showing his paintings in Amiens as a reflection of the general success of the program. ElDahab and Sorer, *Oblique Time*, 78.
63. "L'homme/l'architecture," *Mobile* 8, October 1972.
64. *Courrier picard,* "Le 'praticable' de Claude Parent: un lieu (oblique) de communication," December 23, 1972.
65. Parent considered Amiens to be the model for all other such programs, and he attributed its success to the commitment of the cultural center's director Dominique Quéhec and his artistic staff. Parent, *Entrelacs de l'oblique,* 93.
66. Parent, *Architecte*, 181–86.
67. "Le vernissage de l'exposition Claude Parent, a marqué le départ d'un mois de travail et de réflexion sur l'architecture oblique," *Le Courrier*, February 5, 1973; see also "Le manifestation Claude Parent s'est ouverte hier à la bibliothèque municipale," *Le progrès*, February 4, 1973.
68. "Les Gautriats: la dernière pierre," *Mâcon revue municipale*, no. 6, October 1970, 19.
69. "Une maison de la culture' méconnue: la bibliothèque municipale," *Mâcon revue municipale*, no. 1, January 1968, 25–29.
70. As a side note, Levasseur worked with Pierre Sonrel—the architect of the Maison de la culture d'Amiens—on the design of the Rouen Opera House, built in 1962.
71. Demoriane, "Le tour de France de Claude Parent," 59.
72. The building was designed by the department architect Henri Palazzi and eventually became entirely dedicated to the Archives départementales de Saône-et-Loire after the library facilities moved out in 2000.
73. "Samedi au C.R.E.P.S. de Mâcon, débat de haut niveau sur la fonction oblique: Une architecture pour les hommes." *Le courrier, le journal de Saône-et-Loire,* May 21, 1973.

74. "Samedi au C.R.E.P.S."; also "Débat sur l'architecture oblique en présence de nombreux artistes du C.R.E.P.S.," *Le progrès*, May 20, 1973.
75. The full schedule of all associated programs is included in the event pamphlet, the newsletter published by the Maison de la culture de Douai as well as local press.
76. Project credits in the Maison de la culture de Douai newsletter acknowledge the contribution of city workers for the construction as well as the scaffolding company Entrepose–Lille. *Présences*, no. 11, September 1973, 1.
77. Parent, *Entrelacs de l'oblique*, 102.
78. "Ce soir, à l'hôtel de ville, deuxième conférence de l'architecte Claude Parent sur la fonction oblique' architecture du possible," *La voix du nord*, September 12, 1973.
79. "Amour, même: mime libre sur espace oblique par Alain Hullot," *Présences*, no. 11, September 1973, 2.
80. "Le corpse et l'oblique," *Présences*, no. 11, September 1973, 2.
81. "Occuper la rue," *Présences*, no. 11, September 1973, 2–3.
82. "Foire de Douai, September 73," Maison de la culture, Douai (schedule pamphlet); see also Parent, *Entrelacs de l'oblique*, 94.
83. Parent, *Architecte*, 178.
84. Parent, *Entrelacs de l'oblique*, 102.
85. Parent, *Architecte*, 178–79.
86. Parent, *Entrelacs de l'oblique*, 102.
87. According to one poster, the exhibition started on September 15, 1973 and was on view until the end of October. The opening would have overlapped with the exhibition in Douai, which, according to the Maison de la culture de Douai's program was on view until September 16, 1973. It is not clear whether the dates were ultimately adjusted or if the two exhibitions overlapped, however, it is certain that the events in the two cities, nearly five hundred kilometers apart, were chronologically close to one another.
88. Petit's collaborators credited for the building design included Claude Harlaut and Camille Demangeat. For additional information about the building, see Klein, *Les maisons de la culture*, 34.
89. The cultural center eventually became the Espace des arts, renamed as such in the 1980s, which is how it continues to function in the present.
90. Between 2015 and 2018 the building was renovated by the Atelier d'architecture Pierre Hebbelinck, and the main entry into the building has since been moved to the ground level, while the original concrete stair was demolished. As such, new stairs leading up to the foyer were placed inside the building.
91. Interestingly, the main artwork in the foyer was a sculpture titled *Sur pivot III* (1971), a massive volume made from pink travertine resting on a matching pedestal at a point designed to mechanically rotate, by the artist Morice Lipsi who was among the founding members of Architecture Principe and who made several functional elements for the interior of the St. Bernadette Church.
92. *L'inclisite* was the name of a series of studies for housing, first developed with Virilio in the mid-1960s, which sought to combine cellular housing units with continuous circulation. In 1974, Parent also developed a design as an entry for the PAN competition with two of his studio collaborators, Pierre Aioutz and Irène Labeyrie, using the same strategy of oblique cells clustered in section.
93. A flyer made by the Maison de la culture de Chalon-sur-Saône and the Groupe de travail urbanisme du conseil culturel (the urban working group and cultural council) advertising a meeting with the architect for the evening of Thursday, October 11, 1973, states:

    > Claude Parent's approach is to seek ongoing dialog with all those who are ready to experiment with a future way of living. The discussion after each presentation will focus on the main concerns of the residents of each neighborhood, enabling a more immediate approach to the Oblique Function.
    > Slide projections.

    My translation.
94. "Mois d'octobre 1973," Maison de la culture, Chalon-sur-Saône, 1973. Schedule pamphlet.
95. Parent, *Architecte*, 176.
96. "Samedi, à la Maison de la culture, l'architecture oblique: Thème d'une conférence passionnante présentée par Claude Parent, architecte urbaniste." *Courrier*, October 19, 1973.
97. Parent, *Architecte*, 176.
98. Parent, *Architecte*, 177.
99. Parent, *Architecte*, 177.
100. "De janvier à mars, les associations cannaises expérimenteront la " fonction publique " dans les foyers du théâtre," *Ouest-France Caen, June 22, 1974*.
101. Demoriane, "Le tour de France," 59.
102. In 1954, the city initiated the process of designing a new theater to replace the old building destroyed in 1944. The first design for the modern municipal theater was produced a year later. So after André Malraux's 1958 launch of the program to construct new cultural centers throughout France the municipal project became a p of this statewide initiative, adjusti its name to the Théâtre–Maison de la culture. The theater/cultural center opened to the public as su in 1963. Klein, *Les maisons de la c ture*, 36–37.
    After 1968, the relationship betwe the municipality and the state dissolved and the venue effectively reverted to its original function as the city theater. By the time Parent arrived, the center had bee renamed the Théâtre municipal de Caen. See also "1963–68: la folle histoire de la maison de la culture, *Ouest-France*, April 24, 2013 and "L'histoire du lieu," Théâtre de Ca https://theatre.caen.fr/lhistoire -du-lieu.
103. Bourbonnais originally designed entire project, but the original tra parent façade that he proposed w rejected in the initial design process. Carpentier was thus brough on board to handle the design of t much more solid exterior building shell. Klein, *Les maisons de la cul ture*, 37.
104. This was not Parent's first time working in the space. For the sam foyer, he produced the design for exhibition of photographs by his f quent collaborator and friend Gill Ehrmann on view from June 19 to September 20, 1965.
105. "De janvier à mars, les associations cannaises expérimenteront 'fonction publique' dans les foyer du théâtre," *Ouest-France Caen*, June 22, 1974; see also *Paris–Normandie*, "Dans tout le foyer du théâtre: Les plans inclinés de l'architecte Claude Parent iront à rencontre du public," June 23–23 1974.
106. The model is a part of the permanent collection at FRAC Centre–V de Loire in Orléans. Unlike most other models of various practicables that were made of paper and of which only photographs remain—and other instances whe the designs were, at best, uneven documented—this model was ma of wood and thus more durable ar conducive to longer-term archivir Likewise, thanks in part to its dur bility, it is among the most widely known practicables even if it was never actually built. Because the model renders existing and proposed conditions equally—withou

distinction in material or color—the design appears more complex and architecturally complete than some of the other seemingly more modest schemes.

Parent, *Entrelacs de l'oblique*, 103.

"Les tribulations de Claude Parent à Caen: On discutera de l'architecture en avril, mais on ne vivra à l'oblique qu'en septembre," *Liberté: Caen-Normandie*, March 15, 1975.

According to the article, the fair theme was to be "La femme et l'information," meaning, in English "women and information" or possibly "women and the news." In preparation for the event, Parent was to work with a women's organization on further development of the practicable design, which was to respond to the new function as a space where a group of women live there over a ten-day period (there is no further explanation as to what "living" in the space would entail). Meanwhile, the standing promise was to have much of the previously scheduled live programming, including engagement with local schools, the youth center, theater groups, the municipal library, as well as Alain Hullot's mime performance, also take place on the revised practicable.

ON INTERIORITY

The exception was the outdoor practicable in Douai as discussed elsewhere in the book.

Mark Pimlott, *The Public Interior as Idea and Project* (Prinsenbeek: Jap Sam Books, 2016), 9.

Richard Sennett distinguishes interiors as a spatial condition and interiority as a matter or subjectivity. He theorizes departures from standard accounts of their overlap. According to convention, interiority unfolds in private; what requires attention are the accounts of subjectivity unfolding in public. While Sennett references the street as public space and urban design as the field responsible for shaping this domain of everyday life, his thinking can be translated to the space of the *maison de la culture* as a public interior and the practicables as a design tool for engaging subjectivity. Richard Sennett, "Interiors and Interiority," *A+T: Interior Matters (SOLID Harvard GSD Series)* 47 (2017): 10–19.

Claude Parent, "Nevers, a crypt leaning above the ground," in *Nevers: Architecture Principe—Claude Parent, Paul Virilio*, ed. Frédéric Migayrou (Paris: Éditions HYX, 2010), 16.

5. Brayer, "Interview with Paul Virilio," 21.
6. Virilio, "Instabilisation," 6.
7. Parent, *Vivre à l'oblique*, 47.
8. Parent, *Vivre à l'oblique*, 45.
9. Parent, *5 réflexions sur l'architecture*, 35.
10. For a broader discussion on the overlaps between interior space and individual interiority, see Ewa Lajer-Burcharth and Beate Söntgen, "Introduction," in *Interiors and Interiority*, ed. Ewa Lajer-Burcharth and Beate Söntgen (Berlin/Boston: De Gruyter, 2016), 4.
11. Parent, *Vivre à l'oblique*, 43.
12. Parent, *5 réflexions sur l'architecture*, 36.
13. Walter Benjamin "Paris, Capital of the Nineteenth Century (1935)," in *The Arcades Project*, trans. Howard Eiland and Kevin McLaughlin (Cambridge, MA: The Belknap Press of Harvard University Press, 1999), 8–9. On the significance of Benjamin's work in relation to contemporary studies of the emergence of the modern interior, see also Charles Rice, *The Emergence of the Interior: Architecture, Modernity, Domesticity* (London: Routledge: 2007), in particular the chapter "Irrecoverable Inhabitations: Walter Benjamin and Histories of the Interior."
14. Parent, *Vivre à l'oblique*, 45.
15. Penny Sparke, "Taste and the Interior Designer," in *After Taste: Expanded Practice in Interior Design*, ed. Kent Kleinman, Joanna Merwood-Salisbury, and Lois Weinthal (New York: Princeton Architectural Press, 2012), 24.
16. Parent, *Vivre à l'oblique*, 39.
17. Parent, *5 réflexions sur l'architecture*, 38.
18. Claude Parent, "Le 42e Salon des Artistes Décorateurs," *Aujourd'hui: Art et architecture*, no. 33, October 1961, 92. Unless otherwise noted, all translations are my own.
19. Parent, "Le 42e salon," 92.
20. Parent, "Le 42e salon," 92.
21. Marc Emery, "Le design," *L'architecture d'aujourd'hui*, no. 155, April/May 1971, 2.
22. Claude Parent, "Face à face: Architecture et design," *L'architecture d'aujourd'hui*, no. 155, April/May 1971, 19. Unless otherwise noted, all translations are my own.
23. Parent, "Face à face," 19.
24. Parent, "Face à face," 20. Italicized words are part of the original text.
25. The legacy of promoting consumption can in part be traced back to figures like Christine Frederick (1883–1970), who encouraged planned obsolescence as part of managing the modern home. Through the concept of "creative waste," Frederick encouraged regarding household goods as disposable items that needed to be cyclically replenished as a matter of contributing to a productive industrial society. In France, a similar figure to Frederick, who was American, was Paulette Bernège (1896–1973). These two contemporaries impacted the conceptualization of the modern home and as an environment to be designed and managed and decorators, particularly women, played an important part in these aspects of twentieth-century life in the United States, France, and other parts of the industrialized world.
26. Parent, "Face à face," 23.
27. Alexandra Midal, *Design by Accident: For a New History of Design* (Berlin: Sternberg Press, 2019), 188.
28. Alberto Arbasino, "Gae Aulenti: New Force in Italian Design," *Vogue*, July 1970, 123.
29. Midal, *Design by Accident*, 174. See also Joe Colombo, "Antidesign," *Casabella*, no. 342 (November 1969): 28.
30. Midal writes: "The emancipation of design as a discipline, and the threat that this represented to architecture's monopoly over the home, drew strength from design's newfound visibility. However, the transition was far from a smooth one, with architects continuing to perpetuate the modernist conception of design as a concentrated expression of their discipline." Midal, *Design by Accident*, 164.
31. Midal, *Design by Accident*, 173.
32. Midal, *Design by Accident*, 185.
33. Midal, *Design by Accident*, 185.
34. In the 2010 monograph *Claude Parent: L'œuvre construite, l'œuvre graphique* the renovation is listed as Parent's first ever project, realized between 1950 and 1952, when he was in his late 20s.
35. "Construction 4: Pour aménager un studio à Neuilly elle a utilisé des toits de garage," *Maison et jardin*, no. 50, February 1958, 46–47.
36. Among the projects in which Parent most extensively applied these interests is Villa Bloc in Antibes, designed for and in collaboration with André Bloc. It was realized in 1962, not long before his interests shifted to oblique architecture. For Parent's relationship to Case Study houses, as well as the influence of Mies van der Rohe and Japanese design, see Jean-Lucien Bonillo, *La villa Bloc de Claude Parent/*

architecture et sculpture (Marseille: Éditions Imbernon, 2011). For Parent's reflections on the influence of Theo van Doesburg and de Stijl in his early work, see Claude Parent, "J'oublie et me souviens de van Doesburg," *L'architecture d'aujourd'hui*, no. 287, June 1993, 38.

37. In her book *The Modern Interior,* Penny Sparke writes: "A couple of decades later the Modernist architects and designers were to reject decoration, however, seeing it as synonymous with nineteenth-century bourgeois domesticity and social aspiration. Ironically, though, given their clear and frequently articulated distaste for the interior, several of them had begun their careers in that field." This included Le Corbusier, Walter Gropius, Eileen Gray, and others. Penny Sparke, *The Modern* Interior (London: Reaktion Books, 2008), 93.
38. In the apartment for the editor Jean Baillais, for example, the flooring was made of hexagonal terracotta tiles that clearly predate the 1954 renovation. Rough patches of missing tile, where existing partitions were partially removed, remain visible upon the completion of the renovation.
39. Reporting from the ninth CIAM Congress, which took place in Aix-en-Province in 1953, Parent and Ionel Schein conclude, on the topic of the synthesis of art and architecture, that what is needed is more than the placement of autonomous art objects in space. Instead, the architects demanded that painters and sculptors provide them with elements with which they can then shape space. Ionel Schein and Claude Parent, "9e Congrès des C.I.A.M.," in *Claude Parent: L'œuvre construite, l'œuvre graphique*, 148.
40. Brayer, "L'aventure créatrice," 45–54.
41. Parent, "J'oublie et me souviens," 38, my translation.
42. Even in ground-up architecture commissions from this period, the use of furniture frequently appears as a substantial design consideration. Photographs of a scaled model of the Maison Gosselin house, for example, show an array of miniature furnishings occupying the interior, the detailed layout for which is also reflected in the project's floor plans.
43. Pierre Gueguen, "Appartement de Claude Parent ou l'intégration des arts," *Aujourd'hui,* no. 30, 1961, cited in Brayer, "L'aventure créatrice," 46.
44. Brayer, "L'aventure créatrice," 46, my translation.
45. Le Corbusier, *The Decorative Art of Today* (Cambridge, MA: MIT Press, 1987), 90.
46. Parent, *Lettre tapuscrite, présentation du projet.*
47. Marie-Claude Dumoulin, "Appartement Bellaguet," *Journal de la maison,* April, 1972, 86. My translation.
48. Although this is rarely highlighted, the apartment was inside a residential building in Neuilly-sur-Seine also designed by Parent and completed in 1969. The relatively conventional midrise residence reveals hints of Parent's preoccupation with diagonals in certain details, such as the zigzagging balcony parapets and angled mailboxes in the foyer. Incidentally, this is also one of the projects that, according to building images archived at the Kandinsky Library, Jean Nouvel assisted with at the start of his career.
49. These same paintings were also exhibited at the Maison de la culture d'Amiens as a part of Parent's program in the winter of 1972–73.
50. In an article about Bellaguet's apartment for the seasonal pamphlet published by the Maison de la culture d'Amiens, the painter says that living in an oblique environment not only eliminates the need for furniture but also clothing. If not to be enjoyed nude, the space at the very least inspires taking off shoes and putting on more comfortable clothes in which one can be both relaxed and more mobile. "Un appartement selon l'oblique," *Mobile,* no. 10, December 1972.
51. Rem Koolhaas, ed., *Elements of Architecture* (Cologne: Taschen, 2014), 2305.
52. By private, I refer first and foremost but not only to the domestic realm. Private domains can also include privately owned commercial spaces, such as retail and hospitality venues, which have sufficiently been theorized as sites of interiorization and subjectivity. The spaces that Parent engaged were public in terms of both access and ownership and it is this realm that I am referring to when using the term "public."

5. OTHER ANGLES

1. Parent, *Vivre à l'oblique* , 5–7.
2. Parent, *Vivre à l'oblique*, 79.
3. Parent's use of the term "archeology" in *Vivre à l'oblique* follows the publication of Michel Foucault's *The Archeology of Knowledge* just one year earlier and can in relation to this text be regarded as an inspired attempt t invent the oblique function's intellectual history. The use of archeol ogy as a metaphor for architectur layered relationship to existing conditions has a lineage in it own right, from Peter Eisenman's *Citie of Artificial Excavation* (New York: Rizzoli, 1994) to the recent use of the term "archeology of the future by the architect Lina Ghotmeh as a framework for her practice; see, for example, Lina Ghotmeh, "Livir in Symbiosis – Archaeology of the Future," public lecture, Novembe 6, 2023, posted November 14, 20 by Harvard GSD, YouTube, 1:26:5 https://youtu.be/rVNNzvbD-cAQ?si= bqeY6IroZuLNt9wC.
4. Béatrice Simonot, "Claude Parent present in posterity," in *Nevers: Architecture Principe—Claude Parent Paul Virilio*, ed. Frédéric Migayrou (Paris: Éditions HYX, 2010), 164.
5. Joseph Giovannini, "Claude Pare Visionary Architect of the Oblique Dies at 93," *New York Times*, February 26, 2016, https://www.nytimes.com/2016/03/01/arts/design/claude-parent-architect-c-the-oblique-dies-at-93.html.
6. Frank Gehry, "Claude Parent," in *Claude Parent: Visionary Architec* 17.
7. For Foucault, the construction of genealogy is "gray, meticulous, ar patiently documentary," requiring knowledge of details, and a vast amount of source material. Michel Foucault, "Nietzsche, Genealogy, History," in *Language, Counter-Memory, Practice: Selected Essay and Interviews*, ed. D. F. Bouchard (Ithaca: Cornell University Press, 1977), 76. To suggest that a creati or applied practice like architectu aims to go beyond giving an accou of a genealogy is to also recognize that the patient, meticulous labor is invested differently, whereby the genealogy may be provisional and incomplete, a byproduct of a process rather than its primary objective.
8. In relation to Arakawa and Gins, se Léopold Lambert, "Architectures of Joy: A Spinozist Reading of Parent/Virilio and Arakawa/Gins' Architecture," The Funambulist, https://thefunambulist.net/editorials/philosophy-architectur-of-joy-a-spinozist-reading-of-parentvirilio-and-arakawagins-architecture; Sara Hendren's gra uate thesis at the Harvard Gradua

School of Design completed in 2013, from which the project evolved, included a part that she referred to as "a deep genealogy of the inclined plane," of which Parent is inevitably a part. See https://www.gsd.harvard.edu/project/slope-intercept/; also Sara Hendren, "Notes on the Inclined Plane—Slope : Intercept," in *Disability, Space, Architecture: A Reader*, ed. Jos Boys (New York: Routledge, 2017), 279–86.

Parent's writing from the early 1970s is unapologetically anthropocentric. In the essay "Le rapport de l'architecture au lieu" (Architecture's Relationship to Place) from *5 réflexions sur l'architecture*, he rejects the notion that nature exists apart from human activity or that preserving it in a particular state should take precedence over transforming it according to human self-interest. Parent, *5 réflexions sur l'architecture*, 12–20. The notion of nature as a construct—and thus something that can be deconstructed according to human need—is also echoed in Architecture Principe's early texts published in the magazine.

10. Rem Koolhaas, "Ramp II: Claude Parent," in Koolhaas, *Elements of Architecture*, 2305.
11. Marie Laurberg, "The Museum Walk: Olafur Eliasson at Louisiana," in *Olafur Eliasson: Riverbed*, ed. Michael Juul Holm and Anna Engberg-Pedersen (Humlebaek: Louisiana Museum of Modern Art, 2014), 18.
12. Eliasson says: "We don't take in the exhibition. We produce it by walking through it." "Olafur Eliasson Interview: A Riverbed Inside the Museum," Louisiana Museum of Modern Art, posted November 26, 2014, by Louisiana Channel, YouTube, 42:14, https://www.youtube.com/watch?v=ZLUX3AI2Uic.
13. "Walter De Maria: the New York Earth Room (1977)," Dia Art Foundation, New York. Brochure.
14. "Delcy Morelos," La Biennale di Venezia, accessed August 22, 2024, https://www.labiennale.org/en/art/2022/milk-dreams/delcy-morelos.
15. *The Rite of Spring* is a 1913 ballet by the composer Igor Stravinsky, with the original choreography by Vaslav Nijinsky. Early versions of scenic design consisted of more conventional painted backdrops, including the original staging featuring a painting by Nicholas Roerich. Rather than depicting a bucolic scene in a flat painting or image, as such earlier versions of the set design did, Bausch collaborated with Rolf Börzik on a scenography that treated the stage as a tactile, physically interactive material landscape. In theatrical terms, one can refer to such a three-dimensional scenic element (as opposed to a two-dimensional representation) as practicable.
16. Luca Cerizza, "Mediating Experience: A conversation between Olafur Eliasson and Luca Cerizza, Berlin, 6 July 2009," in *TYT (Take Your Time), Vol. 2: Printed Matter* (Berlin: Studio Olafur Eliasson; Cologne: Verlag der Buchhandlung Walther König, Köln, 2009), 51.
17. Eliasson, "Interview: A Riverbed Inside the Museum."
18. "Sun & Sea," Hammer Museum, accessed August 29, 2024, https://hammer.ucla.edu/programs-events/2021/sun-sea.
19. Pierre Huyghe's site-specific large-scale project was realized for the 2017 Skulptur Projekte, a decennial exhibition in Münster, Germany, curated by Kaspar König.
20. Jerry Saltz, "Can You Dig It?" *New York Magazine*, November 21, 2007, https://nymag.com/arts/art/reviews/41266.
21. Luxloop, who consulted on technical aspects of the project, states "AR that responded to real-time on-site data from the rink such as the temperature, animal movement, and precipitation. The ruleset controlled the AR creatures' movement, colonization, death rates, and birthrates, allowing the system to live autonomously and be influenced by conditions in the environment." "After ALife Ahead," Luxloop, accessed June 26, 2024, https://www.luxloop.com/projects/afteralifeahead.
22. Andrew Russeth, "Constant Displacement: Pierre Huyghe on His Work at Skulptur Projekte Münster," *ARTnews*, June 26, 2017, https://www.artnews.com/art-news/artists/constant-displacement-pierre-huyghe-on-his-work-at-skulptur-projekte-munster-2017-8602.
23. Parent, *Vivre à l'oblique*, 43.
24. Keller Easterling, "Floor," in Koolhaas, *Elements of Architecture*, 10.
25. Nataša Petrešin-Bachelez and Nora Razian, *Let's Talk about the Weather: Art and Ecology in a Time of Crisis* (Beirut: Sursock Museum, 2016), 13. Exhibition catalog.
26. Migayrou, "Critical Architecture," 63.
27. For further explorations of the punctuation mark "/" and its spatial consequences see the end of this chapter as well as Igor Siddiqui, "Slashed Interiors: Text/Space," *Interiority* 3, no. 1 (2020): 5–20.
28. Jeanroy, "Pratiquez l'architecture!," 166.
29. Jeanroy, "Pratiquez l'architecture!," 166.
30. Architects who build houses for themselves, of course, put themselves inside their own work, but that is a different matter even if such efforts (including Parent's house discussed in Chapter 4) can be part of an experiment. The focus here is on the architect's public presence, whether it be mediated or live in format.
31. Charles Aubin and Carlos Minguez Carrasco, eds., *Bodybuilding: Architecture and Performance* (New York: Performa, 2019) and Beth Weinstein, *Architecture and Choreography: Collaborations in Dance, Space and Time* (New York: Routledge, 2024). The former omits Parent's work altogether, even though it otherwise treats the early 1970s as a critical moment fo the convergence of architecture and performance; the latter draws on the author's personal interviews with Parent and his relationship to his sister, the choreographer and performer Nicole Parent.
32. Fleur Watson, *The New Curator: Exhibiting Architecture and Design* (New York: Routledge, 2021), 247.
33. Examples of such projects include Hans Hollein's *Mobile Office* (1969), Coop Himmelb(l)au's *The White Suit* (1969) and *Restless Sphere—Basel Contact* (1971), as well as Hans-Rucker-Co's *Oase no. 7* (1972) shown at the Documenta V exhibition in Kassel, Germany.
34. In the essay titled "Radical Architecture," a contribution to the catalog of MoMA's 1972 survey exhibition on Italian design, Celant writes, "The architect is architecture in the making, and the physical traces and residue are of no consequence; the tangible work also need no longer exist, and should even be abolished, or at least suspended." Germano Celant, "Radical Architecture," in *Italy: the New Domestic Landscape—Achievements and Problems of Italian Design*, ed. Emilio Ambasz (New York: Museum of Modern Art, 1972), 387.
35. The siting of Wexler's *Hypar Room* (1999) is particularly poignant given that it was installed at the Contemporary Arts Center in Cincinnati at the time of the

museum's commissioning of the architect Zaha Hadid to design its new, similarly nonorthogonal, building. Hadid's building, the Lois & Richard Rosenthal Center for Contemporary Art, opened in 2003, and among its distinguishing features is the ground-level lobby floor, which sweeps up into a curve and continues as a wall. A sincere thanks to my colleague, curator Andrée Bober, for bringing my attention to Wexler's installation and its oblique properties.

36. Christopher Hawthorne, "Architecture catches the acting bug," *Los Angeles Times*, June 29, 2017, https://www.latimes.com/entertainment/arts/la-ca-cm-building-type-alex-schweder-20170702-htmlstory.html.
37. Hawthorne, "Architecture catches the acting bug."
38. Watson, *The New Curator*, 248.
39. Watson, *The New Curator*, 248; for reference, see also Jean-Luis Boissier, "Toward a Dramaturgy of Interactivity," in *Practicable: From Participation to Interaction in Contemporary Art*, (Cambridge, MA: MIT Press, 2016), 361–76.
40. Watson, *The New Curator*, 248–49.
41. Watson, *The New Curator*, 248.
42. See, for example, the interview with Bruce Nauman in which the artist states: "My conclusion was that I was an artist and I was in the studio, then whatever it was I was doing in the studio must be art." Interview with Bruce Nauman by Ian Wallace and Russell Keziere in *Please Pay Attention Please: Bruce Nauman's Words*, ed. Janet Kraynak (Cambridge, MA: MIT Press, 2003), 194.
43. Claude Parent, "Architecture: Singularity and Discontinuity," in Paul Virilio and Claude Parent, *Architecture Principe 1966 and 1996,* trans. George Collins (Besançon: Les Éditions de l'Imprimeur, 1997), 153.
44. Penny Sparke, "Interior Decoration, Interior Design Interior Architecture Lines of Development in a Professional Field," in *Home Stories: 100 Years, 20 Visionary Interiors*, ed. Mateo Kries and Jochen Eisenbrand (Weil am Rhein: Vitra Design Museum, 2020), 40–41.
45. Kingsley Marshall and Rupert Loydell, "Control and Surrender: Eno Remixed—Collaboration and Oblique Strategies," in *Brian Eno: Oblique Music,* ed. David Pattie and Sean Albiez (London: Bloomsbury Academic, 2016), 177.
46. Brian Eno and Peter Schmidt, *Oblique Strategies*. Cards with instructions for use.
47. Marshall and Loydell, "Control and Surrender," 177.
48. See also Gary Hustwit's 2024 documentary film *Eno* for interviews with Brian Eno in which he discussed the use of the cards while working with David Bowie and others in the recording studio.
49. Marshall and Loydell, "Control and Surrender," 187. One of Cage's principal tools for incorporating chance into his work was the ancient Chinese text *I Ching,* which would subsequently also serve as an inspiration for *Oblique Strategies. The Book of Changes*, as the *I Ching* is also known, describes the process of deriving a numerical code from chance-based action (i.e., the tossing of coins) which corresponds to a series of interpretive scripts, the overall purpose of which is to gain insight, guidance, or prescience. Cage appropriated the oracle text as a compositional tool soon after the 1950 publication of its popular English translation.
50. The cards in this way engage what Edward de Bono refers to as lateral thinking; see Edward de Bono, *The Use of Lateral Thinking* (London: Jonathan Cape, 1967). Eno used the cards while working with Roxy Music, the band that he helped establish in the early 1970s. Later in the decade, in addition to producing his own albums, Eno extensively collaborated with David Bowie whose Berlin Trilogy albums, *Low* (1977), *Heroes* (1977), and *Lodger* (1979), are known to have been recorded under the heavy influence of *Oblique Strategies.*
51. John Kay, *Obliquity: Why Our Goals Are Best Achieved Indirectly* (New York: Penguin, 2010), 48–52.
52. Kay, *Obliquity*, 6–7.
53. Kay, *Obliquity*, 62.
54. The term is the reference to the economists Michael Hammer and James Champy's 1993 bestseller *Reengineering the Corporation*. Kay, *Obliquity*, 12.
55. Lauren Berlant, *Cruel Optimism* (Durham: Duke University Press, 2011), 1.
56. Kay, *Obliquity*, 146.
57. "Rem Koolhaas, "Ramp I: Tim Nugent," in Koolhaas, *Elements of Architecture*, 2270. Koolhaas's cruel provocation cannot be taken out of context: His point about Parent's low impact is meant to amplify the success of another advocate for the ramp, a non-architect, whose work in activism rather than design brought ramps to more buildings than any of Parent's efforts. Koolhaas writes, "Tim Nugent, born January 10, 1923, declared the universal necessity of adapting the ramp to facilitate every type of human body Nugent saw the ramp as a bridge to a society with equal opportunities for all. He worked for more than 40 years on Project 117.1: a life's work for the establishment of architectural design guidelines dedicated to the physically disabled, which has impacted architecture everywhere. Koolhaas, "Ramp I," 2270.
58. The late architect and teacher Larry Doll echoed Juhani Pallasmaa by saying, "students should make friends with uncertainty." Doll often talked about the unknown and transformational effect of travel on architects, but his advice applied more broadly to a sense of openness toward the unanticipated. Larry Doll, "10 Points for Design in the Realm of the Senses," in *Poetics + Pragmatics: A Design Studio Companion,* eds. Smilja Milovanovic-Bertram and Joyce Rosner (Dubuque: Kendall Hunt Publishing, 2018), 80.
59. Abu ElDahab and Sorer, *Oblique Time with Claude Parent*, 82.
60. Keller Easterling, *Medium Design: Knowing How To Work on the World* (New York: Verso Books, 2021), x.
61. Cecil Balmond, "Informal Space," lecture held at The University of Texas at Austin, September 6, 2017. The quoted text in italics indicates my own emphasis.
62. Easterling, *Medium Design*, 10.
63. Kay, *Obliquity*, 162.
64. Anne Curzan, "Slash: Not Just a Punctuation Mark Anymore," *The Chronicle of Higher Education*, April 23, 2013, https://www.chronicle.com/blogs/linguafranca/slash-not-just-a-punctuation-mark-anymore
65. It is in part thanks to Jane Rendell's feedback at the Unmentionables Symposium in Los Angeles in 2019, hosted by Woodbury University, that I pursued the obliqueness of punctation, eventually resulting in the publication of my journal article article: Siddiqui, "Slashed Interiors: Text/Space."
66. Colomina, *Manifesto Architecture*, 28.
67. Colomina, *Manifesto Architecture*, 38.
68. As a verb, "queer" can in this instance be interpreted as an act of making something inclusive of queer identities or legible explicitly from such perspectives.
69. Sara Ahmed, "Orientations: Toward a Queer Phenomenology," *GLQ: A Journal of Lesbian and Gay Studies*

12, no. 4 (2006): 560.

. "The Unmentionables Symposium," hosted by Woodbury University Department of Interior Architecture at WUHO Gallery on April 6, 2019, accessed November 27, 2024, https://www.unmentionablessymposium.com.

. I recounted this process in an earlier publication, of which this paragraph offers a modified version. See Igor Siddiqui, "Oblique/Interior," in *Appropriate(d) Interiors*, ed. Deborah Schneiderman, Anca I. Lasc, and Karin Tehve (London: Routledge, 2021), 126–27.

. Claude Parent, *Errer dans l'illusion* (Paris: Bernard Chauveau Édition, 2023), 45.

. The book's title may be translated to English as *Wandering in Illusion*, although it has so far only been published in French. References to *Errer dans l'illusion* in this chapter are based on the 2023 published version of the original text.

. Parent, *Errer dans l'illusion*, 87–88.

. Parent, *Errer dans l'illusion*, 13; my translation.

INDEX

Page numbers in bold refer to figures.

A

B

C

D

E

F

G

H

I

U

V

W

Z

CREDITS

over: All images © Igor Siddiqui

6, 61, 62–63, 64–65, 114, 115, 116–17, 8 (bottom), 119, 120, 121 (top and bot-m), 127 (top, middle, and bottom): © aude Parent Archives. Photo © Pierre érenger

7: © Artists Rights Society (ARS), New ork / c/o Pictoright Amsterdam

10, 88 (top and bottom), 90–91: Digital nage from *La ligne de plus grande ente: Projet pour le Pavillon français de Biennale de Venise* (1970), a slideshow onsisting of 285 ektachomes, by Gilles hrmann. © FRAC Centre-Val de Loire, rléans

11, 52 (top), 52 (bottom), 106 (top nd bottom), 134 (top; bottom, left and ght), 136–37, 144, 145 (top and bottom): gital Image © CNAC/MNAM, Dist. MN-Grand Palais / Art Resource, NY

12 (all), 13, 22, 26, 29 (top and bottom), 0 (top and bottom), 89 (top and bot-m), 158 (all), 159 (top and bottom), 162 op): © Claude Parent Archives

15, 31 (bottom), 37, 38–39, 40–41, 0 (top and bottom), 55 (left and right), 6 (all), 57 (all), 58 (left and right), 183: hoto: Igor Siddiqui

16: © Claude Parent Archives. Photo © aad Parent

18: Digital Image © CNAC/MNAM, Dist. MN-Grand Palais / Art Resource, NY. hoto: Pierre Bérenger

21: © Claude Parent Archives. Photo © trice Goulet

23, 30, 59, 66 (left and right), 67, 69, 0–73 (all), 79 (top and bottom), 82 ottom), 108, 118 (top), 122 (all), 123, 126 op), 135 (left and right), 138 (left and ght), 146 (all): Courtesy Claude Parent chives

25, 51, 76–77, 84–85, 100–01, 110–11, 4–25, 130–31, 140–41, 148–49, 154–5: © Igor Siddiqui

31 (top): Digital Image © CNAC/MNAM, st. RMN-Grand Palais / Art Resource, Y. Photo: Paul Virilio

P. 32, 53 (top), 92, 93 (top and bottom), 94–95, 96–97, 98, 176, 177, 178–79, 180–81: Digital Image © CNAC/MNAM, Dist. RMN-Grand Palais / Art Resource, NY. Photo: Gilles Ehrmann

P. 35: © Les Éditions de l'Imprimeur

P. 43: © FRAC Centre-Val de Loire, Orléans

P. 44–45, 86–87, 112–13, 132–33, 142–43, 150–51, 152 (all), 153, 156–57, 160–61, 162 (bottom): © Fonds Claude Parent. SIAF/Cité de l'architecture et du patrimoine / Archives d'architecture du XXe siècle

P. 53 (bottom): © Nicole Parent and Éditions Robert Lafont. Courtesy Claude Parent Archives

P. 78, 102, 103 (right), 104–05: Digital Image © CNAC/MNAM, Dist. RMN-Grand Palais / Art Resource, NY. Photo: Daniel Gaujour

P. 81: © Claude Parent Archives / © Louis Monier

P. 82 (top): Digital Image © CNAC/MNAM, Dist. RMN-Grand Palais / Art Resource, NY. Photo: Louis Monier

P. 103 (left): © Claude Parent Archives / © Daniel Gaujour

P. 126 (bottom, left and right): © Claude Parent Archives. Photo © Alain Planchon

P. 128 (top and bottom): Courtesy Archives départementales de Saône-et-Loire

P. 132 (bottom): © Claude Parent Archives. Photo © Patrick Doppelt

P. 168: Courtesy Demisch Danant. Photo: Thierry Depagne

P. 170: Courtesy Kartell Museum, Milan. Photo: Valerio Castelli

P. 173 (top): Photo © Janet and Frank Beyda

P. 173 (bottom): Digital Image © CNAC/MNAM, Dist. RMN-Grand Palais / Art Resource, NY. Photo: Janet and Frank Beyda

P. 174 (top): © Claude Parent Archives / © Janet and Frank Beyda

P. 174 (bottom): Digital Image © CNAC/MNAM, Dist. RMN-Grand Palais / Art Resource, NY. Photo: Etienne Bertrand Weill

P. 186 (top): © 2008 Reversible Destiny Foundation. Photo: Robert L. Bowen

P. 186 (bottom): Courtesy the artist. Photo: Justin Knight

P. 188–89: © 2014 Olafur Eliasson. Courtesy the artist; Queensland Art Gallery | Gallery of Modern Art; The Josephine Ulrick and Win Schubert Charitable Trust. Photo: Iwan Baan

P. 190–91: Photo: Jean-Pierre Dalbéra, CC BY 2.0, https://commons.wikimedia.org/w/index.php?curid=85487849

P. 192–93: © Pierre Huyghe. Courtesy the artist and Esther Schipper Gallery, Berlin

P. 195: © Joana Hadjithomas & Khalil Joreige. Photo: Audrey Laurans

P. 196 (top): © Vito Acconci / Artists Rights Society (ARS), New York. Courtesy Maria Acconci

P. 196 (bottom): Courtesy the artist. Photo: May Xiong

P. 198: Courtesy the artists. Photo: Richard Barnes

P. 200: Courtesy the artist

P. 208: Courtesy the artist and Participant Inc., New York and Galerie Isabella Bortolozzi, Berlin. Photo: Igor Siddiqui

P. 209: © Adagp Paris, 2025. Courtesy the artist. Photo: Martin Argyroglo

The author and publisher gratefully acknowledge the permission granted to reproduce the copyright material in this book. Every effort has been made to trace copyright holders and to obtain their permission for the use of copyright material.

ACKNOWLEDGMENTS

My interest in Claude Parent's work developed during the years of having the privilege to teach, starting in 2012, in a Paris-based studio program offered by the School of Architecture at The University of Texas at Austin and conducted in collaboration with the École nationale supérieure d'architecture de Paris-Belleville. In 2017, on the first of several summer road trips between my native Croatian coast and France, my now-husband Olivier organized a surprise stop at the St. Bernadette of Banlay Church in Nevers. This visit was made possible by Christophe Joly, a local architecture expert and steward of Parent and Virilio's 1966 masterpiece, who provided us with access to the building and generously shared his insights about its history.

After a handful of attempts to write and publicly speak about obliqueness as an interior condition, I was awarded the Faculty Research Assignment at UT Austin, allowing me to fully dedicate the Spring 2021 semester to this research. I am grateful to Michelle Addington, former dean of the School of Architecture, along with faculty members and colleagues Phoebe Lickwar, Juan Miro, and Vincent Snyder, whose review and endorsement of my initial proposal helped make this award possible. After this research phase, the writing of the manuscript was supported by the Provost's Authors Fellowship from 2022 to 2023. My gratitude goes to Provost Sharon Wood for this extraordinary support, as well as colleagues and authors Christina Bain, Paul Bonin-Rodriguez, Pramit Chaudhuri, and Laura Gutierrez, who were part of our writing group over the course of fifteen months. Funding from the School of Architecture through the Gene Edward Mikeska Endowment for Interior Design, the Emily Summers Excellence Fund for the History of Interior Design, and the Interior Design Endowed Excellence Fund provided essential resources throughout the various stages of research and production that eventually led to the publication of this book. My thanks also goes out to Dean Heather Woofter for her empathy and interest in this project as it approached the finish line.

This research took off in earnest too late to have benefited from direct contact with the architect that inspired it. I am, however, profoundly grateful for the opportunity to get to know the Parent family, in particular Mr. Parent's daughter Chloé and grandson Laszlo whose support and friendship I appreciate and cherish. They graciously opened Mr. Parent's studio to me and shared materials from their archives, offering many clues and answering many questions along the way. Their generosity, genuine interest, intellect, sense of humor, and beautiful humanity put me in contact with the qualities that I am certain Mr. Parent possessed too. Over the years,

Naad Parent collected nearly every newspaper clipping that mentioned her architect-husband, and the sum of such records turned out to be an indispensable vehicle for the kind of time travel that this book required. It is also thanks to the Parent family, and the privately held Claude Parent Archives that they maintain, that many of the visual materials were able to be included in this book. Thank you for all that you have done to help bring this project to fruition, Chloé.

Throughout my research for the book, including site visits to cultural centers, archives, and other venues, I encountered many helpful individuals, including Patrick Foll at the Théâtre de Caen, Cécile Mariotte at the Archives départementales de Saône-et-Loire in Mâcon, Corinne Dumont at the Éspace des arts in Chalon-sur-Saône, and others. Graduate students Chloe Jones and Marija Ivić assisted with early iterations of digital models for each practicable. Also, thanks to peer reviewers and editors of publications in which earlier versions of this research appeared, including *THE PLAN Journal*, *Interiors: Design/Architecture/Culture*, *Appopriate(d) Interiors* as well as the Unmentionables Symposium at Woodbury University and Interior Provocations at Pratt Institute. Odile Decq at the Confluence Institute in Paris, along with Nicolas Hannequin and the late Colin Fournier, provided useful conversations about the work at a critical time. Countless colleagues and friends, including Gaëlle Breton, Tarek El-Ariss, Nerea Feliz, Kate Green, Daniel Koehler, Clay Odom, Jean-François Renaud, Virginia San Fratello, Deborah Schneiderman, Allan Shearer, Meredith TenHoor, Danilo Udovički-Selb, Jonathan VanDyke, Cathrine Veikos, Lois Weinthal, Diana Welch, Jeff Williams, and others provided their support, advice, insight, expertise, wisdom, and kindness in countless ways during and beyond this project. Big thanks to Catherine Gavin for her review of early versions of the chapters; to Lucas Freeman for his thoughtful input and edits of the manuscript; to Luke Bulman for giving the book its final graphic form; and to all the artists whose images appear in the book with their permission. Assistance from UT Austin School of Architecture staff Brandi Brokmeyer, Lauren Crowe, and Josette Lehman during the final stretches is also much appreciated. Finally, my gratitude goes to Gordon Goff, founder and publisher of ORO Editions, for his support of this project and the opportunity to make this book, along with Jake Anderson and Federica Ewing who were instrumental in moving *Oblique Experiments* into print.

I dedicate this book to my family, whose journeys across continents and over generations continue to shape my understanding of the world. My husband Olivier has helped me navigate the nuances of French culture, language, people, and places throughout this research, and this is but the start of a never-ending list of ways in which his patience, enthusiasm, openness, curiosity, tenderness—and so much love—make life beautiful. My mother, Dubravka, and my brothers, Zoran and Tomislav, never fail to provide a sense of togetherness even when we are far apart. They seem to understand what I am doing even when I do not think I do. When I tap into this sense of connection—and my dedication to those who support me—I also always feel the loving presence of my grandparents, *nono* Lujo and *nona* Ivanka, who gave me the gift of trust in my own creativity, resilience, self-determination, and future and who are never not with me.

Published by Applied Research
and Design Publishing, an imprint
of ORO Editions.
Gordon Goff: Publisher

www.appliedresearchanddesign.com
info@appliedresearchanddesign.com

Author: Igor Siddiqui
Book Design: Office of Luke Bulman
Project Manager: Jake Anderson

10 9 8 7 6 5 4 3 2 1 First Edition

ISBN: 978-1-966515-22-7

Prepress and Print work by ORO Editions Inc.
Printed in China

AR+D Publishing makes a continuous effort to minimize the overall carbon footprint of its publications. As part of this goal, AR+D, in association with Global ReLeaf, arranges to plant trees to replace those used in the manufacturing of the paper produced for its books. Global ReLeaf is an international campaign run by American Forests, one of the world's oldest nonprofit conservation organizations. Global ReLeaf is American Forests' education and action program that helps individuals, organizations, agencies, and corporations improve the local and global environment by planting and caring for trees.